Voyages, the Age of Engines

NEW PERSPECTIVES ON MARITIME HISTORY
AND NAUTICAL ARCHAEOLOGY

UNIVERSITY PRESS OF FLORIDA

Florida A&M University, Tallahassee
Florida Atlantic University, Boca Raton
Florida Gulf Coast University, Ft. Myers
Florida International University, Miami
Florida State University, Tallahassee
New College of Florida, Sarasota
University of Central Florida, Orlando
University of Florida, Gainesville
University of North Florida, Jacksonville
University of South Florida, Tampa
University of West Florida, Pensacola

Voyages, the Age of Engines

Documents in American Maritime History,

Volume II,

1865–Present

EDITED BY JOSHUA M. SMITH AND

THE NATIONAL MARITIME HISTORICAL SOCIETY

University Press of Florida

Gainesville/Tallahassee/Tampa/Boca Raton

Pensacola/Orlando/Miami/Jacksonville/Ft. Myers/Sarasota

14 13 12 11 10 09   6 5 4 3 2 1

Library of Congress Cataloging-in-Publication Data
Voyages, The age of engines : documents in American maritime history,
Volume II, 1865–present / edited by Joshua M. Smith and the National
Maritime Historical Society.
p. cm.—(New perspectives on maritime history and nautical archaeology)
Collection of edited historical documents and companion volume to Voyages,
The age of sail.
Includes bibliographical references.
ISBN 978-0-8130-3305-1 (alk. paper)
1. Navigation—United States—History—Sources. 2. United States—History,
Naval—Sources. 3. Voyages and travels—History—Sources. 4. Merchant
marine—United States—History—Sources. I. Smith, Joshua M. II. National
Maritime Historical Society (U.S.)
VK23.V689 2009
387.50973—dc22   2008033949

The University Press of Florida is the scholarly publishing agency for the
State University System of Florida, comprising Florida A&M University,
Florida Atlantic University, Florida Gulf Coast University, Florida Interna-
tional University, Florida State University, New College of Florida, Univer-
sity of Central Florida, University of Florida, University of North Florida,
University of South Florida, and University of West Florida.

University Press of Florida
15 Northwest 15th Street
Gainesville, FL 32611-2079
www.upf.com

Dedicated to the Midshipmen
of the United States Merchant Marine Academy

He who commands the sea has command of everything.

THEMISTOCLES

CONTENTS

PREFACE

Why study maritime history? Consider that more than half the U.S. population lives in coastal counties. The resident population in this area is expected to increase by twenty-five million people by 2015. The world ocean, covering more than two-thirds of the earth's surface, is the engine that drives the planet's environment. The Great Lakes possess about 20 percent of the earth's surface freshwater. Ocean shipping carries 90 percent of the nation's commerce. The United States Navy is the largest and most powerful in the world by far. There are many institutes of higher learning dedicated entirely to working with or on the nation's waters, including three of the five federal service academies and five state-run merchant marine academies. Yet Americans cannot be said to have a firm grasp of the importance of the oceans, Great Lakes, and major rivers. *Voyages* is part of an effort by the National Maritime Historical Society and the David M. Milton Charitable Trust to remind Americans just how large a role our nation's waterways have played in our history.

There are few events in American history that cannot be said to have a maritime element. But maritime history has suffered as a field for decades because it has had no textbook or standardized curricular resources, such as a published document collection. *Voyages* is an attempt to establish a usable, portable, and interesting set of documents on America's maritime past that revolve around historically significant themes. The impetus behind this collection is that documents and images stir students to think more deeply about the impact of all things marine on American society. By providing a body of documents that they themselves analyze, *Voyages* enables students to move beyond being passive participants and to become active learners, putting together patterns from the clues left in these documents and images. Whenever possible, maritime events are linked with larger trends impacting American history.

Voyages consists of almost one hundred and fifty sources divided into two volumes, of which this is the second. Each chapter is broken down into historically significant themes based on three to four items arranged in chronological order. Furthermore, each item is accompanied by three "questions for discussion" that serve to further focus student learning, and possibly to form the basis of student assignments. Most of these documents are edited from versions found in published sources, although a few are the result of archival research or the loan of personal papers. Numerous alterations have been made to enrich their educational value. Spelling has been modified in many instances for clarity, and sections cut out for the sake of brevity. Footnotes have been added, removed, or altered to better inform students with background information. All ship names have been italicized. They should in no way be considered as accurate duplications of the originals, but as excerpts edited for educational value. In all cases, the source used has been cited.

DOCUMENT-BASED LEARNING

Historians are often compared to detectives because they must reconstruct past events out of evidence that is often difficult to put together. Typically, historians rely on written documents such as letters, diaries, government reports, and the like. More recently, historians have reassessed maps and images as primary documents, too; this is a particularly useful discovery given that about half of all students are more visually oriented, while the other half is more comfortable with text. But not all documents are created equal. While some evidence is reliable, some is less trustworthy but may have value nonetheless. While evaluating the evidence and interpreting its meaning is difficult, most historians relish this task as a complex riddle that, when solved, will reveal new insights into the human experience. In maritime terms, think of it as a hunt for buried treasure.

Interpreting historical documents is a basic skill that hones students' analytical skills. It is not a new idea; Harvard history professor Albert Bushnell Hart began publishing collections of documents for student interpretation over a century ago. But in the twenty-first century, with American textual literacy apparently declining, the skills gained through document-based research remain more important than ever. Ideally, after reading the document closely, students will respond constructively and analytically to the ideas advanced in the text. Many students may find it useful to ask themselves a series of analytical questions in order to assess a historical document. The following list is but a sample of how these questions might be conceived:

1. Who was the author of the document? How did their position, rank, or viewpoint influence how they saw events?

2. When was the document created? What other events occurred around the same time that may have influenced the author?

3. Why was the document or image created? What sort of evidence did the document's author present to support their views?

4. How reliable is the document as a source of factual information? Does its author have any sort of bias?

5. What is the document's historical significance? How does it reflect on major themes in American history?

6. What questions does this document leave unanswered?

Instructors and students reading the documents in *Voyages* should realize that four major themes run through this collection. These themes have slowly evolved in teaching a course called *History of American Sea Power* at the United States Merchant Marine Academy in Kings Point, New York. This is a mandatory course taken by all first-year students in order to awaken them to the importance of maritime matters in shaping the nation's history. While obviously this is important knowledge for future ship's officers, groups such as the National Maritime Historical Society believe this is important for all Americans to understand.

THEMES

The first theme is that maritime trade was a crucial element in the historical development of the United States. Columbus sailed across the Atlantic in search of a trade route. Most European settlements came into existence for commercial purposes. The African slave trade has many ramifications for American history, but it must be recognized that economic demands and desires lay at its root. Differences over maritime trade contributed to the American Revolution, and spilled over into the political debates that shaped the Constitution and early American politics. Maritime developments shaped westward movement and the industrial and transportation revolutions. America is a commercial nation, and seaborne commerce has played a significant role in our economic development. Male and female merchants and entrepreneurs, such as Keziah Coffin, Robert Fulton, Robert Dollar, Henry J. Kaiser, and Malcolm McLean represent the aggressive commercial spirit that has made this nation wealthy.

Wealth, however, needs protection, and American writers such as Alfred Thayer Mahan remind us that navies are inextricably linked with commercial development. To paraphrase Admiral Stephen B. Luce (founder of the

Naval War College in Newport, Rhode Island), military sea power is the off-spring of commerce, not its parent. John Paul Jones was a great naval leader not because he captured HMS *Serapis*, but because he brought confusion and destruction to Britain's merchant fleets. When Oliver Hazard Perry defeated a British fleet on Lake Erie, it was important because it opened the Great Lakes to American enterprise, first agricultural and later industrial. In World War II, German U-boats threatened to isolate this industrial nation from supplying its Allies and receiving raw materials. More recently, threats to American security include attacking oil tankers or planting a nuclear bomb in a container ship. Securing seaborne shipping thus remains a crucial element in protecting American business interests, our standard of living, and even the lives of ordinary citizens in our commercial centers, many of which are ports, whether on the ocean, Great Lakes, or western rivers.

The second theme found in this book is power and authority versus degradation, slavery, or powerlessness. Indeed, few scenarios evoke the arbitrary power of one human being over another as much as the often-brutal relationship between the master of a ship in the age of sail and the vessel's crew, or more pointedly, a human cargo of enslaved Africans. The reaction against this power imbalance was often violent, including mutiny, piracy, and militant labor union unrest.

Slavery is one of the most shameful and contentious episodes in American history and is arguably the best example of a power imbalance. Several documents in this collection relate to slavery, including the important memoirs of Olaudah Equiano, an African enslaved on the Guinea coast who endured the hellish "middle passage" to America and later became a sailor. Other documents relate to South Carolina's controversial decision to imprison "colored" seamen while in port, still others relate to the efforts of abolitionists to free slaves by using a coastal schooner to transport them northward.

While African slavery was an important element of race relations, they are far more complex than a dichotomy between black and white. All races and many ethnic groups faced discrimination at some point. On the West Coast, Chinese faced legalized discrimination for many decades under the Chinese Exclusion Act of 1882. It was only with the advent of radical labor unions like Joe Curran's National Maritime Union (NMU) that discrimination began to decline on merchant ships, albeit slowly. The U.S. Navy also struggled with racial integration well into the 1970s.

The third theme revolves around the complex relationship of human communities to the environment. From the early days of European exploration of the Americas, the natural bounty of its lands and waters has been viewed with an eye toward exploitation. As a result of over-harvesting, fish stocks and whale populations have plummeted. Understanding the use of marine resources reveals a great deal about human society. For example, whaling in the early nineteenth century was often seen as a metaphor for the struggle between American civilization and nature. So, too, knowing who claimed the right to act as the arbiter of the use of natural resources can inform us about racial inequalities. In California in the late 1800s, for example, the legislature created laws ostensibly to conserve valuable fisheries, but in reality they were meant to exclude Chinese immigrants from the West Coast.

In the late twentieth and early twenty-first century these debates became more heated as fish stocks shrank and environmental awareness grew. But questions remain. For example, can American efforts to regulate offshore fisheries during the Cold War be best understood as an environmental concern, or was it just another episode in U.S.-Soviet competition? Do nineteenth-century treaties with Native Americans give them the right to hunt whales in the 1990s, and is it racist for environmental groups to oppose those whale hunts? How are the Great Lakes supposed to deal with invasive species brought in by commercial shipping? These are the sort of questions that will continue to haunt the American relationship with its marine environment.

The fourth theme is one of the basic underpinnings of all historical approaches to interpretation, acknowledging persistence or change in human society. In terms of persistence, Native Americans have consistently asserted their separate identity from the rest of American society, despite five hundred years of effort to eradicate or assimilate them. In terms of change, maritime labor unions have fought for society to accept seafarers as first-class citizens, with the same rights and privileges as land-based workers.

Some of the most powerful recent historical scholarship has focused on gender and sexuality in American society. In many ways these studies focus on power imbalances, but another powerful element in them is their focus on change and continuity in gender roles. The relationship between men and women continues to change and raises many questions. Should institutions such as the U.S. Naval Academy cling to its traditional culture, or should it accept women as fully capable of combat roles?

Many of these documents incorporate elements from one or more of these four themes. Indeed, the most powerful of these documents incorporate elements of all four. The questions at the end of each source often reflect the four themes outlined above.

ACKNOWLEDGMENTS

The genesis of this book began with discussions with Burchenal Green of the National Maritime Historical Society. Without her kind encouragement, this project (which has taken some curious twists and turns along the way) would never have gotten off the ground. So, too, the generosity of the David M. Milton Charitable Trust has made this project possible.

Librarians are the unsung heroes of any book, and this is no exception. The staff of the Schuyler Otis Bland Library at the United States Merchant Marine Academy in Kings Point, New York, provided stellar service. In particular, Dr. George Billy, Donald Gill, and Marilyn Stern gave significant contributions in terms of time and effort. So, too, the staff of the Naval Historical Center, especially Ed Marolda and Michael Crawford, proved enthusiastic supporters of this project, as did Bob Browning and Bill Thiesen of the Coast Guard Historian's Office. Colleagues and fellow scholars have played an important role in collecting these documents. John Hattendorf, Brian Payne, Mike Butler, Danny Vickers, Chris Magra, Kenneth Blume, Hans Carlson, Tim Lynch, Arthur Donovan, Walter Lewis, and Bill Bunting helped provide materials or constructive criticism. Scholars may not like to admit it, but administrators are important in the creation of any written work. Dean Warren Mazek and Dr. Gary Lombardo of the U.S. Merchant Marine Academy both provided encouragement. Historians rarely get to speak directly with their sources, but J. Robert Lunney and Keith Johnson were kind enough to permit me to use documents they authored. As usual, my wife Jea has been more than patient in enduring her husband's writing process, as has my daughter Dorothea.

Compiling a work such as this is fraught with peril, but the responsibility for all choices, errors, mistakes, and omissions in compiling *Voyages* are entirely mine.

1

POSTBELLUM

The time after the Civil War witnessed a marked decline in high-seas activity. The war had devastated the American merchant fleet, and the few commercially viable vessels left found it increasingly hard to compete internationally as market conditions and technology changed. So too, the U.S. Navy—the world's third greatest in 1865—quickly went into decline after the war, hamstrung by budget concerns and uncertain of its mission. With few prospects at sea for ambitious young Americans, many of whom were drawn to westward expansion, shipping no longer attracted the nation's youth as it had before the war.

Little effective action was taken to resurrect the merchant fleet. While lobbyists and congressmen debated the merits of "free ships" or subsidies, both American shipping and the allied shipbuilding industry all but collapsed. Only on the banks of the Delaware River did iron and later steel shipbuilding continue.

As the status and profits of seafaring declined, American-flagged ships in blue-water trades increasingly had foreign-born crews, who were treated increasingly harshly by their officers. American vessels developed a reputation as "hell ships" officered by psychotic "bucko mates." In the face of these horrible conditions, maritime labor unions began to agitate for legal reforms that would protect them from vicious "bucko mates" afloat and avaricious "crimps" ashore.

Things fared better on inland and coastal waterways. The postbellum period saw shipping on the western rivers such as the Mississippi reach its peak. On the Great Lakes, waterborne commerce thrived and saw major innovations in ship construction and cargo handling. The coastal trade also boomed, especially for coastal steamers that carried passengers from one coastal city to another.

The American relationship with the sea began to change in this period, too. Seafaring remained dangerous, but the government increasingly stepped in to regulate and protect mariners. The popular media often celebrated mariners as heroes and role models.

By the 1880s, the Navy began to reshape itself, finding a new mission, a new kind of ship, and perhaps most importantly, a new intellectualism that provided greater training, professionalism, and purpose. The utility of this new steel navy made itself clear in the Spanish-American War, in which the American fleet easily swept aside the obsolete Spanish Navy. With this victory came a renewed interest in shipping as a strategic element, demands for an Isthmian canal, and a fierce debate about whether the United States should become an imperial power.

INLAND NAVIGATION

While American transoceanic shipping declined following the Civil War, shipping on the Great Lakes and western rivers flourished as never before. Distinctive marine cultures evolved on America's inland waterways, with their own jargon, ship designs, and folkways. Cities like Chicago and St. Louis experienced rapid growth, in no small part because of their functions as ports. As the value of the commerce on these inland waterways grew, so did efforts to regulate shipping and tame the waters, making transportation safer and more convenient. American citizens increasingly looked to the federal government to perform this function.

The Great Lakes in the postbellum period were important maritime highways for immigrants, grain, timber, iron and copper ores, coal, and lime. Chicago became the nation's second city in terms of population during this period, and other lakeside communities such as Buffalo, Duluth, Milwaukee, Detroit, Cleveland, Toledo, and others grew rapidly as manufacturing or distribution centers that benefited from the cheap transportation the Lakes offered. Nor were these inland seas restricted to supporting heavy industry; they had their own fashionable summer resorts like Mackinac Island and its famous Grand Hotel. But the expansion of navigation came at a cost; the Great Lakes were just as dangerous as the world's oceans, and maritime disasters were common events.

The Mississippi and other western rivers remained the main highways in the West for a decade after the Civil War. The late 1860s and early 1870s were the heyday of the riverboats. Passengers and freight moved up and down the Mississippi, and steamboats on the Missouri transported cargoes as far west as Montana. But the coming of the railroads soon took away much of their business. Many steamboats were converted to traveling showboats featuring plays, opera, and vaudeville acts.

Commercial traffic on the river grew increasingly valuable, but largely consisted of bulk materials such as coal, cotton, and grain moved by tug-boats towing strings of barges. The river's infamous floods frequently in-terfered with river commerce, and by the 1880s the U.S. Army Corps of Engineers had begun to take action to control the waters of the western rivers.

Especially on the Great Lakes, with its growing heavy industries, the key figures were the engineers. These might be the engineers who oversaw the operation of the complex boilers that powered the steamships that increas-ingly dominated the Lakes. But they also might be the civil and military en-gineers who oversaw the design and construction of canals, port facilities, and riverside levees.

Alfred Guthrie, "Eighth Supervising District" (1865)

After the Civil War, the Great Lakes grew in importance as a center of mari-time commerce. Shipping traffic increased greatly and with it an increase in accidents. There were a total of 421 disasters on the lakes and nearby rivers in 1865, distributed as follows: Lake Michigan, 107; Lake Huron, including Georgian Bay, the Straits, and St. Clair river, 98; Lake Superior, 12; Lake Erie, including Detroit river and the Welland canal, 134; Lake St. Clair, 22; Lake Ontario, 48. These represent a loss of more than $1.3 million in ship-ping tonnage and many lives lost.

Government officials advocated for better safety through regulation. The most noted figure in this push was Alfred Guthrie (1805–1882), an engineer who lived in Chicago. Alarmed by the many steamboat accidents on the Great Lakes and western rivers, Guthrie pushed for the passage of the 1852 Steamboat Inspection Act, which called for the inspection of all steam-powered vessels and licensing of steamboat engineers. He also served as the regional superintendent for inspecting steamboats on the Lakes, the Eighth Supervising District of the U.S. Steamboat Inspection Service. In this account, Guthrie reports on the steamboat accidents in his district and makes some recommendations to improve safety on Lakes steamers.

There has been inspected in the Eighth District during the year ending September 30, 1865, 199 steamers, including all classes, pas-senger, ferry and tugboats. There is still remaining something over 20 uninspected, arising from the fact that for a large part of the year there was virtually no Local Board at the port of Chicago. The salary was so small, being only $500, that no competent person could be found who would accept the office, and consequently so much labor was thrown upon me that some of the boats are not yet inspected, but as I have now a board there, these boats will be early attended to.

A large number of steamers in this district have not yet been measured under the new law, but the aggregate tonnage will probably be about 28,600 tons; the approximate sum of what will be derived from certificates of inspection of these steamers will be $8,600.

Three hundred and twenty-four pilots and three hundred and nine engineers have been licensed during the year. For these licenses there has been collected and paid over to the proper authorities the sum of $6,330, making in all, for certificates of inspection of the steamers and the licenses of engineers and pilots some where close upon $14,500. The salaries of two Local Inspectors at Detroit at $800 each, at Chicago $500 each, the Supervising Inspector at $1,500, makes $4,100. After deducting this, together with the necessary traveling and other incidental expenses, there will still remain a very handsome sum to the credit of the government over former years and this year's expenses.

Of these inspections and licenses, the Local Board at Chicago have inspected 52 steamers of all classes, with an approximate tonnage of 6,000 tons, and licensed 53 pilots and 80 engineers.

The Local Board at Detroit have inspected 91 steamers, with a tonnage of 18,000 tons, and licensed 170 pilots and 160 engineers.

The Supervising Inspector has inspected 56 steamers with about 4,200 tons, and has licensed 101 pilots and 67 engineers.

There has been but one accident to passenger steamers in this district the past year in which the lives of any passengers have been lost this was in the propeller[1] *Pewabic* on Lake Huron. There has been four explosions of tug boats and one propeller, with a loss of ten of the officers and crews. Two steamers have been totally destroyed by fire while lying at their docks; five or six have been on fire, but not seriously injured; two have been sunk, but on these no lives were lost. There has been a few collisions but of no serious moment, and are not reported.

The first accident that occurred after the report of the last annual meeting was in the explosion of the propeller *Tonawanda* on the Chicago river, on the 24th of October, in which three persons were lost, the second engineer who was on duty, a fireman and another person.

---

1   Propeller: a Great Lakes term for a propeller-driven steamship.

A very careful investigation into the causes of the explosion was made by the Local Board at Chicago, and reported it to be from want of sufficient water in the boiler. This was attributed partially to an improper arrangement of the pipes and valves leading the water from the forcing pump to the boiler, and also to carelessness or negligence of the engineer in charge. . . .

In this instance the boat was only moving from one dock to another to finish up her freight, and it was not deemed necessary to fire but one boiler. The inference of the inspectors was that the engineer thought he had effectually closed the valve leading to the cold boiler and was deceived, or that he had forgotten it altogether, and that on discovering his mistake or neglect he then closed the valve and forced the cold water upon the heated boiler, and that by a sudden generation of steam beyond the safety-valve to discharge, or the boiler to withstand, an explosion followed, and the boat sunk almost instantly. Against the idea of low water the captain swore that there was so much water that he observed the engine was working water and throwing large quantities out upon the deck. This was explained by the inspectors that as both boilers were connected by the same steam pipe to the engine, it was probable enough that one boiler was entirely full, and its water passed over through the engine as the captain swore.

The inspectors hoped to find, by examining the valves, a verification of their opinion, but they were so much injured that nothing could be determined. Some expected to find the body of the engineer at the valve when the boat was raised, but he was found standing with the starting bar grasped in his hand. Another defective and reprehensible arrangement was found here, the pipe of the steam gauge led from the steam pipe between the throttle valve and the engine so that no pressure would be indicated from the boiler while the engines were not running.

It was also found upon inquiry that four steamers had been supplied with this arrangement of pipes and valves, and that certainly three of them had exploded in the same manner, and one of them was the ill-fated *Globe* that exploded with such terrific violence in Chicago river a few years since, the fragments of which this Board visited with me soon after.

The Local Board recommend that no boiler hereafter be passed, unless the steam gauge be open at all times to the pressure in the boiler.

The tugboat *Success* exploded her boiler in the Chicago river in May last, by which the engineer and three others lost their lives. The engineer lived to give a full and satisfactory explanation of the cause. He says the water had been getting low for some time from some obstruction to the pump or pipes, but hoping he could find and correct the difficulty before any accident should occur, he ventured to keep running instead of stopping, as he ought, until it was too late; that he knew well enough what the consequences would be if he continued; in the midst of this the bell rang to stop; he then told the captain that his water was low and he dare not stop, but as the captain only wanted to stop to hitch on to a vessel, and it would be but a moment or so he stopped, and when he started again the explosion came, the boiler leaving the boat and falling into the river some way off. This was a regularly licensed engineer, and was supposed to be competent, but as it proved he like many others, it is feared, had not the ability to say *no*, though he knew well enough his life was at stake.

This boiler has since been taken up, and was found, contrary to the expectation of the Board of Local Inspectors, to have given way down in the lower part of the fire-box, the farthest it could be from the fire, and where, if there had been any water in the boiler it would have been there, and that part where it would have been overheated it had not given out, and this led the board to doubt the correctness of their former opinion, notwithstanding the statement of the engineer.

My attention being called to it, I gave it as careful an examination as I could, and found that all the lower part of the boiler, near the place which gave way, had become much weakened by rust, not being much over one-half of its original thickness, and that this being the weakest part of the boiler it must of course yield there without any reference to stronger parts of the boiler, whether weakened by fire or otherwise, and hence it is my opinion that the engineer told the truth, and that the explosion was occasioned from want of a sufficient supply of water until the interior portions had become over-heated, and then by some means water was thrown upon the heated plates, and a sudden generation of steam followed which the safety-valve could not relieve. I am confirmed in this still more by the testimony of the engineer, who stated that he was looking at the steam gauge and the hand flew rapidly over as far as it could go, and the explosion followed.

The tugboat *Fanny Stafford* exploded her boiler in the Chicago river on the 19th of June. This was the most complete and destructive explosion that I have known; scarcely any vestige of the boat was left. The boiler left the boat ascending high into the air, passing over a five story building, across one of the public streets and down through the roof and two floors hanging in the third one from the roof. The boiler turned inside out and stripped to pieces in every direction. The engineer and three or four others were lost. The engineer was but a few days before refused a license for incompetency, but, regardless of the law, he still continued to run the boat, and the owners to employ him. I had found it out fully a week before the accident, and had made the proper complaint for his arrest, and had every day urged the officers to arrest him, but some way it was neglected until too late. By this neglect I have no doubt that three or four lives and the boat, worth about $12,000, were lost.

The tugboat *Fanny White* exploded her boiler in Saginaw river, in the State of Michigan, on the 9th of June, in which one or two persons were killed. In this case the boiler had been inspected the year before, but unbeknown to the inspectors it had been materially altered and changed in its construction, and when first fired up it exploded. Supposed cause, imperfect workmanship in putting on the new dome which blew off.

A collision occurred on the evening of the 9th of August off Thunder Bay Light, on Lake Huron, between the propellers *Meteor* and *Pewabic*, by which the *Pewabic* was sunk and thirty-three of her passengers, with seven of the officers and crew were drowned. This collision, occurring upon a clean, open lake, in a smooth sea—each vessel provided with proper and excellent signal lights, in full view of each other; and when the lights were first made, if each had kept her proper course, would have passed full a mile away; yet, approaching each other and colliding under full steam, at a speed of ten or twelve miles an hour, without ever signaling each other by whistle or otherwise, presents apparently a case of most aggravated wrong.

The public very properly called upon the inspectors to give it the most impartial and searching investigation, which was done by the Local Board of Detroit, and the licenses of Captains George P. McKay and George Cleaveland were revoked for mismanagement, and Mr. Cleaveland arrested and put in prison.

The facts substantially are as follows:

The two steamers made each others lights when five or six miles off, and without change of course, would have passed full a mile apart.

Each vessel made the others green and bright light. The *Meteor* very properly continued straight forward in her proper course. The *Pewabic* changed her course a little, but not enough to show her red light, and a little more insensibly crowding up towards the *Meteor* until within two lengths of her, when she suddenly put her wheel hard-a-port and showed her red light for the first time, crossing the *Meteor's* bows, the next instant the collision occurred. On the instant of showing the red light, the captain of the *Meteor* gave one blast of the whistle, that he would go to the right or starboard; rang to stop the starboard engine, and put his wheel hard a-port. The time of all this did not exceed one minute, or perhaps a half. The engineers were both at their posts at the instant the engine stopped, and reversed instantly, and without embarrassment, and as soon as it was discovered that the *Pewabic* was sinking, the life-boats of the *Meteor* were lowered in good order, and life-preservers thrown over for any who might need them; and in fact, everything was done by the officers and crew of both vessels, after the collision, that coolness and good judgment could do the *Meteor* remaining all night in rendering assistance.

The conduct of Captain Wilson and all his officers and crew were highly commended by the Board of Inspectors, and the course he pursued throughout the whole, was approved.

It may be proper to add, that these boats were among the very best of their class anywhere almost new, and supplied with everything required for the safety of passengers life-preservers, life-boats, fire equipment, pumps, &c. The reason why so many were drowned was that the boat sunk so quick, that many were unable to get out of the cabin. Most of those who were taken out of the water had life-preservers on. One or two women were found floating with their heads above the water, but dead, showing the efficiency of the preservers, if not in these instances of saving the life, at least floating the body.

Captain McKay, of the *Pewabic*, whose license has been revoked for mismanagement in the case of the collision, appealed to the Supervising Inspector for a re-hearing, which was given, and it appearing satisfactory that he was regularly and properly off watch, until within one or two minutes of the collision, and that under the existing circumstances he found a collision inevitable, and that he took the best measures he could to ease off the shock and save as far as possible, his vessel, the decision of the Local Board was reversed.

The steamer *Traveler* was burned at the dock at Eagle Harbor, Lake Superior, on the 17th of August—no lives lost; cause unknown. It was well secured from fire around the boilers.

The steamer *J. P. Ward* was burned at her dock at Bay City—no lives lost. No cause ascertained. License of master revoked for not reporting.

The passenger steamer *Huron*, running from East Saginaw to Goderich, Canada, run upon a rock at the mouth of the Saginaw river, and is a loss except the engines and boilers, which are being taken out—no lives lost. No report made. License ordered to be revoked for neglect.

The steamer *Planet*, when within two miles of Mackinaw, about 10 o'clock on the night of the 13th of September, was discovered to be on fire in the hold of the vessel and around the boiler. The flames spread so rapidly that the engineer could not reach the pony engine,[1] which was also in the hold. The pipes conveying the water to the upper decks were put together with soft solder, and were soon melted apart, so as to be entirely useless. The mate immediately got the forward and after pumps at work throwing water upon the fire where it could be reached. The vessel was stopped on the first alarm, so as to not fan the flames, and a sufficient number of the life-boats were lowered into the water, and all the ladies were sent ashore without accident. The engineer, Mr. La Fleur, then turned the steam into the hold, which enabled him to go down far enough with the fire-hose and direct it upon the flame until finally it was extinguished the passengers, in particular, working with their utmost good will. Mr. La Fleur attributed the saving of the vessel mostly to the steam thrown into the hold. He recommends that no pony engine be placed in the hold, or that the pipes be put together with soft solder, if it can be avoided.

The steamship *Detroit* collided with a sail vessel in the harbor of Milwaukee; no very serious injury was done, and no lives lost or persons injured.

The propeller *Governor Cushman* has been ashore two or three times, and met with some injuries to her machinery, but no lives have been lost, and the injuries soon repaired.

---

1   Pony engine: sometimes known as a *donkey engine,* a small auxiliary engine used for pumping water or powering winches.

The boiler of the *F. W. Bashus*, on testing it in the spring, gave way under the hydrostatic test and was ordered to be repaired, and when done it stood the test, and she reserved her certificate.

One license has been refused for writing, or permitting some person to write upon his license, changing its conditions.

A license was refused to Edward McGlennon by the Local Board at Detroit, because he was not a citizen of the United States, as required by a resolution of this Board. A mandamus was issued by Judge Wilkins of the United States District Court to the Board of Inspectors, to appear and show cause why they withheld a license from Edward McGlennon. They appeared in court and plead an order by the Board of Supervising Inspectors prohibiting licenses to other than citizens of the United States. After a hearing of the case, the Judge ordered them to issue immediately the license as requested by the said McGlennon, with which, I believe, the Local Board intended to comply, but by some accident McGlennon was drowned immediately after, and before any license was issued.

The propeller *Dean Richmond* collided with the propeller *Illinois*, which was reported to the Local Board at Detroit, and was them referred to the Inspectors at Buffalo.

The propeller *Meteor*, after the collision with the *Pewabic* proceeded on her way to Lake Superior. When arriving at Sault St. Marie, twenty-four hours afterward, she was found to be on fire in the forward hold. Her fire-pumps were immediately set at work to extinguish the flames, but it was found impossible. The hatch-ways were all fastened down to keep the flames from bursting out, but of no avail, and in order to save the vessel, she had to be scuttled and sunk. The Local Board at Detroit were directed to investigate the case, but were unable to ascertain the cause. They reported that she had fifty barrels of unsacked lime in her hold, but the captain, mate and engineer all swear that there was no water near the lime, but I am firmly impressed in the belief that the lime was the true cause, and that some water unbeknown to them did reach the lime. I recommend that no lime be allowed to be carried in the hold of any steamer hereafter.

The propeller *Stockman* took fire at her dock, and burned to the water's edge, and was a total loss.

The tug-boat *Emerald* took fire but was extinguished. Two other tug-boats have also been on fire. The frequency of these fires has led some to believe that there is a organized band of boat burners, but no evidence of it has been adduced. Several of the steamboat owners are keeping extra watchmen on this account.

ALFRED GUTHRIE,

Supervising Inspector.

Questions for Discussion:

1. What does this document reveal about seafaring on the Great Lakes?

2. According to Guthrie, what was the biggest danger to Great Lakes shipping?

3. What does this document reveal about government efforts to impose safety regulations?

United States Steamboat Inspection Service, *Proceedings of the Fourteenth Annual Meeting of the Board of Supervising Inspectors of Steam Vessels held at St. Louis, MO., October 11th, 1865* (Baltimore: James Lucas & Son, 1865), 52–60.

Currier and Ives, "Ol' Man River" (1863–1884)

Following the Civil War there was a tremendous upsurge in southern appreciation for its distinct culture, which engendered an artistic and literary blossoming that celebrated antebellum life on the Mississippi River. The most enduring of these efforts were Mark Twain's novels and autobiographical accounts, but there were others, too, such as the 1927 musical *Show Boat*, which featured the song "Ol' Man River," a lament about race relations in a seemingly unchanging South.

In the images shown here, the Yankee firm of Currier and Ives attempts to capture the spirit of the Old South in a number of lithographs produced after the Civil War. But the images themselves may raise more questions than they answer. Do they show the South before the war, or after? Do they show an idyllic, slow-paced agrarian society, or the hustle and bustle of a commercial region? Are the African Americans in these images meant to be slaves or free, and how are they interacting with white southerners? The ambiguity may have a purpose in that these images depict an ideal rather than an actuality. David Anderson addresses this southern nostalgia in his important article "Down Memory Lane," which explores how white southerners coped with defeat in the Civil War by looking back to an idyllic past.[1]

1 David Anderson, "Down Memory Lane: Nostalgia for the Old South in Post–Civil War Plantation Reminiscences," *The Journal of Southern History* 71, no. 1 (February, 2005): 105–36.

"'Wooding Up' on the Mississippi," 1863. Lithograph by Currier and Ives, courtesy of the Library of Congress # LC-DIG-pga-00976.

"Low water in the Mississippi," ca. 1867. Lithograph by Currier and Ives, courtesy of the Library of Congress # LC-USZC4-1563.

"Bound down the River," 1870. Lithograph by Currier and Ives, courtesy of the Library of Congress # LC-USZ62-5.

Questions for Discussion:

1. What do these images reveal about the maritime culture of the Mississippi River?

2. What ideals about the Old South do these images attempt to convey?

3. What do these images reveal about racial relations in the South?

Library of Congress Prints and Photographs Division, LC-USZ62-5; LC-DIG-pga-00976; LC-USZC4-1563; LC-DIG-pga-00809.

Anonymous, "Proposed Ship Canal at Sturgeon Bay" (1870)

Isaac Stephenson (1829–1918), in writing his autobiography *Recollections of a Long Life*, recalled that for much of his career as a lumberman, sailor, and entrepreneur the harbors and aids to navigation on the Great Lakes were in terrible shape. He compared navigating a ship on the Lakes to blazing a trail through the forest; there were few charts and many dangers. As one of the largest stockholders in the Peshtigo Company (a huge lumber concern that moved enormous amounts of timber on the Lakes), he was especially concerned about creating safer navigation for Peshtigo's fleet. The document below, which may well have been produced by the Peshtigo Company, argues that the federal government should assist in creating a canal to better connect Green Bay with Lake Michigan. The Peshtigo Company, and particularly Stephenson, managed the construction of the canal, which opened in 1873.

Proposed Ship Canal at Sturgeon Bay, Wisconsin, to Connect Green Bay with Lake Michigan and Open a New Harbor on the West Shore of the Lake.

Reasons why Congress should grant lands to aid in its construction.

1st. The proposed ship canal will shorten the voyages from Green Bay to Chicago on each round trip about two hundred miles, or one fifth of the entire distance.

2d. It will avoid the present dangerous channels through the Islands at the north end of the peninsula called "Porte du Mort," or "Death's Door," where many valuable vessels and their cargoes are annually lost.

3d. It will, by means of the breakwater to be built on the Lake shore, give to the entire shipping traversing Lake Michigan a safe harbor on the west shore of the Lake, much needed at that point, enabling vessels, with the assistance of powerful steam tugs, to be constructed for that purpose, to run into Sturgeon Bay, proverbial for being the most commodious and the finest harbor on the upper Lakes, it being eight miles long, with an average width of more than one mile, and thus adding a new harbor on the Lake shore without Congress appropriating one dollar in money for constructing the same.

4th. The length of the proposed canal is one and a half miles, to be built not less than one hundred feet wide nor less than fifteen feet deep.

5th. The quantity of lumber that would annually pass through the canal is estimated at 150,000,000 feet.

6th. The quantity of cord wood, tan bark, staves, cedar posts, railroad ties, telegraph poles, shingles and shingle bolts annually passing through the canal, estimated in cord bulk, would be 50,000 cords.

7th. This immense quantity of freight is carried by about seventy to one hundred vessels, and would make over three thousand passages annually through the canal.

8th. The development of the Lake Superior region, now rapidly progressing, and the system of railroads now being constructed, designed to bring the mineral ores to Green Bay for shipment, will soon largely increase the number of vessels seeking an outlet from Green

Bay into the Lake, and not only the present but the future enormous traffic of that region requires the opening of this new channel into the Lake as a link in the great chain of new routes and lines of communication demanded by the opening up of the inexhaustible lumber and mineral resources of northeastern Wisconsin and Lake Superior.

9th. The estimated cost of constructing the canal and breakwater is $500,000.

10th. The average number of vessels annually lost on the Islands, at the channel of "Death's Door," is estimated at eight, and the value of the same and their cargoes at $75,000.

11th. Many grain-laden vessels, on their passage from Chicago (and other grain ports) down the lakes, are lost at "Death's Door," in trying to take shelter under the Islands in stormy weather.

12th. There is a strong current setting through "Death's Door," dangerous to vessels navigating it, many vessels having been lost in consequence thereof, even in moderate weather, by being drifted on to the shores, which, being rock-bound, is certain destruction to the craft going ashore.

13th. The official map of survey made by the United States Government, a copy from which is now in the hands of your Committee on Public Lands, show the location of Sturgeon Bay, with soundings, &c., and profile of the dividing ridge and of the point of rocks putting out into the Lake, on which it is proposed to build the breakwater, (and the light-house for which Congress made an appropriation a few years ago, but which will be of no practical use on that part of the coast until the ship canal is completed.) The map of the survey, &c., shows the canal to be a perfectly feasible project.

14th. The Substitute Bill now before your committee provides that the donation of lands asked for shall be made to the State of Wisconsin; limits the time for the commencement and completion of the work, and embodies carefully guarded provisions to regulate the grant, and protect the public domain and treasury of the nation in the event of failure on the part of the State to complete the work.

15th. It is an important public work, involving but a small grant of the public lands to consummate a great public improvement, which, when completed, will be hailed with joy and satisfaction, not only by the great lumber interests of Green Bay, but by thousands of shippers, captains, seamen, and shipowners of the Upper Lakes.

16th. To show more fully the dangerous navigation of the "Death's

Door" channel, it is only necessary to state that within the last few years the Government has been under the necessity of removing the light-house from Plum Island to Pilot Island, and only last fall added to the present lighthouse a "fog-horn," worked by caloric power, to warn vessels trying to make the passage. These wise precautions are commendable; but the true remedy is for Congress to give to the mariner, and the large and increasing interests concerned, a safe channel that looks as though Nature intended should at some day be made through the portage at Sturgeon Bay.

Questions for Discussion:
1. What does this document reveal about the economy of the Great Lakes?
2. What does this document reveal about navigation on the Great Lakes?
3. What does this document reveal about relations between businesses like Peshtigo and the federal government in postbellum America?

Anonymous, *Proposed Ship Canal at Sturgeon Bay, Wisconsin, to Connect Green Bay with Lake Michigan* (Washington, D.C.: McGill & Witherow, 1870), 1–4. Library of Congress, Rare Book and Special Collections Division.

Edward King, "Down the Mississippi" (1874)

The steamboat remains a powerful icon of the Mississippi's heyday as a highway for southern commerce, both in terms of passengers and cargo; with their enormous thrashing paddlewheels and belching smoke they were a dramatic sight. A prime example of a riverboat is the *Robert E. Lee*, built in 1866. It could carry a cargo of nearly six thousand bales of cotton as well as passengers. In 1870 the *Robert E. Lee* won a contest against the steamboat *Natchez* in a 750-mile race between St. Louis and New Orleans, which the *Lee* completed in three days, eighteen hours, and fourteen minutes. Because of hard usage in races and daily service, the danger of shipboard fire or boiler explosion, and generally light construction, the lifespan of most riverboats was only five years, after which owners usually scrapped them to build more modern boats. Furthermore, the frequent floods on western rivers created havoc ashore and afloat. On June 28, 1879, Congress established the Mississippi River Commission to coordinate flood-control efforts on the rivers. The continuing impact of the efforts to control floods is explored by John McPhee's purposefully titled *The Control of Nature*.[1]

In this colorful account of travel on the Mississippi, Edward King

---

1   John McPhee, *The Control of Nature* (New York: Farrar, Straus, Giroux, 1989).

(1848–1896), a reporter from Massachusetts, recounts his extensive travel through the South, much of it by steamboat. King notes both the distinctive culture associated with the western rivers and the damage created by floods.

"O, starboard side!"
"Oo-le-oo-le-oo!"
"Nudder one down dar!"

The roustabouts were loading sacks of corn from one of the immense elevators at East St. Louis into the recesses of that mammoth steamboat, the *Great Republic*, and singing at their toil. Very lustily had they worked, these grimy and uncouth men and boys, clad in soiled and ragged garments, from early morning, and it was full midnight as we stood listening to their song. In their voices, and in the characteristic wail with which each refrain ended, there was a kind of grim passion, not unmixed with religious fervor. The singers' tones seemed to sink into a lament, as if in despair at faulty expression. But the music kept them steadily at their work, tugging at the coarse, heavy sacks, while the rain poured down in torrents. The "torch-baskets"[1] sent forth their cheery light and crackle, and the heat-lightning, so terrible in Missouri, now and then disclosed to those of us still awake the slumbering city, with its myriad lights, and its sloping hills packed with dark, smoke-discolored houses, beyond the river.

Toward morning, the great steamer turned swiftly round, the very spray from the boiling water seeming crowded with oaths, as the officers drove the negroes to their several tasks; and the *Great Republic* glided slowly, and with scarcely a perceptible motion, down the stream. The blinking lights of the ferries behind us faded into distance. We passed tug-boats fuming and growling like monsters, drawing after them mysterious trains of barges; and finally entered upon the solitude which one finds so impressive upon the Mississippi.

A journey of 1,200 miles by water was before us. We were sailing from the treacherous, transition weather of Missourian March to meet loveliest summer robed in green, and garlanded with fairest blooms. The thought was inspiring. Eight days of this restful sailing on the gently-throbbing current, and we should see the lowlands, the Cherokee rose, the jessamine, the orange-tree. Wakeful and pacing

---

1   Torch-baskets: open iron baskets filled with combustible material for lighting.

the deck, across which blew a chill breeze, with my Ulster[1] close about me, I pondered upon my journey and the journey's end.

The *Great Republic* is the largest steamer on the Mississippi river, literally a floating palace. The luxuriantly furnished cabin is almost as long and quite as ample as the promenade hall in the Hombourg Kursaal,[2] and has accommodations for 200 guests. Standing on the upper deck or in the pilot-house, one fancies the graceful structure to be at rest, even when going at full speed. This is the very luxury of travel. An army of servants come and go. As in an ocean voyage, breakfast, dinner and tea succeed each other so quickly that one regrets the rapid flight of the hours. In the evening there is the blaze of the chandeliers, the opened piano, a colored band grouped around it and playing tasteful music while the youths and maidens dance. If the weather is warm, there are trips about the moonlit wilderness of decks and flirtations.

The two-score negro "roustabouts" on the boat were sources of infinite amusement to the passengers. At the small landings the *Great Republic* would lower her gang-planks, and down the steep banks would come kaleidoscopic processions of negroes and flour barrels. The pilots, perched in their cosy cage, twisted the wheel, and told us strange stories. Romantic enough were their accounts of the adventures of steamers in war time, how they ran the gauntlet here, and were seized there; and how, now and then, Confederate shells came crashing uncomfortably near the pilots themselves. The pilots on the Western rivers have an association, with head-quarters at St. Louis, and branches at Louisville, Pittsburgh, and Cincinnati. Each of the seventy-four members, on his trip, makes a report of changes in the channel, or obstructions, which is forwarded from point to point to all the others. They are men of great energy, of quaint, dry humor, and fond of spinning yarns. The genial "Mark Twain" served his apprenticeship as pilot, and one of his old companions and tutors, now on the *Great Republic*, gave us reminiscences of the humorist. One sees, on a journey down the Mississippi, where Mark found many of his queerest and seemingly impossible types.

Our first night on the river was so extremely dark that the captain

---

1   Ulster: a heavy woolen overcoat.
2   Hombourg Kursaal: Hombourg was a town on the border between France and Germany (now in France) known for its spas and casinos, which featured a palatial meeting hall or *kursaal*.

made fast to a shelving bank, and the *Great Republic* laid by till early
dawn. Then we sailed down past the fertile bottom lands of Missouri
and Illinois, past Grand Tower, with its furnaces and crowded villages,
past the great cypress swamps and the wooded lands, until we came
to Cairo, in Illinois, at the junction of the Ohio and Mississippi. One
broad lake spread a placid sheet above the flat country at the Ohio's
mouth. The *Great Eastern*[1] might have swung round in front of the
Illinois Central tracks at Cairo. Stopping but to load more bags of
corn and hogsheads of bacon, with hundreds of clamorous fowls, we
turned, and once more entered the giant river, which was then beginning to show a determination to overflow all proper bounds, and
invade the lands upon its banks.

When the rains have swollen its tributary rivers to more than their
ordinary volume, the Mississippi is grand, terrible, treacherous. Always subtle and serpent-like in its mode of stealing upon its prey, it
swallows up acres at one fell swoop; on one side sweeping them away
from their frail hold on the main land, while, on the other, it covers
plantations with slime, and broken tree trunks and boughs, forcing
the frightened inhabitants into the second story of their cabins, and
driving the cattle and swine upon high knolls to starve, or perhaps
finally to drown. It pierces the puny levées which have cost the States
bordering upon it such immense sums, and goes bubbling and roaring
through the crevasses, distracting the planters, and sending dismay to
millions of people in a single night. It promises a fall on one day; on
another it rises so suddenly that the adventurous woodmen along the
border have scarcely time to flee. It makes a lake of the fertile country
between the two great rivers; it carries off hundreds of woodpiles,
which lonely and patient labor has heaped, in the hope that a passing
steamer will buy them up, and thus reward a season's work. Out of
each small town on its western bank set too carelessly by the water's
edge, it makes a pigmy Venice, or floats it off altogether. As the huge
steamer glided along on the mighty current, we could see families
perched in the second stories of their houses, gazing grimly out upon
the approaching ruin. At one point a man was sculling from house
to barn-yard with food for his stock. The log barn was a dreary pile
in the midst of the flood. The swine and cows stood shivering on a

---

1   *Great Eastern*: an enormous British ship built in 1858 that could carry some four thou-
    sand passengers.

pine knoll, disconsolately burrowing and browsing. Hailed by some flustered *pater-familias*[1] or plantation master bound to the nearest town for supplies, we took him to his destination. As we got below the Arkansas and White rivers, the gigantic volume of water had so far overrun its natural boundaries that we seemed at sea, instead of upon an inland river. The cottonwoods and cypresses stood up amid the water wilderness like ghosts. Gazing into the long avenues of the sombre forests, we could see only the same level, all-enveloping flood. In the open country the cabins seemed ready to sail away, though their masters were usually smoking with much equanimity, and awaiting a "fall."

While we are gossiping of the river, let us consider its peculiarities and the danger of its inundations more fully. Below the mouth of the Missouri, the great river takes a wholly different appearance and character from those of the lovely stream which stretches from Lake Pepin down; and some of the old pilots say that section of it below St. Louis should have been called the "Missouri" rather than the Mississippi. The Missouri, they claim, gives to the Father of Waters most of the characteristics which dominate it until it has been reinforced by the Ohio, the Arkansas, the White and the Red. The river is forever making land on one side, and tearing it away on the other, the bends in its course not permitting the current to wash both banks with equal force. The farmer on the alluvial bottoms sees with dismay his corn-field diminish year by year, acres slipping into the dark current; yet the ease with which corn, cotton and sugar are raised in their respective localities along its banks is such that they willingly run the risk. The pilots complain bitterly of the constant changes in the channel, which it requires the eyes of Argus almost to detect. They say that the current might be made to bear more upon the rocky shores, thus avoiding disastrous losses of land and many "crevasses," as the gaps made in the levées by the encroaching water are called. The stream is so crooked that a twenty miles sail by water is sometimes necessary where the distance across the promontory, round which the steamer must go, is not more than a mile. Sometimes the current, tired of the detour, itself brushes away the promontory, and the astonished pilots see a totally new course opened before them.

---

1   Pater-familias: Latin term for *father of the family*, in this case meaning the male head of a household.

The occasional inundations of the alluvial lands are so little understood, and the general course of the Mississippi is comprehended by so few, that a little idea of its progress downward to the Delta country may prove interesting.

At the junction of the Mississippi and Missouri rivers properly begins what is known as the Lower Mississippi, although the name is not usually applied to the stream until it has crossed the grand "rocky chain" or bed extending across its channel between St. Louis and Cairo. All below this "chain," in the Mississippi valley, is alluvium, through which the river meanders from one bluff to another the bluffs being from forty to one hundred miles apart. Touching these bluffs at Commerce, Missouri, on the west bank, it courses across the valley, passing the vast prairies of Lower Illinois, known as "Egypt," on the east, meets the Ohio at Cairo, then strikes the bluffs again at Columbus, on the eastern or Kentucky shore. It skirts these bluffs as far as Memphis, having on its west the broad earthquake lands of Missouri and Arkansas. It then once more crosses its valley to meet the waters of the White and Arkansas rivers, and skirts the bluffs at Helena in Arkansas, flanking and hemming in the St. Francis with her swamps and "sunk lands." Reinforced by the White and Arkansas, it again crosses its valley to meet the Yazoo near Vicksburg, creating the immense Yazoo reservoir on the east bank, extending from the vicinity of Memphis to Vicksburg, and the valleys and swamps of the Macon and Tensas, on the west side. These latter have no terminus save the Gulf of Mexico, as the river does not approach the western bluffs after leaving Helena. From Vicksburg to Baton Rouge the river hugs the eastern bluffs, and from Baton Rouge to the mouth is the pure "delta country," for a distance of more than 200 miles.

All of this valley below the rocky chain crossing the river channel lies lower than the high water line of this powerful current, and the efforts of men to stay an inundation seem very puerile. The valley is divided into several natural districts, one embracing the lands from the chain to the vicinity of Helena, where the St. Francis debouches; another from Helena nearly to Vicksburg on the east bank, for the Yazoo valley; a third comprises the country from the Arkansas to the Red river, known as the Macon and Tensas valley; a fourth runs from the Red river to the Gulf, on the west side; and a fifth from Baton Rouge to the Gulf on the east side.

Some of these districts have been imperfectly levéed; others have never been protected at all, and the general opinion is that when high water does come the fact that there are a few levées increases the danger of a complete inundation, as the stream, finding itself restrained, breaks the barriers which attempt to control its current. Under the slave system, the planters on the lowlands were able to guard against ruin by water by elaborate preparation and vigilance, which they cannot summon now; and it is believed that nothing but the execution of a grand national work by the General Government will ever secure to the delta that immunity from ruin so desirable for people already savagely stripped by war and political knavery.

Yet the inundations do not come with alarming frequency. In 1867 the lowlands were overflowed and distress ensued; and in this year, 1874, the confusion, distress, and trepidation have been terrible to witness. Starvation has stood at thousands of doors, and only the hands of the Government and charity have saved hundreds from miserable deaths. Below Memphis, and in a wide belt of country round about, along the bottomlands in the State of Mississippi, and throughout the Louisiana lowlands, there has been immense damage. In an hour the planter is doomed to see a thousand acres, which have been carefully prepared for planting cotton, covered with water two or three feet deep. The country round about becomes a swamp, the roads are rivers, the lakes are seas.

As the Mississippi valley, south and north, will in future be one of the most populous sections of the American Union, and as the great network of rivers which penetrate to the Rocky Mountains, and the mighty cañons of the *Mauvaises Terres*[1] are so well adapted for commercial highways; as a score of States and Territories border on the Mississippi alone, why should not the National Government at once undertake the control and care of the stream and its tributaries?

Questions for Discussion:
1. What dangers did the Mississippi pose to those who either navigated its waters or lived on its banks?
2. How did the author regard nature and the environment in this account?
3. What does this account reveal about racial relations after the Civil War?

Edward King, *The Great South: A Record of Journeys* (Hartford, Conn.: American Publishing Company, 1875), 357–63.

1   *Mauvaises Terres*: the White River Badlands of Nebraska. French-Canadian trappers called this region *Le Mauvaises terres a traverser*, which means "bad lands to travel across."

FREE SHIPS AND PROTECTIONISM

The postbellum period was an era of rapid technological advancement, and maritime endeavors were certainly a part of that story. Increasingly powerful and efficient steam engines, durable iron and later steel hulls, more capacious ships, and improved safety, communications, and comfort all changed the way Americans conducted seaborne commerce.

Despite these new technologies, American shipping and shipbuilding suffered after the Civil War. Not only was the high seas merchant fleet shrinking, but technologically the country fell behind competitors like Britain in iron shipbuilding. Commentators noted that American ships were disappearing from the world's oceans while congressmen and businessmen debated the necessity of subsidizing private shipping firms with federal money. A fierce debate ensued about subsidizing the construction of American-built ships versus allowing market forces to work unfettered on the shipping industry. In the end little was done, and America quickly declined as a maritime power after 1865.

John Codman, "The Injustice of Granting Subsidies" (1871)

Many Americans wanted to see American shipping revived, but they disagreed on how to go about it. Many American shipping executives wanted the federal government to assist them in rebuilding the merchant marine by providing subsidies. The primary means of subsidizing American shipping was through mail subsidies. For example, the Pacific Mail Steamship Company offered to provide additional monthly mail-steamship service to Japan and China if it received a subsidy of half a million dollars a year beyond what it already received. A protracted debate followed in Congress over the utility of subsidizing an American-built and -flagged merchant marine.

Some American mariners, such as Captain John Codman (1814–1900), advocated a major change in American oceanic policy. Codman came from an influential New England family; unusually for a sea captain, he was a college graduate. A lifelong Democrat, Codman was the primary advocate for a "free ships" policy that would allow American shipping companies to purchase and use cheap foreign-built ships, rather than one that would subsidize American shipbuilding or favor certain companies with mail contracts. That policy was fiercely fought against by Republican congressmen from shipbuilding states such as Maine, and Congress never adopted a "free ships" policy. In the item below, which was probably a flyer produced to influence Congress, Codman makes a strong argument for "free ships."

THE INJUSTICE OF GRANTING *SUBSIDIES*
TO STEAMSHIP COMPANIES.

Of the many patriotic offers to relieve the Treasury of its money, it is sufficient to mention two of the most prominent, the "American Mail and Ocean Transportation Company" and the "American and European Steamship Company;" the one to enjoy perpetual franchise, and the other to continue for fifty years!

The first proposes to obtain Treasury endorsement of its bonds for $20,000,000, and the second demands immense sums for postage, with extensive land grants in addition.

Each intends to monopolize all the ocean shipbuilding and ship-owning of the country.

Ship-builders and ship-owners alike should protest against such an outrage upon their rights.

Suppose that these subsidy schemes are not mere stock-jobbing operations, and that they will really build a dozen or even twenty steamers at such enormous and uncalled-for expense to the community.

They ask for two years to complete the job. In those two years more than 500,000 tons of iron steamships will be built in Great Britain in shipyards not one of which is subsidized by government.

But in this would-be monopoly-shop of ours which shuts off all other builders, and the influence of which will be used to deprive American merchants of the right to supply themselves in the cheapest markets when they have completed their allotted number of ships, what then? Why, more relief from Government!

They must have it to the extent of $80 or $100 dollars per ton on every succeeding ship, or they must close their works, content with the proceeds of their bonds.

Now, is the encouragement of such individual speculation as this, for the sake of two or three operators, (the other names in these bills being mere cats'-paws), an encouragement to "revive American commerce"?

Does it give any relief to the importer who prefers to own a cheap ship, wherein to bring his goods from Calcutta or China, rather than to pay, as our laws now oblige him to do, freight money to the foreign ship-owner, whose government is more liberal and far-seeing than ours?

Does it give any relief to the owners of Liverpool, London, and

Havre packets who find that their old wooden ships pay no longer, because the iron screw-steamers, which they are not permitted to buy, have taken their business away from them?

Does it give any relief to the hundreds of Americans who are obliged to own ships under foreign flags, because they are not allowed to hold them honestly under their own?

Does the gift of employment to a dozen shipmasters give any relief to a multitude of others who are obliged to remain on shore or to take service with foreigners?

Does it give "relief" to *anybody* excepting a few stockjobbers and speculators?

SUBSIDY is claimed as a necessity for saving our workshops and shipyards from ruin, and for enabling us, in time of war with England, to build ships wherewith to fight her. . . .

We have been humbugged long enough with talk of "the decadence of American commerce." There is an apparent decadence of *all* commerce, or rather of all navigation, because steam has taken the place of sails.

But, according to the figures of this accurate and indefatigable investigator, *the United States has now more steam tonnage by* 97,803 *tons than is possessed by the whole British Empire!*

True, it is almost entirely domestic. Foreign tonnage we have not, because the ocean being free to the world we cannot compete with England upon it, and we are not permitted to divide with England the profits on sailing the ships which we cannot prevent her from building for her own use and for that of other nations wiser than ourselves.

Domestic tonnage we have in abundance for all our requirements, because our shipbuilding for coastwise and inland trade is an absolute monopoly, from which we have kept all foreign interference away, and we shall continue to do so.

Who, then, will make the absurd pretence, that in case of need the mechanics who built this million of tons for home use cannot build ironclads to fight England as they built them to conquer the rebellion? Moreover, if that event is ever anything more than a bugbear, where is the harm of purchasing ships in time of peace that can be used to capture others in time of war?

It is said that "England built up her steam marine by subsidies."

Denied. She gives subsidies for postal communication with her colonies not for ship-building. But let it be admitted that she did so in the beginning, when wooden side-wheel steamers could not carry freight advantageously. Ship-building has now improved so that only one in eighteen of the British steamers in foreign trade is subsidized. The testimony of the Cunard company is, that their "unsubsidized ships pay quite as well as the others."

Why, then, should we begin where England has left off? All her improvements are for us as well as for herself. If her unsubsidized ships have arrived at such perfection that they rival her own that are subsidized, would they not also rival ours?

There is only one straightforward, honest course to pursue that followed in this respect by all nations but the United States *buy what we cannot build, and continue to buy until we can build.*

Let our ship-builders have their materials free of duty, and thus let them *all* fairly compete with foreigners. If they are willing to reduce their price of labor, or if as they pretend their labor is superior, so that they can furnish us with ships as cheaply as they can be bought elsewhere, they will certainly command the preference. But until they can do this, are the rights of American ship-owners to be ignored, and are mechanics at large to be deprived of labor that a single shop may be built with their money for a stock-jobbing monopoly?
Washington, *January* 27, 1871.

Questions for Discussion:
1. What do Codman's arguments reveal about American attitudes toward the relationship between government and business?
2. What were the author's views on British steamships and subsidies?
3. Why did the author want to permit foreign-built ships to enter the American merchant marine?

John Codman, *The Injustice of Granting Subsidies to Steamship Companies* (Washington, D.C.: 1871). Library of Congress, Rare Book and Special Collections Division. Printed Ephemera Collection; Portfolio 206, Folder 15.

F. B. Norton, "Iron Shipbuilding" (1872)

One of the few American shipbuilding companies that seriously attempted to build iron ships after the Civil War was William Cramp & Sons of Philadelphia. Started in 1830 as a traditional wooden shipyard by William Cramp (1807–1879), the company began building iron vessels for the United States Navy during the Civil War and continued making iron-hulled steamships for commercial use thereafter. Cramp's successful transition from wood to iron was relatively rare, in part because it represented a change from shipbuilding as a craft, based on traditions, instincts, and handmade models, to an engineering-based industry with highly trained naval architects who used abstract mathematics to create ship designs. Historian William H. Thiesen, in *Industrializing American Shipbuilding*,[1] has examined that transition in detail.

Cramp's yard became a major employer in Philadelphia, producing both naval and merchant vessels. Notably, Cramp and his son Charles understood shipbuilding both as a business and a statement of national pride and competed keenly with British shipyards.

Philadelphia, April 5, 1872.

Among the many industrial establishments which make this the foremost manufacturing city of the world, yielding an annual product of nearly $400,000,000, none possesses greater interest than the iron shipyard of William Cramp & Sons. As I write, I am seated in an office in the midst of this shipyard, which commands a view of the entire establishment, and as I have a few moments' leisure I know not how I can better employ them than by giving a brief description of this, the busiest place on the continent, and stating a few facts in regard to the important subject of ship-building, about which so much is said and so little is known. Along the side of the enclosure toward the city is a two-story building some hundreds of feet in length. The ground floor is occupied with ponderous machinery for rolling, shearing, punching, and otherwise preparing the plates and bars for their various positions in the ship. The side toward the river is left open to admit the ready transfer of the heavy plates and the long ribs and beams. The second story is one long hall devoted to drawing plans and making patterns. All the lines which go to make up the graceful ship are traced upon this floor, crossing each other in every direction and making a seemingly inextricable labyrinth, until the floor looks as though every problem in plane and spherical trigonometry had been demonstrated upon it without erasing any lines.

At one end of this building are long furnaces for heating the angle irons, which are drawn out upon a large cast-iron floor and here bent to the proper shape for the ribs of a ship. At the other end are forges,

---

1   William H. Thiesen, *Industrializing American Shipbuilding: The Transformation of Ship Design and Construction, 1820–1920* (Gainesville: University Press of Florida, 2006).

and machine and boiler shops. On the river side rise the huge skeletons of four massive ocean steamers, each 355 feet in length, and 3016 tons burden, on which scores of workmen are busily engaged in attaching the ribs to the staunch keel or in riveting the massive plates to the frame. Boys run from their little forges with the red-hot bolts, which are speedily and skillfully riveted by the busy hammermen. It cannot be said of these ships that they are built "without sound of hammer or any tool of iron." Stout teams come, drawing ponderous loads of iron which has been rolled in the mills of adjacent towns. Hundreds of men are seen on every side drawing the iron on trucks, as firemen used to drag engines, with a long rope, or carrying it upon their shoulders up the ascending platforms to the ship's side, and performing a hundred processes one cannot describe. Indeed, I would as soon undertake to make an iron ship without learning the art as to attempt to give any adequate description of the multitudinous sounds and sights and processes of this noisy, busy place.

So far as the great problem of regaining our commercial prestige on the ocean is concerned, the importance of this place cannot be overrated, for here it has found its true solution. The free traders, who persistently attribute all our misfortunes to the tariff, with about as much reason as our ancestors charged theirs to the witches, have made the most of the decline of our ocean commerce. If the multitudes who have believed their false statements, and who have been waiting for free trade to revive a commerce which it, along with secession, destroyed, will visit this shipyard, they can witness for themselves the revival of our commerce by the aid of the very tariff they so lustily abuse. It was not for cheap British iron we were waiting, for every practical ship-builder knows that it is an absurdity to talk of building iron ships of imported materials, but for concentrated capital powerful enough to cope with the rich foreign lines backed up by the patronage of their governments. When, prior to the war, English steamers sought to compete with our clipper ships, we made one feeble, half-way effort to maintain our prestige through the Collins line. But the change from sail to steam necessitated a change from wood to iron. The English government saw this, and gave the needed aid in the repeated efforts which finally were successful. Free trade had depressed our iron industry and impoverished our government, and it was then, before the decline in our tonnage, that Mr. Henry C. Carey predicted that unless we adopted the policy of developing our iron and other industrial interests by adequate protection, we should soon be without a single steamer in the foreign trade. The war only consummated what free trade had begun.

The Pennsylvania Central Railroad has become the most powerful corporation in the world simply by aiding in the development of the great protected industries of Pennsylvania and the country, till it now has acquired the power to push its road across the ocean, and has ordered these four large iron steamships for the European trade. The commercial supremacy of England is the direct result of her manufacturing supremacy, and if history proves anything, it is that manufacturing industry is the only solid basis of a profitable and permanent commerce. As free trade has delayed the introduction of iron ships into our foreign commerce some fifteen years, so now it would speedily ruin the commencement so favorably made. Let it depreciate railroad stocks and business as it did in 1857 and the Pennsylvania Road would soon sell these ships to foreigners. But if this venture is sustained by a prosperous home industry, it will not only be successful, but the precursor of greater things.

The land has been filled with the cry of our decaying shipyards, as though iron shipbuilding was among the "lost arts," so far as America is concerned. But I fail to detect any signs of decay here. The old yard used for many years by this firm became too small, and this one has been added in the past few months. They have turned away numerous orders, and the six yards on this river are now building at least twenty iron ships. Nor need we ask any aid from England in the way of iron, or skilled workmen, or of perfect models. Here is one of the best builders from one of the largest yards on the Clyde, who says he never saw so good iron put into ships before. Our workmen receive better wages, and do more and better work than those abroad. These ships, when completed, will do more work with forty tons of coal per day than an English steamer with one hundred tons. Much has been said as to how wondrous cheaply iron ships can be built abroad, and surely some of them are poor enough to be worthy of low prices; but Messrs. Cramp & Sons state that they will take a contract for any iron ship complete at ten percent advance in currency on the British price for the same. . . . The change from wood to iron in our coasting trade is rapid, and our leading ship owners would scarcely take a wooden steamer as a gift if they were obliged to run it for ten years.

Mr. Franklin B. Gowen, the president of the Reading Railroad, stated to the writer that if the protection was not taken away from our tariff, he alone would build one hundred iron colliers for the coasting trade. England is deeply anxious to prevent the successful establishment of this most valuable branch of industry in our country. She has many ships superseded by the Suez Canal, and others containing old style engines, she would be glad to sell very "cheap," but like her rotten rails and shoddy woolens, they would be dear at any price. There has been a powerful and persistent lobby in Washington, for the past two years, using every possible means to break the tariff on shipbuilding materials, for the sake of gaining their real and ulterior object of free foreign ships, which would close every shipyard in the United States. The West has just as much interest in averting this calamity as the East, for the change from wood to iron has already commenced on our lakes and rivers, and promises to be a profitable and useful branch of industry. Iron vessels and boats have been built at Pittsburgh, Cincinnati, Dubuque, Buffalo, and Wyandotte, and a company has just been organized in St. Louis for building iron steamers. It should be remembered that our Western lakes and rivers furnish many points more favorable to building iron steamers for the ocean than the old shipyards of the seaboard. Mr. Bell's yard in Buffalo has furnished two iron steamers for the Atlantic during the past year, and it was the opinion of John Player, the eminent English engineer who planned the splendid blast furnaces at Milwaukee, that the Ohio River would prove to be the best point in this country for building iron ships for the ocean. I am told that Milwaukee proposes to build iron propellers, and this firm has had serious thoughts of establishing an iron shipyard at your city, in connection with the extensive iron works at Bay View.

Questions for Discussion:

1. What arguments does F. B. Norton put forward supporting protectionism?

2. What does this document reveal about American industrialization in the postbellum period?

3. Why were iron ships so important for American shipping?

F. B. Norton, "Iron Ship-building in the United States," (Philadelphia: 1872). Library of Congress, Rare Book and Special Collections Division. Printed Ephemera Collection; Portfolio 159, Folder 48.

John Roach, "Shall America Build Ships?" (1881)

The one region of the country that proved capable of building modern iron and steel commercial vessels and warships was the Delaware River region near Philadelphia. Historian Thomas R. Heinrich analyzes how proprietary shipyards such as those owned by the Cramps and others survived and adapted to the new form of industrial corporate capitalism that arose in the postbellum period in *Ships for the Seven Seas*.[1]

One of those shipyard owners was John Roach (1813–1887), who in many ways represents the idealized "rags-to-riches" story. Born in Ireland, he came to America as a penniless immigrant. Through hard work and perseverance Roach prospered in the shipbuilding business, and by 1872 operated his own shipyard in Chester, Pennsylvania. Roach prospered as a builder of iron ships, both commercial and naval. An ardent Republican and advocate of protectionism, he was a bitter opponent of the "free ships" advocates, and authored many pamphlets on the subject.

YES. By reason of our position and products, we ought to be the first ocean-carrying nation in the world. To become that, we must build ships. National ambition, prosperity, and self-defense alike are involved in the answer, Yes.

Our early history proves us worthy of that position. When we achieved independence and began as a nation, we began as a nation of ship-builders. Among the first acts of our earliest statesmen was the passage of protective navigation laws, to meet those of England. Starting out with the sturdy spirit of self-reliance, though with bankrupt treasury, no national credit, but a large national debt, only some three millions of people, and a wilderness to conquer, we made such progress in ship-building as the world never saw before.

It was not until we had 46,000,000 of people, resources superior, and foreigners dependent on us for bread, that it was declared we must go abroad to buy ships, and buy them of our great commercial rival at that.

From 1789 to 1812 our tonnage grew from 280,000 to 1,100,000 tons, an increase so remarkable that England, jealous of us as ocean rivals, from the first, made war upon our commerce—for the war of 1812 was nothing else. But in twenty years from the date of peace our

---

1   Thomas R. Heinrich, *Ships for the Seven Seas: Philadelphia Shipbuilding in the Age of Industrial Capitalism* (Baltimore: Johns Hopkins University Press, 1997).

commerce had doubled, and our tonnage increased yet more largely, till in 1850 it was 3,335,454 tons, and we had sold over 400,000 tons of ships abroad, besides. We built the fastest and cheapest wooden ships, and the well-known Yankee clippers were seen in every port all over the world. In 1860 we had 5,350,000 tons, and of our total foreign trade $437,190,000 was carried in American bottoms, against $160,057,000 in foreign ships. Then came our civil war and England's opportunity.

Our growth had been wholly in the wooden sailing ship. But in 1840, seeing the impossibility of competing with us in building the wooden ship, and knowing no nation could be great on the sea that did not build its ships, England found a new factor of success in the introduction of the iron steam-ship. She encouraged the large invest-ment of capital required by establishing steam-ship lines, with ample mail compensation; thus skillfully opening at once new markets, and by increased trade creating new demand for ships. She also gave naval contracts to private ship-builders, to enable them to build up iron shipyards. And from the time she began this policy we began to lose, through not meeting her wisely in this as we had twice met her when it was a question of war; and the rebellion effectually prevented us from continuing a competition in which we had previously been so successful. So the carrying trade of the North Atlantic passed out of our hands.

Since the civil war, laboring under disadvantages spoken of later on, it is not to be wondered at that the American carrying trade has not been revived. The wonder is that we have any shipping left. But who can doubt that if in 1865 our statesmen had recognized the imperiled position and vital importance of this great interest, and had adopted a judicious policy to restore us gradually to our proper place on the sea, millions on millions of dollars annually would have been saved to our country, millions paid to American labor, the day of resumption hastened, and much of the distress of the late "hard times" averted?

Looking at the present and future interests of our country, there-fore, I say that Americans shall and must build ships. But there seems to be some difference of opinion about our ability to do it. Practical men, men who own ships and want to own more, say we can. Theo-rists and "free ship" men, who neither build nor own ships, nor intend to own them, say we cannot. To get at the difference clearly, let us see on what points all are pretty well agreed. These may be set down as:

1. That the United States need more ships than any other nation, having more surplus products to be carried in them.
2. That no nation has ever been a great ship-owning nation that did not build its own ships.
3. That we have natural resources superior to those of any other country for building either wooden or iron ships.
4. That we have the most energetic and intelligent class of workmen in the world.
5. That ninety percent of the ship's cost is labor; and
6. That labor is free, and we can import it from any part of the world without duty or restriction.

What, then, divides the American people on this great national issue? I can see nothing but discriminating laws and the labor question. The one difficulty claimed by the "free-ship" advocate is the difference in the ship's first cost. What does this difficulty amount to? The difference in the first cost of American and English built iron ships is: in the sailing ship eight percent and in the steam-ship from ten to fifteen. What causes it? The greater cost of American labor. It is true we are free to import labor from the European countries, where it is cheap; but the moment the working-man gets here, he seems to imbibe our national idea of the elevation of man, becomes Americanized and wants American wages. I say this is right. But shall we, then, leave our forests and mines undeveloped and thousands of working-men unemployed, because it has ever been and is the policy of our Government to furnish labor with more favorable conditions than it knows elsewhere? Is there no way to build up American shipping other than to crush down American labor, or to buy the ships from a nation which has no advantage over us in ship-building, save as she applies her policy of crushing down labor? I will leave that question for the American people to answer.

But it is not the first cost that prevents us from building ships. Rather let us look at facts like these: 1. The great revolution on the ocean,—from wood to iron, from sail to steam, from the ordinary engine to the compound,—and the start England had of us in the use of these advantages. 2. Our difficult position today through not being able to avail ourselves in other years of these new conditions, by reason of internal strife. Every businessman knows the almost impossibility of raising capital to compete with large capital already in possession of the business. 3. Our enormous system of taxation, different from that of any other nation, and in reality prohibitive of ship owning. 4. Lack of a definite policy which would create a demand for ships in the opening of new markets,—our Government offering no inducements or facilities for reaching the world's markets where our products could be sold, and leaving our merchants to rely on sailing ships or on foreigners for transportation. If it was profitable for the foreigners to open the markets to us, they did so; if not, we went without. 5. The terrible wrong inflicted on American capital invested in the foreign trade by compelling its ships to carry the mails for postage. 6. Exorbitant tonnage dues and consul fees and pilot-wages. These, with other existing burdens, are reasons sufficient why we cannot afford to own ships. And, of course, until we can profitably own ships, we shall not build them.

The "free ship" advocate has plenty to say about a lost carrying trade and antiquated laws. Why is he always silent about these practical, tangible grievances? Why has he nothing to offer but forever the same two remedies—"free ships" and "free material"? Let us see of what sort these remedies are.

1. "Free ships," or the right to buy ships where we choose. That means to buy of England; for no other nation has them to sell, or can build them. It means for a nation having abundant resources and ability to supply itself with ships for its use in peace and defense in war, to become dependent for ships upon a single foreign nation. If we become dependent this year, shall we not be more so next? When shall we emancipate ourselves under this policy? Let us not forget, too, that all nations are interested in having more than one nation able to supply them with iron ships. Again, it means to starve American and feed foreign labor; to take millions on millions of dollars out of circulation among our people; to build up a foreign government and beat down our own. It means inevitable national humiliation and disgrace sooner or later. The statesman who advocates "free ships" ought to come out frankly and admit that, in whatever form he recommends relief for our carrying trade, he means England shall be the gainer. For "free ships" is to depend upon her for them, as I have said; and "free material" used in ships can only be supplied by England. What kind of a plan is that for Americans to propose?

Curiously enough, too, the "free-ship" man is always ready for a bargain. He will give you free material, but you must give him "free ships." Or he will give you a postal contract, but you must give him the right to buy ships in the cheapest market. But if you offer him relief from taxation, he doesn't want that, nor does he want encouragement. What he evidently does want is the English ship, and nothing else will do.

Take the history of the three wars we have fought for independence, for equal rights on the sea, for the preservation of the Union, and I ask you, could we have afforded then to be dependent upon England for ships, and if we had been dependent, what would have been the result? To simply point out the effects of such a condition in our late civil war: Where lay the strength of the North? Was it not chiefly in her ability to at once send sixty thousand trained men from the private shipyards into the navy-yards; to send thousands more of skilled mechanics from our workshops into the arsenals, and in the private shipyards to build the "ninety-days" gun-boats; besides being able, through the work of those left at home, to supply the wants of the people and support our armies in the field? Of what value was it to us that we were able to send out the little *Monitor* from a private shipyard in New York in one hundred days? Had she been four days later, the capital of the nation would doubtless have been captured.

Where lay the weakness of the South? Was it not in her undeveloped condition, without shipyards, or engine-works, or rolling-mills, or factories, or the means in any way to supply the wants of her people or maintain her army either in clothing or implements of war? She never surrendered until we blockaded her coast and shut off her chances to get supplies from England. In our three wars, what should we have done but for our ability to build ships?

But, looking at free ships as a matter of business, what has the difference in first cost to do with our ship owning? Let us compare the ship on the sea to the factory on the land. Both require capital for the plant and men to operate them. Now, what businessman does not know of instances where two men are engaged in the same line of manufacture, and where one of them paid from fifteen to twenty percent more for his plant than the other? But has any business man ever heard of a man's closing up his factory and ceasing competition merely because his plant cost him more, all other things being equal? No, it is not the first cost that drives a man out of the business. But suppose the one man's taxes were twenty times more, the wages of his hands twenty-five to forty percent higher, than those of the other—

why, he would fail, though you gave him his plant for nothing. What man could buy a cheap English factory and run it on the American principle of high taxes, high capital, and high labor? So, in ships, it is not what it costs to get the ship afloat, but what it costs to keep her there, under American rates of taxation, interest, and labor, that prevents us from owning ships in competition with foreign owners, who employ capital under no such disadvantages. . . .

The whole question resolves itself into this: Whether this country, with more goods to carry, with more need of ships, with more raw material to use, with better natural advantages, with the best skilled labor, and with more coast to defend, than any other country, shall be independent and build its own ships, thus encouraging all its industries and protecting its own labor, on which the foundations of this Government were laid, or shall become dependent entirely upon a foreign nation for ships, and let its own working-men shift for themselves when the bread has been taken from their mouths? To do the latter would be to refuse the advantages God has given us. Make this issue, and when the people come to understand it, there will be no question how they will decide.

Questions for Discussion:
1. What does this document reveal about the differences between advocates of "free ships" and protectionism?
2. What does this document reveal about the process of industrialization in the United States?
3. According to Roach, what prevented American shipyards from competing successfully with the British?

John Roach, "Shall America Build Ships?" *The North American Review* 132, no. 294 (May 1881): 467–82.

WEST COAST RACIAL CONCERNS

The decades between the end of the Civil War and 1900 were difficult ones for immigrants and Native Americans. Prejudice was rife in America and existed not only between different racial groups, but also between different ethnicities. Yet at the same time, the United States was also desperate for immigrant labor to open up the undeveloped lands of the West. Northern Europeans generally faced an easier time than other groups. The Chinese who came to port communities like San Francisco on the West Coast, set apart by their appearance, culture, and language, confronted a great deal of discrimination, including lynching and laws that prevented them from acquiring citizenship.

This period also saw the last of the conflicts between Native Americans and settlers moving West. These conflicts sometimes had a maritime element to them, especially in Alaska, where Native groups dominated access to valuable natural resources. For Alaskan Natives, contact with white civilization could be devastating, as trading ships brought disease and alcohol that decimated entire communities.

These racial concerns are exemplified by the career of Captain Michael "Hell Roaring" Healy (1839–1904) of the U.S. Revenue Cutter Service. Healy took part in the punitive expedition against Native Alaskans in 1882, yet he also crusaded to save the same peoples from white liquor smugglers. As a resident of San Francisco and an officer in the Revenue Cutter Service, he was aware of the antipathy against Chinese immigrants and was obligated to enforce the "Chinese Exclusion Act." Historian James O'Toole considers Michael Healy, his equally remarkable siblings, and their complex attitudes and reactions to racial issues in his award-winning book, *Passing for White*.[1]

William G. Morris, "The Navy Shells an Alaskan Village" (1882)

In 1867 the American government purchased Alaska from the Russian Czar. For the first seventeen years following its purchase, there was no government in Alaska outside of that provided by the Army, the Navy, the Revenue Cutter Service, and customs collectors in coastal towns—and the Army withdrew in 1877. In 1880 the census bureau found only 430 non-Natives in the territory.

For about five years in the 1880s, administration of Alaska fell to the Navy. Thrust into this unfamiliar constabulary role, the Navy and Revenue Cutter Service's reaction to disorder by Native Alaskans proved harsh. In response to threats against the Northwest Trading Company, the Navy shelled a Native Alaskan village, killing seven villagers outright while six children burned to death when a landing party torched the village's houses. Compelled by this incident, Congress finally moved to create a civilian gov-

---

1   James M. O'Toole, *Passing for White: Race, Religion, and the Healy Family, 1820–1920* (Amherst: University of Massachusetts Press, 2002).

ernment for Alaska. The following report was made by William G. Morris, a federal customs collector stationed in Sitka.

CUSTOM-HOUSE, SITKA, ALASKA,

COLLECTOR'S OFFICE, *November 9, 1882.*

SIR: On the 28th of last month I had the honor to transmit to the department the following telegram:

"SITKA, *Oct. 28, 1882.*

"SECRETARY TREASURY.

Washington, D.C.:

"26th inst. Hoochenoo[1] Indians becoming troublesome, capturing property from whites, Commander Merriman[2] repaired thither in *Corwin.*[3] Became necessary to shell and destroy village, canoes, and make prisoners. Severe lesson taught. Particulars by mail."

It is presumed that all essential information has already been rendered the department by the report of the commander of the *Corwin* himself, and that as the expedition was a joint one upon behalf of the Navy and Treasury Departments, that the report of the naval commander will also reach the head of this department, hence it will be unnecessary for me to enter into general details, but merely to give a synopsis of what I saw myself as an eye witness, and my opinion of the necessity which existed for adopting such stringent measures.

It has been a custom for many years in this territory, when an Indian has been killed or injured by another, or by a white man, for his surviving relatives to demand at the hands of the parties who injured him a certain payment or tribute, consisting generally of blankets. When this levy is made it means potlatch (pay) or die. It has been attempted by the Navy to break up this practice, but without effect.

Shortly previous to the case at bar, whilst an Indian was cutting down a tree for the Northwest Trading Company at Killisnoo, he was warned of the danger, and continued in a position of peril. The tree fell and killed him. Immediately a certain number of blankets were levied as a fine upon the company by his relatives, and payment demanded. The company refused, of course. Matters remained *in statu*

---

1   Hoochenoo: sometimes *hootzenoo,* an illegal homemade form of rum distilled by both whites and Natives in Alaska. Morris is assuming the villagers were drunk.
2   Merriman: Commander E. C. Merriman of the U.S. Navy.
3   *Corwin:* The U.S. revenue cutter *Thomas Corwin,* commanded by Michael Healy.

quo until the *Adams*,[1] Commander Merriman, arrived in these waters. He touched at Killisnoo on his way to this port, and complaint was made to him of the exaction by the superintendent of the company. He informed the Indians that in future no such payments should either be demanded or enforced as far as white men were concerned; that if they persisted in such course he would punish them severely, and that in this instance the company would and should not pay. They submitted with bad grace.

On the night of October 22, whilst this company were whaling in the Kottzenoo Lagoon, a bomb, shot from the whale-boat at a whale, accidentally exploded and killed an Indian *shaman*, who composed one of the crew; whereupon the latter immediately arose, and aided by about one hundred Indians, overpowered the two white men in the boat and took them prisoners; captured the boat, nets, whaling gear, and steam launch of the company, valued at several thousand dollars, and demanded payment of two hundred blankets for the dead man. The white men were kept close prisoners. A plan was formed to murder the engineer of the launch, who fortunately did not take the trail expected.

Capt. J. M. Vanderbilt, the superintendent, at once got up steam on the company's[2] tug-boat *Favorite*, and started with his family post haste to Sitka for aid from the naval commander. The Indians endeavored to cut off the *Favorite*, but failed.

As soon as Vanderbilt reported the facts to Commander Merriman, the latter put a howitzer and Gatling gun on the *Favorite*, sought the co-operation of the revenue-marine steamer *Corwin*, then in port, and as early as practicable, with a force of about one hundred marines and sailors, started himself for the scene of action, picking up his large steam launch on the way. I accompanied the expedition.

Upon arriving at the lagoon, matters were found exactly as represented by Vanderbilt; the men still prisoners; the Indians increasing in force and very much excited. Commander Merriman lost no time in arresting the ringleaders, and got the two principal chiefs of the tribe on board the *Corwin*, and informed them that, instead of the Northwest Trading Company paying anything to them, he should inflict

---

1   *Adams*: USS *Adams*, a single-screw, wooden-hull, bark-rigged Navy warship much bigger and more heavily armed than the revenue cutter *Corwin*.
2   Company: Northwest Trading Company.

upon them a fine of four hundred blankets, payable the next morning, under the penalty of having their canoes destroyed and principal village shelled and burnt.

So temporizing has been the policy pursued within the past two years by the Navy towards the Siwashes that they evidently thought this a game of bluff. They were surly and impertinent, and affected not to think Commander Merriman would put his threat into execution. They, however, took the precaution to make use of the intervening night in taking to a place of security their large canoes and valuables.

On the following day, the Indians having failed to come to time, Commander Merriman made good his threat, destroyed their canoes, shelled and burnt their village.

My object in addressing the department upon this subject is for the purpose of placing my opinion on record as to the propriety of this measure and the absolute necessity which existed for such harsh measures being adopted.

The Hoochenoos are a rich and warlike tribe, very insolent and saucy towards the whites. Not long since they proceeded to Wrangell and attacked the Church Indians there, killing several, amongst them Toyatt, a missionary Indian, a very useful and intelligent man.

As long as the native tribes throughout the archipelago do not feel the force of the government and are not punished for flagrant outrages, so much the more dangerous do they become, and are to be feared by isolated prospecting parties of miners. Once let it be understood by the Siwashes that the life of a white man is sacred, and that they will be severely handled if they harm him, there will be no danger or difficulty in small parties traversing the country in search of mineral and other wealth.

The punishment has been most severe, but eminently salutary, and in my judgment the very thing that was needed, and unhesitatingly, in my opinion, is the prompt and energetic action of Commander Merriman to be applauded, and this occasion is sought to express great confidence in the result of his action and general management of the Indians since he has been on this station.

Owing to the heavy draught of water needed for the *Adams*, the presence and co-operation of the *Corwin* were most opportune.

The conduct of Lieutenant Healy in command of said vessel, is especially to be commended, as that of an officer and a gentleman and a credit to the service. His officers and men conducted themselves well throughout the whole affair, and deserve therefore special mention.

I am, respectfully, your obedient servant.

WM. GOUVERNEUR MORRIS.

Collector

Hon. CHAS. J. FOLGER,
Secretary of the Treasury, Washington, D.C.

Questions for Discussion:

1. What does this document reveal about racial relations in Alaska in the 1880s?

2. What does this document reveal about the Navy's role in governing Alaska?

3. What sort of problems does this document have for historians attempting to understand this event?

William G. Morris to Charles J. Folger, November 9, 1882. U.S. Congress. House. "Alleged Shelling of Alaskan Villages," 47th Cong., 2nd sess., ex. doc. no. 9 (Washington, D.C.: Government Printing Office, 1883). Found at Naval Historical Center, http://www.history.navy.mil/library/online/alaska.htm#i.

Congress, "Chinese Exclusion Act" (1882)

Sometimes a document is the event, as in the case of many laws. In this instance, the 1882 Chinese Exclusion Act is a remarkable example of the combination of racism and anti-immigrant bigotry, especially on the West Coast. In California, working-class whites feared that Chinese would take their jobs at slave wages and complained, "These cheap slaves fill every place. Their dress is scant and cheap. Their food is rice from China. They lodge twenty in a room, ten by ten. They are wipped curs, abject in docility, mean, contemptible and obedient in all things." It was a patently unjust law—no other nationality was ever targeted so openly. One Chinese woman protested, why us and not the Irish "who were always drunk and fighting?" Nonetheless the law passed, although the Chinese proved adept at avoiding its provisions in a number of ways, such as creating "paper sons."[1] Ronald

---

1   Paper sons: a means of illegal immigration whereby Chinese immigrants forged papers claiming they had a son in China whom they wanted to come to America.

Takaki considers these aspects of the Asian American experience in his book *Strangers from a Different Shore.*[1]

The Chinese Exclusion Act was primarily concerned with controlling the seaborne arrival of Chinese laborers. Note the special emphasis on immigrants arriving by ship and the penalties for ship captains found with Chinese immigrants on board their ships. Anti-Chinese feeling had remarkable persistence: this law continued in force until 1943.

Preamble. Whereas, in the opinion of the Government of the United States the coming of Chinese laborers to this country endangers the good order of certain localities within the territory thereof: Therefore,

Be it enacted by the Senate and House of Representatives of the United States of America in Congress assembled, That from and after the expiration of ninety days next after the passage of this act, and until the expiration of ten years next after the passage of this act, the coming of Chinese laborers to the United States be, and the same is hereby, suspended; and during such suspension it shall not be lawful for any Chinese laborer to come, or, having so come after the expiration of said ninety days, to remain within the United States.

SEC. 2. That the master of any vessel who shall knowingly bring within the United States on such vessel, and land or permit to be landed, and Chinese laborer, from any foreign port of place, shall be deemed guilty of a misdemeanor, and on conviction thereof shall be punished by a fine of not more than five hundred dollars for each and every such Chinese laborer so brought, and may be also imprisoned for a term not exceeding one year.

SEC. 3. That the two foregoing sections shall not apply to Chinese laborers who were in the United States on the seventeenth day of November, eighteen hundred and eighty, or who shall have come into the same before the expiration of ninety days next after the passage of this act, and who shall produce to such master before going on board such vessel, and shall produce to the collector of the port in the United States at which such vessel shall arrive, the evidence hereinafter in this act required of his being one of the laborers in this section mentioned;

---

1   Ronald Takaki, *Strangers from a Different Shore: A History of Asian Americans* (Boston: Little, Brown, and Company, 1989).

nor shall the two foregoing sections apply to the case of any master whose vessel, being bound to a port not within the United States by reason of being in distress or in stress of weather, or touching at any port of the United States on its voyage to any foreign port of place: Provided, That all Chinese laborers brought on such vessel shall depart with the vessel on leaving port.

SEC. 4. That for the purpose of properly identifying Chinese laborers who were in the United States on the seventeenth day of November, eighteen hundred and eighty, or who shall have come into the same before the expiration of ninety days next after the passage of this act, and in order to furnish them with the proper evidence of their right to go from and come to the United States of their free will and accord, as provided by the treaty between the United States and China dated November seventeenth, eighteen hundred and eighty, the collector of customs of the district from which any such Chinese laborer shall depart from the United States shall, in person or by deputy, go on board each vessel having on board any such Chinese laborer and cleared or about to sail from his district for a foreign port, and on such vessel make a list of all such Chinese laborers, which shall be entered in registry-books to be kept for that purpose, in which shall be stated the name, age, occupation, last place of residence, physical marks or peculiarities, and all facts necessary for the identification of each of such Chinese laborers, which books shall be safely kept in the custom-house; and every such Chinese laborer so departing from the United States shall be entitled to, and shall receive, free of any charge or cost upon application therefore, from the collector or his deputy, at the time such list is taken, a certificate, signed by the collector or his deputy and attested by his seal of office, in such form as the Secretary of the Treasury shall prescribe, which certificate shall contain a statement of the name, age, occupation, last place of residence, personal description, and fact of identification of the Chinese laborer to whom the certificate is issued, corresponding with the said list and registry in all particulars. In case any Chinese laborer after having received such certificate shall leave such vessel before her departure he shall deliver his certificate to the master of the vessel, and if such Chinese laborer shall fail to return to such vessel before her departure from port the certificate shall be delivered by the master to the collector of customs for cancellation. The certificate herein provided for shall entitle the Chinese laborer to whom the same is issued to return to and re-enter the United States upon producing and delivering the same to the collector of customs of the district at which such Chinese laborer shall seek to re-enter; and upon delivery of such certificate by such Chinese laborer to the collector of customs at the time of re-entry in the United States, said collector shall cause the same to be filed in the custom house and duly canceled.

SEC. 5. That any Chinese laborer mentioned in section four of this act being in the United States, and desiring to depart from the United States by land, shall have the right to demand and receive, free of charge or cost, a certificate of identification similar to that provided for in section four of this act to be issued to such Chinese laborers as may desire to leave the United States by water; and it is hereby made the duty of the collector of customs of the district next adjoining the foreign country to which said Chinese laborer desires to go to issue such certificate, free of charge or cost, upon application by such Chinese laborer, and to enter the same upon registry-books to be kept by him for the purpose, as provided for in section four of this act.

SEC. 6. That in order to the faithful execution of articles one and two of the treaty in this act before mentioned, every Chinese person other than a laborer who may be entitled by said treaty and this act to come within the United States, and who shall be about to come to the United States, shall be identified as so entitled by the Chinese Government in each case, such identity to be evidenced by a certificate issued under the authority of said government, which certificate shall be in the English language or (if not in the English language) accompanied by a translation into English, stating such right to come, and which certificate shall state the name, title, or official rank, if any, the age, height, and all physical peculiarities, former and present occupation or profession, and place of residence in China of the person to whom the certificate is issued and that such person is entitled conformably to the treaty in this act mentioned to come within the United States. Such certificate shall be prima-facie evidence of the fact set forth therein, and shall be produced to the collector of customs, or his deputy, of the port in the district in the United States at which the person named therein shall arrive.

SEC. 7. That any person who shall knowingly and falsely alter or substitute any name for the name written in such certificate or forge any such certificate, or knowingly utter any forged or fraudulent certificate, or falsely personate any person named in any such certificate, shall be deemed guilty of a misdemeanor; and upon conviction thereof shall be fined in a sum not exceeding one thousand dollars, and imprisoned in a penitentiary for a term of not more than five years.

SEC. 8. That the master of any vessel arriving in the United States from any foreign port or place shall, at the same time he delivers a manifest of the cargo, and if there be no cargo, then at the time of making a report of the entry of vessel pursuant to the law, in addition to the other matter required to be reported, and before landing, or permitting to land, any Chinese passengers, deliver and report to the collector of customs of the district in which such vessels shall have arrived a separate list of all Chinese passengers taken on board his vessel at any foreign port or place, and all such passengers on board the vessel at that time. Such list shall show the names of such passengers (and if accredited officers of the Chinese Government traveling on the business of that government, or their servants, with a note of such facts), and the name and other particulars, as shown by their respective certificates; and such list shall be sworn to by the master in the manner required by law in relation to the manifest of the cargo. Any willful refusal or neglect of any such master to comply with the provisions of this section shall incur the same penalties and forfeiture as are provided for a refusal or neglect to report and deliver a manifest of cargo.

SEC. 9. That before any Chinese passengers are landed from any such vessel, the collector, or his deputy, shall proceed to examine such passengers, comparing the certificates with the list and with the passengers; and no passenger shall be allowed to land in the United States from such vessel in violation of law.

SEC. 10. That every vessel whose master shall knowingly violate any of the provisions of this act shall be deemed forfeited to the United States, and shall be liable to seizure and condemnation on any district of the United States into which such vessel may enter or in which she may be found.

SEC. 11. That any person who shall knowingly bring into or cause to be brought into the United States by land, or who shall knowingly aid or abet the same, or aid or abet the landing in the United States from any vessel of any Chinese person not lawfully entitled to enter the United States, shall be deemed guilty of a misdemeanor, and shall, on conviction thereof, be fined in a sum not exceeding one thousand dollars, and imprisoned for a term not exceeding one year.

SEC. 12. That no Chinese person shall be permitted to enter the United States by land without producing to the proper officer of customs the certificate in this act required of Chinese persons seeking to land from a vessel. And any Chinese person found unlawfully within the United States shall be caused to be removed there from to the country from whence he came, by direction of the United States, after being brought before some justice, judge, or commissioner of a court of the United States and found to be one not lawfully entitled to be or remain in the United States.

SEC. 13. That this act shall not apply to diplomatic and other officers of the Chinese Government traveling upon the business of that government, whose credentials shall be taken as equivalent to the certificate in this act mentioned, and shall exempt them and their body and household servants from the provisions of this act as to other Chinese persons.

SEC. 14. That hereafter no State court or court of the United States shall admit Chinese to citizenship; and all laws in conflict with this act are hereby repealed.

SEC. 15. That the words "Chinese laborers," whenever used in this act, shall be construed to mean both skilled and unskilled laborers and Chinese employed in mining.

Approved, May 6, 1882.

Questions for Discussion:
1. What does this document reveal about popular attitudes toward race and immigration in the late nineteenth century?
2. Under the provisions of this law, what penalties were there for shipmasters who brought Chinese immigrants into the country?
3. How is this law similar or different from the experiences of other immigrant groups that came to America?

William MacDonald, *Select Statutes and Other Documents Illustrative of the History of the United States, 1861–1898* (New York: Macmillan, 1903), 389–94.

Michael A. Healy, "Whisky Traffic" (1884)

Native Alaskans suffered cruelly from the introduction of disease and alcohol by American traders. Standing between the traders and the Native

Alaskans was the U.S. Revenue Cutter Service (USRCS), the forerunner of the U.S. Coast Guard. The USRCS played a major role in late-nineteenth-century Alaska, a topic considered fully in Truman Strobridge and Dennis Noble's *Alaska and the U.S. Revenue Cutter Service.*[1] This role was a policing one: protecting marine resources, pursuing smugglers, and bringing justice in general to a frontier region. But the USRCS also played a humanitarian role by assisting Native Alaskans and rescuing shipwrecked mariners.

In this document, Captain Michael Healy (1839–1904), commander of the revenue cutter *Corwin*, reports on his efforts to stop the illegal liquor trade. There is some cruel irony in this report: Healy himself was an alcoholic, and he was not white. Born to a slave mother and an Irish father, Healy "passed" as white due to his light skin color. Healy struggled with both liquor and racial prejudice throughout his life, yet he here attempts to protect Alaskan Natives from white liquor traffickers. The story of this enormously complex individual is admirably recounted in Maria Brook's documentary film, *The Odyssey of Captain Healy.*[2]

Owing to the continued and determined efforts of the *Corwin*, and notwithstanding the lax enforcement of the law regarding liquor permits to vessels clearing for this Territory, I am happy to state that the whisky traffic in northern Alaska has almost entirely ceased. The beneficial effects of our annual cruises are apparent in the changed condition of the Eskimos. Sickness has decreased; the people are better clothed; more attention is paid to their boats; food is plentiful; furs, bone, and ivory for trade are abundant, and the large number of healthy young children in every village dissipates former fears that the race might become extinct.

Satisfactory as is the present state of affairs, it can be continued only by constant and united work. If efforts to restrain the trade once cease the natural appetite of the natives for alcohol, aided by the white man's greed for gain, will soon cause it to revert to its former terrible condition.

Most of the whalemen desire to see its total suppression, as it places those men who, from conscientious motives and a desire to comply

---

1 Truman R. Strobridge and Dennis L. Noble, *Alaska and the U.S. Revenue Cutter Service: 1867–1915* (Annapolis, Md.: Naval Institute Press, 1999).
2 Maria Brooks, *The Odyssey of Captain Healy* (Waterfront Soundings Productions, 2000).

with the law, will not sell it at a disadvantage with the unscrupulous in competition for the trade in bone, ivory, and furs.

The natives fully understand that we come to suppress this trade and that no liquor can be got on board the *Corwin*, even if they beg for it on their knees, as they frequently have done. When they see our flag they point to it and say, "Oo·mi-ak'-puck pe 'chuck ton'-i-ka" (no whisky ship), and in describing us to others they generally use this expression. Naturally peaceful, of a kindly and hospitable disposition, and seldom, if ever, quarrelsome when sober, under the influence of a small quantity of liquor they become demoniac. The most brutal fights occur when they are in this condition. Their long, sharp hunting-knives make frightful wounds, and their rifles are used without stint and often with deadly effect. In former years our surgeon has often been called upon to dress these wounds. On the bodies of several Indians I have seen marks of bullet wounds received in these drunken brawls, and the omalik of the Diomedes, a comparatively young man, bears three deep scars which he proudly told me he had received in fights, and as proudly boasted of having killed two men while drunk.

The wives of these natives, who are usually treated with more consideration than we should expect they would receive from their savage lords, are frequently brutally beaten when liquor has frenzied the men, and it was with unmixed pleasure that, on the single occasion where we were called upon to make a seizure this year, I noticed that the women recognized us as their friends, used every exertion to assist us in our search, and seemed grateful that powerful friends were among those who were ready and willing to do what could be done to soften the hardships of their savage life. When I think that citizens of my own country have been the prime means of adding this great burden to the load these simple people have to bear, I feel that no exertion can be too great and no vigilance too exacting if it will but bring to punishment these unprincipled traders. If captured, no leniency should be extended to them.

The only trouble that has ever occurred between the whites and native has been when the latter were under the influence of liquor. There is a grain of consolation in the fact that usually those who furnished the whisky were the ones to suffer.

In order that the Department may be fully informed of all phases of this nefarious trade, I would state that some of the "whalers" had been accustomed in the "between seasons" to purchase in Honolulu, and in the summer to sell in these waters, a vile compound called Honolulu rum, thus adding to their violation of the Indian trade law the crime of smuggling. This liquor is useless as medicine, serving it to the crew would be a species of villainy, and its presence on board should subject a vessel to seizure, as it virtually carries with it the intention to trade. Two or three of the whaling captains openly boasted of having thrown overboard one to two hundred gallons of this rum when they heard the *Corwin* had reached the Arctic before them.

I would respectfully recommend that the Department fix upon some quantity of liquor as sufficient for ship's uses and medicinal purposes of these vessels; that the present law in regard to procuring a permit to carry liquors from a collector of customs be rigidly enforced, and that masters of vessels be required to carefully account for every gallon they take on board. Vessels then found in these waters without a permit or with more than the authorized quantity of liquor on board can be seized and sent to San Francisco.

At present it is exceedingly difficult to determine what quantity of alcohol should subject a vessel to seizure, and I should hesitate to break up what might be a profitable voyage for a small quantity of liquor that perhaps might be considered reasonable by another.

Questions for Discussion:
1. What does this document reveal about racial attitudes in the 1880s?
2. How did Alaskan Natives react to the Revenue Cutter Service's efforts to break up the contraband liquor trade?
3. How does this document reflect or distort the concerns of the greater American public in this era?

<hr>

Michael A. Healy, *Report of the Cruise of the Revenue Marine Steamer* Corwin *in the Arctic Ocean in the Year 1884* (Washington, D.C.: Government Printing Office, 1889), 17–18.

MARITIME DISASTER AND RESCUE

Americans in the Victorian era were fascinated with disasters and rescues, and shipwrecks and natural disasters held a morbid fascination for many. But shipwrecks also cost many lives, and hurricanes destroyed valuable property. After the Civil War, the federal government gradually took an increased interest in preventing maritime disasters by supporting aids to navigation like lighthouses and buoys, by creating a service dedicated entirely to saving shipwrecked mariners, the U.S. Life-Saving Service (USLSS), and by instituting scientific research to understand and predict destructive weather systems. These efforts were not unique to the United States; rather they should be seen as part of an international effort to make navigation safer. Aids to navigation and lifesaving efforts represented a growing interest in technology to preserve human life and the growth of government agencies that went beyond the traditional roles of collecting taxes, administering justice, and waging war.

In social terms, what was really interesting about these efforts to save lives was the idealization of rescuers in the popular media. Newspapers and illustrated magazines held up members of the USLSS as "heroes of peace," comparing their actions to fighting a war. Journalist Gustav Kobbé wrote in 1898, "There is one power that wages a ceaseless war against whomsoever ventures upon its domain—the sea. No enemy is more pitiless. Wind and snow and fog are its weapons. It neither asks nor gives quarter." Melodramatic accounts such as this thrilled Victorian readers. Beyond the adventure stories, accounts of shipwreck and maritime disaster give historians a valuable insight into Victorian society—what personal attributes it valued, how it regarded the roles of men and women, and even the influence of advertisements on American society.

Sumner Kimball, "Manful Efforts" (1877)

Sumner Kimball (1834–1923), the official who almost single-handedly created the USLSS in 1871, was well aware of society's morbid fascination with maritime disasters and shrewdly promoted his service by publicly awarding medals to USLSS members and the public. In this instance, he rewards a passenger and crewmember of the yacht *Mohawk*, a 140-foot-long centerboard schooner of 330 tons, owned by William T. Garner, the New York Yacht Club's Vice-Commodore and owner of a steamship line. Garner, his wife, and five others drowned in this tragic accident.

Two life-saving medals of the first class, and six life-saving medals of the second class, have been awarded during the year under the provisions of the act of June 20, 1874.

The medals of the first class were awarded to Col. J. Schuyler Crosby, of New York, at this date the American consul at Florence, and Carl Fosberg, a seaman belonging to the yacht *Mohawk*, in recognition of their extraordinary gallantry upon the occasion of the sudden sinking of that vessel in New York Harbor on the afternoon of the 20th of July, 1876. The horror which this dreadful catastrophe diffused for days through New York and its environs was only relieved by their action, which revealed some of the noblest traits of the human soul. The *Mohawk* was the largest and costliest of the fleet of pleasure-vessels belonging to the New York Yacht Club. She was the property of Mr. William T. Garner, a wealthy merchant of New York, residing near New Brighton, Staten Island, and was sumptuously furnished and appointed. On Thursday afternoon (July 20, 1876) she lay at her anchorage in New York Bay, off Stapleton, Staten Island. At about half past three o'clock Mr. Garner arrived on board with a party of friends, consisting of Mr. Gardiner G. Howland, Mr. Louis B. Montant, Col. J. Schuyler Crosby, Mr. Frost Thorne, together with Mrs. Garner, Miss Adele Hunter, and Miss Edith May, arrangements having been made for a sail down the bay. The day had been somewhat dark and cloudy, with occasional squalls and showers, and at the time of the company coming on board, a thunder-storm was rising in the southwest, of which no other notice was taken by the guests than to retreat into the cabin from the already-dropping rain. The order had been given by Mr. Garner to get under way, and under the direction of the sailing-master, Rowland, the anchor had been lifted from the bottom, but was still in the water, and all the working sails were set except the flying jib. The neighboring craft, of which there were a number, had all taken in sail, and the men upon their decks waited to see how the *Mohawk* would behave in the coming squall. At that moment although there was hardly a breath on deck, a wind smote the upper sails, and the sailing-master gave orders to let go the fore-sheet, the jib-sheets, and the fore-topsail. The order had only been obeyed in respect to the fore-topsail, when the squall struck the yacht with such fury that she careened, and lurched violently to port.

There was an instant tumult of cries, and the gentlemen rushed up on deck from the cabin. In a moment the vessel was on her side with the water pouring over the rail. While she was going over, Mr. Garner and Colonel Crosby hurried back into the cabin to save the ladies. Miss May was far over to the port side as they entered, and Colonel Crosby, calling to her to get out as quickly as possible, met her half way as she came across, got her to the companion-way, where be pushed her up to Mr. Howland and Mr. Montant, and sprang back into the cabin. The bravery of this action will be realized when it is stated that the water was then pouring down the companionway in a steady stream.

To enter the filling cabin down this narrow way, in a vessel keeled over on her side and rapidly sinking, seemed certain death. This Colonel Crosby did, and with equal courage, the seaman Fosberg rushed in with him. The scene in the cabin was frightful. The rich and heavy furniture had shifted, and Mrs. Garner and Miss Hunter were caught and pinioned by it against the sideboard. Mrs. Garner was screaming and her husband was making frantic efforts to release her and her companion, by throwing off the heavy articles which held them down. In these endeavors Colonel Crosby and Carl Fosberg desperately joined, pulling away the furniture and handing it up to Mr. Montant and Mr. Howland, who threw it out on deck. The water, meanwhile, continued to pour in and the cabin rapidly filled. Although nearly submerged, the three men never stopped their perilous work while it could be continued. Their labors were, however, ineffectual, and were ended by the sinking of the vessel. It was only four minutes from the moment she capsized till she went down. Mr. Garner was drowned, clinging to his wife, whom he would not leave. Colonel Crosby and Carl Fosberg, toiling to the last second, were engulfed, and nearly lost their lives. Swallowed by the flood in the cabin, they only escaped by swimming upward, guided by the faint light shed through the water from the broken skylight. The aperture was fortunately large enough to enable them to pass through, and they reached the surface, and were picked up by one of the many boats which at once began to gather around the sunken vessel.

The yacht sank so rapidly that Miss May, after being saved by Colonel Crosby from the cabin, was again placed in the greatest danger. She had not instantly quitted the vessel, being advised to remain by Mr. Montant, who, with Mr. Howland, was engaged in throwing the cabin furniture out on deck from the companion-way. Consequently, when the vessel went down, they were all three caught between the companion way and the furniture, which was now washed back into the cabin, and were completely covered by the rushing flood. Fortunately, Miss May had her arm outside the companion-way, which prevented her from being swept back into the cabin, and Mr. Montant, in his struggles, losing hold of her, she was enabled to swim, and with a few strokes gained the surface of the water, coming up near Mr. Howland, who supported her till they were picked up by a boat from a neighboring yacht. Mr. Montant also escaped, though unhappily he did not long survive the shock of the disaster.

The gold medals of the life-saving service have never been awarded more deservedly than in this instance. It was no common courage and humanity that impelled these two brave men to plunge within the sinking vessel, where in the half darkness, amidst the confusion of huddled furniture and rushing water, they strove for the lives of the unfortunate victims. The perfect behavior of the one in his manful efforts for his friends is matched by the action of the other in imperiling his life for strangers. Writing of him to the department, Colonel Crosby expresses a true feeling, the utterance of which adds new honor to his own conduct, in these words: "Too much cannot be said in favor of this man, who was governed simply by his own brave instincts rather than the hope of any reward. Nor did be have friendly or loyal considerations to prompt him to risk his own life, which he did by remaining to the last moment on board."

It deserves to be stated in this connection that Mr. Carl Fosberg completed his gallantry by his modesty. After the affair in which be behaved so well, he kept out of the way. When reporters sought him he hid. It was with difficulty, and after some time, that be could be found to give him the medal to which his conduct had entitled him.

Questions for Discussion:
1. What does this report reveal about gender roles on board the *Mohawk*?
2. According to this report, what ideal manly qualities did Crosby and Fosberg possess?
3. What does this report reveal about popular American attitudes and concerns circa 1877?

United States Life-Saving Service, *Annual Report of the Operations of the United States Life-Saving Service for the Fiscal Year Ending June 30, 1877* (Washington, D.C.: Government Printing Office, 1877), 53–55.

S. C. Brock, "Wreck of the Steamer *Metropolis*" (1878)

Few areas of the Atlantic Coast are as treacherous as the Outer Banks of North Carolina. While today they are summer playgrounds, in the past mariners widely feared them, especially in the winter when fierce storms pushed many vessels ashore. Men of the U.S. Life-Saving Service, stationed every few miles along the beach, attempted to assist mariners unfortunate enough to wreck on the Outer Banks. If the seas were sufficiently calm, they launched specially designed surfboats to rescue crew and passengers. If that was impossible and the vessel was close enough to shore, they resorted to shooting a line to the vessel and attempting to rescue the shipwrecked sailors one by one in a breeches buoy or similar device. It was a perilous process that put rescuers in a great deal of danger. Little wonder then that the USLSS's unofficial motto was, "you have to go out, you don't have to come back."

The USLSS stations on the Outer Banks prove especially interesting to scholars not only because of the heroic duties they performed, but also because of the composition of the crews. Some of the stations were manned by African Americans (Pea Island being the most famous), others by whites. Historians David Wright and David Zoby have recently examined how these stations came to be segregated in their book, *Fire on the Beach*.[1]

The document below reveals the activities of one (presumably all-white) USLSS crew on the Outer Banks. In this instance a civilian gives testimony of the efforts of a USLSS station to rescue the passengers and crew of the steamer *Metropolis* in the winter of 1878.

S. C. Brock, of Hobbs Woods, and residing on the Sound shore, Currituck Beach, North Carolina, being duly sworn, deposes and says:

At about eight o'clock on the morning of January 31, I was on the marsh near my house and heard at short intervals peculiar cries, like the sound of many human voices, and stopped to listen. The wind was from the eastward, thick weather, and the sounds seemed to proceed from the direction of the ocean. Just at this time I was called by James E. Capps, a boy, who was in one of the upper windows of my house. I went with all speed to the house. I found my horse ready to be saddled. The boy said he had been to the beach and that there, was a steamer ashore just abreast of my house, and that he thought there were women aboard. I mounted my horse and galloped to the beach abreast the wreck, waved my hat to the people on board to let them know assistance would be rendered, and galloped up the beach to give information to Station No. 4.

I noticed that the steamer was lying about 100 yards from the shore (it being then low water) and heading about west-southwest. She was square-rigged forward, fore-and-aft rigged aft, and her mainmast had fallen, also her smoke-stack. There were many people on board,

---

1   David Wright and David Zoby, *Fire on the Beach: Recovering the Lost Story of Richard Etheridge and the Pea Island Lifesavers* (New York: Simon & Schuster, 2001).

a great number of them with cork jackets on. They were crying and screaming for help. The sea was very heavy, about as heavy as we usually have it here, and was breaking over the vessel, which had careened over slightly toward the sea to the southeast.

On my way to Station 4, about one-half mile to northward of wreck I noticed a metallic boat on the beach all burst to pieces. I supposed it was one of the steamer's boats. I had got within about one-quarter of a mile from the station when I met one of the patrol of Station 4 coming south. I asked him how far it was to the station. He said about a quarter of a mile. I told him there was a vessel ashore just abreast my house, and rode on toward the station, the man following. I arrived at station about half past eight, as near as I can judge; did not see Keeper Chappell, but told his crew there was a vessel ashore just abreast my house, and they immediately commenced preparations. Just then Captain Chappell came up from the beach, and I reiterated my information. He told the boys to get ready as soon as possible. He asked me if I thought he could get his boat down there in time. I told him I did not, the distance being great and the vessel fast breaking up. He then put the mortar apparatus in the hand-cart, and taking the medicine-chest, he and I started for the wreck, leaving the crew to follow with apparatus.

I soon after relieved the keeper of the medicine-chest and took it on my horse until within a mile of the wreck, when the keeper took the chest and told me to ride on quickly and see if I could relieve or assist those coming off the wreck. I went on with all speed, and on my arrival found about twenty people ashore alive, and sent a number to my house to be cared for; part went to N.E.K. Jones's. They all had on cork jackets when they came ashore. Saw no persons washing ashore at this time. I took off my hat and waved to those on board to let them know that assistance was coming from Station 4. I then went to my house, as my wife was sick, where I found a number of the survivors. Others had been there, and having warmed themselves, had gone back to the beach to render assistance.

I immediately went back to the beach ready to lend a hand, and commenced making fires, as it was chilly, and numbers were only partially dressed. About half past twelve o'clock the life-saving crew arrived with the mortar apparatus. By this time the wind had shifted to southwest, and the mortar apparatus was put in position ready for firing. The mortar was aimed to windward, as I supposed, to allow for drift. The first shot went over and to windward of the foremast, but the bight of line drifted to leeward, and the mainmast being gone there was nothing to fetch up the bight of the line and it passed over the stern of the vessel and overboard.

The line was then hauled in with shot attached by the life-saving-crew, the mortar reloaded and fired again. The second shot was fired with apparent success, passing over the port fore-topsail yard-arm, the topsail being set and the jib stay. Saw a man go aloft to get the line, whom I afterward learned was the second mate; passed the line down to the crew on deck, who began pulling on it. They had got the tail-block, with tally-board attached, within about 150 feet of the side of the vessel when the line parted, there being a heavy current setting to the northward, and bringing, according to my judgment, a heavy strain upon the whip. The shot-line, minus the ball, was hauled in a second time by the crew of Station 4, together with the whip and tail-block.

Everything was got ready for a third shot, when the keeper found he was out of powder. I immediately sent to my house for powder. The mortar was then loaded for a third time and fired, when the line parted at once near the ball. The mortar was loaded with third and last ball, fired, and cut the line at the ball as before without taking any of the line.

Just at this moment the first officer of the stranded vessel came up and asked the crowd if there was any possible way of getting information to the adjacent station south; also to a telegraph-operator. Nothing was said for awhile. I noticed this and said, Yes, there is a way, that I had a horse and man whom I would send on horseback to Mr. Poyner, who would forward the telegram if he could; if not, I would see that the message was sent on. I sent the officer's telegram to Mr. Poyner, who sent word back that he would send the telegram on at once. This was about three in the afternoon. There was no one washing ashore at this time; they seemed to be waiting or holding on, evidently expecting assistance. So far as I know there was no attempt made by the people on board to send a line ashore by a cask or spar, but they hallooed and made motion to the effect that we were to look out for a line, and I learned afterward from one of the survivors that a man did jump overboard with a line in his teeth, intending to swim ashore with it, but they did not pay out the line fast enough to him, and he was compelled to relinquish his hold, and he swam ashore without it.

Keeper Chappell asked me if I could send a man back to the station for more balls. I told him I could not, as my horse had gone south with a telegram. Chappell then said he didn't know what he should do. So far as I know there was no horse to be had in the vicinity. No immediate assistance being rendered, the people began to jump overboard on doors and other fragments of joiner-work from the vessel. Then the station crew, assisted by N.E.K. Jones, James E. Capps, and myself, waded into the surf and rescued the drowning men. My dog (a large Newfoundland) also went in and dragged one man out.

Shortly afterward a number of citizens arrived from the mainland and elsewhere, among whom were Thomas J. Poyner, Captain Everton, wreck-commissioner, John Saunders, Alonzo Williams, Buchanan Williams, Thomas Litchfield, Sanford Dunton, John Dunton, and others. All united with us in saving life. Clearly if not quite all of those saved had on cork jackets. There was a strong current running to the northward carrying everything in that direction. There was one man swimming ashore who had on a cork jacket. He doubtless would have been saved, but a heavy sea breaking threw a lot of drift-stuff over him and he drowned. The beach was strewn with fragments of the wreck for a distance of at least two miles. About this time the captain of the stranded vessel came in toward the shore. Keeper Chappell and myself seized hold of him and brought him ashore. He had on a rubber suit (Merriman's).

Shortly after this (just before sunset) the foremast fell, covering a number of people under the sail and killing and crippling a great many and knocking them overboard. A few minutes after this the vessel broke up and disappeared almost entirely. There was a great struggle now to save life, as everybody who had remained on the vessel up to this time was overboard. We all pitched in and did our best. Don't know how many were saved in all, but think at least one hundred. At about sunset I left the beach; I was lame, having been struck by a drifting door while endeavoring to save life. I took the captain of the steamer to my house, where the purser and twelve others (survivors) were being properly taken care of. About seven in the evening a surfman from Station 5 came up and asked me if I could take care of a woman, one of the survivors. I told him yes, if they could get her here.

I gave them my wife's cloak. Mr. Josephus Baum's cart being on the beach, she was taken to his house and properly taken care of.

When I left the beach saw a great number of survivors round the fires. There were a great many more people there than I could take care of. I remained home all night, and next morning (Friday, 1st) went back to the beach, saw a number of the shipwrecked people, who said they had had nothing to eat for two days. I sent a number of them to my house at different times throughout the day for food and shelter. There was one man lying down on a bench by a fire suffering very much, having been injured internally by the wreck. I told Keeper Chappell of this, and he took his medicine-chest, went immediately to the man, gave him some brandy, and applied mustard-plasters. Josephus Baum soon came in a cart, took the man to his house, and properly cared for him. John Baker and others contributed clothing for the man.

The captain of the steamer directed me to employ hands to gather up the property and take care of it, and bury the bodies. We buried about twenty-three; all those whose names could be ascertained I wrote with a pencil or red chalk on the head boards; and they are so buried as to be quickly and easily identified by myself. Jimmy Williams, Joshua Beaseley, Benjamin S. Harrison, and two others (names I don't remember) assisted in burying the dead. I saw no jewelry or trinkets of any kind on any of the bodies.

Joshua Beaseley told me that while they were burying the bodies one of the survivors came up and said he was searching for his chum; that he had $13 or $15 on him, and he wanted to get it and take it to his wife. He found his chum, knew him, and found the money, and took it from him in Beaseley's presence. We got through burying the bodies just before night. It was said there was a great deal of provision aboard, but I saw very little of it. What I did see was a few barrels of hard bread.

On Friday night I took care of sixteen persons, among whom were George A. Yoke, Thomas Cogan, B. J. White, B. Clark, and A. W. Newton.

This is all I know of the wreck of the steamer *Metropolis*.

S. C. BROCK.

Personally appeared before me and testified
to the foregoing this 4th of February, 1878.

WALTER WALTON,

Assistant Inspector and Acting Superintendent.

Questions for Discussion:

1. How can this report of a shipwreck be compared to a battle report?

2. What were the greatest aids and the greatest hindrances in rescuing the passengers and crew of the *Metropolis*?

3. What strengths or weaknesses does a sworn deposition such as this have for historians attempting to understand an event?

Deposition of S. C. Brock, in United States Life-Saving Service, *Annual Report of the Operations of the United States Life-Saving Service for the Fiscal Year Ending June 30, 1878* (Washington, D.C.: Government Printing Office, 1878), 92–95.

Paine's Celery Compound, "Gallant Ida Lewis" (1893)

Female lighthouse keepers were relatively common in the postbellum era, yet until recently their story was obscure. Books such as *Women Who Kept the Lights*[1] give a wealth of detail about the careers, lives, and families of lighthouse keepers.

The most famous female lighthouse keeper was Ida Lewis (1842–1911), a household name in postbellum America. The daughter of a lighthouse keeper who manned a small lighthouse in Newport, Rhode Island, Lewis came to public attention for several dramatic rescues in that harbor. Even in her own time, the press struggled to place Lewis within the separate spheres men and women were supposed to inhabit, one editor asking "Is it 'womanly' to tug and strain through a tempest, and then pull half-drowned men into a skiff?" Many men clearly thought it was feminine; suitors from as far west as Ohio proposed to the famous lifesaver, sight unseen.

Idolized as a lifesaver, her private life was less happy; her marriage lasted only a few short weeks, and financial security proved elusive despite her position as a lighthouse keeper. This may have been what drove her to endorse "Paine's Celery Compound," a widely available patent medicine that promised to cure all ailments. In fact, Paine's Celery Compound was 21 percent alcohol and had no medical benefit at all, but it did have a very successful advertising scheme based on endorsements by various personalities.

CELERY COMPOUND

GALLANT IDA LEWIS.

America's Grace Darling, The

Brave Woman Who Keeps The

---

1   Mary Louise Clifford and J. Candace Clifford, *Women Who Kept the Lights: An Illustrated History of Female Lighthouse Keepers* (Williamsburg, Va.: Cypress Communications, 1993).

Lime Rock Light—Her Boat, "The Rescue," Exhibited
At The World's Fair—Heroine Who Saved 18 Lives, Tells How
Her Own Life was Saved—Congress Gives Her A Medal.

Newport, R.I., Nov. 10—America's Grace Darling,[1] the heroine of 18 life-saving exploits, a woman for whom Congress has cast a gold medal of the first class, the first of the kind ever given to a woman, keeps the Lime rock light.

It was when the Russian warships were lying at peaceful anchor in Newport's beautiful harbor, that a small company from the hotel Aquidneck went out in a sail boat to pay a visit to this brave woman, whose life-boat, the *Rescue*, has been one of the most talked-of exhibits at the world's fair. The story told by Miss Lewis of how her own life has been saved, amply repaid the visitors for their journey.

Lime rock lighthouse, the home of this world-famous heroine is within the harbor and is a short sail from the New York yacht club's house. At high tide an ordinary cat-rigged sailboat cannot land at Lime rock, and a rowboat must be used, from which a landing is effected by climbing up the face of the perpendicular rock upon a ladder lashed with fetters of iron to the stone.

At low tide the rowboat is guided toward a pebbly beach through the sword grass that cuts against its sides like slashing martial blades.

But the lighthouse is the blessed symbol of peace on earth and sea, saying good will to men, this saving station of wrecked mariners. And the fair woman to whom the visitors listened told a true narrative for every other brave and good woman in the country—a narrative for every woman in this country to heed and profit by.

Ida Lewis looks to be in her thirties as to age, with a highly nervous temperament, slight figure, bright eyes, with a dash of color in her face.

"It is 35 years since we came to Lime rock, six in family, and now there are but two of us left, my brother Rudolph, who helped you up the rocks, and myself," said she. "My father was a cripple for 17 years, in which time he never cut a mouthful of food for himself; my mother died 10 years ago of a cancer, and my sister six years ago with consumption.

---

1   Grace Darling: A British woman (1815–1842) who became internationally famous for rescuing sailors in an 1838 shipwreck. Like Ida Lewis, she was the daughter of a lighthouse keeper.

"I have never been well in my life until now. My trouble was in chest and lungs, and I have always had a cough from a child. What has done me more good than anything else in the world is Paine's celery compound.

"I have always been miserable in summer, and I believe I should have died this season if I had not taken Paine's celery compound. I began with it last February, and this summer I have been splendid," and her eyes flashed as she warmed to the subject. "And I am delighted to tell it," she continued, "for it is the truth. I have had so many doctors and so many doctor's prescriptions that I had lost faith in them, and I have tried so many patent medicines that I dreaded the summer. But I read about Paine's celery compound and went to see the gentlemen who testified, and they were loud in its praise. My brother Rudolph said that I had better not try it, as I would be disappointed again, and then I would feel worse than ever, but I went ahead; it seemed as if the Lord directed me, and I received benefit from the very first bottle.

"O, you should have seen me last summer. I was short of breath, easily tired out, and had a cough and night sweats, and my doctor told me I had heart trouble. I was so thin, and I was wearing black, and my friends said that I looked like a ghost. Now I am excellent, and I feel proud to tell it and give the credit to Paine's celery compound. I have faith in it because there is nothing like it. I know so many people that have been helped. I am so much improved that my friends did not know me this summer. I have taken eight bottles since February, and the longer I take it the better I get. I have to live economically, and I do all my own housework, washing and ironing, and even the painting of the woodwork outside. I enjoy doing it now, but I believe I should be dead if I had not taken Paine's celery compound."

Besides the gold medal presented her by the United States of America, a silver medal was presented by the humane society of Massachusetts: "To Ida Lewis, the heroine of Lime rock, for her many heroic and successful efforts in saving human lives." Another, also of silver, was presented by the life saving benevolent association of New York: "To Miss Ida Lewis, as a testimonial of her skill, courage, and humanity in rescuing two men in the harbor of Newport, R.I., during a severe storm."

Not only on these several special occasions, however, has Miss Lewis shown the courage and fortitude that have made her famous, but also in the faithfulness and regularity with which her daily round of duties are performed, for they are not few. No lighthouse on the coast is better kept than hers, and not one has a better record.

"People think when they come and find things in perfect order that there is nothing to do here," said she. "But they do not know how early we start in the morning and how many little things have to be done. The lamps have to be cleaned every day, the lenses kept clean, and the brasses polished, to say nothing of keeping the house in order."

Not alone are the "brasses polished" on the light, but the shining copper pump in the kitchen and the row of brass candlesticks on the mantle behind the stove all testify to the success and industry of the thrifty champion of life and strength.

Ida Lewis is called the bravest woman in America. But there are many brave women who have suffered as she has done, who are nearly broken down, who need today a true food for the brain and nerves, and whom Paine's celery compound will make well again. Thousands of other women have been saved by this wonderful remedy.

Questions for Discussion:
1. What is the advertiser's purpose in using Ida Lewis as a sponsor, and how did that impact what was included or excluded in this piece?
2. How does this article idealize Ida Lewis as a woman and a role model?
3. What clues does this advertisement give about the conditions and attitudes women experienced in the late nineteenth century?

"Gallant Ida Lewis," *Newark Daily Advocate* (Newark, N.J.), November 11, 1893.

FISHING WOES AND WORRIES

Fishing remained an important maritime activity after the Civil War. Technological changes permitted greater catches, and improved transportation and preservation techniques, such as the use of ice to preserve fish and railroads that provided rapid and predictable transportation, meant that the public demand for fresh fish expanded rapidly. It was not long before the increased value of the fisheries and better technology meant increased strain on the marine environment.

Overharvesting increasingly became a problem. The first warnings of this came in the form of wildly fluctuating annual catches, but the competition over increasingly scarce resources also meant that fishermen sometimes resorted to violence to protect fishing grounds that they considered "their" property. Examples of this include riots between American and Newfound-land fishermen, "Oyster Wars" between Maryland and Virginia oyster fish-ermen, and the exclusion of Chinese fishermen from West Coast fisheries. Those involved in these incidents were not eager to die for the fisheries, but they proved quite willing to kill for them. Violence—even gunplay—became an increasingly common event on fishing grounds and, in some cases, be-came the focus of international diplomatic efforts.

James Black Groome, "Oyster Troubles" (1874)

Competition between Virginia and Maryland for the resources of Chesa-peake Bay dates as far back as the 1600s, but the improved technology of the postbellum period brought renewed conflict between the two states. As early as the 1860s, it became apparent that the Tidewater's oyster popula-tion was under strain. Both Virginia and Maryland created armed oyster police forces to guard this resource against so-called oyster pirates who used destructive methods to harvest ever-larger amounts of the shellfish. The problem was caused by the ill-defined boundary between Maryland and Virginia on the Pocomoke River. Both states claimed jurisdiction and could not agree on which oyster beds belonged to which state. The result was increased violence. The *New York Times* viciously lampooned this dis-pute as a miniature Civil War, but the conflicts were serious: oystermen were frequently wounded in clashes with state authorities, and deaths were not unheard of as Virginia and Maryland boatmen struggled to sustain their way of life. The standard narrative of these oyster wars, which flared up in-termittently until after the Second World War, remains John Wennersten's *The Oyster Wars of Chesapeake Bay.*[1]

This piece, part of the correspondence between Maryland and Virginia's governors, concerns an event that presaged the more serious "Oyster Wars" of 1882–1883.

STATE OF MARYLAND,
Executive Department,
Annapolis, October 2d, 1874.

His Excellency James L. Kemper, Governor of Virginia:

Sir:

Complaint has been made to me that upon the eleventh ultimo, Thomas Riggin, an unresisting and unarmed citizen of Maryland, was

---

1   John R. Wennersten, *The Oyster Wars of Chesapeake Bay* (Centreville, Md.: Tidewater Publishers, 1981).

approached by an armed canoe, believed to be commanded by William P. Curtis, an oyster inspector of the state of Virginia, and fired upon and wounded severely.

Mr. Riggin, at the time, was engaged in taking oysters on that side of the Pocomoke river, or sound, or bay, (as that body of water is variously termed) most remote from Accomac county, in the state of Virginia, and within a mile of the nearest shore, which, although of late claimed by the state of Virginia, forms a part of the territory out of which the state of Maryland, which has always held it in actual possession and subject to her jurisdiction, created Somerset county. After being thus so severely wounded as to be rendered helpless, he was abandoned to his fate, and was driven by the winds and waves upon the Somerset shore.

The crew of the said armed canoe on the same day captured four canoes occupied and owned by citizens of Maryland, who were taking oysters in the same locality. These canoes were removed to Onancock in your state, where they are still held, as I am informed, under the alleged authority of the commonwealth of Virginia, and their owners, Edward Horsey, John H. Garrison, Henry Curtis, and a Mr. Lewis, were lodged in Drummondtown jail, where, with the exception of Mr. Lewis, who succeeded in procuring bail, they still remain.

Maryland has always claimed for her citizens, and they have always exercised, the right to take oysters in common with the citizens of Virginia in every part of the Pocomoke river, sound or bay, and that claim was, as I am informed and believe, never disputed until during the late war.

That Maryland still asserts her right to jurisdiction over a large part of the Pocomoke is shown by the resolution passed at the last session of the general assembly, which was laid before the general assembly of your state by the Honorables John W. Davis, Isaac D. Jones, and James M. Dennis. That resolution proposes as a compromise that the boundary line between the two states shall be drawn from the center of Cedar straits "by a right line in a southerly direction to the channel of Pocomoke bay or river nearest to Cedar straits; thence up, by and with the channel of the Pocomoke bay or river nearest to a point thereon, opposite to the place on the east shore of said river ascertained by De La Camp," &c.; "the right of fishing and taking oysters in Pocomoke sound or bay and river to be common to the citizens of both states and subject to concurrent regulations by the two states;

or if preferred by the commonwealth of Virginia, this latter provision may be omitted."

And that Maryland's claims to jurisdiction over the whole or a large part of the Pocomoke, has been recognized by Virginia herself, as entitled (until the true boundary between the two states is ascertained and established by some competent tribunal) to respectful consideration is shown by the Compact of 1785, section 10th, which secures the trial of offences committed "on that part of the Pocomoke river within the state of Virginia, or where the line of division between the two states is doubtful," in some cases to the tribunals of the one state, and in other cases to those of the other according to certain rules therein established. And the bona fides of the claim, if not the existence of the right, set up by Maryland on behalf of her citizens to take fish and oysters in common with the citizens of Virginia in the Pocomoke, has also been recognized by the general assembly of your state. As instances of this kind of legislation, I refer to chapter 255 of the act passed in 1819, by the general assembly of your state, which reserves the right of "taking and transplanting of oysters as heretofore from the waters of the Potomac and Pocomoke where these rivers are the common territory of the states of Maryland and Virginia; and so title 29, chapter 101, section 59 of your Revised Code, which, while forbidding under a heavy penalty, any person, other than a citizen of Virginia, from taking terrapins[1] in the rivers Pocomoke and Potomac, provides that "this section shall not extend to a citizen of Maryland taking terrapins in the said mentioned waters."

The Lovett and Davidson line, as you are well aware, extends no further on the east than the centre of Cedar straits, and fixes no temporary boundary on the Pocomoke river, sound, or bay between the two states. It was the hope of the general assembly of Maryland, when proposing to the general assembly of your state, to submit the whole question of the disputed boundary between the two states to arbitration, that the general assembly of your state would take such action as should be deemed necessary to secure, pending the arbitration, "to the citizens of Maryland equal rights with the citizens of Virginia to take oysters and terrapins in the waters of Pocomoke bay, and sound, and river; and the verbal report of the Maryland commissioners on their return from your capital as to the general disposition shown by

---

1   Terrapins: edible turtles found in fresh or brackish water.

the individual members of your assembly to concede all that Maryland desired, strengthened that hope. When the act of your general assembly, providing for the appointment of arbitrators was laid before the general assembly of Maryland, although it was found to be silent in regard to the rights of citizens of Maryland in the Pocomoke, the general assembly of the latter state did not hesitate to pass a law identical in terms with the Virginia act; and believing that pending the arbitration, which is speedily and forever to settle all disputes as to the true boundary, Virginia would not jeopardize the peace of the two states by attempting by the use of armed force to maintain a claim to the exclusive right to take fish and oysters in the Pocomoke, and to deprive the citizens of Maryland of its use in common with the citizens of Virginia, and which they had so long enjoyed and claimed as their right, the Maryland assembly made no provision for securing what it believed to be the right of Maryland citizens therein.

In consideration, then, of the fact that the persons arrested by the armed canoe and placed in Drummondtown jail, were only taking oysters where from time immemorial citizens of Maryland, sustained by the belief of their state in the right to do so, have been accustomed to take them; and of the fact that all disputes will soon be set at rest by the decision of the arbitrators already selected; and that any attempt, by either state, to assert, pending said arbitration, a claim by force is likely to endanger the friendly relations which have long existed, and which should always be cultivated between our states, and perhaps, result in serious loss of life; and of the further fact that when in last March I received information from you that citizens of Maryland had trespassed on the Virginia side of the Lovett and Davidson line, I forthwith, without waiting to ascertain for myself the existence of the grievances of which your officers complained, issued my proclamation warning the citizens of Maryland that the Lovatt and Davidson line must be respected by them:

I respectfully request that you will promptly direct the release from imprisonment of the citizens of Maryland arrested while taking oysters in the Pocomoke, and now in Drummondtown jail; and that the boats seized at the same time, and now detained at Onancock, may be restored to their Maryland owners.

And I further request that if there be in existence a law of the state of Virginia which is intended to secure to the citizens of your state the exclusive right of taking fish, oysters and terrapins in the Pocomoke river, sound or bay (the right to pass and enforce which is denied by the state of Maryland), that no attempt may be made to enforce said law, pending the decision of the arbitrators as to the true boundary between the states. Or, if you prefer it, I ask that a temporary line of division between the two states in the waters of the Pocomoke may be agreed upon, to be binding on both states, until the ascertainment by the arbitrators of the permanent boundary line.

I further request to be informed whether or not the commander of said armed canoe, when firing upon and severely wounding a citizen of Maryland, under the circumstances already detailed, was acting under authority conferred by the laws of Virginia, or in excess of said authority and of his instructions?

Accompanying this letter will be found several affidavits detailing the circumstances attending said shooting, and showing that until the late war there was no attempt to interfere with Marylanders taking fish, oysters and terrapins in all parts of the Pocomoke, in common with Virginians. Because of the delay incident to obtaining these affidavits this letter has not been earlier written.

Desiring most sincerely that the excitement which has been engendered in southeastern Maryland, by the arrest of Maryland oystermen in the Pocomoke may be speedily allayed by some settlement, alike fair and honorable to both states, and which will restore and strengthen the friendly relations which it is my hope may ever exist between our respective states, and with sentiments of the highest regard for you, personally,

I am, sir, your obedient servant,
JAMES BLACK GROOME,
Governor of Maryland.

Questions for Discussion:
1. What does this document reveal about life on Chesapeake Bay in the late nineteenth century?
2. What clues are there in this document that reveal contemporary attitudes toward marine resources?
3. What does this document tell us about the economic importance of the Chesapeake Bay oyster fishery?

Virginia House of Delegates, *Correspondence of the governor of Virginia with the governor of Maryland and the authorities of Accomac County, Va.* (Richmond, Va.: R. F. Walker, 1874), 4–6.

Various, "Fortune Bay Outrage" (1878)

American fishermen had long fished the waters off Newfoundland, and they traditionally bought their bait from Newfoundland fishermen. But in 1871 American and British diplomats radically altered this localized trade. The United States and Great Britain signed the Treaty of Washington, which created a system of free trade for fish and free access to inshore fishing grounds in North America. Between 1871 and 1887, when the United States repealed the free fishing articles of the Treaty of Washington, Americans had free and unrestricted access to all inshore fishing grounds under British jurisdiction.

Yet in the fall and winter of 1876–1877, local fishermen in Newfoundland took exception to the presence of American fishermen in their inshore waters. When the American fishermen fixed their seine nets to the shore, a process known as barring, and did so on a Sunday (both acts were prohibited by colonial legislation in Newfoundland), local fishermen in Fortune Bay banded together and violently opposed the American fishermen. They cut and burnt several seine nets and released the catch the Americans had already made.

The American fishermen protested to their government, which in turn complained directly to British authorities in London, claiming that the international agreement between the United States and Great Britain superseded colonial legislation, and thus colonial legislation amending fishing rights held no jurisdiction over American fishermen. Newfoundland authorities maintained that they had the right to preserve their fishery resources. London agreed, declaring that while Americans had a right of access, they must still obey local laws.

After extensive negotiation, Britain paid a compensation to the American government for the damages done by the Newfoundland fishermen but claimed that the compensation in no way represented a submission to the American claim or that Americans could continue to ignore local legislation in their prosecution of the international resource.

What follows is four affidavits—two from American fishermen and two from Newfoundland fishermen—in reference to what the Americans labeled the *Fortune Bay Outrage*. These documents illustrate the emerging debate regarding proper jurisdictional authority over a resource that spanned national and international space.

Gloucester, Mass., March 7, 1878

Respectfully represent John Pew, Charles H. Pew, and John J. Pew, all of Gloucester, county of Essex, and the commonwealth of Massachusetts, copartners under the firm style of John Pew & Son, that they are American citizens, and engaged in the fishing business at said Gloucester, and were and are owners and fitters of fishing vessels. That they are the sole owners of the American fishing schooners *Ontario* and *New England*, of said Gloucester, and were such owners in the months of November, December, and January last past.

That both of said schooners were fitted for the herring fisheries in the month of November, 1877, and for voyages to Newfoundland, and provided with seines for catching herring. That said schooner *Ontario*, whereof Peter McAulay was master, sailed on the first day of December, 1877, from said Gloucester, and the said schooner *New England*, whereof John Dago was master, on the twenty-eighth day of November, 1877; that both schooners had a full supply of men and outfit for said voyage. That said schooner *Ontario*, when she sailed from said Gloucester on said voyage with her outfits and seine, was worth the sum of seventy-five hundred dollars; and the said *New England*, with her outfits and seine, was then and there of the value of eighty-five hundred dollars. That said schooners both returned to said Gloucester from said voyage, on the seventeenth day of February, without any herring, except that the said *Ontario* had about fifty barrels purchased by her.

And we further represent that we are informed by the masters and crews of said schooners, and believe the same to be true, that the reason why they returned without any herring and made disastrous voyages is that they arrived at Long Harbor, Fortune Bay, Newfoundland, on or about the sixteenth day of December, 1877, and found herring scarce, and were unable to obtain any considerable quantity of herring; and that the masters and crews of said schooners waited at said Long Harbor until the sixth day of January, 1878, to catch or purchase herring, as they might be able to do; that on said sixth day of said January, "the signs for herring being good," the masters and crews of both of said schooners joined their purse seines, thereby making a double seine, which was of the value of at least fourteen hundred dollars, and making a seine of about twenty-four hundred feet long and one hundred and fifty feet deep: that the masters and crews of said schooners threw said double-seine at said Long Harbor and caught and secured therein a very large quantity of herring, amounting to at least two thousand barrels of herring, and more than sufficient to load both of said schooners.

That the masters and crews of said schooners were pursuing their business of catching herring at said Fortune Bay in a lawful manner, and were not in any manner or form interfering with the rights of any party or parties at said Newfoundland, and that the action of said parties in destroying said seine was a most wanton destruction of the property of said firm, and was without the least justification in law or good conscience, and was intended to be a warlike demonstration against the American vessels, their owners, masters, and crews, and to intimidate them and prevent them from prosecuting the herring fisheries in the waters of Newfoundland by catching herring, and thereby compel them to buy herring of the inhabitants of Newfoundland, if they would obtain them, at such prices as said people of Newfoundland might ask for them. That all the American vessels at said Newfoundland on said sixth day of said January were from said Gloucester and were there for herring, and among them were the schooners *Moses Adams, Herbert M. Rogers, John W. Bray, F. A. Smith, Hereward, William E. McDonald, Moro Castle, Edward E. Webster, Bonanza, Wildfire, Bunker Hill,* and *Isaac Rich.* That said schooners *Ontario* and *New England* were, by reason of the destruction of said seine and the freeing of the herring therein, were, both prevented from obtaining cargoes for said schooners.

That at about four o'clock of said sixth day of said January some two hundred men, who belonged about Fortune Bay and had gone ashore from English vessels in said Long Harbor, made a warlike demonstration against the masters and crews of said schooners and seized hold of said double seine, tore it in pieces, and carried it off, and thereby freed all of said herring and prevented the masters and crews of said schooners from obtaining them, and thereby destroyed all hope of their obtaining a cargo for either of said vessels. That of said two hundred men some sixty took hold of said seine and destroyed it, and the others were participating in the destruction of the seine by inciting and encouraging those who were destroying it.

That after the destruction of said seine, as above set forth, the said parties who had destroyed the same returned to their vessels, and on the evening thereafter, to wit, on the evening of the sixth day of said January, they made a jubilant demonstration, blowing horns, firing guns, and shouting as if celebrating a victory, to impress upon the masters and crews of American vessels in said harbor that they were prepared to stand by and justify what had been done, and that the Americans might expect to be treated in future in the same manner should they attempt to catch herring in Newfoundland waters.

And we further respectfully represent that in view of the treatment of the American fishermen by British subjects at said Newfoundland, it is wholly unsafe for American vessel owners to fit vessels for and send them to Newfoundland waters to catch herring, and that it is unsafe for American fishermen to attempt to catch fish in said waters, and that the demonstration against the American fishing-vessel owners, masters, and crews is of such a character as to make it a public violation of the rights of the citizens of the United States wishing to catch herring and attempting to catch herring there. That the loss to the said firm by reason of the warlike demonstration of the people of Newfoundland hereinbefore set forth, and the destruction of said seine in the voyages of said two schooners *Ontario* and *New England*, amounts to at least the sum of sixty-seven hundred dollars.

John Pew.

Charles H. Pew.

John J. Pew.

I, Peter McAulay, of Gloucester, county of Essex, and the commonwealth of Massachusetts, master mariner, on oath depose and say that on the first day of December, A.D. 1877, I was master of the fishing schooner *Ontario*, of said Gloucester, of the burthen of ninety-one tons and twenty-nine one hundredths, and on said first day of said December I sailed on a voyage from said Gloucester to Fortune Bay, on the southwest of Newfoundland, for a cargo of herring, and back to same port of discharge in the United States; that said schooner *Ontario* was fully titled for said voyage, and had on board a mate and five men, making in all seven men; that I arrived with said schooner on said voyage at Fortune Bay, Long Harbor, about the sixteenth day of said December; that I found herring very scarce, and up to the sixth day of January, A. D. 1878, had not been able to obtain, by purchase or otherwise, more than fifty barrels of herring.

That on the sixth day of said January, there being "good signs for herring," and the schooner *New England*, of said Gloucester, being a fishing schooner from said Gloucester, and provided with seine, which said schooner belonged to the firm of John Pew & Son, of said Gloucester, the same parties to whom the said *Ontario* belonged, the masters and crews of both of said schooners threw the said seine to catch herring to load both of said schooners.

That of said seine being thrown, took a large haul of herring, amounting, at least, to two thousand barrels of herring, and more than sufficient to load both of said schooners. That said herring being fully secured in said seine, and said schooners and said seine being at Long Harbor, this affiant saw about two hundred men on the shore at about four o'clock in the afternoon of said sixth day of said January, while the seine was in charge of the masters and crews of said schooners *Ontario* and *New England*, make an attack upon said seine in the most violent manner, and tear up and carry off the seine, and thereby let the herring out of said seine, and prevent the masters and crews of said schooners from obtaining any of said herring. . . . That the men who made said attack upon and destroyed said seine prevented the masters and crews of said schooners from protecting said seine, and some sixty of said two hundred men took hold of said seine, while all the rest of them were inciting and encouraging those who had hold of said seine and were destroying it. That the said men so destroying said seine and inciting those destroying it used threats and violence towards both the masters and crews of said schooners and fully overpowered them, so that they could not protect said seine and save the herring therein. That most of said two hundred men landed from boats in the said bay, and were men belonging in and about said Fortune Bay. That said men who made said attack upon said seine and destroyed the same had been fishing with nets during the day and with seines in the same neighborhood, and had taken quite a large quantity of herring.

And this affiant further says that both he and his crew and the master and crew of the schooner *New England* were pursuing their business in a peaceful and lawful manner, and were not interfering in any manner or form with the rights of any party at said Newfoundland. That the attack upon said seine by said persons from the shores of Fortune Bay was wholly without justification or excuse, and was a warlike demonstration against the American vessels there, which amounted to some fifteen in number, and were all from said port of Gloucester, among which were the schooners *F. A. Smith, Moses Adams, Here-*

ward, William E. MacDonald, Moro Castle, Edward E. Webster, Bonanza, Wildfire, Herbert M. Rogers, Bunker Hill, Isaac Rich, and *John W. Bray.*

That this affiant believes that the only reason of said attack and demonstration by the said persons from the shore was to intimidate the American fishermen there and to prevent them from catching herring, so that the said parties on the shore of Newfoundland might sell herring to the vessels from the United States at a high price and keep the whole control of the herring fisheries in their hands, and wholly deprive the citizens of the United States from prosecuting said fisheries at Newfoundland or obtaining the herring there in any other manner than by purchase.

Commonwealth of Massachusetts, Essex
Peter McAuley.

Deposition of Alfred Noel, Newfoundland, Central District, St. John's

I am master of the schooner *Nautilus* of this port, and on the 19th day of December last I was at Long Harbour, in Fortune Bay, in the *Nautilus,* which was anchored off Woody Island. I had a crew of seven men, and I was there engaged in the herring fishery. There were several American schooners; seven of them were lying off Woody Inland, and two French vessels. This island forms the harbour within half-a-mile of the narrows of Long Harbour; and other American schooners and Newfoundland fishing craft were inside Woody Island, which is the inside part of Long Harbour. All the crafts there, English and American, were hauling herring in seines and nets, and the Americans were purchasing herring from the English. Everything went off quietly, and the greatest harmony prevailed until Sunday, the 6th day of January, when about 2 o'clock in the afternoon five seines, belonging to the American schooners, were put into the water by their crews at the beach on the north-east side of Long Harbour. I know two of the captains by name, Dago and Jacobs, belong to Gloucester, United States, but do not know the names of their schooners. The whole five seines were barred full of herring, when the English crews of the crafts belonging to Fortune Bay ordered them to take their seines up or they would take them up for them; and the Fortune Bay men, finding they would not do as they were requested, then hauled up two of the American seines, but without any damage or injury, and two were at the same time taken up by the Americans; and the same time a seine belonging to Captain Dago was taken up by the Fortune Bay men, the herring thrown out, and the seine was torn up and destroyed. Before this occasion on the said Sunday, one of the American schooners had a seine barred with herring on the beach at Long Harbour for seven days, and it was not at any time meddled with by the Fortune Bay men or any one. Some of the Fortune Bay men had nets out in the water on that Sunday, and the same had been there during the week, but none of the Newfoundland fishermen attempted to haul herring on Sunday at any time while I was at Long Harbour. The Americans' practice had been until lately to purchase herring from the Newfoundland fishermen in Fortune Bay, but this year and last year the American have brought their own seines to haul herring for themselves. The American seines are 30 fathoms deep and 200 fathoms long. These American seines are used for barring herring in deep water, such as the Fortune bay Harbours, viz, Long Harbour, Bay del Nord, and Rencontre. Our fishermen never bar herring, and herring have never been barred in Fortune Bay, to my knowledge, until the Americans brought the large seines I have alluded to into Fortune Bay and used them there to the disadvantage of our fishermen. This mode of barring herring in such harbors as I have mentioned is most destructive and ruinous to the herring fishery in those localities. I do not know the names of the persons who destroyed the seines; there were about eighty vessels from different harbors of Fortune Bay at Long Harbour at the time the seine was destroyed by a great lot of people. I left Long Harbour for St. John's on the 31st day of January and arrived here on the 4th instant.

Alfred Noel.

Deposition of John Ramsey, Central District, St. John's

On or about the 14th of November last I sail from St. John's to Fortune Bay for a cargo of herring. I arrived in Long Harbour, Fortune Bay, about Christmas last. I found about 200 schooners there looking for herring; twelve of the schooners were Americans; my schooner was called the *Briton*, six hands all told. I got most of my herring between Christmas and the 8th January. Most all the schooners in Long Harbour lay inside of Woody Island. Woody Island is about three miles from the entrance of Long Harbour. On the northern side, rather above the island, there is a line beach about a mile long. This is the best hauling place in Long Harbour, and most of all the herring were taken there. It is only this year and last year that the American schooners have brought down very large seines for catching herring. I have been informed that some of these seines were 350 fathoms long and 35 fathoms deep. The seines which our Newfoundland fishermen use are about 120 fathoms long and from 8 to 13 fathoms deep. In the first week in January there were four or five American schooners who had the beach above mentioned barred for herring. The mode of inbarring for herring is as follows when a place is selected, generally a smooth beach with deep water outside free from rocks, a party is sent ashore with a long line from one end of the seine; the seine-boat then goes off with the seine, makes a long sweep, and the other end of the seine is then brought into the beach also; then the crew begin to haul together on both ends of the seine with long seine lines running fore and aft up and down the beach, four or five seines thus barring herring would cover all the hauling ground on this long beach I have spoken of, and would occupy all the best ground for hauling herring in Long Harbour. On the first Sunday in January the beach was barred by four or five large American seines. On that day, after dinner, a large number of people belonging to the crews of the Fortune bay schooners then in Long Harbour went over to the beach, and I was informed there were 600 or 700 Newfoundland fishermen there. The Americans had barred the herring, and were hauling on their seines on the Sunday morning. The Newfoundland fishermen told the American captains to take up their seines or they would take them up for them. All the American seines were then taken up which were set on a Sunday except one; this one the American captain who owned it refused to take up. The Newfoundland fishermen then hauled it ashore, took the herring out of the seine, and according as they hauled the seine out of the water they tore it up. I saw the seine the next day, Monday, on the beach, and it was completely destroyed; it was an old second-hand seine, and very rotten. I have been for thirteen or fourteen years carrying on the herring fishery in Fortune Bay, and during that time I have never known our Newfoundland fishermen to haul herring on Sunday. If the American fishermen were permitted to bar herring in the way that they were doing at Long Harbour Beach, all the rest of the craft would be deprived of the best place in the harbour to haul herring; and such a mode of fishing for herring is most injurious to the fishery and must in time ruin the herring fishery there. The Americans in hauling their long seines often remove the Newfoundland fisher-men's nets when they came in their way. I have known the American last year to have herring barred in for a fortnight. Barring kills a great many herring, and makes those who are barred in very poor. I have seen the bottom covered with dead herring after the seine had been barred for a week. The American schooners heave out their ballast in the channel between Woody Island and the shore, and if not prevented, will soon destroy the anchorage there.

John Rumsey.

Questions for Discussion:
1. What do these affidavits reveal about attitudes toward the environment in 1878?
2. What do these affidavits reveal about international efforts to control access to marine resources?
3. What concerns might a historian have in considering these affidavits as evidence?

U.S. Congress, *Executive Documents of the House of Representatives for the Third Session of the Forty-Sixth Congress, 1880–1881, vol. 1: Foreign Relations* (Washington, D.C.: Government Printing Office, 1881), 557–60; 573–74.

David Starr Jordan, "Chinese Fishermen" (1887)

Fishery conservation is not new; lawmakers have been trying to discourage wasteful practices and protect diminished fish stocks for hundreds of years. But altruistic preservation of natural resources was not always the goal of conservation laws. Environmental historian Arthur McEvoy found, in his book *The Fisherman's Problem*, that California's remarkably effective and progressive fishery regulations after the Civil War had far more to do with excluding the Chinese than with preserving fish stocks.[1] David Starr Jordan (1851–1931) composed the following piece for the "Goode Report," a multivolume government record of the nation's fish stocks, fishing methods, fishing industry, and fishing communities. When Jordan wrote this report, Chinese immigrants faced all manner of discrimination. The federal Chinese Exclusion Act of 1882 almost entirely stopped Chinese immigrants from entering the country, and state legislation curtailed ownership of property

1   Arthur F. McEvoy, *The Fisherman's Problem: Ecology and Law in the California Fisheries, 1850–1980* (Cambridge: Cambridge University Press, 1986).

and increasingly limited Chinese participation in the fishing industry, often under the guise of environmental protection. This discrimination continued into the mid-twentieth century.

On the Pacific coast of the United States, and on the banks of rivers on which salmon canneries are established, there are about 4000 Chinese engaged in catching fish, or in fish drying and fish-canning. Of this number about 463 Chinamen are living in the maritime countries of California and Washington Territory, while the remainder are engaged in the salmon canneries, probably not less than 3000 being employed on the Columbia River, Oregon, and about 600 on the Sacramento and other salmon rivers.

SAN DIEGO COUNTY, CALIFORNIA.—In San Diego County, California, are thirty-seven Chinese. They settled there about the year 1870, and by the use of very fine meshed seines have driven out the Italians who were there at the time of their advent. They are divided into eight companies, which are scattered along the coast between San Diego and Cerros Islands. At San Diego all the fishermen, excepting four Americans and their employés, are Chinamen. Upon their arrival they went to work at catching fish, which they salted and dried; these they shipped to China, their methods of fishing being probably the same as those now in use in China. They seek especially sheltered bays, which they sweep clean with their seines, usually commencing operations in the early part of the night. Some of the Chinamen live entirely on their boats, visiting their houses on land perhaps once a month. The upsetting of their junks[1] is a matter of frequent occurrence, the result usually being a reduction in the number of that particular colony to which the junk belonged. The Chinese take risks in stormy weather which no white man in this region would dream of taking. The two colonies here were established with a special view to fishing—one at Roseville in 1875, and the other in the town of San Diego about 1870. The latter consists of about a dozen houses, arranged in two rows, nearly at right angles to each other, while in close proximity are stagnant pools, stands for drying fish, outhouses and piles of

---

1 Upsetting of their junks: Jordan here notes: "in 1881 this colony owned four large junks, besides three smaller boats."

rotten fish, and all manner of abominations full of crawling maggots, all of which tend to give the colony an extremely unsavory odor. The head man of the colony furnishes the greater part of the fishing capital, and the fishermen prepay him out of the proceeds of their catches. The Chinese of these two colonies use seines, imported from China, about 300 by 10 feet, with a 1 inch mesh. When new these are worth about $100. Along the coast of this county are gathered, principally by the Chinese, about 700 tons of abalones. North of Cerros Island the Chinamen have stripped the whole coast of this shell. Until latterly the Mexican Government paid no attention to the depredations of the Chinamen, but now a license of $60 for each boat is charged upon all coming from the United States in search of abalones, and to collect that tax a Mexican consulate has been established at San Diego. The origin of the abalone business was as follows: The Chinese in China dry the fish of *Haliotis* (or some other related genus), and fishing that animal in California, they commenced the same industry there about the year 1873. Later, white men began to gather up the shells thrown away by the Chinamen, and the use of them for ornaments soon created a demand for them. Thereupon the Chinamen saved the shells, and for three years or so the abalone-shell business has been very extensive. By the excessive working of this industry the abalones have been nearly exterminated in all accessible places, and American dealers now ship Chinamen to the neighboring islands difficult of access, receiving in return the shells, the Chinese retaining the meat.

LOS ANGELES AND VENTURA COUNTIES, CALIFORNIA.— In Los Angeles County are about 30 Chinamen, all of whom are engaged in collection abalones. They ship to San Francisco annually about 150 tons of shells.

In Ventura County, at Point Magie, 9 miles south of Hueneme, is a colony of 6 Chinamen. They settled there in 1877. Two of the number were recently drowned by the upsetting of a junk.

At San Buenaventura there are a few Chinese engaged in fishing from the wharves.

SANTA BARBARA COUNTRY, CALIFORNIA.—There are about 25 Chinamen in Santa Barbara Country engaged in fishing. At Goleta there is a party of 3 employed in fishing with the seine. Many colonies of Chinamen are transported to the neighboring islands in the schooner *Surprise*, belonging to Rogers Brothers, for the purpose of collecting abalones, the meat from which they salt, dry, and ship to

China, paying for their transportation to and from the islands with shells. On the Santa Cruz Islands as great a quantity as 50,000 pounds of fish have been caught in a season by Chinamen.

SAN LUIS OBISPO COUNTY, CALIFORNIA.—At Port Harford, San Luis Obispo County, there is a colony of 8 Chinamen, 6 men and 2 women, and at San Simeon and other places there are 50 Chinamen engaged in collecting abalones, the shells of which they ship to San Francisco, retaining the meat for shipment as food.

MONTEREY COUNTY, CALIFORNIA—There are two extensive colonies in Monterey Country, one at Pescadero, the other at Punta Alones. The colony at the former place, which is in the northwest corner of Carmelo Bay was established in 1868, and is composed of 40 persons, living in eight houses. A considerable proportion of these are fishermen. The others attend to housework and to drying and preparing the fish. They use boats built by themselves, obtaining at Soquel anchovies for bait.

Spaniards, who never fish, are hired to cart the fish from the boats to the drying shores and, again, when dry and prepared, to the point of shipment.

The colony at Punta Alones, which is a mile and a half west of Monterey, settled there in 1864 and consists of 25 fishermen. This is a somewhat larger colony than the one at Pescadero. Some of the women here go fishing with the men. Others stay at home and dress the fish, which operation is aided by a heavy hatchet-like knife. One of the Chinamen at Punta Alones is an American citizen and speaks English well. Others have been hotel cooks. This colony compares favorably with any other one the coast. They ship daily to San Francisco, in fine weather, from 200 to 800 pounds of fish. The member of this colony, as well as those at Pescadero, dry and ship to China an unknown quantity of abalone meat and sell the shells. At certain seasons they also dry many tons of different devil-fish, squids, &c.

SANTA CRUZ COUNTY, CALIFORNIA.—Between Soquel and Aptos, Santa Cruz County, is a large colony of Chinese. There are about 50 of them, all men and all engaged in fishing. They ship to San Francisco and to San José direct, especially in summer. Those not so shipped are sent to Soquel, where they are taken to San Francisco by steamer. The Soquel fishermen make great complaint of the violation of the fish laws by the Chinese, as the latter use fine-meshed seines and take large quantities of young flounders and shad, which are never returned to the water, the Chinese caring nothing for the future fisheries. These fish are either salted and dried, or are left to spoil on the beach. The waste is said to be enormous.

SAN MATEO AND SAN FRANCISCO COUNTIES, CALIFORNIA.—In the town of San Mateo is a company of 7 Chinamen. They fish with seines and ship their fish to San Francisco or peddle them fresh in the neighborhood.

In San Francisco County the Chinese fishermen devote their attention to catching shrimp with purse-nets. With the shrimp small fish of other species are taken and afterwards salted and dried. At Bay View there is a Chinese colony consisting of about 24 men, who, with a hundred seines and eleven junks, are engaged in shrimping. There is another colony of 10 Chinamen 2 miles farther south. The Chinamen arrange the large shrimp, after removing the carapace, on two sticks of cane parallel to each other; these sticks passing through the flesh of the shrimp. These they sell for 30 cents per pound. Others are sold with the carapace and legs removed, simply as meats. The total catch of shrimp and prawn for this county is estimated at 30,000 pounds.

In former years of the Chinamen in San Francisco County were accustomed to eat shark fins, both fresh and dried, which were by them esteemed a great delicacy. The entire business of shrimping was then in the hands of the Chinese. There operations extended from Mare Island to Angel Island. The bulk of the shrimp caught by the Chinese with their fine-meshed nets was shipped to China in sacks. Large quantities of shrimp were sold also to oyster dealers in San Francisco who, after boiling them, would set them before their customers whilst waiting for oysters, thus to temporarily satisfy their appetites. The shells of the shrimp were shipped by Chinamen to China, who paid to the owners of the fishing-grounds a tax of from 50 cents to $1 a month. They also used to catch sturgeon, from whose backbone they would pull with a hook the inside nerve; this, which resembles a piece of macaroni and is nearly 3 feet long, is dried and shipped to China as a rare tid-bit for the epicures.

In 1876 the Italian Fishermen's Union of San Francisco addressed a letter to one of the State Senators, the main object of which was to direct attention to the ruinous methods employed in fishing by the Chinese, their total disregard of the size of the fish they caught, and their waste of all the sturgeon they took, exception the one nerve in the back above referred to. They fished so excessively that often they would ship to China as much as $12,000 worth of shrimp and dried fish per month. The Italians, therefore, asked that the Chinese fishermen be compelled to adopt a system less destructive.

ALAMEDA COUNTY, CALIFORNIA.—In Alameda County there were established in 1870 Chinese fishing colonies which are now deserted. These fisheries were principally for the capture of smelt and herring from the wharf, which they carried on by the aid of very fine square nets, from which not even the very smallest minnows could escape. They would drop their net about every twenty minutes; when hauled up, a boat would be pushed out under the net, and the contents of the net dumped into the boat. Thousands were thus taken every day.

MARIN COUNTY, CALIFORNIA.—Near Point San Pedro, Marin County, there are two colonies of Chinese, numbering in all about 112 persons, who fish for shrimp. These they ship to San Francisco, after having dried them on the hill-sides and threshed them, in Chinese style, in order to separate the hull from the meat.

As will have been noticed, the peculiarity in the construction of the nets used by the Chinamen is that the meshes are extremely fine, the end in view being the capture of all fish, large and small, young and old; and many complaints have been made regarding their use for their use of this style of net, especially by the fishermen at Soquel, Santa Cruz County.

AVARICE OF CHINESE FISHMEN.—With a view to illustrate the extreme avarice of the Chinese fishermen, as shown by their exclusive use of very fine-meshed nets, it may be stated here that Mexican Government has found it necessary to station a consul at San Diego who is instructed to charge every boat coming in search of abalones $60 per annum, their depredations in this fishery having been so extensive as to almost exterminate the species.

SURF-FISHING.—The peculiar method of surf-fishing at Punta Alones and Pescadero in vogue amongst the Chinamen is one entirely unknown to American fishermen, and is described by Professor Jordan, as follows: "At Punta Alones and Pescadero the Chinese fishermen carry on a fishery for the capture of surf-fish [*Embiotoca lateralis*, *Damalicthys vacca*, &c.], and their methods, being characteristically oriental, are of much interest to a stranger. The gill-nets are placed among the kelp-covered rocks, not far from shore, and the boat goes around among the nets to frighten the fish into them. The old man plies the oar, sculling the boat. The young man stands in the bow, with a long pole, which he throws into the water at such an angle that it returns to him. The woman sits in the middle of the boat, with the baby strapped on her back. She is armed with two drum-sticks, with which she keeps up an infernal racket by hammering on the seat in front of her. This is supposed to frighten the fish so that they frantically plunge into the nets. Occasionally this is varied by the women taking the oar and the old man the drum-stick."

SHRIMP AND ABALONE FISHERIES.—The principal fishing industries engaged in by the Chinese are the capture and preparation of shrimps and abalones. The grater part of the shrimp are dried, threshed, and sent to market. The hulls are shipped to China and sold at $20 a ton for manure. They are considered by the Chinese to be an excellent fertilizer.

A minor occupation of the Chinese is that of collecting seaweed.

A colony of Chinamen, numbering perhaps twenty-five men, is located at San Pablo, near the mouth of the Sacramento River, on the bay southwest of San Pablo. They are engaged in shrimp fishing, their methods being the same as those employed by the Chinamen about San Francisco.

FISHERMEN'S HOUSES.—The houses of the Chinese colony at Roseville, San Diego, number about ten. They are low, unpainted, dirty-looking buildings, and are surrounded by hen-coops, whose occupants are fed, to a great extent, upon the small fish which the Chinese capture in their fine-meshed seines.

CHARACTERISTICS OF CALIFORNIAN CHINESE.—It is noteworthy that the Chinese, perhaps in mistrust of their own race, never consign their fish to Chinese dealers in the cities, preferring to transact business with the Americans.

A writer in the *San Francisco Weekly Bulletin* of January 27, 1871, says of the Chinese fishermen of California:

"The Chinese fisherman in China is very different from the Chinese fisherman of California and far above him in equipments, habits, and scale of work. Confident of his seamanship and skill he dashes around in his lateen-sailed junk in a reckless manner, and in hours of recreation indulges his fondness for gambling, while the latter tugs painfully at oar and finds his brother fishermen too poor to gamble with him. The Chinaman is a good sailor in his native craft, but in other vessels, when difficult duties are to be performed, needs some one to direct him constantly.

"On the southern bank, and the entrance of the San Antonio Creek, is a small Chinese settlement, consisting of some dozen wooden houses, called China Point. The shores of the creek are covered with smelt and herring, drying in the sun preparatory to being compressed into compact bales to be shipped away; the nets, patched and old, are lying around everywhere drying in the sun, and the whole dirty, filthy, and ill-smelling.

"The fisherman's boat is a long, unwieldy, clumsily-constructed craft, with heavy, ill-shaped oars. They are not shipped in double rowlocks after the American method, but work on a single pin which passes through the loom of the oar. With the nets piled up in the stern, and the crew at their places, the cockswain, using a large steering-oar, guides the boat to the long flats of the Oakland and Alameda shores, the principal fishing grounds, where the shoals of smelt and herring, which abound here at high water, are encircled by the nets. Stationary nets and seines are also used—one to lay all night, or for some hours, and the other for immediate and active work. At sunset, after drawing the nets, they row home and spare the catch on the shore, ready for the next day's drying. The journey home is accompanied by a song, if the catch has been a large one, or only a grunt, if poor.

"The shores of Islay Creek are the choice of the Chinese fishermen who live on the San Francisco side of the bay. Clams, smelt, and shrimp constitute their catch at low tide, and their manner of procuring the former is extremely remarkable. Either a long plank or square pieces of wood are placed under the feet, and using them in the same manner as snow-shoes the fisherman makes very fair time over the mud. His basket or light boat is pushed along to receive the shell-fish as he picks them up, and before the tide has quit falling his shrimp-net does good service. Their cabins border on the creek, and have the same characteristics, though perhaps on a larger scale, as their fellows at the entrance to the San Antonio. But in addition to preparing fish for transportation to China, they supply, in a great measure, the market in the Chinese quarter, but their fishing ground has not the same size or quality of smelt that are found over the flats on the other side."

CHINESE IN WASHINGTON TERRITORY.—In Washington Territory there are thirty-three Chinamen engaged in fishing. About Cape Flattery and Quartermaster's Harbor there are twelve; near Port Madison there are fifteen engaged in drying fish. They also buy from the Indians. Especial value is set upon flounders, but salmon are held by them in small esteem. At Port Gamble and Ludlow there are six Chinamen who occupy their time in fishing from the wharves. They catch a large quantity of dogfish.

CHINESE IN THE SALMON CANNERIES OF OREGON.—On the Columbia River, Oregon, as many as three thousand Chinamen are engaged in the salmon canneries.

After the salmon have been thrown in a heap on the wharf, the Chinamen cut off the heads, tails, and fins, and remove the viscera. Some Chinamen become so expert at this branch of the work that they can thus clean 1,700 fish per day. After the fish have been washed and cut into sections they are split into three pieces by the Chinaman, one piece being large enough to fill a can, the two others smaller. These fragments are placed on tables, at which the Chinamen stand ready to pack them. Other Chinese put on the covers, while yet others solder them, where this operation is not done by machinery.

The Chinese thus do the bulk of the work at the salmon canneries. The supervisors, foremen, and bookkeepers are, however, white men. The fish-cutters, if expert, receive from $40 to $45 per month. The majority receive $1 per day of eleven hours, and work as required; that is, leaving and coming at any hour that may be set, time during which they are actually at work alone being counted. No other race of people could work at such rates and upon such terms as these, and in the present state of things but for Chinese labor the canneries must needs be closed. They come in April and leave in August, and very few return. They are employed directly and without the aid of any agent. The Chinese, as a rule, work very faithfully. They are never engaged in any drunken riot, and their work is uniform. On the other hand, they are not devoted to their employers. If dissatisfied, "they are the hardest class in the world to manage." They would "use a knife for two cents." If their pay should exceed a day's indebtedness, they would very probably resort to foul, mean work. They are inveterate gamblers, and their wages, as earned, go from one to the other to pay their gaming debts. A Chinaman dare not fish in the Columbia, it being an understood thing that he would die for his sport. They are only tolerated because they work for such low wages. Each cannery employs from one hundred to two hundred Chinese.

Questions for Discussion:
1. What does this report reveal about West Coast prejudices against the Chinese?
2. What sort of connections can be made between environmental protection and racism in this document?
3. What problems does this document pose to historians attempting to understand West Coast fisheries in the 1880s?

George Brown Goode and Joseph W. Collins, *The Fisheries and Fishery Industry of the United States. Section 4: The Fishermen of the United States* (Washington, D.C.: Government Printing Office, 1887), 37–42.

MARITIME LABOR CONDITIONS

Seafaring in the late nineteenth century remained a highly dangerous profession and does not seem to have been held in high esteem by society as a whole, which correctly perceived it as dirty, dangerous, and low-paid work. This was true for deep-sea fishermen, laker crews, and deep-sea trades operating out of large ports on both coasts.

The prestige of the profession as a whole declined with industrialization and the alienation of mariners from society as a whole. This was particularly noticeable on the high-seas fleet, where fewer and fewer native-born citizens took up seafaring careers, and increasingly, U.S.-flagged ships had American officers and foreign crewmembers. This was as true for fishing fleets out of Gloucester, Massachusetts, as it was for transpacific steamers. Working conditions on American sailing vessels, which were nicknamed *Yankee Hell ships*, were known to be terrible, especially those officered by *bucko mates* who intimidated their sailors with all manner of violence. William H. Bunting has recently considered these conditions in his thoughtful handling of sailors' journals from this period, *Sea Struck*.[1]

Sailors were not necessarily safe when ashore, either. Port cities could be dangerous places. A special kind of criminal known as a *crimp* preyed on sailors, depriving them of their pay, their self-respect, and often their liberty when they "shanghaied" them—forcing them to serve on ships against their will. The problem was exacerbated by an unsympathetic court system that considered ordinary sailors to lack the same basic rights as other Americans. In the infamous *Arago* decision of 1897, the U.S. Supreme Court even went so far as to proclaim that the Thirteenth Amendment, which ended involuntary servitude in the United States, did not apply to seamen.

Mariners did not take these conditions lying down. Many organized, especially on the West Coast. Union leaders began to appeal to the government to protect them from abusive labor practices. In 1885 coasting sailors formed the Coast Seamen's Union that by 1887 had produced its own newspaper, the *Coast Seamen's Journal*, to advocate for improved conditions on American ships. It was, however, to be a long and difficult fight, opposed tooth and nail by conservative shipowners who had a variety of methods to thwart the developing power of maritime labor unions.

James H. Williams, "The Crimping System" (1895)

One of the primary goals of early seafaring labor unions was to gain control of the hiring process. Opposing them were "crimps," some of whom were honest boardinghouse owners who acted as middlemen in finding sailors positions on board ships, while others were vicious criminals who trapped sailors in a perpetual cycle of debt, desertion, and what amounted to involuntary servitude. It was a long and difficult battle; the crimps were politically well-connected and ruthless in their determination to keep control over the waterfront. The struggle lasted for decades, and it was only in 1915, when Congress passed the Lafollette Seamen's Act, that crimps were eliminated as a factor in sailors' lives. This piece originated as the complaint of James H. "Jim" Williams, an east coast sailor prominent in the Atlantic Coast Seamen's Union in the 1890s.

As a seaman and a representative of seamen, I desire to call the attention of the commissioner of labor statistics and the legislature to

---

1   William H. Bunting, *Sea Struck* (Gardiner, Maine: Tilbury House Publishers, 2004).

certain abuses and violations of the shipping laws as administered in the port of New York.

Right here it will be quite apropos to state that the strict enforcement of these laws would mean a corresponding decrease in the earnings of a certain class of people who trade on the necessities of seamen, and who, therefore, openly violate the express conditions of the law every day in the year, to the great disadvantage of seamen.

These people may fittingly be described as the middlemen of our calling, who, with a view to their own pecuniary advancement, obstruct the free intercourse between shipmasters and seamen when mutually contracting for a voyage.

Owing to the fact that the merchant marine is the natural recruiting source of the navy, the sailor has always in maritime countries been regarded as a ward of the nation, for whose particular needs special legislation has been found necessary. Those governments who possess the strongest navies have invariably done the most for the protection of their merchant seamen and the encouragement of commerce afloat. Indeed, it may be laid down as an axiom that the naval and maritime standing of any nation is in exact ratio to the amount of protection accorded their merchant seamen. In pursuance of this time-honored policy, the Government of the United States has, from time to time, enacted laws for the better protection of our merchant seamen. These laws, although substantially the same as those of other maritime nations, differ from them in that they contain more of punitive and less of protective clauses affecting the seamen, and in being less specific on points where accurate specification is absolutely necessary in order to leave no loopholes whereby unscrupulous people may be enabled to evade the laws. That this very evil, resulting from the defectiveness of our shipping laws, has been brought about is evident from the flourishing condition of the pernicious 'crimping system,' as practiced throughout the United States, and particularly in the port of New York, which robs the sailor of nearly everything he earns.

At the beginning of this statement mention was made of a certain class of people who trade on the necessities of seamen. Legally, and also in parliamentary and nautical vernacular, they are known as 'crimps,' although among their more intimate associates they are dignified by the appellation of shipping masters and agents. Their ostensible occupation in life is to procure crews for vessels. This, in other maritime countries, is a governmental function, the infringement of which by outside parties is considered a criminal offense and dealt with as such. Owing to the neglect of the United States Government to provide proper officers for the performance of this duty the crimps have never experienced any difficulty either in their efforts to rob the sailor or evade the law. So cunning, unscrupulous, and, withal, so powerful, in a political sense, in their respective localities, are these crimps that the smallest loophole in the law through which they can intrude their iniquitous methods speedily becomes a practical negation of the whole. For many years the crimps of New York have been banded together in an association strong enough to control the entire shipping of this port. Not only do they have it in their power to prevent a seaman from securing employment whenever it suits their purpose to do so, but they can also prevent the master of a vessel from getting a crew, unless he is willing to ship his men through their agencies. It is needless to add that they do not hesitate to use this power whenever occasion may require for the promotion of their own interests. Thus, when the master of a vessel wishes to engage a crew, not finding what he wants at the United States shipping commissioner's office, he is, perforce, compelled to apply to a crimp in order to be accommodated. If sailors happen to be scarce at the time the crimp will charge the captain so much per head for supplying him with men. If, on the other hand, sailors should happen to be plentiful, the crimp will not charge the captain anything for supplying him with a crew; in fact, he will even go the length, sometimes, of paying the captain a bonus for the privilege of shipping his men in order to prevent some other crimp from securing his business, taking care, however, to charge the sailor a correspondingly larger fee to make up the deficiency. This fee is known among sailors by the suggestive name of 'blood money.' The suggestiveness of the name does not in the least exaggerate its import. The 'blood money' in the port of New York ranges from $1 to $20, sometimes more, according to the length and nature of the voyage and the rating of the seaman. As the wages paid to seamen in this port seldom exceed $20 and are usually only about $15 per month, it will readily be seen what a hardship the payment of these exorbitant fees works on 'poor Jack.' It is useless for the sailor to make any objection to this treatment. He has either got to pay the 'blood money' or starve in the streets. There is no alternative in the case; neither has he any resource whereby he can secure his rights. The fashion of paying shipowners and masters for the privilege of supplying them with sailors by the crimps has become so common as to be looked upon as an established custom, and is considered by many shipowners and masters as a legitimate source of income; so much so, in fact, that the majority of them positively refuse to employ seamen on any other terms than what is prescribed by the crimps.

Again, owing to the necessity which a seaman is under in consequence of the present United States law of relying on his advance or allotment note of wages for the payment of his board, clothing, etc, while on shore, the sailors' boarding house keepers, who, by the way, are closely allied with the crimps' association, have a fine opportunity, which, as a rule, they are not slow to take advantage of, to charge the sailors exorbitant prices for the accommodations to be paid for out of their advance.

The effect of the advance system has been unqualifiedly bad. So far from being a provision against the seaman's improvidence, it has compelled improvidence by encouraging the crimping system. Wages paid before the beginning of a voyage involve, of course, a proportionate shortage of wages at the port of discharge, which result tends to throw the seaman upon the mercy of the crimps and to keep him in continual subjection to that class. In fact, the seamen in the majority of trades are necessarily working altogether for the crimps, and seldom handle one cent of the money they earn. It will be seen that such a condition compels improvidence, or, to use a more significant term, dissipation, for under the rule of the crimps the proportion of the seaman's wages which he gets over and above what he eats is neither more nor less than the proportion which he dissipates.

As the sailor is invariably compelled to wait from three days to one week after coming ashore before he can receive his wages, he falls an easy prey to the crimps, who, by plying him freely with liquor during the interval, generally succeed in getting him so deeply in debt that it requires all his wages, and sometimes more even, to satisfy his creditors. From this time forward the sailor is not a free agent, but rather a chattel of the crimp. He is not permitted to look for a ship for himself, nor can he have any voice in deciding what his own wages shall be for his next voyage. All these preliminaries are arranged for him by the crimp, whose chattel he is. In addition to this, he must sign an allotment note for the full amount allowed by law, payable to the crimp. Thus it often happens that after a short stay ashore his allotment note of $40 or $50 does not begin to cover his indebtedness; at least that is what his boarding master claims, and he will have to go to sea short of clothing and other necessities.

As a majority of these boarding houses belong to the crimps' association, unless a sailor goes to one of them, it is practically impossible for him to get a ship. It is unnecessary almost to add that the moral influence exercised on the sailor in these vile haunts is none of the best.

In view of the foregoing, and if you have any regard for the future of our country as a naval and maritime power, I beseech you to appoint a committee to investigate the shipping system in the port of New York, which is a libel on our claim of being the foremost civilized nation on earth. The report issued by the Commissioner of Navigation conclusively shows—and figures don't lie, gentlemen—that native American seamen are getting scarcer and scarcer every year. Native Americans refuse to be outraged in every conceivable way by heartless crimps ashore and fiendish brutes afloat; hence their scarcity on board of our ships. When it is borne in mind that the gravest problem which confronts the Navy Department today is the manning of our new war ships, and that our chief dependence for the same is on mercenary foreigners, it is easy to be seen what a serious question this resolves itself into.

Questions for Discussion:
1. What was the role of "blood money" in the crimping system?
2. What impact did the crimping system have on native-born Americans who might have gone to sea?
3. Who was Williams looking to for assistance in abolishing the crimping system?

United States Treasury Department, *Report of the Commissioner of Navigation to the Secretary of the Treasury* (Washington, D.C.: Government Printing Office, 1895), 270–71.

International Seamen's Union, "The Red Record" (1898)

The *Coast Seamen's Journal* was "A Journal of Seamen, by Seamen, for Seamen," produced by the San Francisco–based International Seamen's Union of America, which was usually known by its first three initials, ISU. Its most famous component was the "Red Record," initiated by Andrew Furuseth (1854–1938), which attempted to document the abuses American seamen faced at the hands of their officers. Notably, most of these cases were on sailing vessels rather than steamers. While its accuracy has sometimes been questioned, the overall pattern seems clear: officers could get away with murder, and often did.

Tam O'Shanter, Captain Peabody, arrived in San Francisco, September 6, 1888. First-Mate Swain arrested on three charges of cruelty preferred by Seamen Fraser, Williams and Wilson. Captain defended his mate on the ground of incompetent crew; did not say how he came to sail with incompetent men. Mate released on $450 bond. Case still in the courts.

Hecla, Captain Snow, arrived in Tacoma, November 1, 1888. Sixteen seamen, being all-hands forward, entered complaint of cruelty in the District Court. Near Cape Horn captain attacked the carpenter; struck him with a heavy instrument, breaking his jaw and knocking out several teeth. Captain nearly killed another man, and, with the aid of the first-mate, beat several of the crew. Crew were put in the hold for forty-eight hours and secured in such a manner that they could neither stand erect, sit nor lie down. One man was tied to a stanchion four days and kept without food. The latter was placed within sight, but out of reach. In Acapulco the crew were imprisoned ashore until the ship was ready to sail. Application was made to the Consul for assistance, but the latter refused, saying the only thing to be done was to "rough it." Captain Snow boasted that he had never been beaten in a difficulty with seamen ashore, and refused to pay his crew the wages due them ($600 in all) for the passage from Cardiff.

Solitaire, Captain Sewall (son of the Bath ship-builder and owner of that ilk), arrived in Dunkirk, France, about January, 1889. In the Channel the mate called a seaman from aloft, knocked him down, jumped on his breast and inflicted wounds from which he died next day. The body was kept in the after hatch for four days. When the corpse was so black that the bruises could not be distinguished the story was given out to the authorities that the man died of consumption. Captain beat two men for talking while at work; first-mate also set upon them and broke one man's nose. Second-mate beat one of the boatswains with knuckle-dusters because the latter omitted the usual "sir" from his address. A sick seaman was hauled out of his bunk and made to go aloft. Another seaman accidentally spat on the deck; was made to go down on his knees and lick it up. Boatswains were beaten for refusing, or being unable to beat the seamen. An *old* seaman was given liquor and then plied to tell tales about the crew. With the cues thus received the officers made occasion to beat the seamen. At Dunkirk the second-mate fled to England, and remained in hiding until the *Solitaire* was ready to proceed to sea again.

John F. Kearns, Captain McDonald, New York, February, 1889. Complaints of general abuse. Some of the crew determined to desert the vessel while still lying in harbor. L. Kaldron and three others launched a roughly made raft and endeavored to make the shore. A storm of wind, sleet and snow came on and drove them to sea. Two of the seamen were washed from the raft and drowned. The steamer *Old Colony* picked up the remaining two covered with ice and nearly frozen to death. One of these subsequently died in the hospital.

Llewellyn J. Morse, Captain Lavary, San Francisco, February, 1889. First-Mate Watski charged by Seaman Arthur Connors with striking him on the head with a pair of handcuffs, imprisonment in the lazarette and gagging because the complainant was singing. Captain was present during these inflictions, but refused to interfere. Watski released on $500 bonds. Case dismissed.

St. Andrew, Captain Heckster, New York, March, 1889. Captain, First-Mate Beveridge and Second-Mate Campbell were arraigned before the United States Commissioner charged by six seamen with having caused the death of a half-witted Norwegian named Elias Nelson. Soon after leaving London, the seamen charge, the captain and mates commenced to ill treat Nelson most brutally, knocking him down with marlin-spikes on the slightest pretext. As a result of this treatment the man died on March 20th. Case dismissed.

Solitaire 2,[1] Captain Sewall, Philadelphia, 1889. Warrants were sworn out for the arrest of the captain, First-Mate F. Ryan and Second-Mate J. W. Robbins, on complaints of brutality on the passage from Dunkirk, France. One man was hit aloft by the second-mate and fell eighty feet into the buntlines and was thus saved. Another man was struck off the yard and fell to the deck. He was killed outright. The mates deserted the ship while towing up the Delaware; Captain Sewall

---

1   2: These figures designate the number of cases reported against the same vessel.

also disappeared for a time. It is reported that Captain Sewall "healed the wounds of all complainants" with $440 in cash.

Commodore T. H. Allen, Captain Merriam, San Francisco, 1889. A seaman fell sick and was confined in the carpenter's shop. Diet for the sick man, common ship's fare; medicine salts. For four days he ate nothing. Finally he died. No investigation held.

McLauren, Captain Oakes, New York, 1889. Second-Mate Lily-bridge charged with beating certain members of the crew with a capstan-bar. One man jumped overboard twice in Singapore, but was captured; he finally managed to desert. Lilybridge was held to answer in default of $3,000 bail. Case dismissed.

Finance, steamer, Captain Zollinger, New York, 1889. First-Mate Evelyn arrested for brutally assaulting a seaman named Burke. The First-Mate attacked Burke with a belaying-pin, clapped him in irons and kicked him all over the body. Evelyn was admitted to bail in $1,000 bonds. Case dismissed.

Finance 2, same captain and mate, August, 1889. Captain beat four negro stowaways over the heads with a plank until they bled and pleaded for mercy. Three of these boys were landed on a desert island twelve miles from St. Thomas Island. Captain instructed the boat's crew to pitch the negroes overboard and let them swim. Second-Mate Martin disobeyed this order until within thirty yards of the Island. Then it was discovered that one of the boys could not swim, and if he had not been pulled into the boat again would assuredly have drowned. Captain Zollinger disappeared upon arrival in New York. Case dismissed.

Standard, Captain Percy, San Francisco, 1889. Seaman E. Ander-son complained of ill-treatment from First-Mate Martin. First-Mate knocked Anderson down and kicked him until he was insensible. Mate ordered him aloft; men had to lash him in the rigging to prevent his falling. Warrant sworn out for the mate's arrest; mate disappeared and could not be found.

Commodore T. H. Allen 2, Captain Merriam, New York, 1889. Fred Hall, a green hand, was accorded cruel treatment on the passage to New York, and when he asked the captain for his pay was told there was nothing due him—the crimps had received all in advance and blood-money. Case dismissed.

Reuce, Captain Adams. San Francisco, 1889. Seventeen seamen down with scurvy; one man died from same disease. Rotten and insufficient food was the cause. While some of the men were holystoning[1] the decks they were beaten by the second-mate. The latter officer deserted as the *Reuce* was towing into San Francisco. Case tried in District Court and verdict for $3,600 damages awarded the seamen.

Robert C. Belknap, Captain Staples, New York, 1889. Crew reported hard and continuous work night and day during the passage. Bad food and violence from the officers. A seaman, William Thomas, reported missing. On the arrival of the *Belknap* in New York the second-mate disappeared. All-hands bore marks of scurvy. Case dismissed.

Sterling, Captain Goodwin, San Francisco, 1890. Three seamen were sent to the Marine Hospital with scurvy. All-hands report bad and insufficient food and brutal treatment from the officers.

Edward O'Brien, Captain Oliver, San Francisco, 1890. First-Mate Gillespie charged with most inhuman conduct. Knocked down the second-mate and jumped on his face; struck one seamen on the head with a belaying-pin, inflicting a ghastly wound, then kicked him in the head and ribs, inflicting life marks; struck another man on the neck with a capstan-bar, then kicked him into insensibility; struck the boatswain in the face because the latter failed to hear an order. Gillespie charged and admitted to bail. Case dismissed.

John Harvey, Captain Stewart, New York, 1890. Captain assaulted the man at the wheel; the first-mate, Phelan, assaulted a man while urging the mate to beat the seamen; threatened to shoot any one who tried to interfere. One man interfered and the captain shot him in the temple. The two seamen were then triced[2] up in the rigging for three hours and beaten while in that position, then chained to stanchions in the hold for twenty-three days on bread and water. Young was triced up and afterward put in jail for testifying in favor of the seamen at Barbadoes. Case laid over till the arrival of the *Harvey* in New York. Case dismissed.

Rappahannock, Captain Dickenson, Philadelphia, 1890. Crew complained of vessel being under-manned. Captain went ashore, got crimps aboard and beat the seamen, then put them in irons and locked them in the forecastle, where they remained with little food for

---

1   Holystoning: scrubbing a ship deck with a piece of sandstone, often on hands and knees.
2   Triced: tied to the standing rigging in a painful position.

two weeks. Captain Dickenson examined by the United States Commissioner. Case dismissed on grounds of "justifiable discipline."

Louisiana, Captain Ogilvie, San Francisco, 1890. One seaman being sick begged to be permitted to stay on deck when there was work aloft. Second-Mate Davis answered by striking him on the head with a belaying-pin, then struck him several blows with his fist. Seaman appealed to the captain, who replied by striking him in the face. Another man who complained of ill treatment was put in irons and fed on bread and water for 100 days. One man ran a nail into his foot, causing great pain and swelling; he was compelled to go about the decks walking on his heels. Case dismissed.

Questions for Discussion:
1. What did the "Red Record" reveal about working conditions on American sailing vessels?
2. What did the "Red Record" reveal about American society, both ashore and afloat?
3. What evidence does the *Coast Seamen's Journal* provide to support its allegations concerning the abuse of seamen?

"The Red Record," *Coast Seamen's Journal*, January 26, 1898.

William D. Sewall, "The Decadence of Our Merchant Marine" (1905)

By 1904 it was very clear that the American-flagged merchant marine was in bad shape. Congress responded by creating the Merchant Marine Commission to investigate, appointing Senator Jacob H. Gallinger (1837–1918) of New Hampshire as chairman. Over eight months, the Gallinger commission traveled all over the country, taking testimony from a wide variety of sources. The commission found that Americans were "practically unanimous not in merely desiring, but in demanding an American ocean fleet, built, owned, officered, and so far as may be, manned by our own people." Furthermore, this sentiment was "just as earnest on the Great Lakes . . . as on either ocean."

In this transcript of his testimony before the Gallinger commission, William D. Sewall (1861–1930), a member of a well-known shipbuilding family of Bath, Maine, states some of his opinions on the decline of American seafaring. Sewall is especially outspoken on the loss of status and lack of prospects for young Americans who wanted to pursue a career at sea, a more conservative approach than the labor leaders of the day, many of whom were immigrants themselves. In this transcript of the proceedings, Senator Stephen R. Mallory (1848–1907), a U.S. Senator from Florida, questions Sewall on why it was difficult to find officers for American-flagged merchant ships.

Senator MALLORY. I wish to ask you a few questions on some other matters, on which you are probably better informed than anybody else. It is relative to the question of securing officers for your ships. Do you have any difficulty in securing officers for your ships?

Mr. SEWALL. We have great difficulty today; very serious difficulty.

Senator MALLORY. I refer to masters and mates.

Mr. SEWALL. Masters and mates; not so much just today with the masters as with the mates; but the masters are fast leaving us. In a few years the condition will be very hard.

I can recall, before I took an active part in the firm, when college students would come down into our yards and go before the mast as boys and move up, and they would rise very rapidly and soon become officers, and then become masters, and then they would take an interest in the vessel, putting their money in it; and one vessel would lead to another. Now there is no incentive like that. There is no inducement for the smart young man to follow a seafaring life.

Senator MALLORY. Why is that?

Mr. SEWALL. The captains used to be the aristocracy of the town.

Senator MALLORY. How long ago was that? You are quite a young man.

Mr. SEWALL. That was twenty-five years ago.

Senator MALLORY. That is since the decadence of our merchant marine.

Mr. SEWALL. That was when things were looking brighter.

Senator MALLORY. We were still in a state of inanition, so far as our merchant marine was concerned.

Where do you now get your captains, your first officers, and your second mates? Where do they come from?

Mr. SEWALL. For captains, we rely largely upon the old-time masters of the wooden clipper ships. As those ships drop out, through age and in one way and another, the masters are left.

Senator MALLORY. As a rule are they Americans?

Mr. SEWALL. The masters are.

Senator MALLORY. They are not naturalized citizens, but Americans?

Mr. SEWALL. Americans; good New England stock.

Senator MALLORY. Are they generally trained? What is their novitiate or their preliminary training?

Mr. SEWALL. They took to the sea from the advantages that did accrue in years gone by.

Representative MINOR. They are born web-footed.

Mr. SEWALL. It was a profession where they stood high and in which they secured fine wages.

Senator MALLORY. Am I right in understanding you to say that that class of men is passing away?

Mr. SEWALL. Decidedly so.

Senator MALLORY. What will you do for masters when they are absolutely gone?

Mr. SEWALL. That is what we want you to help us on. We want you to make some incentive for the young men to go to sea again, and if you can give us the sailing ship, which is the nursery of the seamen, and make its operation profitable, the young men will follow, and we will get our officers.

Senator MALLORY. I suppose you have first mates, second mates, and boatswains aboard your ships?

Mr. SEWALL. We do.

Senator MALLORY. All that class of petty officers, I suppose, as a rule, are from your coast; or are they foreigners?

Mr. SEWALL. Not necessarily, so far as the officers go. We have to take them where we can get them. The first officers more especially would come under your assumption.

Senator MALLORY. But among your subordinate officers you have, as a rule, a great many foreign-born men?

Mr. SEWALL. Yes, sir.

Senator MALLORY. What is their nationality as a rule?

Mr. SEWALL. Oh, well, it varies. In this connection I may say we have taken a man from the forecastle, without any education whatever, who had joined us in years gone by when we operated schooners, and made a master of him. We have one now. The particular man whom I have in mind joined on a coastwise vessel. He had no education. The master whom he joined became somewhat interested in him, and after a few years he went off to school. Since then he has been promoted an officer and master of a schooner, a coastwise vessel. Then he went into a square-rigged vessel, and today he is commander of one of our finest ships.

Senator MALLORY. Have you any system of apprentices on board your vessels?

Mr. SEWALL. Our system has been that all who apply are taken care of as far as possible. Our captains are instructed to promote them as rapidly as possible, and give them every advantage.

Senator MALLORY. Have you made any effort in your business to train young men with a view to making them officers eventually?

Mr. SEWALL. We have, decidedly; that is, through our masters. The only way is to secure a berth for them on our vessels and treat them with consideration and promote them as rapidly as possible.

Senator MALLORY. Do you find any considerable response to that effort?

Mr. SEWALL. We have met with more or less response, but of late years the applications have been very much fewer than they used to be. We used to have to turn away boys. We have a special room on our vessels for boys, a special deck house, so that the boys can be separated from the sailors.

Senator MALLORY. Take a vessel of 5,000 tons. Have you any limit to the number of boys you would carry on such a vessel?

Mr. SEWALL. Three or four would be the limit on one vessel—four.

Senator MALLORY. Have you any other vessels than square-rigged vessels?

Mr. SEWALL. We have one.

Senator MALLORY. What is she?

Mr. SEWALL. Steel.

Senator MALLORY. Four-masted or five-masted?

Mr. SEWALL. A five-masted schooner.

Senator MALLORY. What is her tonnage?

Mr. SEWALL. Three thousand tons.

Senator MALLORY. What is the number of the crew on that five-masted schooner?

Mr. SEWALL. About fifteen, all told.

Senator MALLORY. What is the number of the crew on one of your 3,000-ton square-rigged vessels?

Mr. SEWALL. Double the number; around there; say 30. It depends upon the voyage to some extent.

Senator MALLORY. They are New England schooners used in the coastwise trade?

Mr. SEWALL. Yes, sir.

Senator MALLORY. You use donkey engines[1] for hoisting anchors and sails?

Mr. SEWALL. Yes, sir.

Senator MALLORY. You get along with as small a number of men as possible?

Mr. SEWALL. Yes, sir; we reckon on a schooner for about half the number of men a ship would require.

Senator MALLORY. Take a schooner of 3,000 tons. I should like to get this information, and I believe you are the only witness we are likely to have from whom we can obtain it. A schooner of 3,000 tons, as compared with a square-rigged vessel of the same tonnage, so far as operating expenses are concerned, would cost about one-half. Am I right?

Mr. SEWALL. Yes; I think so; less, possibly.

Senator MALLORY. Is there any objection to these large schooners going into the ocean trade; across the Atlantic, for instance?

Mr. SEWALL. We do not feel that there is, but as a rule they have been employed in that direction but very little. But I am inclined to think myself that they will make the voyage much more frequently in the future. In fact, our last vessel was built with the idea of going anywhere over the world.

Senator MALLORY. I should like to ask your opinion as an expert upon the question of the continuance of the use of sailing vessels, fore and afters as well as square-riggers, as compared with steam vessels. From what you said in your previous remarks, I gather you are of the opinion that sailing vessels would last a good many years yet in the trade for heavy traffic—for such cargo as is bulky or heavy and does not require quick transportation.

Mr. SEWALL. On certain long voyages.

Senator MALLORY. It has been said that inside of twenty years—I

---

1 Donkey engine: a small auxiliary steam engine used for hoisting or pumping aboard ship that allowed a smaller crew to do more work.

have heard it said to a committee of the Senate—we would have no merchant sailing vessels to speak of. Is that your opinion?

Mr. SEWALL. We do not feel that that condition ought to exist. We do not think—

Senator MALLORY. That was not with reference to the dying out of our merchant marine generally, but with reference to steam vessels taking the place of sailing vessels.

Mr. SEWALL. I believe, to a limited extent, you will always have need for sailing vessels. . . .

Senator MALLORY. You have spoken of the falling off of interest on the part of our young men in the matter of seafaring life. Have you any reason to which you ascribe that?

Mr. SEWALL. There is no incentive for them to rise. The young man does not see any future. The young man not only wishes to become an officer and master, but he wants to see a future before him.

Senator MALLORY. That is due to the fact that we have not ships enough?

Mr. SEWALL. We have not ships enough and there is no incentive. They are not paying anything. The old-time master of a sailing ship was not only its master, but he became interested in the vessel. He invested his money.

Senator MALLORY. Our wages are high, both for the officers and the crew, you say?

Mr. SEWALL. For American officers.

Senator MALLORY. Is it because they can not get steady employment? Is that a factor in this decline of interest in seafaring life on the part of our young men?

Mr. SEWALL. It is very true that if any considerable number should seek that profession now they could not be taken care of. In fact, there are quite a number of masters, as I have stated, who are available now. But of the officers below, it is not so.

Questions for Discussion:

1. What does Sewall's testimony reveal about working conditions on American vessels?

2. To what does Sewall attribute the lack of interest among Americans in pursuing a seafaring career?

3. What strengths or weaknesses does Sewall's testimony have in revealing working conditions on board American ships?

William Sewall testimony to U.S. Congress Merchant Marine Commission. *Report of the Merchant Marine Commission, Together with the Testimony Taken at the Hearings. Volume 1: Report and Recommendations of the Commission (Including the views of the minority), and hearings on the North Atlantic Coast* (Washington, D.C.: Government Printing Office, 1905), 103–16.

Oswald Christensen, "Discharge book No. 80865" (1912)

Not all sailors served on oceangoing vessels, however. The Great Lakes in the late nineteenth century had a vibrant maritime commerce and culture. Like their oceangoing brethren, these mariners faced alternating danger and routine, and some claimed that their lives were even harder. In order to advocate for better conditions, the Buffalo, New York, "Association of Engineers" opened correspondence in 1874 with other marine engineer associations around the Great Lakes and formed the Marine Engineers' Association. In 1883 this became the Marine Engineer's Beneficial Association (MEBA), which still operates as one of the oldest labor unions in the nation.

Confronting MEBA and other unionized seafarers was the Lake Carriers' Association (LCA). In 1885 vessel owners in Buffalo, New York, founded the LCA to advocate Lakes shipping, especially by lobbying. From its inception, the LCA was associated with heavy industry, especially United States Steel. The LCA in this period also fought against labor unions that wanted a "closed shop" and by 1913 had largely crushed unionization efforts on the Lakes. Today the LCA continues to advocate for American-flagged shipping on the Great Lakes.

The account below illustrates some of the tactics the LCA used to intimidate seamen and prevent their joining unions. It is a sworn statement by a mariner describing how the LCA attempted to control its workers through the use of discharge books, often known as *fink books.*

I, Oswald Christensen, being first duly sworn, state that on September 8, 1911, I went to the Lake Carriers' Association shipping office at South Chicago, to look for employment as a wheelsman. I was informed by the shipping master that in order to get a job I would have to join the Lake Carriers' Association "welfare plan" and secure a discharge book, which would cost me $1. I thereupon signified my willingness to enroll.

The shipping master then made a record of my name, age, place of birth, name of nearest relative, and personal appearance. He instructed me to sign a paper, the contents of which I did not see, and then, upon receiving from me $1 he gave me a Lake Carriers' Association "discharge book" and an "able seaman's card" or certificate, both being numbered 80865, the latter certifying that "upon the application of the holder and the best information available to the Lake Carriers' Association, Oswald Christensen is competent to perform the duties of able-bodied seaman as wheelsman."

A few days afterwards I went to Conneaut, Ohio, showed my certificate and discharge book to the shipping master at that port, and requested that I be given employment on one of the steamers of the Pittsburgh Steamship Co.

No effort was made to ascertain whether or not I was qualified to serve as a wheelsman other than to ask me one question as to how long I had sailed; no questions relating to seamanship were asked, the certificate and discharge book being handed to me without further questioning, and I was told to wait around for an opportunity to ship.

While waiting to secure such employment I made the acquaintance of a number of men in the shipping office or "assembly room," and by them I was informed that when a discharge book was marked "fair" three times, it meant that the holder of such book was on the black list and would not be allowed to ship again.

On September 19, 1911, I was shipped on the steamer *Crescent City*, belonging to the Pittsburgh Steamship Co., the Lake Carriers' Association "commissioner," or shipping master, William Ford, giving me an "identification card," showing name of steamer, name of port, position (wheelsman) it was intended I should fill, the signatures of the "commissioner," and myself, dated "Lake Carriers' Association, September 19, 1911, assembly rooms. Conneaut." On the bottom of the card appeared the following: "Discharge book No. 80865, which is in his possession and must be presented with this card."

Upon arriving on board the mate, Mr. E. C. Bowerman, immediately asked me for my "discharge book," which I handed to him. He examined it, and finding no marks therein, it being a new book, he questioned me as to where I had been sailing. I replied in such a manner as to indicate that I had formerly sailed as a union man. His attitude toward me was unpleasant and overbearing, but I stayed on board the steamer one trip, until arrival back at the port of discharge, Cleveland,

Ohio, when I signified my desire to quit the ship and requested that my discharge book be returned to me.

The mate, Mr. Bowerman, thereupon told me they would not enter "wheelsman" in the "capacity" column of my discharge book, but that the entry would read, "Watchman, fair." I recognized at once that this was for the purpose of preventing me from again obtaining employment upon any of the vessels of the Pittsburgh Steamship Co., since none of the seamen employed on said vessels are rated as "watchmen."

I remonstrated, but it did no good, and I had only the choice of accepting the book which would thereafter show plainly to all shipping masters or commissioners and officers of all ships in the Lake Carriers' Association to whom I might present it in an effort to secure employment that I was considered unfit, or of refusing to accept the book at all, and thus giving up all opportunity of securing employment on any of the association's vessels.

I took the book and went ashore.

I have sailed 15 years on vessels, both steam and sail, in various parts of the world, and am qualified to serve as able seaman, having served in various capacities on board ship, including that of wheelsman, on a considerable number of steamers.

The steamer *Crescent City* carries a deck crew of 10 men (exclusive of licensed officers) as follows: Four wheelsmen and six deck hands. On the aforesaid trip I was one of the wheelsmen; of the other three, one was a licensed officer, and another was an inexperienced man who was unable to steer. The six deck hands were Greeks, who could not understand the English language.

I have just completed a voyage on the steamship *Fort Morgan* as quartermaster, and I am now residing at No. 10 North Warren Street, Mobile, Ala.

OSWALD CHRISTENSEN.

Subscribed and sworn to before me this 3d day of February, 1912.

GLENN L. HAMBURGER,

Notary Public, Mobile County, State of Alabama.

(My commission expires June 14, 1912)

Questions for Discussion:

1. What does this document reveal about relations between labor unions and corporations in 1911?

2. According to Christensen, how did discharge books affect the unionization of Great Lakes seamen?

3. What are the strengths and weakness of such testimony in understanding
shipboard labor conditions?

U.S. Congress, House of Representatives, *United States Steel Corporation Hearings Before the Committee on Investigation of United States Steel Corporation*
(Washington, D.C.: Government Printing Office, 1911), 3019–20.

NAVALISM AND EMPIRE

Federal officials made two momentous announcements in 1890. The superintendent of the Census Bureau announced that rapid western settlement
essentially meant that there was no longer a frontier line, and Secretary of
the Navy Benjamin F. Tracy called for the creation of a radically different
navy, one capable of meeting an enemy fleet on the high seas and smashing
it. Taken together, these two announcements reflected a growing feeling
among Americans that the nation should look beyond its boundaries and
play a larger role in international affairs.

Prior to 1890 the American Navy was a largely obsolete cruiser force,
scattered around the world to protect American commerce and augmented
by monitors for harbor defense. Tracy called for a new force, an oceanic
navy. The heart of this new navy was to be the battleship, a heavily armed
and armored ship with good seaworthiness, range, and speed capable of
destroying anything afloat.

Tracy based his ideas on the writings of Captain Alfred Thayer Mahan,
a naval officer who advocated the creation of a powerful offensive fleet that
would establish the United States as a world-class naval power. Mahan,
Tracy, the up-and-coming Theodore Roosevelt, and Henry Cabot Lodge—
known as *navalists*—were all proponents of a "large policy" that encouraged American expansion overseas now that the frontier was gone.

The navalists won a major victory in 1890 when Congress funded the
construction of three modern battleships and promised to fund several
more in the years to come. Nonetheless, it took a concerted effort by navalists to convince the American taxpayer that the United States required an
expensive battleship fleet designed for offensive operations. Mahan proved
to be a splendid publicist; he convinced the public that there were serious
external threats to the country that demanded a battleship fleet.

The short Spanish-American War of 1898 seemed to vindicate Mahan.
The American victory was complete, largely thanks to the ability of the

U.S. Navy's modern, Mahanian-style fleet. The United States acquired a number of overseas possessions from Spain, including the Philippines and Guam in the Pacific (and Hawaii by annexation), and Puerto Rico in the Caribbean.

But not all Americans were happy to see the United States become an empire. Many Americans, especially intellectuals such as Mark Twain and progressive politicians such as William Jennings Bryan, opposed the idea of what were essentially American colonies in the Caribbean and Pacific. Neither side accorded much respect to the inhabitants of the new possessions. American attitudes toward them were patronizing at best; at worst they were blatantly racist.

The debate was most fierce when it came to the construction of a modern but extremely expensive battleship fleet; expansionists viewed it as an absolute necessity to defend American interests, while anti-imperialists viewed warfare as outdated and the warships themselves as expensive luxuries the tax-paying public could ill afford.

Alfred Thayer Mahan, "The United States Looking Outward" (1890)

Alfred Thayer Mahan (1840–1914) was an American naval officer and the world's most influential naval writer in the nineteenth and twentieth centuries. His seminal 1890 monograph, *The Influence of Sea Power Upon History*, profoundly influenced how naval officers thought about naval warfare, not just in the United States, but in Britain, Germany, Japan, and other nations. The following piece, originally published in *The Atlantic Monthly* in December, 1890, not only called for Americans to think of the world beyond its boundaries, but to fear the completion of the Panamanian canal then being undertaken by the French. Such a canal, according to Mahan, would encourage European navies to establish naval bases in the Caribbean that threatened the eastern seaboard and, because of the canal, the West Coast as well. According to Mahan, the only remedy for this foreign naval threat was a powerful American battleship fleet.

Indications are not wanting of an approaching change in the thoughts and policy of Americans as to their relations with the world outside their own borders. For the past quarter of a century, the predominant idea, which has asserted itself successfully at the polls and shaped the course of the government, has been to preserve the home market for the home industries. The employer and the workman alike have been taught to look at the various economical measures proposed from this point of view, to regard with hostility any step favoring the intrusion of the foreign producer upon their own domain, and rather to demand increasingly rigorous measures of exclusion than to acquiesce in any loosening of the chain that binds the consumer to them. The inevitable consequence has followed, as in all cases when the mind or the eye is exclusively fixed in one direction, that the danger of loss or the prospect of advantage in another quarter has been overlooked; and although the abounding resources of the country have maintained the exports at a high figure, this flattering result has been due more to the superabundant bounty of Nature than to the demand of other nations for our protected manufactures.

For nearly the lifetime of a generation, therefore, American industries have been thus protected, until the practice has assumed the force of a tradition, and is clothed in the mail of conservatism. In their mutual relations, these industries resemble the activities of a modern ironclad that has heavy armor, but inferior engines and guns; mighty for defense, weak for offence. Within, the home market is secured; but outside, beyond the broad seas, there are the markets of the world, that can be entered and controlled only by a vigorous contest, to which the habit of trusting to protection by statute does not conduce.

At bottom, however, the temperament of the American people is essentially alien to such a sluggish attitude. Independently of all bias for or against protection, it is safe to predict that, when the opportunities for gain abroad are understood, the course of American enterprise will cleave a channel by which to reach them. Viewed broadly, it is a most welcome as well as significant fact that a prominent and influential advocate of protection, a leader of the party committed to its support, a keen reader of the signs of the times and of the drift of opinion, has identified himself with a line of policy which looks to nothing less than such modifications of the tariff as may expand the commerce of the United States to all quarters of the globe. Men of all parties can unite on the words of Mr. Blaine,[1] as reported in a recent speech: "It is not an ambitious destiny for so great a country as ours to manufacture only what we can consume, or produce only what we can eat." In face of this utterance of so shrewd and able a public man, even

---

1   Blaine: James G. Blaine, a Republican politician from Maine who in 1890 was secretary of state.

the extreme character of the recent tariff legislation seems but a sign of the coming change, and brings to mind that famous Continental System, of which our own is the analogue, to support which Napoleon added legion to legion and enterprise to enterprise, till the fabric of the Empire itself crashed beneath the weight.

The interesting and significant feature of this changing attitude is the turning of the eyes outward, instead of inward only, to seek the welfare of the country. To affirm the importance of distant markets, and the relation to them of our own immense powers of production, implies logically the recognition of the link that joins the products and the markets,—that is, the carrying trade; the three together constituting that chain of maritime power to which Great Britain owes her wealth and greatness. Further, is it too much to say that, as two of these links, the shipping and the markets, are exterior to our own borders, the acknowledgment of them carries with it a view of the relations of the United States to the world radically distinct from the simple idea of self-sufficingness? We shall not follow far this line of thought before there will dawn the realization of America's unique position, facing the older worlds of the East and West, her shores washed by the oceans which touch the one or the other, but which are common to her alone. . . .

There is no sound reason for believing that the world has passed into a period of assured peace outside the limits of Europe. Unsettled political conditions, such as exist in Haiti, Central America, and many of the Pacific islands, especially the Hawaiian group, when combined with great military or commercial importance as is the case with most of these positions, involve, now as always, dangerous germs of quarrel, against which it is prudent at least to be prepared. Undoubtedly, the general temper of nations is more averse from war than it was of old. If no less selfish and grasping than our predecessors, we feel more dislike to the discomforts and sufferings attendant upon a breach of peace; but to retain that highly valued repose and the undisturbed enjoyment of the returns of commerce, it is necessary to argue upon somewhat equal terms of strength with an adversary. It is the preparedness of the enemy, and not acquiescence in the existing state of things, that now holds back the armies of Europe. . . .

Despite a certain great original superiority conferred by our geographical nearness and immense resources,—due, in other words, to our natural advantages, and not to our intelligent preparations,—the

United States is woefully unready, not only in fact but in purpose, to assert in the Caribbean and Central America a weight of influence proportioned to the extent of her interests. We have not the navy, and, what is worse, we are not willing to have the navy, that will weigh seriously in any disputes with those nations whose interests will conflict there with our own. We have not, and we are not anxious to provide, the defense of the seaboard which will leave the navy free for its work at sea. We have not, but many other powers have, positions, either within or on the borders of the Caribbean, which not only possess great natural advantages for the control of that sea, but have received and are receiving that artificial strength of fortification and armament which will make them practically inexpugnable. On the contrary, we have not on the Gulf of Mexico even the beginning of a navy yard which could serve as the base of our operations. Let me not be misunderstood. I am not regretting that we have not the means to meet on terms of equality the great navies of the Old World. I recognize, what few at least say, that, despite its great surplus revenue, this country is poor in proportion to its length of seaboard and its exposed points. That which I deplore, and which is a sober, just, and reasonable cause of deep national concern, is that the nation neither has nor cares to have its sea frontier so defended, and its navy of such power, as shall suffice, with the advantages of our position, to weigh seriously when inevitable discussions arise,—such as we have recently had about Samoa and Bering Sea, and which may at any moment come up about the Caribbean Sea or the canal. Is the United States, for instance, prepared to allow Germany to acquire the Dutch stronghold of Curaçao, fronting the Atlantic outlet of both the proposed canals of Panama and Nicaragua? Is she prepared to acquiesce in any foreign power purchasing from Haiti a naval station on the Windward Passage, through which pass our steamer routes to the Isthmus? Would she acquiesce in a foreign protectorate over the Sandwich Islands,[1] that great central station of the Pacific, equidistant from San Francisco, Samoa, and the Marquesas, and an important post on our lines of communication with both Australia and China? Or will it be maintained that any one of these questions, supposing it to arise, is so exclusively one-sided, the arguments of policy and right so exclusively with us, that the other party will at once yield his eager wish, and gracefully withdraw? Was

---

1   Sandwich Islands: the Hawaiian Islands.

it so at Samoa? Is it so as regards Bering Sea? The motto seen on so many ancient cannon, *Ultima ratio regum,*[1] is not without its message to republics. . . .

Whether they will or no, Americans must now begin to look outward. The growing production of the country demands it. An increasing volume of public sentiment demands it. The position of the United States, between the two Old Worlds and the two great oceans, makes the same claim, which will soon be strengthened by the creation of the new link joining the Atlantic and Pacific. The tendency will be maintained and increased by the growth of the European colonies in the Pacific, by the advancing civilization of Japan, and by the rapid peopling of our Pacific States with men who have all the aggressive spirit of the advanced line of national progress.

Questions for Discussion:

1. According to Mahan, why was America now seeking to "look outward"?
2. According to Mahan, what is the link between the American temperament and a strong navy?
3. What role did Mahan envision for the U.S. Navy in the future?

Alfred Thayer Mahan, *The Interest of America in Sea Power, Present and Future* (Boston: Little, Brown, and Company, 1898), 3–16.

Navy Department, "Communications and the Battle of Manila Bay" (1898)

The most celebrated naval battle of the Spanish-American War was Manila Bay, fought on the morning of May 1st, 1898. Craig Symonds, in *Decision at Sea,*[2] hails it as one of the five most important actions fought by the U.S. Navy. It was also a crucial test of the Navy's new doctrine of offensive naval power. Within two days of the declaration of war, Commodore George Dewey (1837–1917) and his squadron sailed for the Philippines, and despite the reports of mines, steamed directly into Manila Bay and engaged the anchored Spanish squadron near Cavite. Dewey famously began the engagement by telling USS *Olympia*'s captain, "You may fire when you are ready, Gridley." Dewey's ships outgunned the obsolete Spanish ships, and sank

---

1 *Ultima ratio regum*: translated literally, *the last argument of kings*, meaning that force will decide an issue that cannot be resolved through arbitration.

2 Craig L. Symonds, *Decision at Sea: Five Naval Battles That Shaped American History* (New York: Oxford University Press, 2005).

them all. The Spanish suffered over 370 casualties, while only 9 Americans were wounded, and none killed.

The news of Dewey's victory was met with wild celebration in the United States. It was the first victory for the new Navy and another step toward the creation of an American empire. For some American expansionists, this was a great opportunity to acquire the strategic overseas possessions necessary for the country to acquire the status of a great power. Many of these expansionists, such as President Theodore Roosevelt, were fired by Admiral Alfred Thayer Mahan's writings, which called for American naval bases near the world's major shipping lanes.

WASHINGTON, *January 27, 1898.*

DEWEY, *Olympia, Yokohama, Japan:*

Retain until further orders the crew of the squadron whose terms of enlistment have expired.

CROWNINSHIELD.

WASHINGTON, *February 25, 1898.*

DEWEY, *Hongkong:*

Order the squadron, except the *Monocacy,* to Hongkong. Keep full of coal. In the event declaration of war Spain, your duty will be to see that the Spanish squadron does not leave the Asiatic coast, and then offensive operations in Philippine Islands. Keep *Olympia* until further orders.

ROOSEVELT.

WASHINGTON, *February 26, 1898.*

DEWEY, *Hongkong:*

Keep full of coal—the best that can be had.

LONG.

WASHINGTON, *March 21, 1898.*

DEWEY, *Hongkong:*

The *Baltimore* has been ordered to proceed to Hongkong, upon the arrival of the *Mohican* at Honolulu, with ammunition for the Asiatic Station.

LONG.

WASHINGTON, *April 1, 1898.*

DEWEY, *Hongkong*:

Fill up with provisions purchased on station; then how many days provisions have you on hand? How much soap and tobacco shall I ship?

LONG.

WASHINGTON, *April 4, 1898.*

DEWEY, *Hongkong*:

Can you purchase immediately supply steamer? What will be the cost of?

LONG.

HONGKONG, *April 4, 1898.*

SECRETARY OF THE NAVY, *Washington*:

I have chartered the British steamer *Nanshan*, having over 3,000 tons of coal now on board. Before the outbreak of hostilities can and would purchase this steamer. I request the earliest information in order to conclude arrangements. Can not be made after the outbreak of hostilities.

DEWEY.

WASHINGTON, *April 6, 1898.*

DEWEY, *Hongkong:*

Purchase immediately *Nanshan* and one more vessel for supplies. Charge special appropriation. Send the receipts to the Department. Enlist for special service, if possible, one year, unless sooner discharged, the crew of. Detach and order assume command of each an officer. Arm if possible. War may be declared. Condition very critical.

LONG.

WASHINGTON, *April 6, 1898.*

DEWEY, *Hongkong:*

The receipt of telegram of April 4 is acknowledged. I approve the action. Expedite delivery. April 6 maybe last opportunity.

LONG.

HONGKONG, *April 6, 1898.*

SECRETARY OF NAVY, *Washington, D.C.:*

I have purchased *Nanshan* and I have engaged her crew. Will detail an officer for command. I have ordered three officers, 50 men from *Monocacy* to fill vacancies here. I hope to get another steamer.* * * The receipt of telegram April 6 acknowledged, to expedite delivery.

DEWEY.

WASHINGTON, *April 7, 1898.*

DEWEY, *Hongkong:*

Land all woodwork, stores, etc., it is not considered necessary to have for operations.

LONG.

HONGKONG, *April 9, 1898.*

SECRETARY OF NAVY, *Washington, D.C.*

I have purchased the British steamer *Zafiro*, for supplies, for £18,000 sterling. I will arm, equip, and man vessel immediately.

DEWEY.

WASHINGTON, *April 21, 1898.*

DEWEY, *Hongkong:*

The naval force on the North Atlantic Station are blockading Cuba. War has not yet been declared. War may be declared at any moment. I will inform you. Await orders.

LONG.

WASHINGTON, *April 24, 1898.*

DEWEY, *Hongkong:*

War has commenced between the United States and Spain. Proceed at once to Philippine Islands. Commence operations at once, particularly against the Spanish fleet. You must capture vessels or destroy. Use utmost endeavors.

LONG.

HONGKONG, *April 25, 1898.*

SECRETARY OF NAVY, *Washington:*

The squadron will leave for Manila, Philippine Islands, immediately upon the arrival of the United States consul from Manila.

DEWEY.

HONGKONG, *April 25, 1898.*

SECRETARY OF NAVY, *Washington:*

In accordance with the request of the governor of Hongkong, the squadron leaves today for Mirs Bay, China, to await telegraphic instructions. Address, Hongkong. I will communicate by tug.

DEWEY.

WASHINGTON, *April 26, 1898.*

DEWEY, *Hongkong:*

Following proclamation of the President of the United States is forwarded for your information:

Whereas, by an act of Congress approved April 26, 1898, it is declared that war exists and that war has existed since the 21st day of April, A.D. 1898, including said day, between the United States of America and the Kingdom of Spain; and whereas, it being desirable that such war should be conducted upon principles in harmony with the present views of nations and sanctioned by their recent practice, it has already been announced that the policy of this Government will be not to resort to privateering, but to adhere to the rules of the declaration of Paris: Now, therefore, I, William McKinley, President of the United States of America, by virtue of the power vested in me by the Constitution and the laws, do hereby declare and proclaim: One, the neutral flag covers the enemy's goods, with the exception of contraband of war; two, neutral goods, contraband of war, are not liable to confiscation under the enemy's flag; three, blockades, in order to be binding, must be effective; four; Spanish merchant vessels in any ports or places within the United States shall be allowed till May 31st, 1898, inclusive for loading their cargoes and departing from such ports or places, and such Spanish merchant vessels, if met at sea by any United States ship, shall be permitted to continue their voyage, if, on examination of their papers, it shall appear that their cargoes were taken on board before the expiration of the above term, provided that nothing herein contained shall apply to Spanish vessels having on board any officer in the military or naval service of the enemy, or any coal, except such as may be necessary for their voyage, or any other article prohibited or contraband of war, or any despatch of or to the Spanish Government; five, any Spanish merchant vessel which, prior to April 21, 1898, shall have sailed from any foreign port, or place in the United States, shall be permitted to enter such port or place, and to discharge her cargo, and afterwards, forthwith, to depart without molestation, and any such vessel, if met at sea by any United States ship, shall be permitted to continue her voyage to any port not blockaded; six, the right of search is to be exercised with strict regard for the rights of neutrals, and the voyages of mail steamers are not to be interfered with except on the clearest grounds of suspicion of a violation of law, in respect to contraband or blockade.

In witness whereof I have hereunto set my hand and caused the seal of the United States to be affixed.

Done at the city of Washington on the 26th day of April, in the year of our Lord one thousand eight hundred and ninety-eight, and of the Independence of the United States the one hundred and twenty-second.

WILLIAM McKINLEY.

By the President:

JOHN SHERMAN, Secretary of State.

LONG.

HONGKONG, April 27, 1898.

SECRETARY OF THE NAVY, *Washington*:

Williams, the United States consul from Manila, has arrived. The squadron will sail immediately for the Philippine Islands.

DEWEY.

HONGKONG, May 7, 1898. (Manila, May 1.)

SECRETARY OF THE NAVY, *Washington*:

The squadron arrived at Manila at daybreak this morning. Immediately engaged enemy and destroyed the following Spanish vessels: *Reina Christina, Castilla, Don Antonio de Biloa, Don Juan de Austria, Isla de Luzon, Isla de Cuba, General Lezo, Marquis del Duaro, El Curreo, Velasco,* one transport, *Isla de Mandano,* water battery at Cavite. I shall destroy Cavite arsenal dispensatory. The squadron is uninjured. Few men were slightly wounded. I request the Department will send immediately from San Francisco fast steamer with ammunition. The only means of telegraphing is to the American consul at Hongkong.

DEWEY.

Questions for Discussion:

1. What do these telegrams reveal about the state of communication in 1898?

2. What do these communications tell us about naval warfare circa 1898?

3. What problems did Dewey anticipate, and how did he prepare for them?

George Dewey, *The War with Spain. Operations of the United States Navy on the Asiatic station* (Washington, D.C.: Government Printing Office, 1900), 5–8.

Theodore Roosevelt, "Why the Nation Needs an Effective Navy" (1908)

President Theodore Roosevelt (1858–1919) was an avid advocate for the Navy and one of the foremost imperialists of his day. The source of Roosevelt's views on the importance of the Navy on future American greatness can be directly attributed to the influence of Alfred Thayer Mahan's seminal *The Influence of Sea Power on History*, which forcefully asserted that great powers must have great fleets. Those seeking further reading on Teddy Roosevelt's naval policies may want to consult James R. Reckner's book, *Teddy Roosevelt's Great White Fleet*,[1] which looks at the motives and implications for Roosevelt to send a battleship fleet on a global cruise.

In this speech, an address at the Naval War College, Newport, Rhode Island, on July 22, 1908, Roosevelt preaches his forceful foreign policy to an audience sure to appreciate his calls for a large and powerful navy.

There are only a few things that I desire to say today to the conference, and what I have to say really is said less to the officers present than to the great bulk of my fellow countrymen outside. I could not speak to you technically. I can speak to my fellow countrymen who are deeply interested in the American navy, but who sometimes tend to be misled as to the kind of navy we should have and as to what the navy can and ought to do.

For instance, there are always a certain number of well-meaning, amiable individuals—coupled with others not quite so well-meaning—

---

1   James R. Reckner, *Teddy Roosevelt's Great White Fleet: The World Cruise of the American Battle Fleet, 1907–1909* (Annapolis, Md.: Naval Institute Press, 1988).

who like to talk of having a navy merely for defense, who advocate a coast-defense navy. Such advocacy illustrates a habit of mind as old as human nature itself—the desire at the same time to do something, and not to do it, than which there is no surer way of combining the disadvantages of leaving it undone and of trying to do it. A purely defensive navy, a mere coast-defense navy, would be almost worthless. To advocate a navy merely for coast defense stands in point of rational intelligence about on a par with advocating the creation of a school of prize-fighters in which nobody should do anything but parry. No fight was ever won yet except by hitting; and the one unforgivable offense in any man is to hit soft. Don't hit at all if it can possibly be avoided; but if you do hit, hit as hard as you know how. That applies to the individual and it applies to the nation; and those who advocate a merely defensive navy, a mere coast-defense navy, are advocating that we shall adopt as a national principle the principle of hitting soft. I hope with all my heart that never will this nation of ours hit unless it cannot possibly be helped. I believe that the nation should do everything honorable at all times to avoid any trouble; that it should scrupulously refrain from wronging or insulting any other nation; that it should put up with a good deal in the way of misconduct on the part of others before going to war. But when this nation does have to go to war, such war will only be excusable if the nation intends to hammer its opponent until that opponent quits fighting. You don't hammer an opponent if you keep your fleet along the coast waiting until the opponent takes the initiative and hammers you.

For the protection of our coasts we need fortifications; we need to have these fortifications not merely to protect the salient points of our possessions, but we need them so that the navy can be footloose. A year ago at the time that it was announced that the fleet was to go around the world there were a certain number of newspapers, especially in my own city of New York, that raised a clamorous protest against it. Exactly how close the connection was between this protest against the fleet going around the world and dissatisfaction with the economic policies of the Administration, it is not necessary at this moment to discuss; but the protest was made. It took at one time the form of a mistaken prophecy to the effect that the fleet would not be allowed to go around the world, and one of the reasons alleged was that to let it go around the world would leave New York defenseless in the event of war; the theory evidently being that the fleet, or a portion of it, would be used especially to protect New York and other cities in the event of war. If war comes at any time in the future, that Administration under which it comes will indeed be guilty of folly if they use the fleet to protect any port. Let the port be protected by the fortifications; the fleet must be foot-loose to search out and destroy the enemy's fleet. That is the function of the fleet; that is the only function that can justify the fleet's existence; and that function cannot exist in the case of such a ridiculous fleet as the fleet would be if it were only possible to use it for coast-defense purposes.

Again, as a question of national policy. When statesmen, when the people behind political leaders, embark on any given policy, they build up for themselves a time of humiliation and disaster in the future if they do not prepare to make that policy effective. There is something to be said (from my standpoint, gentlemen, not much, but still something) for the theory that this nation shall never have any interests outside its own borders and shall assume toward other nations an attitude of such meekness that no trouble can ever possibly come. As I say, something can be said for that policy. It would not appeal to me; but still it is a defensible policy. But a wholly indefensible policy would be consistently to work for the assumption of responsibilities without making any provision for meeting the demands necessarily entailed by those responsibilities. To be rich, aggressive, and unarmed, is to invite certain disaster and annihilation.

We have taken the Philippines; but if we had not taken them not a particle of difference would be made as regards the needs of our naval policies. There has been a division among this people as to the taking of the Philippines. There has been no division on the Monroe Doctrine; no division on building, maintaining, policing, and defending the Panama Canal; no division about Hawaii and Porto Rico; no division about keeping Alaska, which, though on the continent, is just as much separated as if it were an island; no division about asserting our superior right to defend and protect Cuba. Not one of the courses of action thus outlined can be followed out excepting with a first-class navy. The Monroe Doctrine was in danger of falling not merely into disuse, but into contempt, until we began to build up our navy. The Monroe Doctrine won't be observed by foreign nations with sufficient strength to disregard it when once it becomes their interest to disregard it, unless we have a navy sufficient to make our assertion of the doctrine good. The Monroe Doctrine, unbacked by a navy, is an empty boast; and there exist but few more contemptible characters, individual or national, than the man or the nation who boasts, and when the boast is challenged, fails to make good. If we have a coast-defense navy only we had better at once turn over the Panama Canal to some stronger and braver nation which would not limit itself merely to a coast-defense navy, and could protect and police it. If we should limit ourselves merely to a navy that would confine us to defensive war—war certain in the end to be unsuccessful—it would be well at once to give up Hawaii, to give up Porto Rico, to give up Alaska, and to say that we had no more interest in Cuba than the smallest outside power. If we intend to claim to be a great nation then we must fit ourselves so that we may be ready at need to make good that claim. That can only be done by building up and maintaining at the highest point of efficiency the United States navy.

There is a curious corollary to what I am just saying. If we are ready to make good the claims, the chances are infinitesimal that it will ever be necessary to do so. The real chance of war for this nation comes only if we combine a policy which disregards the interests or feelings of others, with a policy of helplessness to hold our own if our right to do as we wish is challenged. If, on the other hand, we are ready in very fact to hold our own, the chance becomes infinitesimal that we will be called upon to do so.

I have spoken of our needing an efficient navy because of our possessions that are separated from us by water; because of our advocacy of the Monroe Doctrine; because of our being engaged in building the Isthmian Canal. But constituted as this people is, if we did not have a foreign possession; if we abandoned the Monroe Doctrine; if we handed over to some other power the Panama Canal, it would still be necessary for us to have a navy, and a strong, fighting navy. We do not want any navy at all if it is not a first-class one; and such a navy will be necessary for us just so long as we demand the right to administer our internal affairs as we think best.

This country is yet in its youth. In the process of building up, many hundreds of thousands of immigrants are coming here from all parts of the world, representing many different nationalities, many different strata of cultivation, of civilization. In consequence there are points of friction between this country and other countries such as exist in no other nation than ours. It is a curious fact, and a lesson as to the folly of a portion of mankind, that many of the very people who advocate our following some given course of policy that will be most apt to bring us into trouble with other nations, stoutly protest against our also following the only policy that would make such a course of conduct as that they advocate anything but contemptible in the eyes of the world and disastrous to ourselves.

Ultimately, and I think at not a very distant period, as this country fills up, and as it becomes more and more important that we should keep on the highest possible level the plane of living of our working men—for the chief end of a national policy in this country should be to keep on the highest level the prosperity of the tiller of the soil and the wage-worker, for the prosperity of all other classes will follow their prosperity—therefore, gentlemen, as it becomes more and more important to keep that prosperity at a high level, it is very possible that we shall have to exercise a continually greater supervision, a continually greater exercise of the right of rejection among immigrants that come hither, and shall, as regards it may be many different peoples, take an attitude that will tend at first to provoke friction with them. Now it is our undoubted right to say what people, what persons, shall come to this country to live, to work, to become citizens. It is equally undoubtedly our duty that that right shall be exercised in a way that will be provocative of the least, and not of the most, friction with outsiders. The theory of certain of our fellow citizens that we can permanently follow a policy of peace with insult is erroneous. We must stand up for our rights firmly but temperately and courteously and with all possible respect, not merely for the rights but for the feelings of others; and finally, gentlemen, we must remember that we cannot permanently be certain that we will keep our rights as the world now is unless we have potential force back of them.

We have the right to choose who shall come here from abroad. It is our duty to exercise that right so that it will cause the minimum of offense to any other friendly power, so that it will cause the minimum of friction and will be accompanied with the greatest good-will and friendship and evidences of good-will and friendship on our part toward other powers. But it is absolutely necessary that if we claim for ourselves the right to choose who shall come here, we shall be in trim to uphold that right if any power challenges it; and it cannot be upheld by words, it cannot be upheld by a coast-defense navy, by a navy that will parry but that won't hit.

It can be upheld only by the possession of an efficient fighting navy, a navy able to preserve the honor and the interest of the United States, not by inviting attack on our shores and then seeing if we cannot repel it, but by taking such action as shall guarantee us against our shores being attacked.

Now, what I have said naturally has no special interest for you. I am a layman. Speaking to professional men, I could not tell them anything about their profession. But I can say to my fellow laymen and to all my countrymen, civilians, sailors, or soldiers, what are certain great lines of policy which we should follow. At the present day the Monroe Doctrine is unchallenged, and the people abroad who used to sneer at it now say it is a pretty good doctrine after all, a useful doctrine on the whole for the peace of the world. What has produced that change? Words? Not a bit of it. Diplomacy? Only in so far as diplomacy rested on the substantial basis of potential force. The voyage of the sixteen battleships around South America, through the Straits of Magellan, from Hampton Roads to Puget Sound—that was the most instructive object-lesson that had ever been afforded as to the reality of the Monroe Doctrine.

Now, gentlemen, the possibilities of misapprehension, of misconstruction, of what one says are infinite, especially when they are accompanied with something of design. I wish to reiterate, and to say with just as much earnestness as I have spoken today on other subjects, that I want a first-class fighting navy because it is the most effective guaranty of peace that this country can have. Uncle Sam can well afford to pay for his peace and safety so cheap an insurance policy as is implied in the maintenance of the United States navy. There is not a more paying investment that he makes. All of the leaders of our people are fond of assuring this people that it is a great people; they are fond of assuring it of that fact even when they are advocating policies that if carried out would assuredly make the fact merely a memory. We are a great people. That ought not to be a subject for boastfulness; it ought to be a subject for serious consideration because of the heavy responsibilities that go with it. We cannot help playing a great part in the world, but we can very easily help playing that part well; and to be a great people and make a great failure is as unattractive a spectacle as history affords. We are one of the great world-powers—in situation, in population, in wealth. We are such a power because of the spirit and purpose of our people. It is not open to us to decide whether or not the career that we lead shall be important; it has got to be important. All we can decide is as to whether our success shall be great or our failure great; we are sure to make either a great failure or a great success. I would not pretend for a moment, gentlemen, to you or to anyone else that merely military proficiency on land or sea would by itself make this or any other nation great. First and foremost come the duties within the gates of our own household; first and foremost our duty is to strive to bring about a better administration of justice, cleaner, juster, more equitable methods in our political, business, and social life, the reign of law, the reign of that orderly liberty which was the first consideration in the minds of the founders of this Republic. Our duties at home are of the first importance. But our duties abroad are of vital consequence also. This nation may fail, no matter how well it keeps itself prepared against the possibility of disaster from abroad; but it will certainly fail if we do not thus keep ourselves prepared. And I ask our people to take the keenest and most intelligent interest in the affairs of the navy and to watch closely those at Washington, in the Executive Department and in the Legislative Department as well, who are concerned with the affairs of the navy, because as a nation we need greatly in the interest of peace, in the interest of true national greatness, that the United States navy, with its ships, its officers, its enlisted men, shall at every point be kept in the highest possible condition of efficiency and well-being.

Questions for Discussion:
1. What does Roosevelt's speech reveal about American attitudes about international relations in the early 1900s?
2. How does Roosevelt frame his argument to make it more effective?
3. What arguments did Roosevelt provide for an effective U.S. Navy?

Theodore Roosevelt, "Why the Nation Needs an Effective Navy," in *Memorial Edition: Works of Theodore Roosevelt*, vol. 15, *American Problems*, ed. Hermann Hagedorn (New York: Charles Scribner's Sons, 1926), 250–57.

Lucia Ames Mead, "What Our Navy Costs Us" (1909)

Not all Americans bought into the idea of building an enormous battleship fleet. Intellectuals and reformers wrote powerful arguments against naval expansion. One such opponent of the battleship fleet was Lucia Ames Mead

(1856–1936), an outspoken anti-imperialist, pacifist, and feminist who devoted much of her life to social reform. She served as a vice president of the Anti-Imperialist League, an officer of the Women's Peace Party, and in 1926 represented the Women's International League for Peace and Freedom on the committee supporting a Washington, D.C., conference of the All-America Anti-Imperialist League. Ames was a firm believer in international cooperation and the power of arbitration over war. In this article, Mead considers the enormous cost of maintaining a large U.S. battleship fleet versus the benefits those same tax dollars could bring to American society.

Most men and most women have no more visual image before their minds when reading large figures than have the infants of the kindergarten. Millions and billions mean much the same to many very intelligent people. "As many persons every day die of tuberculosis in this country as were killed in the Italian earthquake,"[1] asserted an exceptionally charming and intelligent lady in a recent conversation. "Impossible," was the reply, "only one hundred and sixty thousand die of that annually." "Oh, well," she responded, "I suppose I ought to say 'every year' instead of 'every day.' I read so many statistics it confuses me." One hears people talk of "billions and billions" of people on the globe, with no comprehension that the total population is only one and a half billion. The cleverest persons in adding columns with lightning rapidity and in dealing accurately with figures are often the widest from the mark when they attempt to visualize and compare statements of concrete acres, pounds, dollars or people. Alfred Wallace, the English scientist, well suggested that every school should have one room whose walls should be marked off in tiny squares with a dot in every other one, the total dots numbering a million, which would give the little future taxpayers and voters some comprehension of the amount which today seems to be the norm of comparison in the business world as a "thousand" was to our forefathers.

In no matter is this more evident than in the stupidity with which nations, whose achievements in physical science are enormous, deal with other nations with whom they desire and must have business relations. The assumption that these customers and old friends may at any moment, out of mere wanton cupidity, pounce upon each other, might have had excuse in years past. Today it is puerile folly, so far

---

1   Italian Earthquake: southern Italy experienced a massive earthquake in 1908.

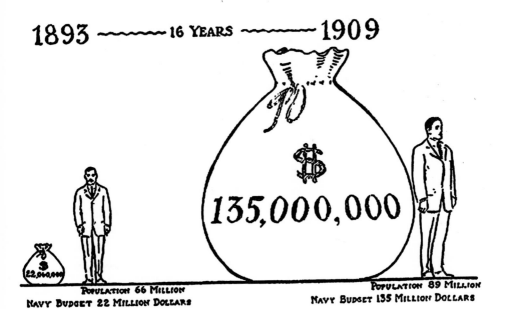

Growth of the Navy Budget, 1893–1909, *The World Today* 16 (April 1909).

FOR WHICH PURPOSE WILL UNCLE SAM BE MOST PLEASED TO SPEND HIS MONEY?
Bartholomew, in the Minneapolis *Journal*

The World Today 16 (April 1909).

as any danger to the United States is concerned, a country that since the adoption of the Constitution has never been attacked, that has begun every one of its three foreign wars,[1] that has not an enemy in the world and is capable, as many other nations are not, of feeding its own people.

A well-known clergyman has recently declared that the presentation of the economic argument will never deter from providing huge armaments. This is true, perhaps, so long as huge armaments are supposed to be necessary for security, and no substitutes for war are known to be available. Such a condition, it is easy to show, no longer exists. The United States will never fight England again so long as the frontier between Canada and the United States—the safest borderline in the world—remains unguarded, as it has been for over ninety years. It will have no occasion to fight Spain or Mexico again unless it provokes a war as wicked as the Mexican War was declared to be by General Grant. It can as easily keep the peace with all other nations in the future as it has done in the past. When it grants the independence to the Philippines that is promised by President-elect Taft, it can secure their neutralization by mutual agreement of the nations and free us with honor from the one weak spot within our possessions. Pending the granting of independence, no nation will pay the hundreds of millions of dollars necessary to wrest this white elephant from us. Least of all, will Japan do it, with reference to which President Roosevelt has said: "The national government has been able to achieve a completely satisfactory solution of all possible difficulties that could be at issue between our people and the Japanese." No difficulty can arise with any nation which now can not be arbitrated if we choose.

Today a huge navy offers a temptation to settle questions in a more spectacular way than quiet arbitration, especially if jingo journalism decides that a little blood-letting would be interesting and promote certain vested interests. War is far more likely with a huge navy than without it. Naval expenditures have swelled so preposterously in the last ten years, not from increased need but from increased desire for prestige, and from a timidity and scare carefully worked up by the navy cranks, who go up and down the land sowing suspicion and en-

---

1   Three foreign wars: the War of 1812, Mexican War, and Spanish-American War.

mity to men of other lands, in order to get large naval appropriations passed.

Consider: We are patting ourselves on the back for our generosity to Italy in her dire distress. Yet, all the United States Government has given—$800,000—is $70,000 less than the annual cost of running one great battleship in time of peace.

It should be emphasized that the supposed preventative of war, a huge navy, is fast becoming as terrible as war itself. In 1908 we spent as much for armaments in time of peace as we spent in war ten years before. The war in Cuba and the Philippines, in which only about four thousand Americans were killed, cost a sum of money which, rightly spent, might have saved one hundred million unnecessary deaths by typhoid and tuberculosis, allowing $600 for each patient. The armament extravagance is a question of life as well as money. For money means health to the sick, education to the ignorant, decent conditions of living for the crowded slum which breeds crime; it means life instead of death.

The House of Representatives has just voted $135,000,000 for this year's support and enlargement of the navy in a time of profound peace. This is $100,000,000 more than we spent a few years ago, and yet we had then a greater sense of security than we have today. We sleepily read these figures and lazily guess that the government probably knows what it is about; at all events we feel that we must keep up with the procession and follow the fashion of the world even if it does cost a good bit. Meanwhile we are getting alarmed about our forests and we lament that Congress will not give one cent from the treasury to save our mountains from erosion, our valleys from desolation and our mill-wheels from alternate drought and flood.

Let us see what could be done by saving the cost of one of the two huge battleships of twenty-six thousand tons just ordered. The lamentable fact is not so much their cost as their size, which sets a new standard for the world and means throwing out of service the ship of ordinary size, and forcing all nations to drain their resources to the uttermost to match our ships. Yet it was President Roosevelt who suggested at the National Peace Congress in New York in 1907 that the first step toward limitation of armaments might well be the limitation of the size of battleships. Now we are forcing the world into incalcu-

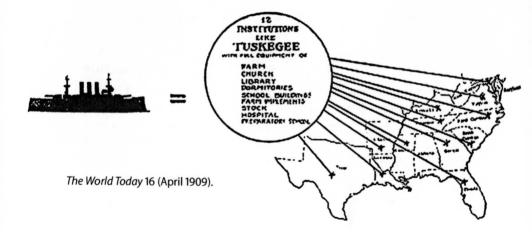

The World Today 16 (April 1909).

lable increase of expense without one particle of increased security after the first year or two of our start.

These new battleships will cost $10,250,000 each. The cost of one battleship expended for constructive, useful work could do any one of the following things:

1. It would put a Tuskegee, with its full equipment of farm, church, library, dormitories, school buildings, farm implements and stock, in addition to a hospital and preparatory school, into Maryland, Virginia, North Carolina, South Carolina, Georgia, Florida, Mississippi, Louisiana, Texas, Arkansas, Kentucky and Tennessee, and thus provide twelve permanent great factories of good citizenship; and each of these would be destined to create several smaller ones and indefinitely to fight the enemies of ignorance, shiftlessness and crime, far more deadly than any supposititious enemies beyond sea.

2. It would supply two permanent trade schools or churches or Young Men's Christian Association buildings at $100,000 each to

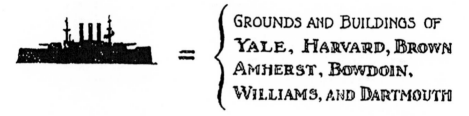

The World Today 16 (April 1909).

every state and territory, the District of Columbia, Alaska, the Philippines and Puerto Rico; these would create others and send forth citizens equipped to add enormously to the wealth and honor of the country.

3. One short-lived battleship equals the cost of five hundred and twelve locomotives at $20,000 apiece.

4. It equals the cost of all the grounds and buildings of Harvard and Yale and Brown universities and of Amherst, Bowdoin, Williams and Dartmouth colleges, the accumulations in some instances of two hundred and fifty years of educational enterprise. Let would-be benevolent women, pottering over their little palliatives on the evils of the body politic, which leave their children and grandchildren the same evils to remedy with the same bazaars and church fairs and entertainments that gain perhaps a thousand dollars after three months' work—let them consider, I say, that the repairs on even one little torpedo boat average $17,000 every year and that the cost of one big cannon shot at target practice costs more than did the whole education of Daniel Webster. Let them pause and consider whether they can not afford a little time and effort to remove this awful folly and cut away the root of poverty, so as to save the world the necessity for half its present charities.

5. It could change the future of this world and end war if rightly expended in influencing the press, and in carrying on a campaign of education on international justice and world organization in colleges, universities, theological and normal schools of the five leading nations. The future leaders who control affairs would know the political and economic facts of which this generation knows scarcely anything. It would not be fooled by exploded fallacies. It would have a new psychological attitude. The whole question is, after all, simply what men think is the best way to get what they want from each other; it is a psy-

The World Today 16 (April 1909).

chological question. Money thus spent would provide international lectureships; interchange of visits of leading men in the different nations; voting regular peace budgets to be spent in promoting international fraternity and in swift publication of facts to silence suspicion should friction arise; it would promote a sounder political economy and lower tariff walls of separation.

Two things are to be noted about armaments: first, their period of utility is yearly shortened. Formerly a battleship could be of use twelve or fifteen years, but, as the *Army and Navy Journal* has pointed out, all this has been changed by England's introducing the new standard of the *Dreadnought*,[1] and now the limit of time is cut down to about six years. Second, fewer men are employed in building a great steel destroyer than would be employed if the money were spent for constructive purposes. It is evident that one hundred and two trade schools at $100,000 each would employ vastly more men to build and to conduct for fifty years than would be employed in building and running a battleship.

The silly talk about armaments "giving employment," which every callow youth instantly advances when protest is made against them, is perhaps the silliest of all the talk in which unimaginative and credulous persons indulge. This talk is rarely heard among trade-unionists. They know better. Women fascinated with brass buttons, men who hobnob with the Navy League or with those who have powder to sell, these it is who tell us that, though we are to have a $125,000,000 deficit this year, if we only spend $135,000,000 on the navy, it will "give employment" and be a good thing.

Said Jean de Bloch, the eminent author of the "Future of War," to the writer, the year he died: "When you talk to people about the evils of all this, don't waste your time telling them how wicked they are; tell them what fools they are."

Questions for Discussion:
1. What is the author's strongest argument against battleships?
2. How does the author treat the alleged economic benefits of battleship construction?

---

1   *Dreadnought*: HMS *Dreadnought*, a revolutionary British battleship that sparked a major naval arms race after its launch in 1906.

3. What does the author anticipate in terms of battleship construction and future wars?

Lucia Ames Mead, "What Our Navy Costs Us," *The World Today* 16 (April 1909): 389–93.

PROGRESSIVES AT SEA

Around the beginning of the twentieth century, reformers questioned the manner in which the nation operated. The nation was clearly wealthier than it had ever been, but there were numerous problems, too. The divide between rich and poor had grown enormously, and industrial workers clamored for an equitable share of the nation's prosperity. When their demands went unmet, some turned to radical politics that promised to redistribute wealth among the working class. Corporations and millionaires seemed to possess a disproportionate amount of wealth and power in a democracy. City governments were often corrupt, and urban centers were crowded, filthy, and disease-ridden. Natural resources that should have been held in trust for the masses were instead extracted in the most wasteful manner possible. Muckraking journalists called attention to the exploitation of child labor, corruption in city governments, the horror of lynching, and ruthless business practices.

The movement to address the nation's economic, political, social, and moral problems is known as Progressivism. This movement had a wide range of implications for American society, including four constitutional amendments that authorized an income tax, provided for the direct election of senators, extended the vote to women, and prohibited the manufacture and sale of alcoholic beverages. In maritime terms, the Progressives attempted to improve working conditions on American vessels and the waterfront, developed a newfound interest in conservation and the environment, and attempted to break up or regulate large corporate trusts.

In these three pieces, three aspects of Progressivism as it impacted maritime matters are revealed. The leaders of Chicago investigated what really happens on Great Lakes steamboats, a woman experiences the horrors of an immigrant passage across the Atlantic firsthand, and the photos of Lewis Hine expose the cruelty of child labor. The one aspect all three share is that they involve a direct investigation by people who disguised themselves to appear as something they were not.

Chicago Vice Commission, "Lake Steamers" (1910)

In March 1910, Chicago Mayor Fred Busse posed a difficult question to the Chicago Vice Commission: should prostitution remain a regulated business in Chicago's segregated vice districts, or should it be outlawed, scattering prostitution throughout the city? Typical of Progressive-era reformers, the commission thoroughly investigated the question and found that there was a strong connection between low wages and prostitution. While the average woman earned six dollars a week, about 40 percent less than the commission deemed necessary for independent living, the average prostitute earned roughly twenty-five dollars per week. The commission's 1911 report, *The Social Evil in Chicago*, although temporarily banned from the U.S. postal system as obscene material, was hugely influential in similar investigations around the world.

The below excerpt is a damning exposé of behavior on the Great Lakes excursion steamers. While the gleaming white exteriors and holiday air made these vessels appear the very embodiment of clean-cut fun, the Chicago Vice Commission finds them to be the sites of underage drinking, gambling, and prostitution. The report disguises vessel names to protect their owners, but an experienced maritime historian could probably discover the ships' names with the information provided below.

There are two classes of boats on the lake, those which carry the holiday crowds and those which cater to the regular vacation traffic.

The excursion boats, as a rule, carry an element which is more or less disorderly. The other boats are less frequented by this element.

There are several classes of these disorderly groups on the holiday boats; first, girls who are evidently professional or semi-professional prostitutes, together with young men whom they find it easy to attract; second, the class of vile young men who make these excursion trips for the purpose of seeking out girl recruits; and third, a group which is very important, especially when the preventive end of the work is considered as conducted by the Juvenile Protective Association.

The following is a typical story which illustrates this last group: A young couple who are sweethearts starts on one of these excursions. The trip is longer than is expected, or the girl is taken sick. A stateroom is secured and this one act may change the whole aspect of the future relationship of these two and may entirely spoil what might have developed into a happy married life.

Of the excursion steamers the (X1044) was the worst and the (X1045) the least offensive. The (X1044), in addition to being a very large boat—capacity approximately 5,000 people—makes a rather long trip. This boat also has a large number of easily acquired staterooms.

Practically all of the boats were equipped with bars and the quantity of liquor sold depended entirely on the character of the crowd aboard. The bar in the (X1047) was extremely popular and liquor was openly sold to both young men and young women who were evidently minors.

Gambling machines were openly used on nearly all of the boats in the early part of the season, but were taken off for some reason in August. A lottery game for selling candy was another means of gambling, but was not nearly so popular with the boys and young men as the nickel gambling wheel.

TYPICAL INSTANCES.

The following are typical instances of conditions found on these boats:

Investigator left South Haven on August 21st at 5:30 P. M. for Chicago on the (X1044). Almost every stateroom on the boat was in use. The decks were crowded, and many of the young men were getting acquainted with the girls. Observation of the staterooms was as follows:

In No. 66 were four men. Two girls visited the room during the trip. In No. 61 there was one girl. She was visited by four men at different times. No. 69 was occupied by two girls and two young men. In No. 21 three men and three girls were in the lower berth.

In the bar room about twenty young girls were drinking beer, five of them not over twelve years of age. One child, eight years old, was drinking beer with older people.

September 3rd 1910, investigator left Chicago on the steamship (X1049) for South Haven, Michigan. In the bar room there were about twenty young girls and boys sitting at tables drinking beer.

In stateroom No. 28, two boys and two girls were lying in the berths and all under the influence of liquor. In room No. 56 were found two men and two girls; one of the girls appeared to be very drunk. Three boys visited stateroom No. 51 during the trip. A young woman was in this room. In stateroom No. 64 a man about sixty-five years old was sitting at the door reading. Later he was seen in the crowd talking very earnestly to a young woman. After a while they went into stateroom No. 64 and locked the door, and did not appear again until the boat arrived in South Haven.

On September 5th, 1910, this boat had a very large crowd on its return trip to Chicago. On the upper deck a man was in earnest conversation with a girl. The girl was very good looking and well dressed. The man had been talking some time when he was heard to say, "I will get a stateroom." She said, "All right, I will see." He went downstairs and when he returned she went with him to stateroom No. 19.

Saturday, July 2nd, 1910, investigator left Chicago for South Haven at 2:00 P. M. on the steamer (X1050). The passengers consisted principally of boys and girls between the ages of twelve to twenty-one. The boat was loaded to its full capacity. One girl and three different men entered stateroom No. 53. Shortly after the boat left Chicago groups of men began to crowd the deck, and one group of six young men, all under age, stood in a circle drinking whiskey. Another party of eight had suit cases filled with beer. They drank the beer and threw the empty bottles overboard saturating the men and women in their vicinity with the froth from the bottles. Sitting on the upper deck were three women talking. Soon a young man came up and said, "The bunch are all down in the stateroom stewed and Arvella is the only girl in the crowd." The number of this stateroom was 71.

The bar room was filled with boys and girls. Two girls in particular could not have been over sixteen years old; were singing in drunken discord, lying in the arms of two men. Sitting at the next table was a young woman with her skirts up to her knees talking to the young men who were sitting next to her. She pounded the table with beer bottles to emphasize her remarks, and to attract the attention of other men in the bar room. In fact the whole boat seemed filled with intoxicated boys and girls.

Some of the staterooms were occupied by boys and others by girls. In stateroom No. 50 there were two boys in bathing suits, and two girls in kimonos, lying in each others arms; anyone passing could have seen them as the door was open most of the time. Room No. 64 was occupied by two boys and two girls; all appeared under the age of twenty. They were lying in each others arms, and at least three dozen empty beer bottles were on the floor and wash stand.

Two girls and two boys were standing in front of stateroom 20. One of the girls refused to enter saying, "I ain't no saint, but I can't do anything like that." Later her companions succeeded in persuading her to enter the room and they did not come out during the entire trip.

For a while investigator stood in front of stateroom No. 71 and watched, a young girl who was in the room with four young boys. One of the boys was very much intoxicated and every time his companions tried to make him stand on his feet he would throw himself back in the berth. This young boy could not have been over eighteen years old.

Returning from South Haven July 3rd at 6:00 P.M. the conditions were very bad. Just before the boat left the dock four couples came up the companion way, all under the influence of liquor.

Stateroom No. 74 was occupied by two girls and two young men: one of the girls was standing in front of the dressing table with nothing on except a dress skirt while the other called to a boy who happened to pass.

Questions for Discussion:
1. What does this report reveal about the ideals and reality of American morality in 1910?
2. What connections between alcohol consumption and prostitution does this report make?
3. What strengths or weaknesses does this document have in assessing events on these steamboats?

Chicago Vice Commission, *The Social Evil in Chicago: A Study of Existing Conditions with Recommendations by the Vice Commission of Chicago* (Chicago: Gunthorp-Warren, 1911), 215–17.

Anna Herkner, "Steerage Women" (1911)

Immigration was a harsh ordeal under any circumstances, but for young women traveling without their families it could be an especially grim experience. Anna Herkner (1878–1959) was a pioneer social worker and labor reformer. Disguised as a Bohemian immigrant, she crossed the Atlantic repeatedly on various foreign-flagged ships to report on the conditions immigrants suffered in *steerage*, the name given to the cheapest and least desirable passenger spaces on a ship. Herkner found that while the new type of ships had decent conditions for immigrants, a number of old ships still operated with truly deplorable conditions. These included inadequate toilet facilities, bad food, and dirty, unhygienic, and crowded conditions in general. Perhaps most deplorable on the old style of ships was the treatment of immigrant women by the crew and male passengers. A Senate committee investigating steerage conditions reproduced Herkner's report, of which a small portion follows.

From the time we boarded the steamer until we landed, no woman in the steerage had a moment's privacy. One steward was always on duty in our compartment, and others of the crew came and went continually. Nor was this room a passageway to another part of the vessel. The entrance was also the only exit. The men who came may or may not have been sent there on some errand. This I could not ascertain, but I do know that, regularly, during the hour or so preceding the breakfast bell and while we were rising and dressing, several men usually passed through and returned for no ostensible reason. If it were necessary for them to pass so often, another passageway should have been provided or a more opportune time chosen.

As not nearly all the berths[1] were occupied, we all chose upper ones. To get anything from an upper berth, to deposit anything in it or to arrange it, it was necessary to stand on the framework of the one below. The women often had to stand thus, with their backs to the aisle. The crew in passing a woman in this position never failed to deal her a blow—even the head steward. If a woman were dressing, they always stopped to watch her, and frequently hit and handled her. Even though they were sent there, this was not their errand.

Two of the stewards were quite strict about driving men out of our quarters. One other steward who had business in our compartment was as annoying a visitor as we had and he began his offenses even before we left port. Some of the women wished to put aside their better dresses immediately after coming on board. As soon as they began to undress he stood about watching and touching them. They tried to walk away, but he followed them. Not one day passed but I saw him annoying some women, especially in the washrooms. At our second and last inspection this steward was assigned the duty of holding each

---

1   Berths: bunks.

woman by her bare arm that the doctor might better see the vaccination.

A small notice stating the distance traveled was posted each day just within the entrance to our compartment. It was the only one posted in the steerage as far as I could learn, and consequently both crew and men passengers came to see it and it served as an excuse for coming at all times. The first day out the bar just within our entrance was used. This brought a large number of men into our compartment, many not entirely sober, but later the bar was transferred.

One night, when I had retired very early with a severe cold, the chief steerage steward entered our compartment, but not noticing me approached a Polish girl who was apparently the only occupant. She spoke in Polish, saying, "My head aches—please go on and let me alone." But he merely stood on and soon was taking unwarranted liberties with her. The girl, weakened by seasickness, defended herself as best she could, but soon was struggling to get out of the man's arms. Just then other passengers entered and he released her. Such was the man who was our highest protector and court of appeal.

I can not say that any woman lost her virtue on this passage, but in making free with the women the men of the crew went as far as possible without exposing themselves to the danger of punishment. But this limit is no doubt frequently overstepped. Several of the crew told me that many of them marry girls from the steerage. When I insinuated that they could scarcely become well enough acquainted to marry during the passage, the answer was that the acquaintance had already gone so far that marriage was imperative.[1]

There was an outside main deck and an upper deck on which the steerage were allowed. These were each about 40 feet wide by 50 feet long, but probably half of this space was occupied by machinery, ventilators, and other apparatus. There was no canvas to keep out the rain, sun, and continual showers of cinders from the smokestack. These fell so thick and fast that two young sailor boys were kept busy sweeping them off the decks. It is impossible to remain in one's berth all the time, and as there were no smoking and sitting rooms we spent most of the day on these decks. No benches nor chairs were provided, so we sat wherever we could find a place on the machinery, exposed to

---

1   ... marriage was imperative: i.e., the woman was pregnant.

the sun, fog, rain, and cinders. These not only filled our hair, but also flew into our eyes, often causing considerable pain.

These same two outdoor decks were used also by the crew during their leisure. When asked what right they had there, they answered: "As much as the passengers." No notices hung anywhere about to refute this. The manner in which the sailors, stewards, firemen, and others mingled with the women passengers was thoroughly revolting. Their language and the topics of their conversation were vile. Their comments about the women, and made in their presence, were coarse. What was far worse and of continual occurrence was their handling the women and girls. Some of the crew were always on deck, and took all manner of liberties with the women, in broad daylight as well as after dark.

Not one young woman in the steerage escaped attack. The writer herself was no exception. A hard, unexpected blow in the offender's face in the presence of a large crowd of men, an evident acquaintance with the stewardess, doctor, and other officers, general experience, and manner were all required to ward off further attacks. Some few of the women, perhaps, did not find these attentions so disagreeable; some resisted them for a time, then weakened; some fought with all their physical strength, which naturally was powerless against a man's. Others were continually fleeing to escape. Two more refined and very determined Polish girls fought the men with pins and teeth, but even they weakened under this continued warfare and needed some moral support about the ninth day. The atmosphere was one of general lawlessness and total disrespect for women. It naturally demoralized the women themselves after a time. There was no one to whom they might appeal. Besides, most of them did not know the official language on the steamer, nor were they experienced enough to know they were entitled to protection.

The interpreter, who could and should be a friend of the immigrants, passed through the steerage but twice a day. He positively discouraged every approach. I purposely tried on several occasions to get advice and information from him, but always failed. His usual answer was, "How in the d—— do I know?" The chief steerage steward by his own familiarity with the women made himself impossible as their protector. Once when a man passenger was annoying two Lithuanian girls I undertook to rescue them. The man poured forth a volley of oaths at, me in English. Just then the chief steward appeared, and to test him I made complaint. The offender denied having sworn at all, but I insisted that he had, and that I understood. The steward then administered this reproof, "You let them girls alone or I fix you ————— easy."

The main deck was hosed every night at 10, when we were driven in. The upper deck was washed only about four times during the voyage. At 8 each evening we were driven below. This was to protect the women, one of the crew informed me. What protection they gained on the equally dark and unsupervised deck below isn't at all clear. What worse things could have befallen them there than those to which they were already exposed at the hands of both the crew and the men passengers would have been criminal offenses. Neither of these decks was lighted, because, as one sailor explained, maritime usage does not sanction lights either in the bow or stern of a vessel, the two parts always used by the steerage. The descriptions that I might give of the mingling of the crew and passengers on these outdoor decks would be endless, and all necessarily much the same. A series of snapshots would give a more accurate and impressive account of this evil than can words. I would here suggest that any agent making a similar investigation be supplied with a kodak[1] for this purpose.

To sum up, let me make some general statements that will give an idea of the awfulness of steerage condition, on the steamer in question. During these twelve days in the steerage I lived in a disorder and in surroundings that offended every sense. Only the fresh breeze from the sea overcame the sickening odors. The vile language of the men, the screams of the women defending themselves, the crying of children, wretched because of their surroundings, and practically every sound that reached the ear, irritated beyond endurance. There was no sight before which the eye did not prefer to close. Everything was dirty, sticky, and disagreeable to the touch. Every impression was offensive. Worse than this was the general air of immorality. For fifteen hours each day I witnessed all around me this improper, indecent, and forced mingling of men and women who were total strangers and often did not understand one word of the same language. People cannot live in such surroundings and not be influenced.

All that has been said of the mingling of the crew with the women of the steerage is also true of the association of the men steerage pas-

---

1   Kodak: a portable camera recently invented by George Eastman.

sengers with the women. Several times, when the sight of what was occurring about me was no longer endurable, I interfered and asked the men if they knew they might be deported were their actions reported on landing. Most of them had been in America before, and the answer generally given me was: "Immorality is permitted in America if it is anywhere. Everyone can do as he chooses; no one investigates his mode of life, and no account is made or kept of his doings."

Questions for Discussion:

1. What information does this document reveal about the immigrants who came to America before the First World War?

2. What clues does this document give about the power dynamics on board immigrant ships?

3. How does the author's viewpoint shape this report?

United States Senate, *Reports of the Immigration Commission: Steerage Conditions* (Washington, D.C.: Government Printing Office, 1911), 21–23.

Lewis Hine, "Canning Factories" (1909–1911)

Lewis Wickes Hine (1874–1940) was one of the foremost Progressive journalists. His métier was photojournalism, and the cause he is best known for was fighting child labor. Hine made no attempt to exaggerate the poverty of child laborers, believing that people were more likely to join the campaign against child labor if his photographs accurately captured the reality of the situation. His work was effective, Owen Lovejoy, Chairman of the National Child Labour Committee noted: "the work Hine did for this reform was more responsible than all other efforts in bringing the need to public attention." But factory owners often refused him permission to take photographs and accused him of muckraking.

Hine found fish factories a rich ground to work in, from New England to the Gulf Coast. Improved canning methods after the Civil War resulted in a huge boom in canned fish products, especially oysters, shrimp, and sardines. Shucking oysters, shelling shrimp, and cutting sardines was grueling labor, demanding long and or irregular hours in unpleasant conditions that resulted in cut, raw, and bleeding fingers. Almost always it was unskilled piecework that demanded speed and paid little. Nonetheless, marginalized groups often sought this labor, in part because it allowed families to work together.

"Oyster shuckers at Apalachicola, Florida, 1909. This work is carried on by many young boys during busy seasons. This is a dull year so only a few youngsters were in evidence." Photo by Lewis Hine, courtesy of the Library of Congress # LC-DIG-nclc-00745.

"The smallest shrimp-picker standing on the box is Manuel, about five years old, who worked here last year also. Cannot understand a word of English. Location: Biloxi, Mississippi," 1911. Photo by Lewis Hine, courtesy of the Library of Congress # LC-DIG-nclc-00823.

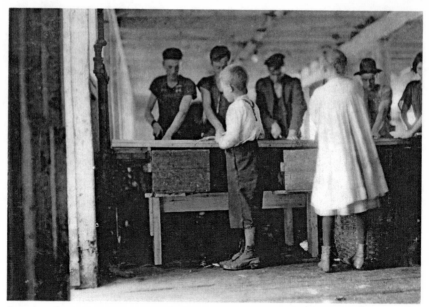

"Interior of a cutting shed in Maine. Young cutters at work, Clarence, 8 years, and Minnie, 9 years. Photo does not show the salt water in which they often stand, nor the refuse they handle. On the low shelf are two of the 'boxes' used as measures, and for which they get 5 cents a box. Location: Eastport, Maine," 1911. Photo by Lewis Hine, courtesy of the Library of Congress # LC-DIG-nclc-00944.

Questions for Discussion:

1. What similarities exist between the oyster shuckers, immigrant shrimp peelers, and child sardine cutters pictured above?

2. What do these photos reveal about the relationship between adults and children in the early 1900s?

3. What did Hine include or exclude to maximize the impact of these photos?

2

WAR, DEPRESSION, WAR AGAIN

The first half of the twentieth century saw American maritime activity fluctuate wildly. The needs of empire after the Spanish-American War, including the construction of the Panama Canal, meant that the federal government and business leaders alike took a renewed interest in maritime matters. The First World War initially brought a burst of commercial interest in shipping as American businessmen sought to profit from neutrality. After the United States joined the war in 1917, the government entered the shipping business to transport soldiers to France. But the 1920s and 1930s saw another dramatic decline in American shipping as business and labor conditions worsened. The approach of World War II brought about a revival of shipping once again, and by 1945 the United States had the world's most powerful navy and merchant marine.

Serious questions attended these maritime developments. Up until the end of 1941, many Americans were unhappy with the creation of a large peacetime navy that seemed linked with imperialism and what some saw as warmongering. So, too, the idea of a government-supported merchant fleet did not sit well with Americans who questioned the economic and strategic benefits of a strong merchant marine. Labor relations were extremely contentious in this period, as shipowners and labor unions engaged in a mutually destructive battle for control of shipping. Most of these questions were put aside when the United States entered the Second World War, only to be picked up again after 1945.

The beginnings of the transformation of American society during the 1920s and 1930s was reflected by the changes in how Americans related to the sea. The city-weary middle class sought the nation's beaches to flee the heat and rediscover nature. Labor unions fought to give seafarers the same rights as those ashore. African Americans looked to a new black-owned and -operated steamship line to assert an identity that was separate from white America.

The approach of war saw the United States once again ill-prepared. Japanese and German aggression was resented, but many, if not most Americans wanted to stay out of the war. President Franklin D. Roosevelt slowly pushed the nation toward preparing for war. He informed Americans that the Atlantic and Pacific oceans no longer protected Americans from tyranny abroad in radio-broadcasted "fireside chats." Even so, the Japanese attack on Pearl Harbor on December 7, 1941, came as a shock to the public and military alike. One startling change was that the demands of a two-ocean war transformed a generation of young women from housewives to factory workers. All in all, the early twentieth century was a deeply troubling time for seafarers and maritime communities, a period from which they would emerge radically changed.

THE GREAT WAR

During the first three years of World War I, the United States attempted to remain neutral and to benefit from supplying materials to both sides. In his monograph, *Wilsonian Maritime Diplomacy*,[1] Jeffrey J. Safford argues that this neutrality did not mean that the United States remained complacent. In fact, maritime matters were a prominent component of President Woodrow Wilson's plan to enhance the power of the United States, by expanding the Navy and the merchant marine.

Wartime conditions proved conducive to the growth of American shipping lines as the war pushed freight rates to extraordinary heights; it was said that the cost of a ship could be paid for in a single voyage to Europe. But this opportunistic approach angered both sides. The British Navy frequently boarded and impounded American-flagged merchant ships on suspicion of supplying the German war effort, and the German Navy repeatedly sank American ships using their terrifying new weapon, the submarine. The American government protested in strong terms when the belligerent powers seized or sank neutral American ships, and the American public became increasingly angry with the German attacks, which often killed civilians. A German submarine attacked and sank the British passenger liner RMS *Lusitania* in 1915, killing 1,198 passengers, including 128 Americans. American opportunism, British blockade, and German unrestricted submarine warfare thus combined to inexorably draw the United States into a war in which most citizens wanted no part.

---

1   Jeffrey J. Safford, *Wilsonian Maritime Diplomacy, 1913–1921* (New Brunswick, N.J.: Rutgers University Press, 1978).

William Jennings Bryan, "Neutral Shipping Rights" (1914)

The British Royal Navy, by far the most powerful fleet afloat in 1914, moved quickly to choke off German supplies at the outset of World War I. The process by which it did so was known as a blockade, using naval ships to intercept all ships entering or leaving enemy ports. But intricate international laws regulated how a blockade was to be conducted, and the British frequently violated those laws in seizing neutral American cargoes. In particular, Britain violated international law when it expanded its definition of contraband to include any sort of foodstuffs. The British blockade and its high-handed implementation increasingly angered American businessmen and farmers as British warships seized American-owned cargoes destined for Europe, detaining the ships themselves for weeks or months.

In this item, the American government protests the British seizure of American cargoes through the U.S. ambassador in London. The American secretary of state protesting the British actions was William Jennings Bryan (1860–1925), three-time Democratic candidate for president and a well-known Progressive and peace advocate. As described in Michael Kazin's *A Godly Hero*,[1] Bryan grew uncomfortable with Wilson's increasingly bellicose attitude toward Germany. He resigned his position in 1915 in protest over President Wilson's handling of the *Lusitania* sinking.

THE SECRETARY OF STATE TO THE AMERICAN AMBASSADOR AT LONDON.
(TELEGRAM.)

DEPARTMENT OF STATE,
Washington, December 26, 1914.

The present condition of American foreign trade resulting from the frequent seizures and detentions of American cargoes destined to neutral European ports has become so serious as to require a candid statement of the views of this Government in order that the British Government may be fully informed as to the attitude of the United States toward the policy which has been pursued by the British authorities during the present war.

You will, therefore, communicate the following to His Majesty's Principal Secretary of State for Foreign Affairs, but in doing so you

---

1   Michael Kazin, *A Godly Hero: The Life of William Jennings Bryan* (New York: Knopf, 2006).

will assure him that it is done in the most friendly spirit and in the belief that frankness will better serve the continuance of cordial relations between the two countries than silence, which may be misconstrued into acquiescence in a course of conduct which this Government can not but consider to be an infringement upon the rights of American citizens.

The Government of the United States has viewed with growing concern the large number of vessels laden with American goods destined to neutral ports in Europe, which have been seized on the high seas, taken into British ports and detained sometimes for weeks by the British authorities. During the early days of the war this Government assumed that the policy adopted by the British Government was due to the unexpected outbreak of hostilities and the necessity of immediate action to prevent contraband from reaching the enemy. For this reason it was not disposed to judge this policy harshly or protest it vigorously, although it was manifestly very injurious to American trade with the neutral countries of Europe. This Government, relying confidently upon the high regard which Great Britain has so often exhibited in the past for the rights of other nations, confidently awaited amendment of a course of action which denied to neutral commerce the freedom to which it was entitled by the law of nations.

This expectation seemed to be rendered the more assured by the statement of the Foreign Office early in November that the British Government were satisfied with guarantees offered by the Norwegian, Swedish and Danish Governments as to nonexportation of contraband goods when consigned to named persons in the territories of those Governments, and that orders had been given to the British fleet and customs authorities to restrict interference with neutral vessels carrying such cargoes so consigned to verification of ship's papers and cargoes.

It is, therefore, a matter of deep regret that, though nearly five months have passed since the war began, the British Government have not materially changed their policy and do not treat less rigorously ships and cargoes passing between neutral ports in the peaceful pursuit of lawful commerce, which belligerents should protect rather than interrupt. The greater freedom from detention and seizure which was confidently expected to result from consigning shipments to definite consignees, rather than "to order," is still awaited.

It is needless to point out to His Majesty's Government, usually the champion of the freedom of the seas and the rights of trade, that peace, not war, is the normal relation between nations and that the commerce between countries which are not belligerents should not be interfered with by those at war unless such interference is manifestly an imperative necessity to protect their national safety and then only to the extent that it is a necessity. It is with no lack of appreciation of the momentous nature of the present struggle, in which Great Britain is engaged, and with no selfish desire to gain undue commercial advantage that this Government is reluctantly forced to the conclusion that the present policy of His Majesty's Government toward neutral ships and cargoes exceeds the manifest necessity of a belligerent and constitutes restrictions upon the rights of American citizens on the high seas which are not justified by the rules of international law or required under the principle of self preservation.

The Government of the United States does not intend at this time to discuss the propriety of including certain articles in the lists of absolute and conditional contraband, which have been proclaimed by His Majesty. Open to objection as some of these seem to this Government, the chief ground of present complaint is the treatment of cargoes of both classes of articles when bound to neutral ports.

Articles listed as absolute contraband, shipped from the United States and consigned to neutral countries, have been seized and detained on the ground that the countries to which they were destined have not prohibited the exportation of such articles. Unwarranted as such detentions are, in the opinion of this Government, American exporters are further perplexed by the apparent indecision of the British authorities in applying their own rules to neutral cargoes. For example, a shipment of copper from this country to a specified consignee in Sweden was detained because, as was stated by Great Britain, Sweden had placed no embargo on copper. On the other hand, Italy not only prohibited the export of copper, but, as this Government is informed, put in force a decree that shipments to Italian consignees or "to order," which arrive in ports of Italy can not be exported or transshipped. The only exception Italy makes is of copper which passes through that country in transit to another country. In spite of these decrees, however, the British Foreign Office has thus far declined to affirm that copper shipments consigned to Italy will not be molested on the high seas. Seizures are so numerous and delays so prolonged that exporters are afraid to send their copper to Italy, steamship lines decline to accept it, and insurers refuse to issue policies upon it. In a word, a legitimate trade is being greatly impaired through uncertainty as to the treatment which it may expect at the hands of the British authorities.

We feel that we are abundantly justified in asking for information as to the manner in which the British Government propose to carry out the policy which they have adopted, in order that we may determine the steps necessary to protect our citizens, engaged in foreign trade, in their rights and from the serious losses to which they are liable through ignorance of the hazards to which their cargoes are exposed. In the case of conditional contraband the policy of Great Britain appears to this Government to be equally unjustified by the established rules of international conduct. As evidence of this, attention is directed to the fact that a number of the American cargoes which have been seized consist of foodstuffs and other articles of common use in all countries which are admittedly relative contraband. In spite of the presumption of innocent use because destined to neutral territory, the British authorities made these seizures and detentions without, so far as we are informed, being in possession of facts which warranted a reasonable belief that the shipments had in reality a belligerent destination, as that term is used in international law. Mere suspicion is not evidence and doubts should be resolved in favor of neutral commerce, not against it. The effect upon trade in these articles between neutral nations resulting from interrupted voyages and detained cargoes is not entirely cured by reimbursement of the owners for the damages, which they have suffered, after investigation has failed to establish an enemy destination. The injury is to American commerce with neutral countries as a whole through the hazard of the enterprise and the repeated diversion of goods from established markets.

It also appears that cargoes of this character have been seized by the British authorities because of a belief that, though not originally so intended by the shippers, they will ultimately reach the territory of the enemies of Great Britain. Yet this belief is frequently reduced to a mere fear in view of the embargoes which have been decreed by the neutral countries, to which they are destined, on the articles composing the cargoes.

That a consignment "to order" of articles listed as conditional contraband and shipped to a neutral port raises a legal presumption of enemy destination appears to be directly contrary to the doctrines previously held by Great Britain and thus stated by Lord Salisbury during the South African War:

> "Foodstuffs, though having a hostile destination, can be considered as contraband of war only if they are for the enemy forces, it is not sufficient that they are capable of being so used, it must be shown that this was in fact their destination at the time of their seizure."

With this statement as to conditional contraband the views of this Government are in entire accord, and upon this historic doctrine, consistently maintained by Great Britain when a belligerent as well as a neutral, American shippers were entitled to rely.

The Government of the United States readily admits the full right of a belligerent to visit and search on the high seas the vessels of American citizens or other neutral vessels carrying American goods and to detain them when there is sufficient evidence to justify a belief that contraband articles are in their cargoes; but His Majesty's Government, judging by their own experience in the past, must realize that this Government can not without protest permit American ships or American cargoes to be taken into British ports and there detained for the purpose of searching generally for evidence of contraband, or upon presumptions created by special municipal enactments which are clearly at variance with international law and practice.

This Government believes, and earnestly hopes His Majesty's Government will come to the same belief, that a course of conduct more in conformity with the rules of international usage, which Great Britain has strongly sanctioned for many years, will in the end better serve the interests of belligerents as well as those of neutrals.

Not only is the situation a critical one to the commercial interests of the United States, but many of the great industries of this country are suffering because their products are denied long-established markets in European countries, which, though neutral, are contiguous to the nations at war. Producers and exporters, steamship and insurance companies are pressing, and not without reason, for relief from the menace to transatlantic trade which is gradually but surely destroying their business and threatening them with financial disaster.

The Government of the United States, still relying upon the deep sense of justice of the British Nation, which has been so often manifested in the intercourse between the two countries during so many years of uninterrupted friendship, expresses confidently the hope that His Majesty's Government will realize the obstacles and difficulties which their present policy has placed in the way of commerce between the United States and the neutral countries of Europe, and will instruct its officials to refrain from all unnecessary interference with the freedom of trade between nations which are sufferers, though not participants, in the present conflict; and will in their treatment of neutral ships and cargoes conform more closely to those rules governing the maritime relations between belligerents and neutrals, which have received the sanction of the civilized world, and which Great Britain has, in other wars, so strongly and successfully advocated.

In conclusion it should be impressed upon His Majesty's Government that the present condition of American trade with the neutral European countries is such that, if it does not improve, it may arouse a feeling contrary to that which has so long existed between the American and British peoples. Already it is becoming more and more the subject of public criticism and complaint. There is an increasing belief, doubtless not entirely unjustified, that the present British policy toward American trade is responsible for the depression in certain industries which depend upon European markets. The attention of the British Government is called to this possible result of their present policy to show how widespread the effect is upon the industrial life of the United States and to emphasize the importance of removing the cause of complaint.

Questions for Discussion:

1. What clues does this document reveal about American attitudes and concerns in 1914?

2. What does this document reveal about seaborne commerce in 1914?

3. What does this document reveal about American efforts to stay out of the First World War?

William J. Bryan, "Seizure of American Cargoes," in *The New York Times Current History: The European War*, vol. 2, *January–March 1915* (New York: New York Times, 1917), 1184–87.

Woodrow Wilson, "The *Sussex* Sinking" (1916)

If British seizure of American property on the high seas angered many, the German policy of unrestricted submarine warfare truly outraged the average American. The basis for this anger was the fact that German submarines attacked unarmed civilian ships with no warning, leading to the deaths of many civilian men, women, and children, including Americans. The Germans, however, maintained that the traditional rules of the sea could not be observed by their submarines, whose main defense was stealth, and declared unilaterally that they had the right to sink any ship suspected of carrying supplies to Britain—a policy known as unrestricted submarine warfare.

The sinking of the large passenger liner *Lusitania* in May, 1915, brought these issues to the fore. President Woodrow Wilson repeatedly and angrily protested that sinking and others to the German government. The protest below was one of Wilson's more effective. Written in the wake of the sinking of an unarmed French steamer with some American passengers on board, Wilson expresses his disgust at what he perceives is a needless loss of human life. The German government, fearing that the United States would enter the war on Britain's side, pledged to stop targeting passenger vessels, to search ships for contraband, and to allow passengers and crew to abandon ships before sinking them, in accord with pre-war agreements.

Ultimatum Delivered to Germany's Secretary of Foreign Affairs, April 18th, 1916:

Information now in the possession of the Government of the United States fully establishes the facts in the case of the *Sussex*, and the inferences which the Government has drawn from that information it regards as confirmed by the circumstances set forth in your Excellency's note of the 10th inst. On the 24th of March, 1916, at about 2:50 o'clock in the afternoon, the unarmed steamer *Sussex*, with 325 or more passengers on board, among whom were a number of American citizens, was torpedoed while crossing from Folkestone to Dieppe. The *Sussex* had never been armed; was a vessel known to be habitually used only for the conveyance of passengers across the English Channel; and was not following the route taken by troop ships or supply ships. About eighty of her passengers, noncombatants of all ages and sexes, including citizens of the United States, were killed or injured.

A careful, detailed, and scrupulously impartial investigation by naval and military officers of the United States has conclusively established the fact that the *Sussex* was torpedoed without warning or summons to surrender, and that the torpedo by which she was struck was of German manufacture. In the view of the Government of the

United States these facts from the first made the conclusion that the torpedo was fired by a German submarine unavoidable. It now considers that conclusion substantiated by the statements of Your Excellency's note. A full statement of the facts upon which the Government of the United States has based its conclusion, is enclosed.

The Government of the United States, after having given careful consideration to the note of the Imperial Government[1] of the 10th of April, regrets to state that the impression made upon it by the statements and proposals contained in that note is that the Imperial Government has failed to appreciate the gravity of the situation which has resulted, not alone from the attack on the *Sussex*, but from the whole method and character of submarine warfare as disclosed by the unrestrained practice of the commanders of German undersea craft during the past twelvemonth and more in the indiscriminate destruction of merchant vessels of all sorts, nationalities, and destinations. If the sinking of the *Sussex* had been an isolated case the Government of the United States might find it possible to hope that the officer who was responsible for that act had willfully violated his orders or had been criminally negligent in taking none of the precautions they prescribed, and that the ends of justice might be satisfied by imposing upon him an adequate punishment, coupled with a formal disavowal of the act and payment of a suitable indemnity by the Imperial Government. But, though the attack upon the *Sussex* was manifestly indefensible and caused a loss of life so tragical as to make it stand forth as one of the most terrible examples of the inhumanity of submarine warfare as the commanders of German vessels are conducting it, it unhappily does not stand alone.

On the contrary, the Government of the United States is forced by recent events to conclude that it is only one instance, even though one of the most extreme and most distressing instances, of the deliberate method and spirit of indiscriminate destruction of merchant vessels of all sorts, nationalities, and destinations which have become more and more unmistakable as the activity of German undersea vessels of war has in recent months been quickened and extended.

The Imperial Government will recall that when, in February, 1915, it announced its intention of treating the waters surrounding Great

---

1 Imperial Government: the German government, which was headed by the *kaiser*, or emperor.

Britain and Ireland as embraced within the seat of war and of destroying all merchant ships owned by its enemies that might be found within that zone of danger, and warned all vessels, neutral as well as belligerent, to keep out of the waters thus proscribed or to enter them at their peril, the Government of the United States earnestly protested. It took the position that such a policy could not be pursued without constant gross and palpable violations of the accepted law of nations, particularly if submarine craft were to be employed as its instruments, inasmuch as the rules prescribed by that law, rules founded on the principles of humanity and established for the protection of the lives of noncombatants at sea, could not in the nature of the case be observed by such vessels. It based its protest on the ground that persons of neutral nationality and vessels of neutral ownership would be exposed to extreme and intolerable risks, and that no right to close any part of the high seas could lawfully be asserted by the Imperial Government in the circumstances then existing.

The law of nations in these matters, upon which the Government of the United States based that protest, is not of recent origin or founded upon merely arbitrary principles set up by convention. It is based, on the contrary, upon manifest principles of humanity and has long been established with the approval and by the express assent of all civilized nations.

The Imperial Government, notwithstanding, persisted in carrying out the policy announced, expressing the hope that the dangers involved, at any rate to neutral vessels, would be reduced to a minimum by the instructions which it had issued to the commanders of its submarines, and assuring the Government of the United States that it would take every possible precaution both to respect the rights of neutrals and to safeguard the lives of noncombatants.

In pursuance of this policy of submarine warfare against the commerce of its adversaries, thus announced and thus entered upon in despite of the solemn protest of the Government of the United States, the commanders of the Imperial Government's undersea vessels have carried on practices of such ruthless destruction, which have made it more and more evident as the months have gone by that the Imperial Government has found it impracticable to put any such restraints upon them as it had hoped and promised to put. Again and again the Imperial Government has given its solemn assurances to the Government of the United States that at least passenger ships would not be thus dealt with, and yet it has repeatedly permitted its undersea commanders to disregard those assurances with entire impunity. As recently as February last it gave notice that it would regard all armed merchantmen owned by its enemies as part of the armed naval forces of its adversaries and deal with them as with men-of-war, thus, at least by implication, pledging itself to give warning to vessels which were not armed and to accord security of life to their passengers and crews; but even this limitation their submarine commanders have recklessly ignored.

Vessels of neutral ownership, even vessels of neutral ownership bound from neutral port to neutral port, have been destroyed, along with vessels of belligerent ownership, in constantly increasing numbers. Sometimes the merchantmen attacked have been warned and summoned to surrender before being fired on or torpedoed; sometimes their passengers and crews have been vouchsafed the poor security of being allowed to take to the ship's boats before the ship was sent to the bottom. But again and again no warning has been given, no escape even to the ship's boats allowed to those on board. Great liners like the *Lusitania* and *Arabic*,[1] and mere passenger boats like the *Sussex*, have been attacked without a moment's warning, often before they have even become aware that they were in the presence of an armed ship of the enemy, and the lives of noncombatants, passengers and crew, have been destroyed wholesale and in a manner which the Government of the United States cannot but regard as wanton and without the slightest color of justification. No limit of any kind has, in fact, been set to their indiscriminate pursuit and destruction of merchantmen of all kinds and nationalities within the waters which the Imperial Government has chosen to designate as lying within the seat of war. The roll of Americans who have lost their lives upon ships thus attacked and destroyed has grown month by month until the ominous toll has mounted into the hundreds.

The Government of the United States has been very patient. At every stage of this distressing experience of tragedy after tragedy it has sought to be governed by the most thoughtful consideration of the extraordinary circumstances of an unprecedented war and to be guided by sentiments of very genuine friendship for the people and

---

1 *Arabic*: a German submarine torpedoed the British passenger ship *Arabic* on August 19, 1915, with the loss of two American lives out of a total of approximately forty.

Government of Germany. It has accepted the successive explanations and assurances of the Imperial Government as, of course, given in entire sincerity and good faith, and has hoped, even against hope, that it would prove to be possible for the Imperial Government so to order and control the acts of its naval commanders as to square its policy with the recognized principles of humanity as embodied in the law of nations. It has made every allowance for unprecedented conditions and has been willing to wait until the facts became unmistakable and were susceptible of only one interpretation.

It now owes it to a just regard for its own rights to say to the Imperial Government that that time has come. It has become painfully evident to it that the position which it took at the very outset is inevitable, namely, the use of submarines for the destruction of an enemy's commerce, is, of necessity, because of the very character of the vessels employed and the very methods of attack which their employment of course involves, utterly incompatible with the principles of humanity, the long-established and incontrovertible rights of neutrals, and the sacred immunities of noncombatants.

If it is still the purpose of the Imperial Government to prosecute relentless and indiscriminate warfare against vessels of commerce by the use of submarines, without regard to what the Government of the United States must consider the sacred and indisputable rules of international law and the universally recognized dictates of humanity, the Government of the United States is at last forced to the conclusion that there is but one course it can pursue. Unless the Imperial Government should now immediately declare and effect an abandonment of its present methods of submarine warfare against passenger and freight-carrying vessels, the Government of the United States can have no choice but to sever diplomatic relations with the German Empire altogether. This action the Government of the United States contemplates with the greatest reluctance, but feels constrained to take in behalf of humanity and the rights of neutral nations.

Questions for Discussion:
1. What is the basis of Wilson's argument?
2. What clues does this document reveal about American attitudes and concerns in 1916?
3. What does this document reveal about submarine warfare in the First World War?

Charles F. Horne, *Source Records of the Great War* (New York: National Alumni, 1923) 4: 89–95.

Floyd P. Gibbons, "How the *Laconia* Sank" (1917)

The American public had a grim obsession with being torpedoed, especially after the sinking of the *Lusitania*. Newspapers eagerly catered to this curiosity. In this instance, the *Chicago Tribune* sent one of its star reporters, Floyd P. Gibbons (1887–1939), to cover how submarines sank merchant and passenger vessels. Gibbons, a self-proclaimed headline hunter, volunteered to cross the Atlantic in a British passenger ship, with the expectation that it would be "submarined." Toward that end, he boarded the ship *Laconia* equipped with a special life preserver, a large bottle of drinking water, flashlights, and a flask of brandy. Gibbons correctly predicted the sinking of the *Laconia*, during which about thirteen people died. Gibbons survived and quickly submitted his story to his editors, who published it. In its day, this article was considered a major feat of journalism, an influential piece read aloud in both houses of Congress as evidence of the maliciousness of unrestricted submarine warfare. It remains a lively and vivid account of how a torpedoed ship sank.

QUEENSTOWN,[1] February 26, 1917.

I have serious doubts whether this is a real story. I am not entirely certain that it is not all a dream. I feel that in a few minutes I may wake up back in stateroom B19 on the promenade deck of the Cunarder *Laconia* and hear my cockney steward informing me with an abundance of "and sirs" that it is a fine morning.

It is now a little over thirty hours since I stood on the slanting decks of the big liner, listened to the lowering of the lifeboats, and heard the hiss of escaping steam and the roar of ascending rockets as they tore lurid rents in the black sky and cast their red glare over the roaring sea.

I am writing this within thirty minutes after stepping on the dock here in Queenstown from the British mine sweeper which picked up our open lifeboat after an eventful six hours of drifting and darkness and bailing and pulling on the oars and of straining aching eyes toward that empty, meaningless horizon in search of help.

But, dream or fact, here it is:

---

1   Queenstown: an Irish port on that island's southern coast, known since 1922 as *Cobh*.

The Cunard liner *Laconia*, 18,000 tons burden, carrying seventy-three passengers—men, women, and children, of whom six were American citizens—manned by a mixed crew of two hundred and sixteen, bound from New York to Liverpool, and loaded with food-stuffs, cotton, and war material, was torpedoed without warning by a German submarine last night off the Irish coast. The vessel sank in about forty minutes.

Two American citizens, mother and daughter, listed from Chicago, and former residents there, are among the dead. They were Mrs. Mary E. Hay and Miss Elizabeth Hay. I have talked with a seaman who was in the same lifeboat with the two Chicago women and he has told me that he saw their lifeless bodies washed out of the sinking lifeboat.

The American survivors are Mrs. F. E. Harris, of Philadelphia, who was the last woman to leave the *Laconia*, the Rev. Father Wareing, of St. Joseph's Seminary, Baltimore, Arthur T. Kirby, of New York, and myself.

A former Chicago woman, now the wife of a British subject, was among the survivors. She is Mrs. Henry George Boston, the daughter of Granger Farwell, of Lake Forest.

After leaving New York, passengers and crew had had three drills with the lifeboats. All were supplied with life-belts and assigned to places in the twelve big lifeboats poised over the side from the davits of the top deck.

Submarines had been a chief part of the conversation during the entire trip, but the subject had been treated lightly, although all ordered precautions were strictly in force. After the first explanatory drill on the second day out from New York, from which we sailed on Saturday, February 17, the "abandon ship" signal—five quick blasts on the whistle—had summoned us twice to our life-belts and heavy wraps, among which I included a flask and a flashlight, and to a roll call in front of our assigned boats on the top deck.

On Sunday we knew generally we were in the danger zone, though we did not know definitely where we were—or at least the passengers did not. In the afternoon during a short chat with Captain W.R.D. Irvine, the ship's commander, I had mentioned that I would like to see a chart and note our position on the ocean. He replied: "O, would you?" with a smiling, rising inflection that meant, "It is jolly well none of your business."

Prior to this my cheery early morning steward had told us that we would make Liverpool by Monday night and I used this information in another question to the captain.

"When do we land?" I asked.

"I don't know," replied Capt. Irvine, but my steward told me later it would be Tuesday after dinner.

The first cabin passengers[1] were gathered in the lounge Sunday evening, with the exception of the bridge fiends[2] in the smoke-room.

"Poor Butterfly" was dying wearily on the talking machine[3] and several couples were dancing.

About the tables in the smoke-room the conversation was limited to the announcement of bids and orders to the stewards. Before the fireplace was a little gathering which had been dubbed as the Hyde Park corner—an allusion I don't quite fully understand.[4] This group had about exhausted available discussion when I projected a new bone of contention.

"What do you say are our chances of being torpedoed?" I asked.

"Well," drawled the deliberative Mr. Henry Chetham, a London solicitor, "I should say four thousand to one."

Lucien J. Jerome, of the British diplomatic service, returning with an Ecuadorian valet from South America, interjected: "Considering the zone and the class of this ship, I should put it down at two hundred and fifty to one that we don't meet a sub."

At this moment the ship gave a sudden lurch sideways and forward. There was a muffled noise like the slamming of some large door at a good distance away. The slightness of the shock and the meekness of the report compared with my imagination were disappointing. Every man in the room was on his feet in an instant.

"We're hit!" shouted Mr. Chetham.

"That's what we've been waiting for," said Mr. Jerome.

"What a lousy torpedo!" said Mr. Kirby in typical New Yorkese. "It must have been a fizzer."[5]

---

1   First cabin passengers: first-class passengers, who paid the highest ticket prices for better staterooms and meals.

2   Bridge fiends: people addicted to playing bridge, a complex card game involving four players.

3   Talking machine: a record player, a relative novelty in 1917.

4   Hyde Park corner: a reference to the north-east corner of London's Hyde Park, where radicals often gathered to speak and protest. The people referred to were probably political radicals or pacifists.

5   Fizzer: a torpedo that failed to explode or did so only feebly.

I looked at my watch. It was 10:30 P.M.

Then came the five blasts on the whistle. We rushed down the corridor leading from the smoke-room at the stern to the lounge, which was amidships. We were running, but there was no panic. The occupants of the lounge were just leaving by the forward doors as we entered.

It was dark on the landing leading down to the promenade deck, where the first class staterooms were located. My pocket flashlight, built like a fountain pen, came in handy on the landing.

We reached the promenade deck. I rushed into my stateroom, B19, grabbed my overcoat and the water bottle and special life-preserver with which THE TRIBUNE had equipped me before sailing. Then I made my way to the upper deck on that same dark landing.

I saw the chief steward opening an electric switch box in the wall and turning on the switch. Instantly the boat decks were illuminated. That illumination saved lives.

The torpedo had hit us well astern on the starboard side and had missed the engines and the dynamos. I had not noticed the deck lights before. Throughout the voyage our decks had remained dark at night and all cabin portholes were clamped down and all windows covered with opaque paint.

The illumination of the upper deck on which I stood made the darkness of the water sixty feet below appear all the blacker when I peered over the edge at my station, boat No. 10.

Already the boat was loading up and men were busy with the ropes. I started to help near a davit that seemed to be giving trouble, but was stoutly ordered to get out of the way and get into the boat.

We were on the port side, practically opposite the engine well. Up and down the deck passengers and crew were donning life-belts, throwing on overcoats, and taking positions in the boats. There were a number of women, but only one appeared hysterical—little Miss Titsie Siklosi, a French-Polish actress, who was being cared for by her manager, Cedric P. Ivatt, appearing on the passenger list as from New York.

Steam began to hiss somewhere from the giant gray funnels that towered above. Suddenly there was a roaring swish as a rocket soared upward from the captain's bridge, leaving a comet's tail of fire. I watched it as it described a graceful arc in the black void overhead, and then, with an audible pop, it burst in a flare of brilliant white light.

There was a tilt to the deck. It was listing to starboard at just the angle that would make it necessary to reach for support to enable one to stand upright. In the meantime electric flood lights—large white enameled funnels containing clusters of bulbs—had been suspended from the promenade deck and illuminated the dark water that rose and fell on the slanting side of the ship.

"Lower away!" Some one gave the order and we started down with a jerk towards the seemingly hungry rising and falling swells.

Then we stopped with another jerk and remained suspended in mid-air while the man at the bow and the stem swore and tussled with the lowering ropes. The stem of the lifeboat was down, the bow up, leaving us at an angle of about forty-five degrees. We clung to the seats to save ourselves from falling out.

"Who's got a knife, a knife, a knife!" shouted a sweating seaman in the bow. "Great God, give him a knife!" bawled a half-dressed, jibbering negro stoker, who wrung his bands in the stern.

A hatchet was thrust into my hand and I forwarded it to the bow. There was a flash of sparks as it crashed down on the holding pulley. One strand of the rope parted and down plunged the bow, too quick for the stem man. We came to a jerky stop with the stern in the air and the bow down, but the stern managed to lower away until the dangerous angle was eliminated.

Then both tried to lower together. The list of the ship's side became greater, but, instead of our boat sliding down it like a toboggan, the taffrail caught and was held. As the lowering continued, the other side dropped down and we found ourselves clinging on at a new angle and looking straight down on the water. . . .

Many feet and hands pushed the boat from the side of the ship and we sagged down again, this time smacking squarely on the pillowy top of a rising swell. It felt more solid than midair, at least. But we were far from being off. The pulleys twice stuck in their fastenings, bow and stem, and the one ax passed forward and back, and with it my flashlight, as the entangling ropes that held us to the sinking *Laconia* were cut away.

Some shout from that confusion of sound caused me to look up and I really did so with the fear that one of the nearby boats was being lowered upon us.

A man was jumping, as I presumed, with the intention of landing in the boat and I prepared to avoid the impact, but he passed beyond us and plunged into the water three feet from the edge of the boat. He bobbed to the surface immediately.

"It's Duggan!" shouted a man next to me. I flashed the light on the ruddy, smiling face and water-plastered hair of the little Canadian, our fellow saloon passenger. We pulled him over the side. . . .

As we pulled away from the side of the ship, its ranking and receding terrace of lights stretched upward. The ship was slowly turning over. We were opposite that part occupied by the engine rooms. There was a tangle of oars, spars, and rigging on the seat and considerable confusion before four of the big sweeps could be manned on either side of the boat.

The jibbering, bullet-headed negro was pulling directly behind me and I turned to quiet him as his frantic reaches with his oar were hitting me in the back. In the dull light from the upper decks I looked into his slanting face, eyes all whites and lips moving convulsively. Besides being frightened the man was freezing in the thin cotton shirt that composed his entire upper covering. He would work feverishly to get warm.

"Get away from her; get away from her," he kept repeating. "When the water hits her hot boilers, she'll blow up, and there's just tons and tons of shrapnel in the hold!"

His excitement spread to other members of the crew in the boat. The ship's baker, designated by his pantry headgear, became a competing alarmist, and a white fireman, whose blasphemy was nothing short of profound, added to the confusion by cursing everyone. It was the give way of nerve tension. It was bedlam and nightmare.

Seeking to establish some authority in our boat, I made my way to the stern and there found an old, white-haired sea captain, a second cabin passenger, with whom I had talked before. He was bound from Nova Scotia with codfish. His sailing schooner, the *Secret*, had broken in two, but he and his crew had been taken off by a tramp and taken back to New York. He had sailed from there on the *Ryndam*, which, after almost crossing the Atlantic, had turned back. The *Laconia* was his third attempt to get home. His name is Captain Dear.

"The rudder's gone, but I can steer with an oar," he said. "I will take charge, but my voice is gone. You'll have to shout the orders." There was only one way to get the attention of the crew and that was by an overpowering blast of profanity. I did my best and was rewarded by silence while I made the announcement that in the absence of the ship's officer assigned to the boat, Captain Dear would take charge. There was no dissent and under the captain's orders the boat's head was held to the wind to prevent us from being swamped by the increasing swell.

We rested on our oars, with all eyes turned on the still lighted *Laconia*. The torpedo had struck at 10:30 P.M. According to our ship's time, it was thirty minutes after that hour that another dull thud, which was accompanied by a noticeable drop in the hulk, told its story of the second torpedo that the submarine had dispatched through the engine room and the boat's vitals from a distance of 200 yards.

We watched silently during the next minute, as the tiers of lights dimmed slowly from white to yellow, then to red, and nothing was left but the murky mourning of the night, which hung over all like a pall.

A mean, cheese-colored crescent of a moon revealed one horn above a rag bundle of clouds low in the distance. A rim of blackness settled around our little world, relieved only by general leering stars in the zenith, and where the *Laconia* lights had shone there remained only the dim outline of a blacker hulk standing out above the water like a jagged headland, silhouetted against the overcast sky.

The ship sank rapidly at the stem until at last its nose stood straight in the air. Then it slid silently down and out of sight like a piece of disappearing scenery in a panorama spectacle.

Questions for Discussion:
1. How does the author emphasize his sense that this incident seemed unreal to him?
2. What does this document reveal about American attitudes and society circa 1917?
3. What are the strengths and weaknesses of Gibbons's account for historians studying the First World War?

Floyd P. Gibbons, *How the* Laconia *Sank: The Militia Mobilization on the Mexican Border. Two Masterpieces of Reporting* (Chicago: Daughday and Company, 1917), 11–25.

SEA AND SAND

The beach has long been a focus of American recreation. As the nineteenth century progressed, Americans increasingly flocked to the beach to escape overheated cities. By the early twentieth century, going to the beach was a well-established pastime on the nation's shores, both seaside and on lakes. More and more surfers and sport fishermen took to the beach, but bathing remained the primary activity. All three activities slowly crept into the American psyche, forever changing how Americans related to the maritime environment.

Surfing evolved into more than a sport. It has become a distinct subculture (even a counterculture) that revolves around the love of surfing, the desire for the ultimate ride, an almost spiritual appreciation of life in and around the ocean, distinctive dress and speech patterns, and even a type of popular music. While surfers respect those with decades of experience, surfing is generally thought of as associated with tanned, muscular, and fun-loving youth.

Surf fishing—and sport fishing in general—is also a subculture in American society, although not a counterculture. Its goal is escape from the stress of modern life. Unlike surf culture, fishing is often associated with middle age (and beyond) and a contemplative, even cerebral, appreciation of the outdoors and hard-earned skill.

Most Americans experience the beach for bathing on hot summer days. Bathing suits underwent considerable change for both men and women in the early decades of the century. For men it was less controversial, but as late as the early 1930s men were required to cover their torso at the beach. For women the transition was more dramatic. In the early 1900s society demanded that women cover their shoulders and wear stockings and skirts while swimming. While a handful of reformers, like Annette Kellerman (1887–1975), advocated the one-piece bathing suit as a practical garment, many communities deemed it shockingly revealing and immoral.

Jack London, "Surfing: A Royal Sport" (1907)

Surfing is an ancient Hawaiian sport, but by the start of the twentieth century it had all but died out, partly at the urging of Christian missionaries who encouraged the native Hawaiians to give up it up. A renewed interest in Hawaii shortly after the United States absorbed those islands captured the imagination of American writers such as Mark Twain and Jack London (1876–1916). London saw surfing as an antidote to the increased effeteness of American bourgeois society in the early twentieth century. His article excited interest in both Hawaii and the mainland United States. Duke Kahanomoku (1890–1968), a native Hawaiian, and others revived the sport in Hawaii, while George Freeth (1883–1919), of mixed Hawaiian and Irish ancestry, is credited by some as the *father of modern surfing* for bringing the sport to California's beaches.

That is what it is, a royal sport for the natural kings of earth. The grass grows right down to the water at Waikiki Beach, and within fifty feet of the everlasting sea. The trees also grow down to the salty edge of things, and one sits in their shade and looks seaward at a majestic surf thundering in on the beach to one's very feet. Half a mile out, where the reef is, the white-headed combers thrust suddenly skyward out of the placid turquoise-blue and come rolling in to shore. One after another they come, a mile long, with smoking crests, the white battalions of the infinite army of the sea. And one sits and listens to the perpetual roar, and watches the unending procession, and feels tiny and fragile before this tremendous force expressing itself in fury and foam and sound. Indeed, one feels microscopically small, and the thought that one may wrestle with this sea raises in one's imagination a thrill of apprehension, almost of fear. Why, they are a mile long, these bull-mouthed monsters, and they weigh a thousand tons, and they charge in to shore faster than anyone can run. What chance? No chance at all, is the verdict of the shrinking ego; and one sits, and looks, and listens, and thinks the grass and the shade are a pretty good place in which to be.

And suddenly, out there where a big smoker lifts skyward, rising like a sea-god from out of the welter of spume and churning white, on the giddy, toppling, overhanging and downfalling, precarious crest appears the dark head of a man. Swiftly he rises through the rushing white. His black shoulders, his chest, his loins, his limbs—all is abruptly projected on one's vision. Where but the moment before was only the wide desolation and invincible roar, is now a man, erect, full-statured, not struggling frantically in that wild movement, not buried and crushed and buffeted by those mighty monsters, but standing above them all, calm and superb, poised on the giddy summit, his feet buried in the churning foam, the salt smoke rising to his knees, and all the rest of him in the free air and flashing sunlight, and he is flying through the air, flying forward, flying fast as the surge on which he stands. He is a Mercury—a brown Mercury. His heels are winged, and in them is the swiftness of the sea. In truth, from out of the sea he has leaped upon the back of the sea, and he is riding the sea that roars and bellows and cannot shake him from its back. But no frantic outreaching and balancing is his. He is impassive, motionless as a statue carved suddenly by some miracle out of the sea's depth from which he rose. And straight on toward shore he flies on his winged heels and the white crest of the breaker. There is a wild burst of foam, a long tumultuous rushing sound as the breaker falls futile and spent on the beach at your feet; and there, at your feet steps calmly ashore a Kanaka,[1] burnt golden and brown by the tropic sun. Several minutes ago he was a speck a quarter of a mile away. He has "bitted the bull-mouthed breaker" and ridden it in, and the pride in the feat shows in the carriage of his magnificent body as he glances for a moment carelessly at you who sit in the shade of the shore. He is a Kanaka—and more, he is a human being, a member of the kingly species that has mastered matter and the brutes and lorded it over creation.

And one sits and thinks of Tristram's[2] last wrestle with the sea on that fatal morning; and one thinks further, to the fact that Kanaka has done what Tristram never did, and that he knows a joy of the sea that Tristram never knew. And still further one thinks. It is all very well, sitting here in the cool shade of the beach, but you are a human being, one of the kingly species, and what that Kanaka can do, you can do yourself. Go to. Strip off your clothes that are a nuisance in this mellow clime. Get in and wrestle with the sea; wing your heels with the skill and power that reside in you; bit the sea's breakers, master them, and ride upon their backs as a king should.

And that is how it came about that I tackled surf-riding. And now that I have tackled it, more than ever do I hold it to be a royal sport. But first let me explain the physics of it. A wave is a communicated agitation. The water that composes the body of the wave does not move. If it did, when a stone is thrown into a pond and the ripples spread away in an ever widening circle, there would appear at the center an ever increasing hole. No, the water that composes the body of a wave is stationary. Thus, you may watch a particular portion of the ocean's surface and you will see the same water rise and fall a thousand times to the agitation communicated by a thousand successive waves. Now imagine this communicated agitation moving shoreward. As the bottom shoals, the lower portion of the wave strikes land

---

1   Kanaka: native Hawaiian.

2   Tristram: probably a reference to King Tristram the Younger, whose kingdom sank beneath the sea according to some versions of the King Arthur legends.

first and is stopped. But water is fluid, and the upper portion has not struck anything, wherefore it keeps on communicating its agitation, keeps on going. And when the top of the wave keeps on going, while the bottom of it lags behind, something is bound to happen. The bottom of the wave drops out from under and the top of the wave falls over, forward, and down, curling and cresting and roaring as it does so. It is the bottom of a wave striking against the top of the land that is the cause of all surfs.

But the transformation from a smooth undulation to a breaker is not abrupt except where the bottom shoals abruptly. Say the bottom shoals gradually for from a quarter of a mile to a mile, then an equal distance will be occupied by the transformation. Such a bottom is that off the beach of Waikiki, and it produces a splendid surf-riding surf. One leaps upon the back of a breaker just as it begins to break, and stays on it as it continues to break all the way in to shore.

And now to the particular physics of surf-riding. Get out on a flat board, six feet long, two feet wide, and roughly oval in shape. Lie down upon it like a child on a coaster and paddle with your hands out to deep water, where the waves begin to crest. Lie out there quietly on the board. Sea after sea breaks before, behind, and under and over you, and rushes in to shore, leaving you behind. When a wave crests, it gets steeper. Imagine yourself, on your board, on the face of that steep slope. If it stood still, you would slide down just as a child slides down a hill on his or her coaster. "But," you object, "the wave doesn't stand still." Very true, but the water composing the wave stands still, and there you have the secret. If ever you start sliding down the face of that wave, you'll keep on sliding and you'll never reach the bottom. Please don't laugh. The face of that wave may be only six feet, yet you can slide down it a quarter of a mile, or half a mile, and not reach the bottom. For, see, since a wave is only a communicated agitation or impetus, and since the water that composes a wave is changing every instant, new water is rising into the wave as fast as the wave travels. You slide down this new water, and yet remain in your old position on the wave, sliding down the still newer water that is rising and forming the wave. You slide precisely as fast as the wave travels. If it travels fifteen miles an hour, you slide fifteen miles an hour. Between you and the shore stretches a quarter of mile of water. As the wave travels, this water obligingly heaps itself into the wave, gravity does the rest, and down you go, sliding the whole length of it. If you still cherish the notion, while sliding, that the water is moving with you, thrust your arms into it and attempt to paddle; you will find that you have to be remarkably quick to get a stroke, for that water is dropping astern just as fast as you are rushing ahead.

And now for another phase of the physics of surf-riding. All rules have their exceptions. It is true that the water in a wave does not travel forward. But there is what may be called the send of the sea. The water in the overtoppling crest does move forward, as you will speedily realize if you are slapped in the face by it, or if you are caught under it and are pounded by one mighty blow down under the surface panting and gasping for half a minute. The water in the top of a wave rests upon the water in the bottom of the wave. But when the bottom of the wave strikes the land, it stops, while the top goes on. It no longer has the bottom of the wave to hold it up. Where was solid water beneath it, is now air, and for the first time it feels the grip of gravity, and down it falls, at the same time being torn asunder from the lagging bottom of the wave and flung forward. And it is because of this that riding a surf-board is something more than a mere placid sliding down a hill. In truth, one is caught up and hurled shoreward as by some Titan's hand.

I deserted the cool shade, put on a swimming suit, and got hold of a surfboard. It was too small a board. But I didn't know, and nobody told me. I joined some little Kanaka boys in shallow water, where the breakers were well spent and small—a regular kindergarten school. I watched the little Kanaka boys. When a likely-looking breaker came along, they flopped upon their stomachs on their boards, kicked like mad with their feet, and rode the breaker in to the beach. I tried to emulate them. I watched them, tried to do everything that they did, and failed utterly. The breaker swept past, and I was not on it. I tried again and again. I kicked twice as madly as they did, and failed. Half a dozen would be around. We would all leap on our boards in front of a good breaker. Away our feet would churn like the sternwheels of river steamboats, and away the little rascals would scoot while I remained in disgrace behind.

I tried for a solid hour, and not one wave could I persuade to boost me shoreward. And then arrived a friend, Alexander Hume Ford,[1] a

---

1   Alexander Hume Ford: born in South Carolina, with a career as a Chicago journalist already behind him, Ford became a major promoter of both surfing and Hawaii.

globe trotter by profession, bent ever on the pursuit of sensation. And he had found it at Waikiki. Heading for Australia, he had stopped off for a week to find out if there were any thrills in surf-riding, and he had become wedded to it. He had been at it every day for a month and could not yet see any symptoms of the fascination lessening on him. He spoke with authority.

"Get off that board," he said. "Chuck it away at once. Look at the way you're trying to ride it. If ever the nose of that board hits bottom, you'll be disemboweled. Here, take my board. It's a man's size."

I am always humble when confronted by knowledge. Ford knew. He showed me how properly to mount his board. Then he waited for a good breaker, gave me a shove at the right moment, and started me in. Ah, delicious moment when I felt that breaker grip and fling me. On I dashed, a hundred and fifty feet, and subsided with the breaker on the sand. From that moment I was lost. I waded back to Ford with his board. It was a large one, several inches thick, and weighed all of seventy-five pounds. He gave me advice, much of it. He had had no one to teach him, and all that he had laboriously learned in several weeks he communicated to me in half an hour. I really learned by proxy. And inside of half an hour I was able to start myself and ride in. I did it time after time, and Ford applauded and advised. For instance, he told me to get just so far forward on the board and no farther. But I must have got some farther, for as I came charging in to land, that miserable board poked its nose down to bottom, stopped abruptly, and turned a somersault, at the same time violently severing our relations. I was tossed through the air like a chip and buried ignominiously under the downfalling breaker. And I realized that if it hadn't been for Ford, I'd have been disemboweled. That particular risk is part of the sport, Ford says. Maybe he'll have it happen to him before he leaves Waikiki, and then, I feel confident, his yearning for sensation will be satisfied for a time.

When all is said and done, it is my steadfast belief that homicide is worse than suicide. Ford saved me from being a homicide. "Imagine your legs are a rudder," he said. "Hold them close together, and steer with them." A few minutes later I came charging in on a comber. As I neared the beach, there, in the water, up to her waist, dead in front of me, appeared a woman. How was I to stop that comber on whose back I was? It looked like a dead woman. The board weighed seventy-five pounds, I weighed a hundred and sixty-five. The added weight had a velocity of fifteen miles per hour. The board and I constituted a projectile. I leave it to the physicists to figure out the force of the impact upon that poor woman. And then I remembered my guardian angel, Ford. "Steer with your legs!" rang through my brain. I steered with my legs, I steered sharply, abruptly, with all my legs and with all my might. The board sheered around broadside on the crest. Many things happened simultaneously. The wave gave me a passing buffet, a light tap as the taps of waves go, but a tap sufficient to knock me off the board and smash me down through the rushing water to bottom, with which I came in violent collision and upon which I was rolled over and over. I got my head out for a breath of air and then gained my feet. There stood the woman before me. I felt like a hero. I had saved her life. And she laughed at me. It was not hysteria. She had never dreamed of her danger. Anyway, I solaced myself, it was not I but Ford that saved her, and I didn't have to feel like a hero. And besides, that leg-steering was great. In a few minutes more of practice I was able to thread my way in and out past several bathers and to remain on top my breaker instead of going under it.

"Tomorrow," Ford said, "I am going to take you out into the blue water." I looked seaward where he pointed, and saw the great smoking combers that made the breakers I had been riding look like ripples. I don't know what I might have said had I not recollected just then that I was one of a kingly species. So all that I did say was, "All right, I'll tackle them tomorrow."

The water that rolls in on Waikiki Beach is just the same as the water that laves the shores of all the Hawaiian Islands; and in ways, especially from the swimmer's standpoint, it is wonderful water. It is cool enough to be comfortable, while it is warm enough to permit a swimmer to stay in all day without experiencing a chill. Under the sun or the stars, at high noon or at midnight, in midwinter or in midsummer, it does not matter when, it is always the same temperature—not too warm, not too cold, just right. It is wonderful water, salt as old ocean itself, pure and crystal clear. When the nature of the water is considered, it is not so remarkable after all that the Kanakas are one of the most expert of swimming races.

So it was, next morning, when Ford came along, that I plunged into the wonderful water for a swim of indeterminate length. Astride of our surf-boards, or, rather, flat down upon them on our stomachs, we paddled out through the kindergarten where the little Kanaka boys were at play. Soon we were out in deep water where the big smokers came roaring in. The mere struggle with them, facing them and paddling seaward over them and through them, was sport enough in itself. You had to have your wits about you, for it was a battle in which mighty blows were struck, on one side, and in which cunning was used on the other side—a struggle between insensate force and intelligence. I soon learned a bit. When a breaker curled over my head, for a swift instant I could see the light of day through its emerald body; then down would go my head, and I would clutch the board with all my strength. Then would come the blow, and to the onlooker on shore I would be blotted out. In reality the board and I had passed through the crest and emerged in the respite of the other side. I should not recommend those smashing blows to an invalid or delicate person. There is weight behind them, and the impact of the driven water is like a sandblast. Sometimes one passes through half a dozen combers in quick succession, and it is just about that time that one is liable to discover new merits in the stable land and new reasons for being on shore.

Out there in the midst of such a succession of big smoky ones, a third man was added to our party, one Freeth. Shaking the water from my eyes as I emerged from one wave and peered ahead to see what the next one looked like, I saw him tearing in on the back of it, standing upright on his board, carelessly poised, a young god bronzed with sunburn. We went through the wave on the back of which he rode. Ford called to him. He turned an airspring from his wave, rescued his board from its maw, paddled over to us and joined Ford in showing me things. One thing I learned in particular from Freeth, namely, how to encounter the occasional breaker of exceptional size that rolled in. Such breakers were really ferocious, and it was unsafe to meet them on top of the board. But Freeth showed me, so that whenever I saw one of that caliber rolling down on me, I slid off the rear end of the board and dropped down beneath the surface, my arms over my head and holding the board. Thus, if the wave ripped the board out of my hands and tried to strike me with it (a common trick of such waves), there would be a cushion of water a foot or more in depth between my head and the blow. When the wave passed, I climbed upon the board and paddled on. Many have been terribly injured, I learn, by being struck by their boards.

The whole method of surf-riding and surf-fighting, I learned, is one of non-resistance. Dodge the blow that is struck at you. Dive through the wave that is trying to slap you in the face. Sink down, feet first, deep under the surface, and let the big smoker that is trying to smash you go by far overhead. Never be rigid. Relax. Yield yourself to the waters that are ripping and tearing at you. When the undertow catches you and drags you seaward along the bottom, don't struggle against it. If you do, you are liable to be drowned, for it is stronger than you. Yield yourself to that undertow. Swim with it, not against it, and you will find the pressure removed. And, swimming with it, fooling it so that it does not hold you, swim upward at the same time. It will be no trouble at all to reach the surface.

The person who wants to learn surf-riding must be a strong swimmer, and must be used to going under the water. After that, fair strength and common sense are all that is required. The force of the big comber is rather unexpected. There are mix-ups in which board and rider are torn apart and separated by several hundred feet. The surf-rider must take care of him or herself. No matter how many riders swim out with you, you cannot depend upon any of them for aid. The fancied security I had in the presence of Ford and Freeth made me forget that it was my first swim out in deep water among the big ones. I recollected, however, and rather suddenly, for a big wave came in, and away went the two men on its back all the way to shore. I could have been drowned a dozen different ways before they got back to me.

One slides down the face of a breaker on the surf-board, but has to get started to sliding. Board and rider must be moving shoreward at a good rate before the wave overtakes them. When you see the wave coming that you want to ride in, you turn tail to it and paddle shoreward with all your strength, using what is called the windmill stroke. This is a sort of spurt performed immediately in front of the wave. If the board is going fast enough, the wave accelerates it, and the board begins its quarter-of-a-mile slide.

I shall never forget the first big wave I caught out there in the deep water. I saw it coming, turned my back on it and paddled for dear life. Faster and faster my board went, till it seemed my arms would drop off. What was happening behind me I could not tell. One cannot look behind and paddle the windmill stroke. I heard the crest of the wave hissing and churning, and then my board was lifted and flung forward. I scarcely knew what happened the first half-minute. Though I kept my eyes open, I could not see anything, for I was buried in the rushing white of the crest. But I did not mind. I was chiefly conscious of ecstatic bliss at having caught the wave. At the end of the half-minute, however, I began to see things, and to breathe. I saw that three feet of the nose of my board was clear out of water and riding on the air. I shifted my weight forward, and made the nose come down. Then I lay, quite at rest in the midst of the wild movement, and watched the shore and the bathers on the beach grow distinct. I didn't cover quite a quarter of a mile on that wave, because, to prevent the board from diving, I shifted my weight back, but shifted it too far and fell down the rear slope of the wave.

It was my second day at surf-riding, and I was quite proud of myself. I stayed out there four hours, and when it was over, I was resolved that on the morrow I'd come in standing up. But that resolution paved a distant place. On the morrow I was in bed. I was not sick, but I was very unhappy, and I was in bed. When describing the wonderful water of Hawaii I forgot to describe the wonderful sun of Hawaii. It is a tropic sun, and, furthermore, in the first part of June, it is an overhead sun. It is also an insidious, deceitful sun. For the first time in my life I was sunburned unawares. My arms, shoulders, and back had been burned many times in the past and were tough; but not so my legs. And for four hours I had exposed the tender backs of my legs, at right angles, to that perpendicular Hawaiian sun. It was not until after I got ashore that I discovered the sun had touched me. Sunburn at first is merely warm; after that it grows intense and the blisters come out. Also, the joints, where the skin wrinkles, refuse to bend. That is why I spent the next day in bed. I couldn't walk. And that is why, today, I am writing this in bed. It is easier to than not to. But tomorrow, ah, tomorrow, I shall be out in that wonderful water, and I shall come in standing up, even as Ford and Freeth. And if I fail tomorrow, I shall do it the next day, or the next. Upon one thing I am resolved: the *Snark* shall not sail from Honolulu until I, too, wing my heels with the swiftness of the sea, and become a sunburned, skin-peeling Mercury.

Questions for Discussion:
1. What does this account tell us about London's relationship with the sea?
2. What strengths or weaknesses does this sort of account have for historians?

3. How might this account be appealing to those interested in distancing themselves from mainstream American culture in 1907?

Jack London, "Surfing: A Royal Sport," *The Cruise of the* Snark (New York: Macmillan, 1911): 75–90.

Van Campen Heilner, "Surf Fishing" (1920)

Van Campen Heilner (1889–1970), born to wealth in Philadelphia, found his life purpose in sport fishing, especially surf fishing on the Jersey shore. Heilner had a knack for writing about his fishing experiences and even as a teenager published his fishing stories in popular and influential magazines such as *Field & Stream*. In 1920, when only twenty-one years old, Heilner collaborated with fellow avid fisherman Frank Stick to write *The Call of the Surf*, the first published book devoted exclusively to surf fishing.

Heilner was able to devote his life to fishing and writing about the sport in magazines and books, the most famous of which was his 1937 work, *Salt Water Fishing*. He ranks among other famous authors like Zane Grey and Ernest Hemingway in popularizing sport fishing in the twentieth century. In this excerpt from the first chapter of *The Call of the Surf*, Heilner extols the merits of surf fishing as a healthy outdoor activity for all Americans.

Game and fish are fast disappearing as our remoter sections become settled, as lakes and bayous are drained, and I have been assured that the time is not far distant when we will have degenerated into a race of stoop-shouldered, anaemic creatures, fit only for such mild recreative pastimes as bridge, whist contests and pink teas. But I dislike to harbor the thought, and I do not believe it, not for a minute. I would hate to think of my children, and of my children's children being deprived of those healthful, zestful, and entirely innocent recreations which have been such a big matter in my own life, and which have done much to make this very earthly sphere of ours such an entirely satisfactory dwelling place.

True, a good day's shooting, or a fair catch of trout or of bass, nowadays entails the expenditure of considerable time and money, to the city dweller at least, yet am I buoyed up by the knowledge that one form of sport exists, and with a bit of sane supervision will remain to the sportsmen of the country, and to their descendants for as long as the ocean rolls and its waves beat upon our shores.

The lovers of salt-water angling are legion. Each day of the season fishermen venture seaward from every sizeable town and city along our coasts to dabble with short rods and with hand lines on the offshore banks. If the weather be fair, your shipmates companionable, and your skipper a man of tact and of discretion, this boat fishing is good sport I grant you, but there is better to be had by those who remain behind, providing they know how. Better so far as environment and methods are concerned, and under average conditions, better also in respect to the size and quality of the catch. You will still have the spray in your face and the salt breeze will come sweet to your nostrils, yet the clean sand will be beneath your feet. The vasty deep will roll before your eyes, and the blue sky will arch above your head. The fish you catch will glisten with brine, and the hue of the deep water will be reflected from their shimmering scales, yet storm, or wind, or rain, shall hold no terrors for you.

Surf fishing is by no means a new development of the angler's art; in fact, it is one of the oldest we have any record of, but only of late years has it begun to achieve real popularity. No method of fishing in which I have indulged affords greater diversion, or is more productive of satisfying results. I will go further, and will say that no sport, not even the hunting of big game, has more enthralled me in those pleasurable throes of excitement, which only the outdoorman knows, than have the battles I have waged with those great and goodly fish which so frequently take into their capacious jaws the bait of the surf fisherman.

To feel the lift, the gentle mouthing, and then the irresistible tug and run of a thirty-pound channel bass; to sense the jarring rush of the striper; to see the enormous length of a shark leave the waves in headlong leap, while the line runs like water from your reel; these experiences are sufficient to send the blood pounding through the body, and to lift the sportsman into the ultimate heaven of happiness.

There is a certain individuality and fascination about this particular brand of fishing which is to be found in no other branch of the art in like degree. To the neophyte this statement may sound like an exaggeration, and one who has found his diversion in inland waters may deny it, yet does the fact remain that few who try their hand at the game but become devotees. All forms of angling are pleasurable, to me at least, and yet their appeal may arise from entirely distinct causes. Surf fishing owes its charm to a number of easily perceived allurements, but mainly, I think, to the fact that nowhere else does the element of chance enter so strongly. One casts a fly, and he catches trout, and trout only. In bass or muskallunge fishing it is usually bass or muskallunge that come to net or to gaff, as the case may be. True, a fish of exceptional weight may gladden the heart of the fresh-water fisherman, and after all it is this chance catch which causes him so persistently to continue the sport. I knew a lake in northern Wisconsin, where one could go, supposing he knew the trail, and be assured of catching from twenty to a hundred bass in a few hours' fishing. And yet this lake was rarely visited, for the reason that no fish over two pounds' weight had ever been taken from its waters. We preferred to cast our lures in the larger lakes, where an odd bass or pike of large size might be taken.

In the surf I have captured them of a dozen species, and ranging from a kingfish no more than a pound in weight up to a thirty-five pound bass (and on the same tackle) in the space of a single tide. Once the hook is cast into the ocean, no man can say what finny fellow will venture in from the deep to inspect the bait. It may be some dainty creature, carrying the opalescent colors of coral strands, and with a flavor to his fat sides to delight the senses of a gourmand. Or it may be some weird and rare denizen of the ocean bed, or even a great bass or drum, and not infrequently a shark, which will test the fibre of one's rod. But whatever the fish may be, they all afford good sport, and with scarcely an exception they may be eaten with a relish. No other fishing is quite so apt to bring tremendous, and even startling, results. Upon more than one occasion I have seen a sufficient number of weakfish, croakers, bluefish, and bass beached by a single rod to afford an epicurean feast to a hundred people.

As to the fighting ability of these fish that come inside the breakers—and this would be the first question asked by the average fisherman, I can assure him that there are those among them which will take out five hundred feet of line at a single rush and which, unless the angler protect his hands with thumb stall or drag, will blister the fingers that attempt to halt them. Aye, and more than once, if a man persist in the sport, will he see the last of his nine hundred feet of line disappear from his rod tip as his quarry makes a final run. There are fish in the surf which will cause the rod to jerk and quiver in the grasp as though it were beaten upon by a heavy sledge. Fish which will take the angler half off his feet with the violence of their attack, and cause him to shout aloud in the excitement of the combat. Yes, they are worthy antagonists, these fellows of the blue water, and none need feel compassion in giving combat to them, though we may honor them for their gameness.

When I wade into the surf, and swinging the rod forward, see my weight and bait disappear beneath the water, then there comes a feeling which it is hard for me to describe. A feeling of expectation, certainly, and of hope, and yet with it, something akin to awe. I perceive the wide ocean before me, reaching to my horizon and to an infinity of other horizons beyond. The waves come rolling in, to break far out, to gain in volume and to break again at my feet. Gulls dip and swerve, and hover in their feeding, and their wild cries sound above the roar of waters. And as my eyes sweep over the scene and consider all those great creatures who dwell beneath the waves, and who even now may be investigating my bait, then, as I say, a sensation of something near to awe comes to me. I feel my own unimportance in the scheme of things, my presumption in casting this ineffective hook and slender line into the deep. There are tremendous fishes there in the water before me. Great porpoises have disported close inshore, diving and bounding through the waves like miniature submarines. Huge, man-eating sharks there are, too, for I have both seen and felt them at the end of my line. Tuna perhaps, of a thousand pounds or more; mossy-backed sea turtles and stingarees, and a multitude of others among the kindred of the sea. I meditate upon these facts, when suddenly, as I stand, there comes a sharp jerk to my rod. I set the hook instinctively, before my conscious mind has time to switch to the problem in hand, and all sensations are swallowed up in the joys of the battle.

The fascination of our environments, the widespread ocean, changing constantly with every hour that passes, and with each slightest fluctuation in wind or tide; the wide, clean beach; the broken dunes; and the salt grass, giving to the constant breeze; and the breeze itself, which is of such importance, particularly in summer weather, these things I shall dwell upon at no great length. If you are a fisherman, and follow the call of the surf, you will come to know and to care for it all with an instinctive appreciation, such I suppose as the gray gull feels as he wheels in the wind, and blends his cry with the voice of the waters.

Many times I have been asked to express an opinion concerning the strength and agility of saltwater fish as compared to those which range in fresh water. Time was when I might have given the preference to either the black bass or trout, figuring upon a pound-for-pound basis, and so far as regards the difficulty of bringing to gaff is concerned, the muskallunge would have been my choice. I still believe that fewer muskallunge are landed in proportion to strikes than any fish I have ever caught, with the exception of the tuna. And yet this is mainly because of the peculiar bony construction of the mouth, and the difficulty in setting a hook, and also from the fact that so many muskallunge strike on a short line. The tackle used in the pursuit of salt- and fresh-water fishes and the methods employed vary so greatly that it is hard to compare them with justice to both species. Yet I know that I have landed muskallunge of thirty pounds on a six-ounce rod, and completed the job in less than twenty minutes. Also, I have never known a fresh-water fish to force me to give more than fifty feet of line. Yet in the surf I have seen a channel bass of around thirty pounds take five hundred feet of line in a single run, and this while the fisherman checked him with all the strength of his two arms, while the twenty-eight-ounce rod fairly creaked with the strain upon it. Consider, too, the fact that the saltwater fellow battles against the force and the buffets of tide and wave as well as against heavier tackle. Ninety per cent of the muskallunge which are hooked are killed by dragging behind the skiff of the fisherman after the first few minutes of active battle. On the whole, I am convinced from my own observation that there are at least a dozen salt-water fishes which if hooked up in a tug of war with the best we find in fresh water, would drag them where they willed. So far as the smaller of the salt-water species are concerned, the weakfish, croakers, etc., these I grant you will make a less spectacular fight than do either bass or trout. But try the same fish on light tackle and I believe you will agree with me that there is little to choose between them, and that from a standpoint of strength and endurance, the palm must go to those denizens of the blue water, while the bluefish is unquestionably a stronger, faster, and more spectacular fighter than either the bass or trout.

I have seen a forty-pound muskallunge leap from the water and throw the spoon twenty feet with a shake of his head. But I have also seen a hundred-and-fifty-pound shark surge upward in a succession of headlong plunges, and with his huge, lithe body thresh the water into foam. I have known him to take out eight hundred feet of line, nine hundred, and to keep on going, with, so it seemed to me, his speed increasing with every sweep of his tail.

The methods employed in this surf fishing are scientific and sportsmanlike. It is not a very difficult thing to learn to cast sufficiently well to catch fish when conditions are ideal, but to cast two hundred feet or better is another matter and comes only through conscientious practice. To get one's line out with that springy snap of the rod which sends the bait and weight in a low, graceful arc; to land in the second or third line of breakers; and, above all, to handle reel and line with that degree of expertness which precludes the possibility of a backlash, this is the development not of weeks but usually of years. While the act of casting in itself is not usually either a strenuous or a violent form of exercise, still when combined with the beach tramping and wading, and the exposure to wind and to sun, and to salty spray, which is all a part of the game, it goes to form a recreation which in its health-giving qualities alone is to be seriously considered.

This fishing is not entirely a matter of casting one's bait with ease and grace, and of handling the fish when hooked with complete aplomb. No, there is a great deal more to it than that. It combines a thousand tricks and knacks of the craft, which one gathers up and stores away for future need. There is no form of fishing either that offers greater opportunity for pioneer work in the way of discovering new methods and new applications of old principles. Each season that passes seems to bring some new fish to the attention of the surfman, or at least to suggest to him some fresh method of dealing with old acquaintances.

Questions for Discussion:

1. What does this document reveal about American society's views of nature in the 1920s?

2. Other than fish, what does Heilner seem to be seeking when he goes surf casting?

3. Why would this experience be appealing to ordinary Americans in the 1920s?

Van Campen Heilner and Frank Stick, *The Call of the Surf* (Garden City, N.Y.: Doubleday, Page, 1920), 3–13.

Various, "Bathing Beauties" (1923)

The early 1920s saw the height of a bathing suit controversy. While some women demanded the one-piece "Kellerman" bathing suit as a practical garment to swim in, the establishment of the Miss America contest in 1921 at Atlantic City, New Jersey, linked bathing costumes to ideals of beauty and fashion. Both male and female moralists all over the country deplored these developments as lewd displays of the female body. To make things more difficult, different communities had different standards, and on some beaches officials patrolled and regulated swimwear. Women—and less often, men— could find themselves arrested if they breached a community's standards for bathing suits. There was also often a generational divide among women on the bathing suit issue, with younger women favoring the more practical but more revealing swimsuits, while older women often preferred bathing costumes that were both less practical and less revealing.

The controversy gradually died as some communities, especially in Florida, realized that relaxed swimwear standards could result in additional

New York beauties at Atlantic City carnival, September 8, 1922. Photo by unknown, courtesy of the Library of Congress # LC-USZ62-119722.

Bill Norton the bathing beach policeman measuring distance between knee and bathing suit on woman, Washington, D.C., 1922. Photo by National Photo Company, courtesy of the Library of Congress # LC-USZ62-99824.

tourism. Angela J. Latham, in *Posing a Threat*,[1] has suggested that mass media also played a role in creating a reference point whereby communities could gauge standards of decency. In particular, photos of the Miss America Contest's contestants in bathing suits influenced perceptions of fashion and morality among the American public.

Questions for Discussion:
1. How do the above photos reflect the tensions concerning swimwear in the early 1920s?
2. What challenges do photographs offer to historians in attempting to understand the past?
3. What do these photos reveal about American society in the 1920s?

Library of Congress Prints and Photographs Division, LC-USZ62-99824; LC-USZ62-119722.

---

1   Angela J. Latham, *Posing a Threat: Flappers, Chorus Girls, and Other Brazen Performers of the American 1920s* (Hanover, N.H.: Wesleyan University Press, 2000).

MERCHANT MARINE POLICY

Between 1900 and the Second World War, the United States wrestled with how best to improve its merchant marine. Before the First World War, questions arose regarding the benefits of government ownership of the merchant marine versus private ownership. Ultimately the government did take control of American shipping and built an enormous fleet of cargo vessels for the war effort, though virtually none of them were completed until after the war ended. Saddled with this enormous fleet of expensive ships, the government struggled with what to do with them. The Jones Act of 1920 recognized that they were a national strategic asset and thus could not be sold to foreign buyers. Many were laid up in reserve status, awaiting a future war.

In the meantime, a debate raged in shipping circles: should the government continue to operate merchant shipping as it had during the war, as a government-operated corporate entity, or should the vessels be sold to private shipping companies to operate as private assets? Andrew Gibson and Arthur Donovan, in *The Abandoned Ocean*,[1] found that the Depression proved a difficult time for the shipping industry, adding to the misery of an industry that was already sick. Gibson and Donovan hailed the intervention of Congress in 1936 to reorganize and strengthen the nation's merchant marine as landmark legislation that formed the basis of American maritime policy down to the present day. The Merchant Marine Act of 1936 massively subsidized American steamship lines to provide jobs, improve the nation's economy, and provide sealift capabilities for the armed forces. The Merchant Marine Act of 1936 thus prepared the merchant marine for the coming trials of World War II.

Robert Dollar, "A National Shipping Policy" (1915)

Robert Dollar (1844–1932) was a self-made man. Born in Scotland, as a boy he emigrated to Canada, where he worked in a logging camp, then moved to the United States, where he made a fortune in the lumber business. In the 1890s he moved into shipping and began trading with Asia, especially China. Dollar was a fierce opponent of government regulation and particularly resisted the 1916 Seamen's Act, which regulated shipboard labor conditions, including outlawing the cheap Chinese labor he used on

---

1 Andrew Gibson and Arthur Donovan, *The Abandoned Ocean: A History of United States Maritime Policy* (Columbia: University of South Carolina Press, 2000).

his transpacific service. Like many self-made businessmen, he also opposed labor unions and was a major force in breaking the 1919 seaman's strike in San Francisco. In this piece, dating to the first years of the First World War when the United States was still neutral, Dollar expresses his doubts about government control of the merchant marine, which was one of the options the federal government considered as it prepared for entry into the First World War.

How many of our people realize that in the most essential points upon which the law is expected to enlighten the shipowner, the American statutes relative to shipping are either mute or so ambiguous that there is probably not one ship operator in this country that could offhand tell you in the most general way what is and what is not permissible in the operation of ships, as far as the customs regulations, manning, victualling and equipment are concerned. Our laws are very strict on lifesaving equipment. They provide for a more stringent test of boilers than is the case elsewhere, but although the equipment of lifeboats is minutely defined, there is no law that requires the navigating compasses to be properly adjusted and compensated, while the engine which receives its steam from the boiler that is so carefully tested by the Federal Inspectors does not come in for any mention at all in the book of rules that are enforced upon American ships in the name of safety, but which go so far wide of the mark that the insurance underwriters give no consideration to the steamboat inspection certificates in estimating the worth of a ship for insurance purposes, while Lloyds or other foreign classification certificates are readily accepted. Thus it is possible to build under our laws steamships that defy so much all accepted ideas as to safety in ships, that they would be uninsurable. Hence, no ship is ever built in this country that is not far and away in excess of the requirements of the Steamboat Inspection Service, because ships need insurance and underwriters are quite a bit more exacting than the United States government in their ideas as to what constitutes a safe ship, although they are not so finicky as to the thousand and one trifles that the Steamboat Inspection Service is so keen upon, perhaps for the reason that the rules being so vague about the essentials of proper construction and equipment, it is well that so much attention were paid to the apparatus that comes into play only when it is no longer safe to remain on board a vessel.

American licensed officers, who are better paid than those sailing under any other flag, are submitted before obtaining their certificates to a very strict examination on lifeboat drills, fire drill, etc., but the official requirements in other directions, are very lax. Therefore but few of our officers know anything of such methods of signaling as Morseing or semaphoring, so that when a ship is spoken at sea by those modern methods and she does not reply, it is customary among foreign navigators to remark that "she must be a Yankee." Yet the law now obliges American ships to carry third mates, when in other countries many vessels which would require those officers if operated under the American flag, carry often but an "only mate," the second mate being virtually a boatswain.

Time does not permit complete enumeration of the shortcomings of our laws as regards the most essential points which navigation laws ought to cover, contrasting those deficiencies with the onerous requirements of our statutes. It required the European war to change the regulations as to measurement of ships so as to bring our methods in conformity with the universal usage. And the reason why the regulations were changed was not that they worked an injustice on American ships, but that foreign-built ships put under the American flag under the emergency act would have had their net register tonnage increased that on which shipping dues were paid—if they had been granted new tonnage certificates on the American basis.

I have mentioned the foregoing merely to give you practical examples of the vicissitudes which confront the American shipowner who has to contend in the prosecution of his daily business with the Treasury Department, the Bureau of Navigation, the Steamboat Inspection Service, the Public Health and Marine Hospital Service, the Immigration Service and at times the Department of Justice, to say nothing of a multitude of restrictions imposed by local authorities, as represented by boards of pilots, city and state wharf authorities, etc., so that the life of the operator of American ships bears a strong relationship to that of the little boy whose mother said to the nurse: "See what Thomas is doing in the nursery and tell him he mustn't."

Little wonder that under such conditions the threat of government ownership is sufficient to frighten away all newcomers who see nothing ahead but increased official interference, without obtaining from the government of this country that measure of consideration to which the shipowners of other countries have become accustomed and which has taken such concrete expression as the constant reliance of the public services upon the assistance which the national shipping could render in the ordinary prosecution of its commercial mission.

Thus, England, Germany and Japan dispense with troopships and naval colliers, obtaining such vessels as are needed for the transport of troops to the Colonies overseas and for the transport of coal to the fleet during maneuvers, from the commercial fleet under the national flag that could always be drawn upon for such purposes. Here, on the contrary, as soon as our nation became possessed of outlying dependencies, the transportation of troops to those parts was confided to a fleet of government vessels purchased for that one purpose, while the Navy Department that always voiced the complaint that it was hampered by lack of funds, undertook the construction of a large fleet of colliers built internally like the well-known commercial steam colliers operating on the Atlantic Coast, except that the naval vessels are fitted with mechanical discharging gear for the purpose of delivering coal into the bunkers of warships. Recently the government of the Canal Zone took delivery of two large steam colliers designed to carry coal to the bunkering stations on the Panama Canal. These vessels which are operated on such an extravagant scale that undoubtedly their operation is costing much more than the same service could be obtained for by means of chartered commercial vessels. Unfortunately it has been the consistent policy of our government to proceed always on the assumption that American ships were non-existent or could not be created.

Various remedies have been proposed for the solution of our merchant marine question. The proposals now figuring most prominently before the public may be summed up under three heads: First, government ownership; second, equalization of operating costs, under whatever name may be given to the direct assistance of the state to shipping; third, the development of a truly national shipping policy along lines recommended by a permanent non-partisan shipping board after business-like consideration of the country's real shipping necessities.

Let us examine the first proposition: government ownership is nothing new. It has been in operation in other countries before this, with the same invariable outcome of failure. We are, nevertheless, free to consider without prejudice and without bias, whether the proposal as made to the American people in its newest form, contains any element that ought to recommend its adoption as a national policy, whatever form the policy may take. The intention is, substantially, to acquire a large fleet of merchant ships to be operated in the interest of our foreign trade in such directions as the prospect of immediate profits precludes the free operation of ships run for purely commercial purposes.

We see here a proposition to pay a subsidy of far greater scope than any subsidy policy that has as yet been proposed; for any subsidy contract is necessarily limited as to the amount of money which may be disbursed to the shipowners undertaking the subsidized services, whereas, with the government itself operating the ships on that extravagant scale with which all business men are familiar, there is no limit to the deficit that may be accumulated by the ships performing the services yet to be announced. Therefore, if on the ground of economy only, it would seem to be part of wisdom at least to endeavor to find private shipowners willing to undertake specified voyages for stipulated sums of money, proper guarantees as to the ability of the contractor to continue the service after its initiation being given by the recipients of the subsidies.

This comment relates to the principle of government ownership, which it is impossible to escape whatever form the new government shipping bill may take. At the time this paper was written, the new bill had not been introduced, and it would have been unwise to attempt to discuss unofficial reports that, instead of being confined to government operation, the vessels, constructed by the government, may be leased to private companies for operation in certain trades not yet designated. That all vessels entering American ports will be subject to regulation of freight rates and service, and that the entire lot will be administered, after the government ownership principle has been embodied in it, by the shipping board. This much, however, is fair to say: The government proposes to embark in a business which normally it costs 25 per cent to 35 per cent more to conduct under the American than under foreign flags. Unless the government can perform the service more cheaply than private enterprises, it must incur deficits to be met out of the public treasury. The vessels cannot be leased to private companies unless private companies can operate them profitably.

In other words, the only way the government can induce private companies to operate those ships under the American flag, under the conditions prevailing before the war, and surely will prevail after the war, is to make the leasing price low enough to offset the excess of operating cost over that of our competitors. Somebody must pay, and under the government ownership principle it will be the taxpayer. If, then, the principle of government aid is exercised only through the leasing of government-owned vessels to private companies, the American flag in foreign trade will become a government monopoly.

The increase of our shipping in foreign trade will depend upon the willingness of the taxpayers to increase the appropriations to be made for the new construction, and, possibly, continued deficits in the governmental shipping policy account.

In other words, the shipping policy, requiring continuing and increasing appropriations, will be under debate at each session of Congress. It is easy to see how sectional and political considerations may complicate any shipping progress dependent upon the government ownership policy.

Another and most important consideration remains to be weighed most carefully before we can dismiss this matter of government ownership. We desire ships as another factor in the creation of national wealth for the purpose of retaining for ourselves part of the profits on our carrying trade that we have in the past been disbursing abroad. In what respect, therefore, would government ships run for the obvious purpose of working on unprofitable service constitute an accession to our wealth? As enunciated, the proposal can only result in increasing the burden of federal taxation at a time when the nation is accumulating a deficit.

However, we are told that the foremost consideration in the government ownership and operation of steamship services is for the national defense, as the ships thus created would be available in time of war as naval auxiliaries. This latter point has a strange sound in such times as these, when we see laid up in our own harbors the naval auxiliaries of a great European power,[1] whose inability to maintain her sea power during the conflict now raging, has set at naught all the preparations made in times of peace for the mobilization of its auxiliaries.

On the other hand, what an object lesson is offered to us by the immense requisitions of shipping made by Great Britain since the war began, for the purpose, not only of transporting men and ammunition to the seat of war, but also for the purpose of keeping up her importations of food for her people! It was not the mail contracts under

---

1   Great European power: Germany, then at war with Britain and France.

which certain ships were to be built to Admiralty specifications that gave Great Britain the million tons, or more, of shipping that she has kept constantly under requisition since the war began, maintaining that auxiliary fleet at the highest point of efficiency by the constant interchange of vessels drawn from the immense mercantile fleets that, in the days of peace, carried her coal and manufactures to all parts of the world, and came back laden with raw materials and foodstuffs. It will always be possible to adapt war necessities to the opportunities afforded by the existence of mercantile fleets existing solely as instruments of trade for the procurement of wealth, but to create fleets of commerce-carriers built primarily as naval auxiliaries according to the ideas of naval and military experts whose notions of what constitutes the proper type of ship suited to war requirements, are about as fixed as those of designers of ladies' hats, is the very worst delusion that can be entertained, and one which may bring disaster upon us in the day of need through the false hope which it fosters.

Questions for Discussion:
1. How does Robert Dollar underscore the efficiency of private enterprise versus government regulation?
2. What concerns does Dollar have about the proposed government ownership of the American merchant fleet?
3. According to Dollar, how do foreign nations cope with their strategic needs for shipping in time of war?

Robert Dollar, "Development of a National Shipping Policy," in *Selected Articles on the American Merchant Marine*, ed. Edith M. Phelps (New York: H. H. Wilson Company, 1920), 176–82.

Wesley L. Jones, "American Ships for Our American Trade" (1920)

In the aftermath of the First World War, for which the federal government built an enormous fleet of merchant vessels to defeat Germany, a debate ensued as to the relationship between the federal government and maritime commerce. Wesley L. Jones (1863–1932) was a powerful Republican senator from Washington state who as chairman of the powerful Appropriations and Commerce Committees promoted a strong merchant marine and protectionist economic policies. His most enduring legacy was the Merchant Marine Act of 1920, often known as the Jones Act. This legislation formally enacted cabotage, a principle stipulating that only American ships could carry cargo between American ports—a move popular with Jones's constituents because it made Alaska dependent on Seattle-based shipping firms. But in a bigger sense, the Jones Act was the first time the federal government committed itself to supporting the merchant marine as a strategic asset in both peace and war. Federal support and often ownership of shipping, and cabotage itself, were examples of the economic nationalism that typified international trade relations in the interwar period—and in fact, cabotage is still a cornerstone of American maritime policy. In this article, Jones outlines his ideas about a viable American merchant marine.

No more important problem confronts the American people than that of our merchant marine. We have a direct financial interest in it to the amount of about three billion dollars, which was appropriated and expended at a time when the emergency of the war created a sudden and urgent need for shipping. We get some idea of the meaning of so vast an expenditure when we realize that it exceeded the book value of all the merchant fleets of the world when the war broke out.

It is taken for granted that every patriotic citizen wishes to see a merchant marine under the American flag large enough to carry such part of the world's trade as may be commensurate with our wealth, power, and standing among the nations.

This country needs such a fleet, not only for its commercial growth, but for defense in time of war and for the stability of domestic industry in time of peace. We do not desire, and it is not our purpose, to drive other nations off the sea, but we do want to, and we ought to do, at least our proportionate part of our own and the world's carrying trade, so that our commerce shall have a fair chance on the world's markets.

In the early part of the present year there will be under our flag twelve million tons of shipping for foreign trade, more than two-thirds of which will be owned by the government and paid for by taxes from the people. How to use this great fleet to the best advantage is the problem that confronts us, and it should be solved as soon as possible. We are going to solve it not in the spirit of destruction, but in the spirit of fair play, and with a determination to secure our just portion of the world's maritime trade.

Of course, the nations that have been doing the ocean carrying trade during the last fifty years are not going to give it up without a struggle. They have the experience, the business facilities, and the connections throughout the world that give them a great advantage. Government aid and power will be coordinated with private energy and initiative to maintain their position, and must be met in the same way.

Nations that depend upon foreign fleets to carry their products and to bring them their supplies are in a position of dependence. The peace of the world is not secure so long as one nation wholly dominates the ocean trade. We do not seek to dominate it, but we do seek to do a just and proper part of it, and especially of our own commerce.

If we cannot attain this end now, we never can do it. No halting, hesitating, doubting policy will succeed. We must take risks. We must encourage our capital and energy to go into this worldwide competition, and assure them that we are behind them to build up and sustain rather than to tear down. With this assurance no one can doubt our success.

We want our merchant marine put on a permanent basis and enabled to expand and develop to meet the additional needs of commerce. It is a new field for us. To a greater or less extent we must experiment as to the means and policies to be followed.

We have a large tonnage now, but this alone does not make a successful merchant marine. Steamship lines must be established, and regular, certain, and permanent services must be secured. Commercial agencies must be organized, and business facilities which we do not now have, but which are necessary to success, must be created.

Our ships have been built in a hurry, and many are not the types best suited to our trade. We have built too many of some kinds, and none of others. The fleet should be properly balanced, and then we should maintain it on a par with our commercial growth and in the highest state of efficiency. Worn-out vessels must be replaced with new ones. Our ship-owners and ship-operators must be placed as nearly as possible on an equality with their competitors in operating costs and operating conditions. Otherwise our fleet will be dissipated and our flag driven from the sea, and we shall again be in the same dependent and humiliating position into which we had fallen before the war.

These general considerations moved Congress to pass the bill which became law June 5, 1920. If its provisions are followed, we shall have the foundations for a policy that will maintain an ample American merchant marine under the American flag and ultimately in private ownership.

The sale and disposition of our government-owned ships is not the only or indeed the most important problem to be met. The most important question, and the most difficult one, is to take care of the future of our merchant marine and make it what it ought to be. Not only must this be kept in view in settling the more immediate question of the disposal of our ships, but we must make permanent provision for their successful operation and maintenance in competition with the world.

The act of June, 1920, lays down for the first time in more than fifty years a broad general policy for the development of an American merchant marine. After signing the act, however, President Wilson declined to carry out some of its most important provisions.

For many years, the United States has been prevented, by restrictions imposed upon it through commercial treaties, from taking steps to build up its own merchant marine. There can be no more opportune time to abrogate these agreements and to make new commercial arrangements, if they are deemed desirable, than the present. France has already notified us of her desire to abrogate her treaty with us, and we should put ourselves in a position where we can do whatever we deem necessary to promote our commercial welfare. We may not desire to go back to the policy of our fathers, under which our ships were the nation's pride, but we ought to be free to do it if we want to.

Congress made provision for this by directing the President to give the notice necessary to abrogate such treaties, and I regard it as a national calamity that the provision was not put promptly into force. There may be provisions in the act that ought not to be there. Experience alone, however, will show them, and then they will be removed. There are many things that should be added, and I hope this will be done.

I know the spirit of those who wrote the bill. Partisanship had no place in its consideration. We acted as Americans. Every word, every line, every paragraph, every section, was written solely in the interest of the United States. We know that other governments will look after their citizens and their needs; and if our own business is to be cared for, we must do the same for ours.

We may differ about government ownership, but that can be no issue here. The government owns these ships, whether we will or no.

They cannot be given away; nor must we allow private parties to take the cream of the fleet, leaving the government to close out the remainder at a great sacrifice. Grant that government ownership should end as soon as may be, the transfer must be brought about without unnecessary sacrifice, and just as a private individual would get rid of property which he did not desire to keep, but which he did not have to dispose of at a sacrifice.

Furthermore, the government is interested in the future success of our shipping and the maintenance of a permanent fleet. That object must be kept in view, and the purpose of recent legislation has been the establishment of a policy under which an adequate merchant marine will be developed and maintained under private ownership and operation. Whenever any of the government's ships can be sold so as to promote this ultimate purpose, they should be sold. If not sold, they should be operated privately, when this can be arranged for on fair terms and in a way to promote the general object in view.

Private interest, incentive, and energy bring the greatest efficiency. Efficiency means success—its absence, failure—in business and enterprise.

No one can reasonably hope, however, that, in the face of foreign competition, and handicapped by our lack of experience and of business connections, private capital will be able to take over all this shipping in a short while and establish the world-wide trade system that we ought to have. To serve our present needs, to establish and maintain new lines, and to develop the markets that we must have, additional ships of special type, size, and speed must be built. They will cost large sums of money. Some may be constructed by private capital, but in my judgment, if we are to have them at all, most of them will have to be built by the government. They can be built without new appropriations, and will help to repay what has already been spent. Along with the ships we also have facilities for doing our own construction. It is economy to use them, even if the additional cost of a ship may be a little more—which I very much doubt.

At Camden, New Jersey, for example, the government has a plant for the building of the largest ships in the world, with ways[1] a thousand feet long. This plant, which cost several millions of dollars, is for

---

1   Ways: the space in a shipyard where the ship is actually built and from which it is launched.

all practical purposes a part of the New York Shipbuilding Company's yard. Unless private interests are ready to buy it and pay a fair price for it, the government ought to keep it and use it for building the ships we ought to have, for the construction of which there are probably no other existing facilities.

To sum up the situation, we may as well admit that we are comparatively inexperienced in financing, building, and operating ships; but we ought to have, for national safety and commercial success, at least fifteen million tons of shipping, to be maintained and increased as trade grows, along with ample ship-building and repair yards.

Under the stress and spur of war needs we spent three billion dollars for the building of a merchant fleet. This work was carried on hastily, wastefully, and inefficiently, and investigating committees have developed the unpleasant facts that everyone familiar with the situation already knew.

We are paying today the cost of following the theory that it was better to depend upon those who would carry our products most cheaply, instead of owning our own transportation facilities. When the world war began, we had only 1,076,152 gross tons of shipping out of nearly fifty million tons engaged in the world's trade. American vessels were only carrying about ten percent of our foreign commerce.

The new law is not perfect, nor is it the last word on the question of our merchant fleet. Constructive changes are always in order and always welcome. It has its defects and its dangers. Waste and extravagance are possible under it; but before it is condemned it should have a fair trial. Our ships must be handled and controlled by human agencies, and therefore mistakes cannot be wholly avoided. But it coordinates private initiative, incentive, and patriotism with government power and responsibility, and I hope it may accomplish the great purpose that we all seek.

A Shipping Board[1] of seven men has been provided for, and on this board rests the responsibility of carrying out the provisions of the law. More power and discretion has been given to it than to any other government agency. Success in carrying out our policies will

---

1   Shipping Board: between 1916 and 1933 the Shipping Board oversaw the promotion and regulation of the merchant marine, including the operation of government-owned steamship lines.

depend largely upon the members of the executive agency entrusted with the power to act. It may be well to place some restrictions upon private interests or activities of members of the board; but we should have men upon it of the highest business character and the widest possible experience, and their interest in shipping should be taken as a recommendation rather than otherwise. We should have men on the Shipping Board who know the shipping business, who can meet those dealing with the board on their own ground, and who can anticipate the moves of our competitors.

Every important section of the country should be represented on this great board, and provision for this is made in the Merchant Marine Act of 1920. Men of standing and experience in shipping, commerce, agriculture, labor, and industry should be upon it, for this board will make or mar our merchant marine.

Questions for Discussion:
1. What does this document reveal about the connections between the federal government and maritime trade?
2. What does this document reveal about international trade in the wake of the First World War?
3. Did Jones exclude any obvious factors in his arguments?

Wesley L. Jones, "American Ships for Our American Trade," *Munsey's Magazine* 72 (February–May, 1921): 215–17.

New York American, "Keep the Dollar at Home" (1927)

The 1920s and 1930s are remembered as a period of isolationism, during which the United States largely turned its back on the international community. This image is not altogether correct, however: the United States actively participated in world affairs, and American businesses sought to expand their markets. Nonetheless, appeals to the American public's nationalism often trumped the temptation to purchase cheaper foreign goods or services, and tariffs such as the Hawley-Smoot Tariff of 1930 were the product of an economic nationalism that emphasized protecting domestic markets and production. The following image was initially printed in the newspaper *The New York American* and later reproduced by the federal government's U.S. Shipping Board to promote the use of American ships.

KEEP THE DOLLAR AT HOME

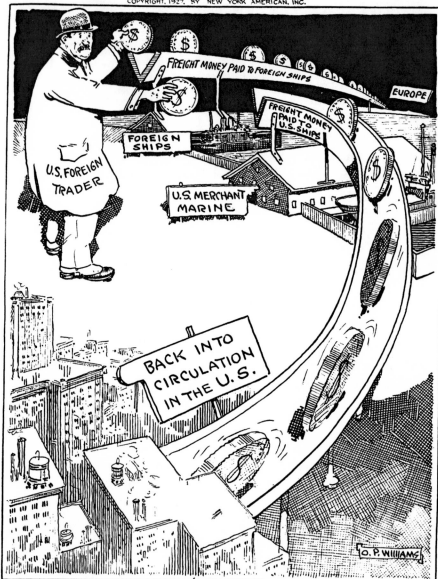

THE AMERICAN DOLLAR SPENT ON OCEAN FREIGHT WILL LAND EITHER ABROAD OR HERE AT HOME. IF IT LANDS ABROAD, IT WILL BENEFIT OUR COMPETITORS. IF IT GOES INTO THE UP-BUILDING OF AN AMERICAN MERCHANT MARINE, IT WILL CIRCULATE AT HOME, BUILDING BUSINESS FOR EVERYBODY. EVEN IN BUSINESS WE NEED MORE LOYALTY TO AMERICA

"Keep the Dollar at Home," 1927. U.S. Shipping Board, *Trade Routes & Shipping Services* (Washington, D.C.: Merchant Fleet Corporation, 1927), 73.

Questions for Discussion:

1. According to this cartoon, how will using U.S.-flagged shipping assist the merchant marine?

2. How could this image be associated with the concept of isolationism?

3. How can this image be associated with the concept of economic nationalism?

_____

U.S. Shipping Board, *Trade Routes & Shipping Services* (Washington, D.C.: Merchant Fleet Corporation, 1927), 73.

Merchant Marine Commission, "The Importance of Shipping" (1937)

The grim years of the Depression proved difficult ones for the American merchant marine. The fleet was aging, the level of professionalism in American crews was low, and profits were slim or nonexistent. President Franklin D. Roosevelt, with an eye toward providing seafaring and shipbuilding jobs for Americans, urged Congress to pass the Merchant Marine Act of 1936. The act completely reformed American shipping by providing generous government subsidies through the new U.S. Merchant Marine Commission directed by Joseph P. Kennedy Sr. (1888–1969), father of future president John F. Kennedy. Kennedy moved quickly to reform the merchant marine, producing a powerful pamphlet entitled *An Economic Survey of the American Merchant Marine*. That pamphlet, reproduced in part below, asked tough questions about the viability of American shipping and concluded that government subsidies could only be justified on two grounds: developing foreign commerce and national defense.

The principal arguments advanced in behalf of shipping, so far as they concern foreign trade, are these:

1. Ships subject to our own control are necessary to insure continued delivery of our goods, both exports and imports.
2. American vessels protect our traders against exorbitant rates.
3. American vessels in a trade tend to improve the service given to our exporters and importers.
4. Domestic-flag competition prevents discrimination against our goods by foreign vessels.

Of these arguments, two appear to have sufficient validity to be worthy of inclusion in a fact-finding report. These are the statements which relate to the continuity and quality of service. The others are either undemonstrable or seemingly at variance with the facts. Nevertheless, the survey indicates that we are justified in concluding that an American merchant marine is of material value in the development of our foreign commerce.

Continuity of service.—The principal advantage which accrues to our foreign commerce from the possession of a domestic-flag marine is that it provides a measure of insurance against possible interruption of service. For more than half a century, prior to the World War, the bulk of our exports and imports was carried by foreign vessels. Several times during that period we were deprived of a considerable part of the foreign fleet which customarily served our trade. In the present unsettled condition of international affairs the United States should avoid undue dependence upon foreign carriers likely to be withdrawn at a moment's notice.

In the event of war, even with the United States remaining neutral, dependence on foreign ships would place our overseas trade at the mercy of other nations. During the World War the withdrawal of alien vessels resulted in a serious dislocation of our foreign trade at a time when we enjoyed an unprecedented opportunity to expand our business with other nations. Total world tonnage was reduced by the destruction of vessels, idleness of the tonnage of the Central Powers, and the use of ships for military purposes by the Allies. American overseas trade was further affected by the diversion of tonnage to the imperative commercial needs of other countries.

The most serious reduction in foreign-flag tonnage occurred in trade routes far removed from the war zone. Direct trade with the Allies was maintained and even improved since these nations looked to the United States for increased supplies. It was necessary, however, for the United States to secure foreign vessels, to recondition old vessels and build new ones, to divert coastwise steamers to overseas trade routes, and to press into service sailing ships and antiquated steamers in order to provide service to foreign markets.

Today we are faced with the threat of a recurrence of the conditions of the last war. Political uncertainty and international tension are on the increase. If the present antagonisms should result in war, we would be confronted again with the problems which beset our commerce in 1914. The disruption of our trade probably would be much greater in the future as a larger percentage of our trade is now being transacted with nations not having their own shipping facilities.

For these reasons it is important that we maintain a merchant marine of some proportions in the international carrying trades.

Rates.—Proponents of a strong merchant-marine policy regard American vessels as a form of protection against exorbitant rates, both in time of peace and during periods of international stress. We find that there is little evidence to support this view. Rates in general seem to have been little affected by the establishment of American lines, although there have undoubtedly been considerable savings to our shippers as a result of direct routing and the elimination of transshipments. American lines commonly join the conferences set up in their respective trades. Shippers have complained that our lines, insofar as they have any influence at all in the conferences, are more likely to stand for higher than for lower rates. Even if our lines were dedicated to the reduction of rates, they could be outvoted in the various conferences where foreign lines predominate.

The whole situation has been obscured by the excessive shipping tonnage available since the war, which has kept ocean-freight rates extremely low. This condition is rapidly disappearing now as international trade expands and as laid-up tonnage is either scrapped or restored to active service. Rates are determined by the law of supply and demand, and are ordinarily the highest the lines can get. They will be "exorbitant" whenever the demand for shipping space increases out of proportion to the vessels available. . . .

Quality of service.—The statement is frequently made that American vessels in a trade tend to improve the service available to our exporters and importers. We find this to be a fact. American shippers, in order to compete successfully, require direct, speedy, and reliable service to their markets abroad. Our experience before the war, when American vessels carried but 10 percent of our foreign commerce, demonstrated only too well the disadvantage of having to depend on foreign shipping service.

Sailings, as a rule, were slow and infrequent, especially to non-European countries. In many cases there was no direct service available between our ports and the ports of other nations, so that goods had to be transshipped. This resulted in many delays, especially when vessels for the final leg of the voyage were not at hand. Indeed, for many years merchandise bound for the east coast of South America actually had to be shipped by way of Europe, although this was later remedied. Only on the North Atlantic run, and to some, extent in the Caribbean, were shipping facilities at all adequate to our needs. Elsewhere, the American exporter labored under a serious competitive handicap.

The development of an American merchant marine after the war greatly improved the service enjoyed by our exporters and importers, and undoubtedly facilitated the striking increase in our foreign trade during this period. In 1914 there were only 19 American-flag services operating to foreign countries and American overseas possessions. In 1930 there were 83 such services. By 1936 the number had fallen to 58, due to consolidations and the abandonment of some lines during the depression, but the service they offered remained materially superior to that available before the war.

The outstanding benefit to the Nation's foreign trade came from the establishment of regular line service in the long-voyage, overseas trade routes which before the war were handicapped by indirect transshipment services, insufficient sailings, inferior vessels, lack of regularity and the concentration of lines at too few American ports. The combined American and foreign line services have now been vastly improved. In several instances the improvement was due entirely to the establishment of regular American line services; in other instances regular services were established by both American and foreign lines. The operation of American lines has made transshipment generally unnecessary. Foreign lines have been forced to establish direct services, and to improve services which were obviously inferior to those enjoyed by rival European exporters.

While part of the improvement in the services would doubtless remain even if existing American lines were replaced by foreign lines, such a situation would again place our traders at a disadvantage. Dependence on foreign lines usually means dependence on lines that are primarily interested in the trade of their own countries. Their services out of American ports are likely to be less certain and permanent, and for the most part inferior to those offered their shippers at home.

Discrimination.—An argument often advanced to support the maintenance of an American merchant marine is the possibility of discrimination against our goods on the part of foreign lines. Despite recurring charges, there is little in the record to substantiate this attitude. Shipping is so highly competitive, and there are so many services available under different flags, that the individual operator can hardly afford to practice outright discrimination against a customer. It is not believed that discrimination is practiced to any appreciable extent today. However, the trend toward nationalized shipping may increase the potentialities of discrimination in the future—a consideration that should not be ignored. In any event, the existence of a domestic-flag fleet gives us a weapon to be used if and when discrimination occurs.

Balance of payments.—There has been a great deal of discussion in connection with the merchant-marine problem about the effect of shipping on the balance of international payments. Merchant marine enthusiasts maintain that money spent for American shipping services is money kept at home, with consequent benefits to American labor, management, and capital. Economists declare, on the other hand, that ship services are a form of export, and that whatever we spend in this way tends to reduce the purchasing power of other nations and may, therefore, diminish exports of some other form. It may, of course, also result in increased imports.

The principal objection to subsidies, of course, is that they tend to misdirect capital and labor into uneconomic channels. . . .

Even more important, perhaps, than its role in the development of commerce is the vital relationship that exists between the merchant marine and national defense. Many authorities regard the latter consideration as the more important of the two, a view which is supported by the fact that national defense is placed ahead of trade as an objective of the Merchant Marine Acts of 1920, 1928, and 1936. It is obvious that national defense is an important, if not the primary, justification for the maintenance of American vessels in foreign trade.

The Commission has had the collaboration of all of the defense agencies of the Government in the preparation of this survey. Although, for obvious reasons, it would not be advisable to divulge the Nation's plans for defense, it is possible to indicate in a rough way our probable shipping requirements should we be so unfortunate as to become involved in a war. These requirements place the merchant service in a position second only to that of the armed forces in the maintenance of an adequate defense establishment.

The Commission believes that, although the United States has renounced war as an instrument of national policy, and although our national policies do not contemplate the sending of expeditionary forces abroad, nevertheless it would be well to be prepared for any contingency, including the contingency of fighting away from our own shores. The policy of the American people has been traditionally a policy of peace. We have not sought, nor do we seek, trouble with any nation. The foreign policy of the United States for the past few years is striking proof of our desire to avoid conflict. Nevertheless, when the United States has been embroiled in war, we have invariably turned to offense as the best means of defense. The same would undoubtedly be true again were we to be forced into another conflict.

The merchant marine is an essential part of naval operations. The United States, with 60 harbors and 7,000 miles of coastline, is peculiarly dependent upon the Navy for defense. Although various claims have been made concerning the percentage of naval strength attributable to commercial vessels, the determination of such percentage is believed to be an impossible and unnecessary task. The question of relative importance, it might be said, is about on a par with endeavoring to determine the comparative value of the lungs and the heart to a human being. For the purposes of this study it is only necessary to state that a large volume of merchant tonnage is necessary to the effective functioning of the armed forces of the Nation in time of trouble.

Over-all requirements.—Careful study of all possible contingencies indicates that the military forces would require, in the event of war with a major power, a minimum of 1,000 merchant ships of all types, aggregating about 6,000,000 gross tons. These vessels would be required in the early stages of a conflict for technical military purposes, and represent but a fraction of the number that would ultimately be necessary in case of prolonged hostilities.

We now have available under the American flag some 1,400 seagoing vessels of 2,000 gross tons or more. Approximately 400 of these vessels are engaged in foreign trade; 800, including 300 tankers, are in the coastwise trade; approximately 200 are in lay-up. It will thus be seen that the thousand vessels considered necessary for minimum military requirements are at present available, although the majority of the ships are old and slow and some do not meet technical requirements with regard to size.

In view of the foregoing figures, it might be argued that the United States should maintain a much larger merchant marine than that now in existence. The Commission has given earnest consideration to this viewpoint. We have been given to understand that the present fleet, if rejuvenated through an orderly replacement program, will meet the principal needs of our defense agencies. It is not believed, however, that we should permit the ocean-going fleet to fall much below its present size, even though, through consolidations and replacements, the efficiency of the various lines is increased.

It has been suggested that the Commission maintain a pool of 200 laid-up vessels for possible use in an emergency. These vessels would prove extremely valuable if foreign carriers, for any reason, should be withdrawn from our trades. This was the case in 1926, when British vessels were tied up by a coal strike. The United States Shipping Board took 100 vessels from lay-up, placed them in various trade routes, and, it has been claimed, increased the national income several hundred million dollars by moving goods which otherwise could not have been exported. The Commission believes that such a pool of vessels should be maintained and has taken steps to keep the present laid-up fleet intact. There are now 113 vessels in this fleet, practically all of which are considered to have sufficient value for commercial and military purposes to warrant their further preservation. These vessels will be kept for an indefinite period, thus giving us a reserve for possible use in time of emergency. Keeping this laid-up fleet off the market will also remove one deterrent to new construction on the part of private operators.

Technical requirements.—Merchant vessels serve the armed forces in many ways. Combination passenger and cargo vessels can be converted into aircraft carriers. Ships to be suitable for this conversion should be capable of supporting a flight deck 600 feet long by 60 feet wide, with an absolute minimum length of 500 feet. These vessels should be capable of 20 knots or better, with a minimum of 18 knots. There are at present 10 such vessels in the United States merchant marine, some of which meet only the minimum requirements. Military authorities believe that there should be at least 20 of these vessels available.

The combination vessels could also be used as auxiliary cruisers. Vessels for this purpose should have a speed of not less than 20 knots, preferably much more, and they should have a large cruising radius. The only vessels under the American flag suitable for such conversion are those already mentioned as possible aircraft carriers.

There is an additional need for troop transports which should have a speed of at least 16½ knots and should be capable of carrying a minimum of 2,000 men and their equipment. This same type of vessel is also suitable for conversion into hospital ships and tenders of various class. There are not sufficient ships of this type under the American flag to meet possible requirements. For that reason it would be necessary, if trouble arose, to utilize vessels of less desirable characteristics for many of the tender conversions.

The American merchant marine is deficient in tankers capable of accompanying the fleet. The Secretary of the Navy has indicated a need for at least 20 such vessels. The Navy would require, for a maximum military effort, a total of some 300 tankers of various types and speeds. The present tanker fleet is considered adequate except for the high-speed vessels mentioned above.

The backbone of any over-water military operation is the general supply or cargo vessel. Although some of these vessels may accompany the fleet, the majority move in convoys or, if the exigencies of the situation permit, by themselves. Inasmuch as the speed of the convoy is limited to that of the slower vessels, which constitute the bulk of the American fleet, there is little justification from the military standpoint for the construction of a large number of fast cargo vessels at this time. Building such vessels would work an economic hardship upon the merchant marine without any great compensating benefits.

It should be recognized, in any consideration of the merchant marine problem, that the dual functions of subsidized shipping—trade and defense—are essentially contradictory. Many of the requirements of defense, such as excessive speed and additional bulkheads, may add to the costs of vessel operation or reduce the effectiveness of the vessel as a commercial carrier, or both. Some of the vessels, considered essential from a military standpoint, may prove to have little or no economic justification. Thus it can be seen that the problem of maintaining an "adequate" merchant marine involves the reconciliation of two vastly different and sometimes antagonistic sets of requirements.

As will be seen from the foregoing, the American merchant marine in its various categories contains most of the vessels considered by defense agencies as the minimum required for an initial military effort. The value of the vessels is greatly reduced, however, by their advanced degree of obsolescence. We are dangerously deficient in the matter of speed, especially with regard to tankers and a small number of cargo vessels capable of accompanying the fleet. Although it is difficult to cite the exact number of each type of vessel that would be required to meet a given situation, it appears that the defense needs of the United States dictate the replacement of the bulk of the present fleet, and that such replacement should include at least 10 combination passenger and cargo vessels, approximately 20 high-speed tankers, and a small number of fast cargo vessels.

The Commission, in conference with the Navy Department, has attempted to differentiate between (a) auxiliaries which accompany the fleet and (b) auxiliaries which need not accompany the fleet. The speed for vessels in the first category is 16½ knots; the speed for the others is 12 knots and upward, as may be found practicable from an economic point of view. The most pressing need for fast vessels is in the tanker field, as the fuel requirements of combatant vessels are far greater than the requirements for other supplies. Combatant vessels generally carry cargo supplies sufficient for 90 days; they can carry fuel for perhaps a third of this period. Therefore, for naval use, tenders, tankers, and the like require the 16½-knot speed, but general supply vessels do not.

The Commission accordingly is negotiating for the installation in new tankers of engines capable of developing a speed of 16½ knots. Inasmuch as there is no economic justification for such speed, it will be necessary for the Government to reimburse the private operator for the increased cost of such installation.

With regard to cargo vessels, the Commission has developed a standardized design for a vessel of 8,800 deadweight tons with a speed, fully loaded, of 15 to 15½ knots. This vessel is considered extremely practical from the standpoint of both trade and defense. Cargo vessels converted to tender use are rarely loaded beyond 50 percent of capacity on a weight basis. So loaded, the Commission's proposed cargo vessel would be able to travel with the fleet. The Commission also has under consideration a design for cargo vessels of a higher speed.

War materials.—In addition to technical military functions, merchant vessels must also serve the demands of commerce in time of war. Enormous quantities of raw materials, many of them vital to the operation of American industries, must be brought in from foreign sources of supply. Other imports should be continued as far as possible in order to avoid disruption of the domestic market and discomfort to the civilian population. To pay for imports, and to preserve our position in foreign markets, it is also necessary to carry on a large export trade.

All of these considerations make it expedient for the United States to maintain a sizable merchant marine in the international carrying trades.

Questions for Discussion:
1. How did the authors of this report see the importance of shipping to the American economy in the 1930s?
2. What was the perceived relationship between the Navy and merchant shipping?
3. How does this report anticipate and recommend changes for future conflicts?

U.S. Maritime Commission, *Economic Survey of the American Merchant Marine* (Washington, D.C.: Government Printing Office, 1937), 5–13.

INTERWAR ISSUES OF RACE AND LABOR

After the First World War, two of the greatest issues facing American society were race and labor relations. For African Americans returning from the Great War, the continuing and even growing racism they faced was a huge disappointment and many turned to the radical vision of Marcus Garvey and the Universal Negro Improvement Association (UNIA), with its "Africa for the Africans" message. The most interesting of Garvey's ideas was setting up industries run by and for those of African descent, including the Black Star Line of steamships. But as Theodore Kornweibel has demonstrated in *Seeing Red*, the federal government stepped in to quash Garvey, whom it considered an "undesirable, and indeed a very dangerous, alien."[1]

The other issue was organized labor. Since the 1870s, organized labor had clashed repeatedly with big business, which often made use of the police to suppress labor unrest. The economically and politically powerful denied the right of labor to organize, collectively bargain, or strike. Many middle-class Americans associated such activities with communism, while for blue-collar workers they were simply attempts to gain decent working

---

1   Theodore Kornweibel, *Seeing Red: Federal Campaigns against Black Militancy, 1919–1925* (Bloomington: Indiana University Press, 1998).

conditions and pay. Industrialists consistently articulated the idea that labor was secondary to capital in the productive process—labor was cheap and replaceable, wages were necessarily low—in order to discipline the workforce. The shipping industry proved especially outspoken in its opposition to labor unions, using ancient laws that defined any labor action as mutiny. *Industrial warfare* is a term used by labor historians to describe the fierce and often bloody struggle between big business and labor movements.

With the stock market crash and the Depression devastating the country's economy, the situation only became worse. Increasingly desperate dockworkers and merchant mariners finally took to the streets of San Francisco in the summer of 1934. Scholars such as Bruce Nelson, in his important labor history *Workers on the Waterfront*,[1] have identified San Francisco's maritime strike of 1934 as a crucial moment in labor history, when labor unions took a strong stand against corporations. Hired thugs, paid informants, police—even the National Guard—were used to suppress union activity, with casualties on both sides. While the unions increasingly grew in power, many strident critics remained, and the public remained divided about the usefulness of organized labor. All in all, it was a tough time to be a mariner, and the term *industrial warfare* seems to be an apt one.

Marcus Garvey, "The Black Star Line" (1920)

Marcus Garvey (1887–1940) was the controversial leader of the back-to-Africa movement, of which the Black Star Line of steamships was supposed to be an important part. Garvey intended that the Black Star Line be an entirely black-owned and -operated steamship company, not only providing employment and generating wealth for the black community, but also connecting black communities in America, the Caribbean, and Africa. In the 1920s, when discrimination and violence against African Americans was rampant, it seemed an attractive idea to many. The venture failed, and a debate still continues as to why. Arguments range from Garvey's incompetence as a businessman to actual corruption on his part to a conspiracy by the federal government to undermine his efforts. The following is a brochure produced late in the short life of the Black Star Line, when the enterprise was already faltering and Garvey was under federal investigation for defrauding the shareholders of his steamship company.

---

1   Bruce Nelson, *Workers on the Waterfront: Seamen, Longshoremen and Unionism in the 1930s* (Champaign: University of Illinois Press, 1988).

AN APPEAL
To the Colored People of New York by
THE BLACK STAR LINE STEAMSHIP
CORP.
56 West 135th Street New York, N. Y.

——

Today We expect Every Negro To Do His Duty! ! !
Men and Women of New York
AWAKE!   AWAKE!   AWAKE!

——

A MESSAGE FOR YOU!

TO THE NEGRO CITIZENS OF THE STATE OF NEW YORK:

The time has come when every colored man and woman in this State as well as in other parts of the Nation must realize the seriousness of the time in which we live. A great industrial change is about to take place which will affect the Negro, and the best thing for the race to do is to prepare itself for the reaction.

INDUSTRIAL EMANCIPATION

THE UNIVERSAL NEGRO IMPROVEMENT ASSOCIATION has mapped out a program for the industrial emancipation of the race and is now concentrating its efforts on the building up of a great industrial commonwealth in the Republic of Liberia, West Africa, and at the same time to start out an active campaign for the establishment of central factories in the State of New York.

MINERALS AND RAW MATERIALS

It is planned to remove from Africa, South America and the West Indies minerals and raw materials and send them to these United States of America aboard the ships of the BLACK STAR LINE to be turned into marketable commodities.

ESTABLISH FACTORIES

The factories that the UNIVERSAL NEGRO IMPROVEMENT ASSOCIATION through the NEGRO FACTORIES CORPORATION, expect to establish in New York will employ hundreds and probably thousands of helpers so as to cope with the demand that will be made for the products. The first thing, therefore, to be contemplated is the financial support of the entire colored population of New York for these projects.

BIGGER SHIPS

Hence, an appeal is here directly made to each and every one to support the BLACK STAR LINE STEAMSHIP CORPORATION so as to render the company able to purchase bigger ships and place them on the African-American-South American route. This corporation desires to run a regular service between New York and Monrovia, Liberia; but the sum of $250,000 is required immediately to meet the demand of purchasing new ships and repairing for good working order those already in service. It is imperative that the support be given immediately.

SUBSCRIBE FOR SHARES

We are asking each and every colored man and woman in the State to subscribe for 5, 10, 20, 50, 100, 200 shares at $5.00 each in the BLACK STAR LINE STEAMSHIP CORPORATION.

Write or call at office of BLACK STAR LINE, INC.

54–56 West 135th St., New York, N. Y.

HELP YOURSELF!

What is the use of complaining about non-employment? What effort have you made to employ yourself? Negroes have always expected others to do for them what they ought to do for themselves. HENCE, the UNIVERSAL NEGRO IMPROVEMENT ASSOCIATION is teaching a lesson of self-help to all the Negroes in the State of New York and throughout the United States of America and the West Indies.

SUPPORT NEGRO CORPORATIONS

If you desire to work in factories, you must build and support your own factories. If you desire to work in offices, you must support your own corporations which will maintain the offices to employ you. These are facts that rule the industrial and commercial life of all people and the Negro should be no exception.

SUPPORT YOUR OWN INDUSTRIES

Owing to the bankrupt state of the world, every race and every people is making effort to conserve its own energy and support its own industries. The Negro, if he is alive to the seriousness of the situation, will now make a desperate effort to place himself in the great commercial and industrial world.

EMPLOY THOUSANDS OF NEGROES

Hence, the UNIVERSAL NEGRO IMPROVEMENT ASSOCIATION has started a campaign to educate the Negroes of the State of New York to the fact that they must get behind industries of their own, finance them, put them on a sound financial basis and thus render them able to employ the hundreds and thousands who are now without employment.

NEGROES MUST PROVIDE FOR NEGROES

Negroes must provide for Negroes; otherwise, there is going to be a great economic stagnation among the race.

The UNIVERSAL NEGRO IMPROVEMENT ASSOCIATION has started its plan of conveying the raw materials from Africa to the United States of America to be manufactured into marketable commodities, for the carrying out of which plan factories have to be built in Harlem and other districts in New York.

But we have to convey the raw materials; and for that purpose the BLACK STAR LINE STEAMSHIP CORPORATION desires to float more and bigger ships for the African-American trade. The Corporation, therefore, asks each and every colored man and woman in the State of New York who can afford to buy shares to do so now.

WILL NEGROES SUBSCRIBE $10,000,000?

$250,000 must be raised in the next thirty days to place another ship on the African route. If all the colored people will but make up in their minds to support this corporation, in another three months its capital of $10,000,000 will be subscribed and we will have at our command twenty ships capable of conveying Negroes from America to Africa, of stimulating the industries of Africa and of conveying the raw materials from Africa to the United States of America for Negroes here to utilize in factories and mills and therefore keep themselves employed.

GO DIRECT TO OFFICE OF BLACK STAR LINE

No serious-minded colored man or woman will stop to argue that now is not the time to give whole-hearted support to the plans of the UNIVERSAL NEGRO IMPROVEMENT ASSOCIATION and the business plans of the BLACK STAR LINE. As you read this circular, therefore, go direct to the office of the BLACK STAR LINE, 56 West 135th St., New York, N.Y., and buy your shares. Buy 5, 10, 15, 20, 30, 50, 100, 200 shares at $5.00 each and help to lay the foundation of your own economic future.

With the necessary tonnage of ships trading between the United States and Africa regularly, the untold wealth of Africa will be exploited, which will make it possible for the shareholders of the BLACK STAR LINE to reap large profits in the near future. Why not help one great Negro Corporation to succeed. Instead of having little corporations here and there, all striving to make success, why not make one great effort of the race to make one big corporation that will be able to lend support and protection to the entire fifteen millions in the country?

Call at the Office of the BLACK STAR LINE, INC., 56 West 135th Street, New York, N.Y., and buy your shares.

CRITICISM IS CHEAP & CANNOT FEED HUNGRY MEN

Many Negroes in New York have criticized the BLACK STAR LINE STEAMSHIP CORPORATION; yet it is the only corporation of importance in the country that has been able to withstand the criticism of the entire world, which proves a strong and capable business management behind the corporation. The BLACK STAR LINE is so firmly established in its determination to succeed that all the critics have become disappointed in seeing the Corporation growing stronger and stronger every day. Yet through the criticisms that have been leveled against the BLACK STAR LINE, a large number of Negroes in the State did not perform their duty in supporting the Corporation by buying shares. Through this negligence on their part, the entire race is made to suffer at this time of industrial stagnation. What have the critics done to help find employment for the Negroes of New York?—Absolutely nothing. But if the people during these years had helped to subscribe their shares to the BLACK STAR LINE and its $10,000,000 of capital had been raised, today the BLACK STAR LINE would have at least twenty ships on the ocean trading between the United States and Africa and the West Indies and South and Central America, bringing in precious cargoes and the rich minerals of Africa to the United States, to the factories that would have been established and which would have employed today the thousands and thousands who are unemployed.

We think that it is a great lesson to the Negro people of New York to understand that the critics do not help them, but rather that they only tend to dishearten and discourage the race. Criticism cannot feed a man. Some man who gets up and writes an article in the newspaper against some corporation or some movement that is endeavoring to do good for the people, cannot help to find bread for the people when they are out of work. But such corporations, if well started and supported, can give employment to hundreds and thousands and relieve any economic situation. This lesson ought to be taken seriously to heart by every Negro in Harlem and other parts of the State of New York.

NEGROES SHOULD STOP BEING CHILDISH

NEGROES should stop being childish in their attitude towards their own success. Stop criticizing and do some constructive work, such as is being done by the BLACK STAR LINE STEAMSHIP COR-PORATION. This Corporation needs more ships. Its capital must be fully subscribed; and before things come to the worst, we are asking every Negro in the State and in the districts of Harlem and Brooklyn to rush to the office of the corporation immediately and buy more shares, so that more ships can be launched upon the seas.

Help subscribe the entire capital of $10,000,000, if possible, within the next few months by buying 5, 10, 15, 20, 30, 50, 100, and 200 shares at $5.00 each. The BLACK STAR LINE Office is open from 9:00 a.m. to 6:30 p.m. If you can't call in person, address your communication to the BLACK STAR LINE STEAMSHIP CORPORATION, 56 West 135th St., New York, N.Y., or call at Liberty Hall, 120 West 138th St., any night at 8:00 o'clock.

BUY YOUR SHARES NOW!

Questions for Discussion:
1. What does this document reveal about the hopes and aspirations of African Americans in 1920?
2. What charges does Garvey level at the critics of the Black Star Line?
3. How does the Black Star Line fit into Garvey's bigger plans for the Universal Negro Improvement Association?

United States, Circuit Court of Appeals for the Second Circuit, Transcript and Record: *Marcus Garvey v. United States* 4: 2564–71.

San Francisco Daily News, "Trouble at the Embarcadero" (1934)

Union victory in the 1934 maritime strike in San Francisco came at a cost. Numerous clashes between union members and the city's police force compelled California's governor to call in the National Guard to assist the police. Labor historian David Selvin, in *A Terrible Anger*,[1] captures the spirit

1   David F. Selvin, *A Terrible Anger: The 1934 Waterfront and General Strikes in San Francisco* (Detroit: Wayne State University Press, 1996).

of the times, contending that one of the reasons the strike was a success was that labor leaders restrained their use of violence, thereby making their opponents look bad, especially after police shot and killed two strikers.

The dock section of that city, known by the Spanish name *Embarcadero*, was the scene of most of the violence. This article from the *San Francisco Daily News* of July 6, 1934, captures some of the tension felt in a waterfront that seemed ready to explode into violence. While there was some violence and even loss of life in melees between union activists and police, eventually the shipowners backed down and gave the dockworkers better pay and working conditions. It was an important victory that encouraged more union activism in the years that followed, including the formation of the powerful California-based International Longshoremen's and Warehousemen's Union (ILWU) in 1937. Leading the strike and later the ILWU was Harry Bridges (1901–1990), the dynamic Australian-born labor leader who made his union one of the strongest in the nation.

Martial law reigned on the waterfront today. Under muzzles of machine guns manned by the National Guard, the Industrial Association and the Belt Line Railway resumed the movement of cargo from strike-crippled piers.

The laws of war automatically went into effect when the militia took possession of the Embarcadero in the wake of Gov. Frank Merriam's[1] proclamation of tumults and riots in the city, Atty. Gen. U.S. Webb rules.

The entire city may be put under martial law, if strike disturbances intensify, the attorney general declared.

So efficient was the protection afforded by guardsmen that the Industrial Association opened a second warehouse for the storage of goods moved from Pier 38.

An odd, and perhaps ominous change in the strikers' tactics became increasingly evident on the scene of yesterday's battles. Quiet prevailed and squadrons of strikers themselves were moving among groups of men ordering them to disperse. "General strike!" was whispered. Strikers, held in check by police and troops, were hoping to be able to wield their last and perhaps most effective weapon to enforce their demands.

---

1 Merriam: Frank Merriam (1865–1955), Republican governor of California from 1934–1939.

Chief Quinn[1] also ordered his men to round up all Communists engaged in distributing subversive literature.

And Gov. Merriam, in calling out the militia, had said that while his proclamation actually embraced the entire city, the National Guard would continue themselves to protect state property along the Embarcadero.

However, when the first truck left Pier 38, a squad of soldiers was patrolling Third st. between King and Berry sts., a machine gun was set up near a pile of bricks which furnished rioters with ammunition Tuesday, another machine gun was posted at King and the Embarcadero and three more machine guns were on the second floor ramp of the state terminal which runs from the Embarcadero to Third and Berry sts. These guns had a full range of the warehouse and adjoining streets.

Machine guns were also located in front of the Matson docks,[2] each manned by a crew of four. On the roofs of Piers 34, 36 and 40 were expert riflemen, posted to keep a watch for snipers.

The consensus among National Guard officers was that for the present the Guard will devote itself to protection of state property. This includes Third and Townsend sts., because the Belt Line tracks run there. Troops on the waterfront were augmented by 390 additional guardsmen, including 250 men of the 184th Infantry from Santa Rosa, Petaluma and Napa and 140 men of the same regiment from San Jose. These additions brought the total militia command on duty here to nearly 2400.

Maj.-Gen. David P. Barrows,[3] commander of the guard, arrived on the waterfront from his Berkeley home and consulted with Col. R. E. Mittelsteadt, commander of the guardsmen. Asked what the guard would do if strikers hurled rocks at the troops across the Embarcadero

---

1   Quinn: Chief of Police William J. Quinn (1883–1963), a major reformer of the San Francisco Police Department, was himself wounded when a rock hit him in the head during this strike.

2   Matson docks: Matson Navigation Company has provided most of the ocean transportation between California and Hawaii from the early twentieth century to the present.

3   Barrows: David P. Barrows (1873–1954), a well-known professor and former president of the University of California who commanded the California National Guard until 1937.

deadline, both men smiled and replied: "We're here to preserve order. Our men, however, will not stand for injury of any kind, even verbal."

Col. Mittelsteadt said that "while this is new to us we have assured Chief Quinn 100 per cent co-operation." "We mean business," the colonel added. "We now have a total of 2000 men on duty on the waterfront and should circumstances necessitate additional men, we have sufficient men in Oakland to bring over here at a moment's notice."

Every pier along the entire Embarcadero had its quota of guardsmen this morning, about 15 men to a pier. Inside the dock houses were their cots, mounted machine guns and a consignment of the dread vomit gas. Outside, 10 men stood ready for duty. Five others were on sentry, maintaining contact with sentries on adjoining piers.

The guardsmen meant business. They had orders, they said, to challenge everyone at 50 feet, to shoot if the challenged one failed to halt. Persons with credentials were able to be allowed to pass, all others were to be ordered off the waterfront.

The National Guard took over the waterfront with perfect military precision.

A campfire glowed beside the railroad tracks, flashing its light on steel bayonets. Neat little, deadly little machine guns peeked out over the sides of bullet-proof trucks. War!

It was war for those picketing longshoremen who sat about the fire near the Belt Line Railroad and watched the California National Guard move onto the waterfront. It was war for those grim faced, nervous boys who had been called to strike duty from their schools, office work and play to protect life and property in San Francisco. It was war, too, for veterans of other campaigns, men who had gone through the World War and had seen action many times. Late at night they moved onto the waterfront and took their posts. There they will eat and sleep for "duration." It was war as the call was flashed out over specially installed telephones from the State Armory at 14th and Mission sts. to the men of the 250th Coast Artillery to report for duty. All during the afternoon they gathered, were issued equipment, full packs with blankets, mess kits—and steel helmets, rifles and bayonets. "Any man who fires a shot into the air will be court-martialed. Shoot to hit!" That was the grim order issued by Col. Mittelsteadt. He declared the guardsmen were not under orders to "shoot to kill," but, on the other hand, they are not to fire in hope of merely frightening their opponents.

Supplementing his order was this from Capt. Bedford W. Boyes, plans and training officer in charge of placing the guard units: "We want strikers to realize that we are soldiers and not policemen. We do not intend to engage in hand-to-hand combat. We are not going to hit anyone on the head with clubs because we are not equipped with them." Neither will the guard use gas, he declared, police experience having proved gas an unreliable weapon due to strong winds that sweep the waterfront. He admitted, however, that troopers were equipped with nauseating and tear gas. On the other hand, a marked lack of gas masks to protect the guard from the fumes was noticed at the Armory as equipment was being issued. Officers were reluctant to comment, but it was learned that sufficient masks were not available.

A post command previously had been set up at the Ferry Building. Delay in starting to the waterfront was attributed to slowness of lunch boxes to arrive at the Armory. Many of the boys flopped on the floor, against gun carriages or on their bedrolls and went to sleep in the chill air.

Col. Mittelsteadt made it clear that wartime conditions existed, that his men are equipped with rifles, bayonets and machine guns and that the Embarcadero will not be a safe place "for persons whose reasons for being there are not sufficient to run the risk of serious injury." Chief Quinn echoed that sentiment when he made a new appeal to citizens to keep away from the waterfront. But a good many policemen, from the chief down, resented the presence of the citizen-soldiers. "We have the situation in hand and I'm afraid the National Guard coming in will result in much bloodshed and many deaths," said Chief Quinn. "In a situation like this, the National Guard sets a deadline and then shoots anyone who crosses it. The strikers don't understand these kind of orders and are quite likely to barge across deadlines. And rifles are being put in the hands of inexperienced men. Then we'll have to deal with the strikers, and the mere presence of those soldiers on the waterfront may make it all the tougher for us." Chief Quinn and little, dynamic Theodore Roche, president of the Police Commission, were in active command during the peak of yesterday's rioting. Both escaped injury by inches when strikers hurled bricks at their cars. Both planned to be in the center of things again today, if any trouble developed.

Questions for Discussion:

1. Does this newspaper article show any bias for or against the maritime workers?

2. How does this newspaper article reflect the idea of industrial warfare?

3. What doubts did the San Francisco Police Department have about National Guard intervention?

"Martial Law Rules Docks," *San Francisco Daily News*, July 6, 1934. Courtesy of the Virtual Museum of the City of San Francisco, http://www.sfmuseum.org/.

Joseph B. Weaver, "The Problem of Seagoing Labor" (1937)

In October, 1937, Joseph B. Weaver, an affluent businessman and former director of the U.S. Bureau of Marine Inspection and Navigation, made this fiery anti-union speech before the Propeller Club, an organization dedicated to promoting the American Navy and merchant marine. President Roosevelt appointed him the director of the Bureau of Navigation and Steamboat Inspection to improve safety at sea after the *Morro Castle* fire of 1934, but Weaver resigned after two years on the job, apparently over disagreements with the Roosevelt administration on labor policies. In this piece, Weaver gives his views on the problems associated with the recently invigorated labor movement in the maritime industry. The views he expresses were fairly typical of middle-class Americans in the 1930s, many of whom viewed labor unions with undisguised suspicion.

Our vessels are a year older. No new tonnage, with the exception of tankers, has been constructed. The labor situation has progressed from bad to worse. Since that time the disastrous West Coast strike has occurred. Since that time discipline has ceased to exist on our ships. It is not necessary to deal in detail with the innumerable instances of insubordination, incipient mutiny, and violence; but in looking over various occurrences that daily are brought to the attention of all of us, one is forced to the conclusion that these are not "irresponsible acts" of Secretary Perkins's "bad boys," but that the combination of these instances can be called with good reason "organized disorder."

The unfortunate struggle between the C.I.O.[1] and the American

---

1   C.I.O.: Congress of Industrial Organizations, an umbrella group of aggressive and sometimes radical unions.

Federation of Labor[1] for the domination of sea-going unions undoubtedly has played an important part in bringing about these conditions. There was a ripe field in some cases for justifiable satisfaction, but nothing in those circumstances can logically account for these continuing occurrences. There seems to be a sinister underlying influence over and above this struggle between the unions that many furnish the predominant motive for these unaccountable occurrences.

Patience and wise administration of the laws enacted would have worked out these problems. But what happened? First, the disastrous West Coast strike.[2] Second, the spread of disorder to the Gulf and to the East Coast; and third, practically a complete breakdown in the enforcement of our maritime laws.

So that at the present day I would say, without fear of contradiction, that the discipline and morale on our vessels is the lowest it has ever been, probably lower than that on any vessels of other flags.

The merchant marine, which should play a most important part in the national defense, has become a liability rather than an asset.

It is not a pleasant picture to contemplate, particularly in view of the fact that we seem to be gravitating gradually toward a participation in world events which may demand all our resources.

If this catastrophe overtakes us soon, there will not be time to build up morale on our ships, because this collapse has been long in the making. It will be too late.

Troops must be transported without interruption, ammunition and supplies must move on scheduled time, fuel for the fleet must make its rendezvous in accordance with pre-arranged plans. This cannot be done if the total irresponsibility of the various labor leaders and their underlings, and the total lack of restraint and discipline on the part of the men themselves continues.

In the past we have seen labor leadership decide where and when our vessels shall sail; and what and to whom they shall carry. Is there any evidence that under present radical labor leadership these conditions will be changed? Is there any evidence that "gentlemen's agreements" and even contracts will not eventually be broken?

Should war come now, there is only one solution. That is, all work-

---

1   American Federation of Labor (AFL): a larger umbrella group of older, more conservative labor unions.

2   West Coast strike: the "Big Strike" of 1934 in San Francisco.

ers in the loading, sailing and repairing of our vessels be enlisted as
part of the United States military establishment and be amenable to
the resulting discipline. The people will demand it. The government
must enforce it.

What a contrast between this picture of chaos and the orderly,
responsible record of the railroad unions. There we have collective
bargaining and collective responsibility—there we have integrity, discipline, and efficiency. There is no fear that our railway transportation
will collapse in such a national emergency.

And why should not the same condition obtain on our ships that
exists on our railroads? There is no reason why there should be a difference. And there is no reason why, with sane, responsible labor leadership, the government should be called upon to enforce the navigation laws which were designed and enacted and which give to the
various governmental agencies all the necessary power and jurisdiction to cope with the present situation. Some restraining influence
has prevented the enforcement of these laws, probably with the hope
that the ordinary common sense of the American laboring man would
result in a realignment and a reorganization of the unions into responsible bodies.

It would seem that the unions cannot extricate themselves from
the present situation and that the time has arrived when the government must exert its full force and authority. Otherwise, the American
merchant ship will disappear from the seas.

It is inconceivable that labor should adopt an attitude which, if carried on for an appreciable time, will kill the very industry in which
that labor is employed.

If our water transportation was the only medium of transportation, there might be a logical reason for imposing on the industry
such conditions. But, in foreign commerce, vessels of foreign flags
ready and only too willing to take up this burden; and in our domestic
transportation, railroads, trucks and aeroplanes are always available;
and, dealing specifically with tankers, there is nothing to prevent the
extension of the already important pipe-line systems so that the need
for the majority of tankers will no longer exist.

The rank and file of our labor should be advised that continuation
of what is now going on will ultimately mean the laying-up of vessels, the abandonment of services, and the loss of employment. They
should know that those who must obtain their livelihood by going

to sea will eventually have to seek employment under foreign flags, where the wages, living conditions, and all other circumstances under which work is performed are so far inferior to the conditions which exist in our American merchant marine, not to mention the conditions which will be provided on new vessels, that there is absolutely no comparison.

The members of the Propeller Club of the United States are familiar with conditions on our ships, but, in the event this discussion reaches others who are not familiar with these conditions, I wish to list a few incidents, for the authenticity of which I can vouch, as typical of every day occurrences on vessels flying the American flag.

Every day for the past year 'sit-down strikes,' otherwise known as 'quickies' in maritime parlance, have occurred in all ports of the country. Vessels cannot be scheduled with certainty as at the last moment any trivial excuse can be trumped up; such as, complaints about the food or coffee; the demand that an elaborate menu be served, in many cases much more extensive than anyone here present would expect or even desire; a non-union man may have been shipped, or a member of an opposing union signed on. Any one of these excuses has been sufficient to stop the operation of our vessels, not only in homeports but abroad as well.

Drunkenness on the part of the crew has resulted in some of the most disgraceful episodes aboard our vessels. Obscenity, profanity, and even nudity have, on occasion, been thrust in the very faces of women and children passengers. Stewards have grossly insulted passengers at the dining tables, even to the extent of deliberately spilling soup over women, and other similar actions. One lady passenger, who had been seasick and not at her table for a day or two, came down to dinner and the steward refused to serve her and stated that "she had better go back and eat her meals where she had been eating them."

On some occasions it has been almost impossible to secure food on some vessels without currently tipping those who were serving.

A personal friend of mine, making a coastwise voyage, came out of his stateroom one night to go to dinner and saw a semi-drunk steward attempting to manhandle a young woman passenger in the corridor. This gentleman, not being controlled by any unions or subject to any penalties, did just what you or I would do. He knocked the steward flat—and as this man weights some 260 pounds, the steward was properly 'flattened.' Had a licensed officer done this, he would have been subject to fine and possibly imprisonment.

Intimidation, violence and bloodshed are the orders of the day on our ships and on the waterfront. Our officers are threatened and, on one occasion, tried by the crew. Retaliation for imaginary grievances on the part of the crew has, in one case, resulted in deliberate murder. This particular instance can more properly be called execution.

I quote from a consular report which is an official document and which sums up, I think, beyond any question of doubt, the lamentable conditions now existing on our ships.

While the statements regarding the deplorable lack of discipline on American ships plying in the Far Eastern waters are unfortunately true, they only act to cause Far East shippers and travelers to use other vessels. During the recent strike many importers dealing in merchandise from the United States were unable to get their orders filled, and several stated bluntly that they never again intended to use American ships, since they could not be relied upon. The publication of such articles as these, in which additional strikes are forecast, cannot help but to deter Far East traders from shipping on American vessels.

The shocking lack of discipline on board American vessels is common talk in the Far East both among Americans and other nationals and predictions are freely made that a marine disaster of the first magnitude will inevitably result if such conditions are allowed to continue.

And again I quote from another consular report, likewise an official public document.

Repeated reports of strikes and difficulty with crews on American vessels plying the Pacific are causing much concern generally, particularly among passengers, who are more and more inclined to patronize ships under other flag because of the existing situation. I will say frankly, from my observation in recent years of the crews of the American lines on the Pacific, I would prefer to have my family travel on other lines. I would feel a greater sense of security if they traveled on other lines. I have myself observed members of the crew of the American seagoing ships discussing their officers and their orders and union activities, using profane language in the presence of passengers and generally giving the impression of lack of discipline and of orderly conduct and ability and skill in their calling.

There does not seem much that I can add, except to state that there is no exaggeration in regard to any of the above; that every one of these instances and many more can be substantiated.

Let us debunk this whole situation.

Radical union leadership has failed. The union hiring halls have proven a menace. Discipline on our vessels is a joke. This leadership has had its opportunity.

We have all the necessary laws and authority vested in definite government agencies to protect the traveling public, to protect the rights of the operators, and to protect the rights of labor. Let those agencies perform their duty promptly, fearlessly, and without passion or prejudice; but, in fairness to these agencies, interference from other government departments must be eliminated.

Let the government set up government hiring halls and perform the duties which, according to law, are mandatory in this connection.

Numerous cases of insubordination, violence and near mutiny are before the government now for decision. Let us hope that all legal technicalities and maudlin sympathies be brushed aside; and let us hope that these agencies, without quibbling, will get down to the fundamental question of whether or not these charges are right or wrong and will impose any penalties fearlessly.

Rid the ships of the undesirables. Stamp out Communism on our vessels. Give the public, the operators and decent labor a chance. Then we will see a prosperous industry out of which will grow responsible unions and more responsible associations of operators. LET US SAVE THE AMERICAN MERCHANT MARINE!

Questions for Discussion:
1. What does this document reveal about attitudes toward labor unions in the 1930s?
2. Why was Weaver so vehemently anti-labor?
3. How did Weaver view the role of labor unions in creating a viable merchant marine?

Joseph B. Weaver, "The Problem of Seagoing Labor," in *Propeller Club of the United States, American Merchant Marine Conference Proceedings: 1937*, 39–42.

Joe Curran, "Our Union Can Be Strong" (1937)

Industrial warfare was far more than the struggle between labor unions and the wealthy shipowners. Unions also fought other unions, and not only with words. Union versus union brawls were common in the late 1930s, especially between left-wing and more conservative unions. Another issue that divided union activists was race. Older unions were strictly segregated, but the East Coast National Maritime Union (NMU) was racially integrated from the start and demanded that shipping companies accept racially mixed crews.

Joe Curran (1906–1981), who led the NMU from its creation until 1973, was a strong advocate of racial tolerance from the time of the first NMU national convention in 1937. In this speech from the 1937 meeting, Curran argues that accepting blacks and Asians on an equal footing will make the NMU stronger in its struggle for better working conditions and urges the membership to incorporate racial equality into the union's constitution. A recent treatment of the NMU and its radical political and racial stances is Gerald Horne's monograph on the NMU's long-time black vice president, Ferdinand Smith, entitled *Red Seas*.[1]

Our Union can be strong only if it seeks to unite every bona-fide seaman within its ranks; every seaman who makes his living going to sea, we must seek to bring into our Union. Those who are not in our Union will be used by the shipowners to fight our Union. This is the general principle with which your trustees have tried to meet a number of questions which we considered of the utmost importance. We have at all times attempted to fight any tendencies that would tend to create divisions within our ranks, and we have done this with some success. One of our biggest achievements is the fact that we have won the support of the colored seamen. To do this we had to combat the propaganda of Grange[2] and others who attempted to win the support of the colored seamen by telling them that if they joined the NMU, then they would be unable to keep the jobs they now have, that the colored seamen would be discriminated against in the NMU.

---

1   Gerald Horne, *Red Seas: Ferdinand Smith and Radical Black Sailors in the United States and Jamaica* (New York: New York University Press, 2005).

2   Grange: David "Emperor" Grange (1890s–1940s), the African American president of the Marine Cooks, Stewards, and Waiters' Union of the Atlantic and Gulf (MCSWU).

The I.S.U.[1] fakers sought to secure the support of the colored seamen by making it seem that only the I.S.U. would give them a square deal. Fortunately, the colored seamen were not confused by these promises because our Union has fought against any form of discrimination whatsoever, and took into consideration that in the past the colored seamen have not always gotten a square deal, and that we could only convince them that the NMU was a real rank and file organization by showing them that our Union fought against the evils that existed and to guarantee that the colored seamen in our Union would have the same rights in our organization as any other bona-fide member of the NMU. The Union must continue to adhere to this policy. We are making headway in putting it into effect. If we are having difficulties, if we are not putting it into effect as rapidly as we would like, then it is because those things which were taught by the employers for years for the purpose of dividing us so that whites would fight colored, and colored fight whites, has not yet been completely eliminated.

The same thing applies to the Filipino brothers who in recent months have begun to give splendid support to our Union. They are doing this because they see that we are not pursuing a policy such as pursued by the I.S.U. officials and other individuals, which threatened to make these Filipinos enemies of the Union. We must recognize certain reactionary legislation adopted by Congress recently which discriminates and attacks the Filipinos and foreign-born seamen, is an attempt to create a division within the ranks of the seamen and at bottom an attack against our Union.

What must be our attitude toward these questions? First, we are accepting for membership all bona-fide maritime workers who are eligible to sail upon American ships; second, we are attempting to secure the repeal of those clauses of the reactionary legislation that disfranchises bona-fide seamen; and this is the way to make the American Merchant Marine one hundred per cent American.

There may be some who might still question such a policy. Our answer to them is this. If people are bona-fide seamen, have been sailing American ships, are ready to declare their willingness to become American citizens, then they belong in the Union and aboard the ships. If they are not with us, then THEY WILL ASSUREDLY BE AGAINST US. We must make it possible for them to be with us.

---

1   I.S.U.: International Seamen's Union, an older, corrupt union that did little for its membership.

If they are not with us; if they do not have the same rights as we do, then—if and when we come out on strike—the shipowners will use them against us. Therefore, in our own interests, and for our own self-protection, and for the purpose of maintaining our Union, our policy must always be to unite all bona-fide seamen.

In building our organization, accepting men into our Union, the membership has taken into consideration the fact that due to the policies of the I.S.U. officials, the activities of stool pigeons and ship-owners' agents and the so-called unofficial character of our strike, which was not called by a referendum vote of the membership because the officials would not permit it; many honest seamen were in the past confused on many questions to such extent, that in some cases they did not participate in many actions. We recognize that the question involved here is not that the man was not a good union man, but was confused, not clear as to the issues involved. In such cases, our policy has been to accept such men into our organization. We can cite hundreds of cases wherein this policy was proven correct; where we now see such crews, former "loyal" I.S.U. members, who are today most loyal supporters of the NMU protecting the Union on the ships and carrying on militant actions to improve their living and working conditions.

There can be no question, but that the majority of these men are honest union men and belong in our ranks—we want them there. It may be true that a few will be phoney, but out of fear of the few who may be phoney, we must not set up barriers to the thousands who are honest. If a few manage to sneak into our ranks, well, we know how to deal with them, and they will be dealt with. Therefore, your trustees recommend that the Union continue to seek the support of all bona-fide honest seamen in the N.L.R.B.[1] elections and of the membership in our Union. If we do not follow this policy, then we will help to foster support by some seamen for Grange and Co. or even for a company union. Finally, there has been one other question that our organization has been forced to meet and answer.

From outside sources there has come the charge that we are a Communist organization. Your trustees have always replied to these union disrupting charges from outside to the effect that our Union is not a political organization; is not committed to the support of any political party and is controlled by the rank and file. We have even heard such

---

1 N.L.R.B.: National Labor Relations Board.

charges from people in the trade union movement. The Union has clearly indicated its policies, and its position is most clearly stated in the following statement, which was published in the Pilot and Voice of Federation and sent to the West Coast Unions.

There is one other point about which you no doubt wish to be informed. Like you, we here in the East and Gulf have at various times been labeled a "bunch of reds." Already Hunter, Scharrenberg[1] and Co., together with some of the shipowners, are charging, the National Maritime Union was "hatched in Moscow." On the Pacific Coast, we understand, there are those who charge that the National Maritime Union is "communist controlled."

In our Union, the same as yours, we have Republicans, Democrats, Communists, Socialists and what not. We intend to unite the seamen, regardless of their political beliefs, and not to divide them because of their race, religion, or political beliefs. Neither Democrats, Republicans or Communists dominate and control our Union—the Rank and File do.

The Trustees and the membership generally have considered the policy of the Union to accept into his ranks every bona-fide seaman regardless of political opinions and we have been and are opposed to any attempt to divide union membership on the basis of their political opinions. We think that the policy of "red baiting" which is pursued by the reactionaries in their attacks against President Roosevelt, against the C.I.O., John L. Lewis,[2] and at times, even against our own union, must be condemned, rejected as a method fostered and encouraged by the shipowners for the purpose of disrupting, dividing and eventually destroying our Union.

We are gathered in this Convention to discuss and to finally adopt a constitution for our organization. At the instruction of our membership, the District Committee, through the Convention Preparations Committee has prepared the draft of such a constitution for your consideration and action. It will be the task of this convention to discuss this constitution; to make amendments that it may see fit and to reject it or adopt it according to the will of this convention. In drafting the constitution, which is being submitted to you, we have attempted to

---

1   Scharrenberg: Paul Scharrenberg (1877–1969), leader of the Sailor's Union of the Pacific.

2   John L. Lewis: an important figure in the creation of the C.I.O., longstanding president of the United Mine Workers of America, and an important ally of Joe Curran.

take into consideration the experiences that we have had in the past and also experiences of the C.I.O. as to what was the most effective form of organization. All the experiences in America, both in our industry and in the C.I.O., show that the most effective means of organization is that form which will tend to unite the workers more and more upon an industrial basis. We have attempted to apply this idea in the preparation of this draft constitution, in order to weld much closer the Cooks and Stewards, Sailors and Firemen into one united union, and at the same time, to do it in such a manner as would ensure that each Division would receive even greater attention to its own particular problems and above all, to ensure the greatest possible degree of democracy within our ranks. Not only does the proposed constitution attempt to bring the crafts closer together, but it also takes important steps forward toward bringing the Union on board the ships.

While insuring the greatest amount of democracy and autonomy, and at the same time uniting our forces in all ports and on all ships into a compact solid organization under a unified program and leadership which will enable the tens of thousands of seamen to act in the disciplined, organized, unified manner, necessary. It is our opinion that the constitution is the application of the C.I.O. principles to our industry and that it will enable us to build what we want, a strong, powerful union. In this light, it is submitted to you for your discussion, consideration and action.

Questions for Discussion:
1. According to Curran, why do shipowners continue to promote racism against "colored" sailors?
2. What bigger ideas does this document reveal about American society in the 1930s?
3. How is this speech related to the idea of industrial warfare?

National Maritime Union, *Proceedings of the First Constitutional Convention of the National Maritime Union* (New York: 1937), 84–87.

SEA STORIES

This section is composed of three life histories compiled and transcribed from 1936 to 1940 by the staff of the Folklore Project of the Federal Writers' Project for the U.S. Works Progress Administration (WPA). The WPA was created specifically to employ Americans during the Depression, and the Folklore Project hired numerous writers to record oral histories of some ten thousand ordinary Americans of different occupations, races, and ethnicities. The pieces in this section highlight maritime workers: seamen, a stewardess on passenger liners, and a Portuguese-American fisherman on Cape Cod. Conducted before the days of tape recorders, the interviewers had to take detailed notes with a pencil and pad of paper. The Library of Congress currently holds the originals of these interviews, maintaining them as a national resource because "Personal recollection has a significance of its own and offers a window onto the ways people shape their identity and see the world around them."[1] The following three samples have been heavily edited from the originals.

Agnes Shipper, "Stewardess on the *President Arthur*" (1925)

Job opportunities for women at sea were limited through most of the twentieth century. One of the few positions open was that of stewardess on board passenger vessels. This document, a WPA oral history conducted at the National Maritime Union headquarters in New York City in 1939, is the account of a woman who identified herself as *Agnes Shipper*. Notably, if she was a member of the NMU in 1939, she probably made a career of working on ships.

The *President Arthur* was the former German steamship *Princess Alice*, seized by the U.S. government when it entered World War I. Owned by the American Palestine Line, Inc., the *President Arthur* was its only ship, and a rather elderly one at that: the vessel was built in 1900. In 1925 this ship transported Jewish Americans directly to Palestine; all food served on the ship was strictly kosher. After only three voyages the company collapsed due to a scarcity of passengers and the shipboard problems outlined below. A number of similar small steamship lines established after the First World War suffered similar fates as inexperienced managers failed to realize the complexities of steamship company operations.

> I was on a ship, the *President Arthur*, a Jewish company had started the Palestine line and they finished by making just three trips and the line was finished. In the office where they were selling tickets, they had beautiful pictures. They would tell the passengers they had a beautiful

---

1   Ann Banks, "Voices from the Thirties: Life Histories from the Federal Writers' Project," http://lcweb2.loc.gov/wpaintro/intro16.html, last accessed June 27, 2008, and based on Banks's *First Person America* (New York: W. W. Norton, reprint 1991).

swimming pool on the ship, beautiful quarters, and it turned out that the pictures they were showing were the pictures of the *Leviathan*.[1] When I joined the ship they had already made one trip.

They only had one ship but they told the passengers they had a raft of them. So when the ship came in, it came in late. The entire crew got off, the way they were treated. So they hired another crew. The crew walked on and saw the condition of the ship. They all walked off again. So they had to take the ship out in mid-stream, come down to the office and get another crew.

So they got the new crew down to the dock and took them out on tugs. So while I was walking around on the ship, trying to find the purser or the chief steward, to get my bags off, while this was happening they took the ship out in midstream. So then the crew wouldn't work. So all these Jewish passengers came on. Ordinarily a ship is very neat. The passenger walks on to a perfect ship. Here the beds were all down, the chambers out, fruit scattered around. So we all had to stay. Even the passengers couldn't get off. I didn't get into a uniform until we were ten miles out to sea.

Then when everybody saw they couldn't do anything about it they made the best of it. The stewards started to make up the rooms and the passengers started to ask where the swimming pool was. Then we told them the swimming pool was in the basins in their rooms, the only swimming pool there was. Then, when we finally got to Naples, they decided to make a ferryboat out of it. They ferried back and forth between Naples and Alexander,[2] about six times, before we came back. We nicknamed the ship the Mediterranean cruiser, or the baloney express.

The ship broke down and had to wait there four weeks longer. The ship's boilers had to be repaired. So I used the time to fall in love with one of the chief engineers and got married. So I made a honeymoon out of it.

So the chief steward, who was a German, after he got all the stores, the victuals, on board, he went ashore to the different store keepers then at four o'clock in the morning the merchants would come alongside, in row boats, and buy the stuff back, half the price, and he made that money. So then, when the engineers found that out, after the coal

---

1   *Leviathan*: SS *Leviathan*, an enormous and luxurious ocean liner operated by United States Lines, and the biggest ship in the U.S. merchant marine in the 1920s.

2   Alexander: Probably Alexandria, in Egypt.

was all aboard, the engineers sold the coal over the side, the same way. So when the sailors found out they started to sell their rope over the side, just leaving enough coal, rope, etc., to get along with.

So then when the stewards heard of that they started stealing the sheets and the silverware. I had a set of silverware myself. Then we started back to New York. When we got several miles out, half way, the coal started to give out. We were going around in circles. They had no coal, no steam, no power. They were using wood, whatever they could find, steamer chairs and everything, to make fires. They had to put in to Halifax to get coal.

Four days before we reached Halifax the food gave out. When the crew heard about it they stole all the food they could and let the passengers go to the devil. So one of the engineers had a lot of oranges in his room and he shared them with us.

Then they discovered that all they had on the ship was dried herring. That made us awful thirsty. Then the crew started to look for some food and away down they found some powdered eggs that was laid there before the ship was laid up. It was all moldy. Then the horrible part of it was the engineers, they were drunk in Naples most of the time and they had failed to put a fresh water supply on. So the fresh water gave out and they had to make tea with salt water and eat herring.

In spite of that we had a wonderful time. We did just as we darn pleased. We knew that we would all be fired. The chief steward got off the ship in Halifax. He knew he would be under arrest.

Questions for Discussion:
1. What does this document reveal about seafaring in the 1920s?
2. Why does this stewardess enjoy a voyage so plagued with problems?
3. Who is responsible in a situation like that on the *President Arthur* and what action should they have taken?

"Seamen's Stories," Library of Congress, Manuscript Division, WPA Federal Writers' Project Collection.

O'Brien, "Interview with a Mariner" (1939)

In the late 1930s, federal workers compiled oral histories from thousands of ordinary Americans. This interview with a mariner, identified only as *O'Brien*, was conducted at the New York headquarters of the new radical

National Maritime Union, an organization with known Communist ties. O'Brien's bitterness toward those better off than himself is clear, but he is also an intelligent man who understands that mariners need to be treated like other American workers. O'Brien was painting the "traveling libraries," or boxes containing sets of books distributed to the crews of different ships when an interviewer found him.

Pride under this system? Don't make me laugh. We're just living a step above the mission stiff.[1] I leave that pride stuff to them long hairs you got in Greenwich Village.[2] You can put pride in the waste-basket as far as I'm concerned. I was born right on the waterfront. I'm no yo-ho-ho an' a bottle of sarsparilla adventurer—you know what I mean? I knew it was a friggin' phony life the first day I tackled it. My old man worked in this industry. Rigged up the first tow-boom ship on the White Star Line. WHY? MAN, I WAS BORN ON THE WATERFRONT DONCHASEE. I'm in a dif'ren class than these adventurers that goes to sea for the kick in it. Be'in a sailor is no life, it's a friggin' unnach'rel life. The seaman knows where he's gonna end up that's what drives him to the bottle. It's an unnach'rel life, y'see. NOW, HERE'S THE REAL STORY AND NO BULL, FELLER. Ninety eight percent of the seamen ain't married. It makes a man high-strung. I'm just goin' off into the sexual line which ain't exactly my line it's a deep subject. But the guy that don't get married is a frigged out article. After years of roamin' around some of 'em try to settle down. It takes 'em years to get used to livin' ashore inna majority of cases an' some of 'em don't ever get used to it nach'r'ly. So the first thing you know you're floatin' back to sea. There's no enticement to hangin' around a furnished room. Hey, here's somethin' you don't know. Do you know what feels like a ship ashore? It's a jail. You wake up in a bunk an' if it wasn't for the bars you'd think it was a ship. So help me Jesus there was a friend of mine that was trustee in a jail over in Jersey City. Three quarter bunks—white sheets—an' the deck was spotless. It was more sanitary than half the ships—sanitary as hell. The windows—this was in the trustees mess room—they were like friggin' French windows. Conditions was so good I bummed a guy for a shave. A ship is like a

---

1 Mission stiff: homeless person in a shelter.
2 Greenwich Village: a part of New York City famed for its artists and bohemian attitudes.

jail, the same kinda life in a way; I'm referrin' to the federal type of jail, y'see, where the conditions is improved over the old type of jail. Sure, we've improved conditions on the ships but here's the story on what has retarded the improvin' of conditions.

Do you know the worst type that goes to sea. It's the adventurers, those friggin' college boys. Nach'r'ly they don't give a damn, y'see. Rotten grub, unsanitary conditions it's all in the fun y'understand. Strange things happening and so on and so forth. China an' Japan an' the South Seas—why I worked under one skipper that had that type spotted. This skipper was after two kinds on the ship. The first was the licensed man that signs on as an A.B. an' then tries to undermine the officers so's he can get the job. Number two if he caught somebody readin' an adventure story that was the end of him. The *Leviathan* was one of the ships that had so many adventurers on it she just managed to stagger into port. These kids from the various colleges—puttin' up with rotten conditions, lousy grub—see what I mean?

It was fellers like them that put the hammers in American ships, them that sailed for a summer and then graduated from the various colleges.

WHAT THE HELL DO THEY KNOW ABOUT GOIN' TO SEA? It was the old-timers that really fought. They knew where they were goin'—everybody turning out the same in the end. They knew they were headed for the Bowery. It put some fight in 'em. I never read an honest book about the sea except one. It was by a guy by the name of Dana.[1] The sonofabitch he was word for word. He was friggin' legitimate. He was tellin' the truth an' he was talkin' about them old sailing ships but it's still true today the most of it. It was word for word."

Questions for Discussion:
1. Why does O'Brien seem so angry with those who sought adventure at sea?
2. What does this document reveal about seafaring in the 1930s?
3. How does O'Brien view a seaman's chance of living a happy life ashore?

"O'Brien," Library of Congress, Manuscript Division, WPA Federal Writers' Project Collection.

---

1   Dana: Richard Henry Dana Jr., author of *Two Years Before the Mast*.

Joseph Captiva, "Portuguese Fisherman" (1939)

The following interview was held in the Provincetown, Massachusetts, home of Joseph Captiva, a Portuguese-born fisherman who came to the United States as a teenager and operated his own fishing boat, and was thus known as *Captain Joe*. The interviewer, Alice Kelly, described Captiva as "around fifty and looks a good deal younger. A little over medium height, he is exceedingly solid and powerful and is considered by everyone who knows him, 'One fine lookin' feller.'" Kelly seems to have had some difficulty capturing Captiva's Portuguese accent, but she clearly admired the man and enjoyed her interviews with him. Captiva, too, enjoyed the interviews, reveling in the role of storyteller.

I wouldn't never be happy without I had a boat under me.

Jeeze! I come near lose my boat. I just fix her up nice—new paint, clean her up, everything. Then I was going put in whole now engine.

Well, I need some tar, so I get her in a bucket, heat up upon fire, see? First thing I know, she catches—goes right up!

My boy he shout. I grab the 'stinguisher and let her have it, but tar she burns terrible. I see I'm going lose my boat. I holler at the boy and the men. They won't go down. You can't blame 'em. The flames she's coming up. But she's my boat. She's all I got, so what could I do?

I go down. I grab the tar bucket, throw her overboard, throw over some parts the engine, take blankets, stamp out the fire. Anyways, I save my boat. If she went, all my work gone—everything.

My hands she hurt preety bad, but I don't think she'll leave no scars. I been out fishing few days ago, but I wasn't no good. My hands she swole all up. Drive me crazy! Was a big catch and I couldn't do nothing. But I was glad get out in the boat again. I'll be out in 'nother week.

The boy's good fisherman. Portuguese boys, they do more like the old man. Some of 'em get these ideas to high school. Don't do them no good, 's I can see, but don't do them no harm neither. Lots these Americans they tell me their boys is in the city. Got jobs here, got jobs there. Me, I like have the boy on my boat. Teach him. Then I know where he is, what he's doing. The boat she'll be his. It's good for him know how to handle her.

I used to go out with my old man when I wasn't bigger than Jo. The old country, we was all fisherman, me and my brothers. My father fish, too. And his father. Some dragging, but mostly with hooks. That's about all they do back there. Fish, and maybe marketing and like that. I could work most as good as a man time I was fourteen. I come over here when I was nineteen. The way I come, we had folks over here. They write to my father, tell him was good money over here. My old man come over and my mother and us four boys. Then we send for other people. That's how we all come.

On land the Portuguese and Americans don't always get on so good. But we fish together all right. It's different out in the boats. There's the same rules for everyone. The rules for a captain and crew are the same everywhere, and we all want the same things—a good catch and a good market. We get on good on the sea.

They find out we're good fishermen. Anybody'll tell you they ain't no men can fish better than the Portuguese. We can always get jobs on the boats. I wouldn't want work on land all the time. Lots of the men do when they get older, but not me. I wouldn't never be happy without I had a boat under me. I'm a good fisherman. Maybe I wouldn't do so good with a regular land job.

The Yankees they fish to get money enough to go ashore, run shops maybe, or do business. The Portuguese he don't like that. He fishes because he wants to. Because he don't want no boss. One time I try stay ashore couple years. I had a good job on a yacht. Good pay, the best of everything, but I didn't like it. Rather be independent. Not say this "yes sir" and "no sir" all the time. The Yankees they don't mind. They run stores, they work for bosses, and they don't care. But the Portuguese, he always a kind of a independent feller.

Of course the skippers are like bosses kinda, but it's not the same. And then you work you can be skipper yourself. I been captain now for a long time. My son, he'll be captain some day too.

I fish always on trawlers. It's hard work, but I don't never get tired. Makes a man hard, that kind of work. The trap boats, they get the bait. That ain't no work. Ain't fast enough for me. I like to fight. Fight wind and cold and weather. I don't feel the cold no more.

A while ago I come in from fishing. I come up on the dock and Jeeze! I was dirty. Stand all night clean fish and it was dirty weather the whole trip after first day. Well, up an the dock the wind was blowing like sixty. I take off my shirt, fill a bucket of water, and I give myself a good wash. Feels good! But they's some city folks come down on the dock and they couldn't get over it, how I stood there wash myself with no shirt and the wind blowing. Say, the wind's my friend—and the water. I feel at home. In a house I'm like a big bull. Jeeze! if I can't feel a boat under me, I want to die.

The Portuguese is great for giving nicknames to every one. More'n the Americans, I guess. The man over at cold storage, that's Bennie Regular. That ain't his name. That's his nickname. They call him that 'cause he's a regular fellow. They call him that since he was little. He's regular. They call me "Pulaski." That means peppy, full of life, full of fun. Then they was a whole family in town. We used call them the "Baubas." Means dumb, kind of foolish. And they's Joe Portygee. That means he's all Portuguese. Just like in the old country.

Then they's my boy. They call him "Kak I." I dunno what that means. And young Morrie over there, he's "Fonda" on account of this Captain Fonda, told such big stories, and "Zorra," that means fox. Zorra's family got that name long time ago, like my family got "Captiva." Zorra's family was awful good fishermen, so where they live they call 'em "Fox of the sea." Then they's a whole family they call 'em "Goddam." Jackie Goddam, Mamie Goddam, and like that. That's cause the old lady she couldn't speak English so good and she'd call the children when they was little, "You come here, goddam." "Don't you do that, goddam." So they call 'em the "Goddams." Then they's lots ain't so nice. The Portuguese they make lots of jokes and they'll name a man because he acts this way or that way, goes this place or that, and sometimes the names they ain't so polite. They's one family, they used to call 'em the "Dirties." I guess the old woman she ain't such a good housekeeper or something. Anyways, that's what they call 'em. You ask, "Do you know Frankie, or Manuel, or Tony?" and they'll say, "You mean one of the 'dirties'?"

Lots old country people changes their names over here. Say old country names is too hard to say. I think that's foolish. Anybody can learn say "Silva" or Captiva or "Cabral." Jeeze! They ain't so hard. Some the Perrys was Perrera, I guess. And here's these two brothers and they change the name, and now one's called Smith and the other Carter. That don't make no sense. Some the Roses was Rosario, but you wouldn't get me to change my name, Captiva. I guess not!

It's the schools does it. They used to keep sending word home— have so much milk, so much orange juice. Must brush teeth. I never brush my teeth in the old country. Nobody did. And I got fine teeth. I send word to the teacher once. I says, "Tell 'em I know them kids when they was little. Their fathers was fishermen just like me. They never had no orange juice and no quarts of milk." But they laugh. Say times is change. I guess so.

The schools is better over here. They wasn't no public schools where I come from. You pay fifty cents a month each child to a teacher and the one man he teach everything. The young people over here, they have a good time. Back home the old folks was strict. Too strict. Young people was all the time running away. My kids they bring their friends home. That youngest girl of mine, she's always after me dance with her, go out places. Kids ain't afraid of the old folks no more. I think that's a good thing. Look at the Fishermen's Ball. It's for the families. My wife was there and my girls. My girl, the youngest one, she likes make me dance with her. She says, "Don't be behind the times, pa." She's a great kid.

It's nice when the whole family goes out that way. That's the way in Portugal. The families make what we call fiesta together. It's not like here, the women out all day, the men out all night. Unless once in a while like Saturday nights the men they go out have a few drinks. Plenty people say the Portuguese don't care for their wives, 'cause they don't make such fuss. They care all right. Sure, they care. Only with us the man's the boss. Everything is for the man. Makes him feel big, I guess. If a woman she's a good wife, has children, keeps the house nice, she's all right.

All the same, with us it's like with all the other countries. The woman she's boss in the house. She runs the house the way she wants, just so she has the meals right and takes care the children.

I think the Portuguese take more interest like in the children. Maybe it's only fishermen, they don't see them so often. The Americans they talk about the kids, but they don't stay around them so much. Sometimes Americans they'll say, "I shouldn't never have married. Just a worry." But the Portuguese he likes a good family.

This is a good season for fish. It's warm, that's why. When it comes cold and they's ice in the bay and like that, the fish they make for warmer waters. Have to chase them all over the place. But now they most jump into the boat.

It's dragging I do. We drag with big nets along the bottom. I don't go out nights much no more, but I got accommodations on my boat so's eight men can sleep on board. Eight men. She's a sloop. That's one mast. But they ain't no sailing now. My new engine she's beautiful.

Raises my profit. Used to cost ten, twelve dollars a day to take the boat out. Now costs only two, three. Much better engine.

I got a good crew, too. Me, I'm captain. Then I got engineer, and a cook. And my boy, he fishes. But we only stay out a day or two.

Used to go to Banks[1] every year. It's just a habit some fishermen's got. They got to go to the Banks every year. That trip to the Banks, it was awful. Stay away six months, work night and day, and then after that you've made three, four hundred dollars, 'tain't worth it. They's just as good fish near home, and not so hard work.

Of course, scalloping, that's different. That's terrible work, too. Out weeks and dragging with big heavy steel nets. But there's big money to it. Big money. But it's awful work. Have to be strong like a horse to stand it.

I don't never get scared. I don't know nothing else, only fishing and the sea. I never think about drowning any more'n you think about danger in the streets. Sure, the women worries, I guess. They used to get down on the beach and yell and pray when the boats was late out there was storms, and the womens always worrying about something, anyways.

My wife now, she worries sometimes about the boy. I tell her he's better off to sea than running around with all these wild crowds. Ain't drowned yet, nor I ain't drowned yet. She wouldn't really want me to come ashore. Her people was fishing folks too. She knows I wouldn't be no good on land.

My boat can hold twenty-five thousand pound. We don't often got that much. Sometimes we do, though. One time we went out seven thirty, eight o'clock at night. Nine o'clock we come back in—full. Twenty-five thousand pound this silver perch. Made a thousand dollar that one night. We fish on shares. I get most because the boat she's mine, all the man takes their share.

We go out nights when we hear the fish she's running good. That's a funny thing. We don't have no regular plan, where we go, but no boat never goes alone. We start out, try all the places where we know fish comes sometimes. Then when we come back, one boat comes up. The Cap says, "You had good catch?" If I say, "Yes," then likely he'll say, "Jeeze, I didn't get nothing. I'm coming with you to-morrow." Or if I didn't do so good, next day I go out with a crowd's got a good catch.

---

1   Banks: the Grand Banks, a fishing ground off Newfoundland.

We start about three, four in the morning. It's dark and boys! is it cold! Well, when we got outside the harbor, not far—couple hours, maybe—and start fishing. It's get light then and they's coffee on the stove. Everybody feels good. I got a beautiful stove on my boat. We cook chowder, oyster stew, make coffee—everything. And plenty of room.

We don't get so tired unless by night we've worked hard. Then maybe we want stretch ourselves, have a little fun. But we don't mind getting up early. People don't need so much sleep 's they think. Look at me. Been fishing thirty years. Sometimes up two, three nights. I always start early morning. But when I get home, I don't want to go to bed. Maybe have a little nap, then work around the house, or go out and see my friends. Have a little drink maybe down to Mac's, have some friends in for supper and a glass of ale. Once I'm off the boat, I want a change.

If I couldn't fry fish and make chowders I'd have starved plenty of times. The Yankees they generally puts salt pork in it. But we use the olive oil. Roll the fish up in flour. Then put your oil in the pan. Let it got real hot, smoking. And don't keep turning the fish, leave it cook one side till she's brown's a pork chop. We make galvanized pork, like this. Take a good pork roast or chops and all day you dip 'em in sauce made with vinegar and garlic and real hot peppers, then you cook 'em like always. Fried fish and galvanized pork—that's real Portuguese.

We made the Cape.[1] We built it up. We're the Portuguese pilgrims. Us and the American fisherman. We make Gloucester too. I was up there a couple years. I fished all over, out of Chatham, out of Gloucester everywhere. When first come here there wasn't nothing, but sand and a few houses and docks and boats. We used dry the codfish out on the Dunes. They'd be pretty near miles of it spread out. The whole place stunk. They was fishermen all up and down the Cape. The old whalers went out then. Captain Avila down here, he found a chunk of ambergris[2] once. And fishing off the Grand Banks was a gold mine. You'd get so much you couldn't load it all. Times you'd be up two, three nights cleaning, up to your knees in it and half frozen. . . .

It's a good life. You got be strong, and there used be big money in it. Not no more, though. Now the middleman he gets everything and

---

1   the Cape: Cape Cod, Massachusetts.
2   Ambergris: a valuable secretion produced in the intestine of sperm whales, sometimes found afloat or cast ashore.

they don't pay the prices anyhow. Sometimes you might as well throw away the catch. It don't keep forever. Give it away or throw it away if you can't sell it. I think it's like this, the government don't know the conditions of fishing. We make a big lot money some seasons, then for a long time we're broke. We got get good prices. Then they's credit. We used get credit eight months, a year maybe. Now it's tough to get three months. Money's scarce, they say, but I don't know. They's plenty for mortgage houses, for projects, for new playground. People don't appreciate the fisherman.

You won't find many nowadays got much of anything saved. We most of us belong to one of these burial insurance societies. But the widows of most of us wouldn't have much if we went. That's why a man's foolish not to buy a house if he can, even if he has to have a pretty big mortgage. And that's why it's good to own your boat. The Portuguese aren't as good for business as the Yankee fisherman.

Pretty soon we got to go down the Cape settle some business. The draggers and the seiners, they're in together like. Now the cold storage's got worried. They use the weirs—like traps—and they trawl. And they don't want us in shore get the silver perch. Last time we have a fight about this, they agree we go three miles out summers. But winters we fish everywheres. That's why they don't like. There's no reason we should go outside winters. The weirs ain't out winters. Summer's different.

But we won't have no trouble. We'll all go up to Boston. Whole bunch of us. They got to have silver perch. Perch's about the only fish they can make money on. It costs three cents a pound freeze the fish, and maybe it's cheap fish, gets only one, two cents a pound. Like that they don't make no money. But they's plenty of fish. They claims we take all the fish. But that ain't so. They just want it all. And it don't make sense we should go outside winters when they ain't fishing.

We don't mind going up to Boston. I guess not. Last time we hired us two buses. Sing all the way, stop have a little drink now and then. Had a good time. And we win, so coming back we felt fine. Was a nice trip. I guess we'll have a good one this time.

Questions for Discussion:
1. How does this fisherman relate to the sea?
2. What does this document reveal about immigrants' expectations for a better life in the United States?

3. What clues does this interview give about this fisherman's relations with his wife and family?

"Portuguese Fisherman," Library of Congress, Manuscript Division, WPA Federal Writers' Project Collection.

WAR ON THE HORIZON

As the 1930s progressed, it became increasingly apparent that Japan and Germany were behaving in a bellicose manner that promised to drag the United States into another world war. Long before the United States actually entered the war, in both the Pacific and the Atlantic, American seamen in the sea services and merchant marine were among the first to fall victim to Axis aggression. For example, leftist merchant mariners fought fascism as volunteers in the Spanish Civil War (1936–1939) in a special unit of American volunteers known as the *Abraham Lincoln Brigade*. So too, the aerial attack in 1937 on three American-flagged oil tankers and their naval escort, the aging gunboat USS *Panay*, was one of the incidents that awoke Americans to the threat posed by the Japanese Empire. The Nazi threat at sea developed after 1939. Neutral American ships such as the SS *Robin Moor* occasionally fell victim to German submarines that even attacked U.S. Navy ships, as in the attempted torpedoing of the destroyer USS *Greer* in 1941. The U.S. Navy, as demonstrated in George Baer's *One Hundred Years of Sea Power*,[1] struggled to adapt to these new threats.

President Franklin D. Roosevelt took these incidents as opportunities to gain public support for American rearmament, but until December 7, 1941, there were still American politicians such as Senator Gerald P. Nye who opposed American preparations for war.

Cordell Hull, "*Panay* Telegrams" (1937)

The *Panay* incident was an attack by Japanese aircraft on three American oil tankers and the gunboat USS *Panay* in the Yangtze River on December 12, 1937, during an offensive by Japan in its war with China. The attack sank the clearly marked American gunboat, killed two men, and wounded forty-three others. The American secretary of state, Cordell Hull (1871–1955), protested the incident through the ambassador to Japan, Joseph C. Grew. Both quickly determined that the Japanese claims that the attack was made

---

1   George W. Baer, *One Hundred Years of Sea Power: The U.S. Navy, 1890–1990* (Stanford: Stanford University Press, 1994).

in error were false. Nonetheless, the American government realized that it was completely unprepared for a war with Japan, and the Japanese government apologized for the attack and compensated the United States for its losses. War was averted in 1937, but the Japanese Empire and the United States were clearly on a collision course in Asia.

Telegram from Secretary of State Hull to Ambassador Grew, December 13, 1937, 8 p.m:

Please communicate promptly to Hirota[1] a note as follows:

"The Government and people of the United States have been deeply shocked by the facts of the bombardment and sinking of the U.S.S. *Panay* and the sinking or burning of the American steamers *Meiping*, *Meian* and *Meisian* [*Meihsia*] by Japanese aircraft.

The essential facts are that these American vessels were in the Yangtze River by uncontested and incontestable right; that they were flying the American flag; that they were engaged in their legitimate and appropriate business; that they were at the moment conveying American official and private personnel away from points where danger had developed; that they had several times changed their position, moving upriver, in order to avoid danger; and that they were attacked by Japanese bombing planes. With regard to the attack, a responsible Japanese naval officer at Shanghai has informed the Commander-in-Chief of the American Asiatic Fleet that the four vessels were proceeding upriver; that a Japanese plane endeavored to ascertain their nationality, flying at an altitude of three hundred meters, but was unable to distinguish the flags; that three Japanese bombing planes, six Japanese fighting planes, six Japanese bombing planes, and two Japanese bombing planes, in sequence, made attacks which resulted in the damaging of one of the American steamers, and the sinking of the U.S.S. *Panay* and the other two steamers.

Since the beginning of the present unfortunate hostilities between Japan and China, the Japanese Government and various Japanese authorities at various points have repeatedly assured the Government and authorities of the United States that it is the intention and purpose of the Japanese Government and the Japanese armed forces to respect fully the rights and interests of other powers. On several occasions, however, acts of Japanese armed forces have violated the

---

1   Hirota: Foreign Minister Koki Hirota of Japan.

rights of the United States, have seriously endangered the lives of American nationals, and have destroyed American property. In several instances, the Japanese Government has admitted the facts, has expressed regrets, and has given assurances that every precaution will be taken against recurrence of such incidents. In the present case, acts of Japanese armed forces have taken place in complete disregard of American rights, have taken American life, and have destroyed American property both public and private.

In these circumstances, the Government of the United States requests and expects of the Japanese Government a formally recorded expression of regret, an undertaking to make complete and comprehensive indemnifications, and an assurance that definite and specific steps have been taken which will ensure that hereafter American nationals, interests and property in China will not be subjected to attack by Japanese armed forces or unlawful interference by any Japanese authorities or forces whatsoever."

Before seeing Hirota inform your British colleague of intended action and text, but do not thereafter await action by him.

We are informing British Government of this instruction to you.

HULL.

Telegram from Ambassador Grew to Secretary of State Hull, December 14, 1937, 6 p.m:

1. At 5 o'clock this afternoon Yoshizawa[1] called on me upon instructions from the Minister for Foreign Affairs and handed me a note of which the following is an informal translation made by the Foreign Office. The translation is accurate in point of substance and corresponds closely to the original Japanese text.

"December 14, 1937.

Monsieur l'Ambassadeur: Regarding the incident of the 12th December in which the United States gunboat *Panay* and three steamers belonging to the Standard Oil Company were sunk by the bombing of the Japanese naval aircraft on the Yangtze River at a point about twenty-six miles above Nanking, I had the honor, as soon as unofficial information of the incident was

---

1   Kenkichi Yoshizawa: Director of the American Bureau of the Japanese Ministry for Foreign Affairs.

brought to my knowledge, to request Your Excellency to transmit to the Government of the United States the apologies of the
Japanese Government. From the reports subsequently received
from our representatives in China, it has been established that
the Japanese naval air force, acting upon information that the
Chinese troops fleeing from Nanking were going up the river
in steamers, took off to pursue them, and discovered such vessels at the above-mentioned point. Owing to poor visibility,
however, the aircraft, although they descended to fairly low alti-
tudes, were unable to discern any mark to show that any one of
them was an American ship or man-of-war. Consequently, the
United States gunboat *Panay* and the vessels of the Standard Oil
Company, being taken for Chinese vessels carrying the fleeing
Chinese troops, were bombed and sunk.

While it is clear, in the light of the above circumstances, that
the present incident was entirely due to a mistake, the Japanese
Government regret most profoundly that it has caused damages
to the United States man-of-war and ships and casualties among
those on board, and desire to present hereby sincere apologies.
The Japanese Government will make indemnifications for all the
losses and will deal appropriately with those responsible for the
incident. Furthermore, they have already issued strict orders to
the authorities on the spot with a view to preventing the recurrence of a similar incident.

The Japanese Government, in the fervent hope that the
friendly relations between Japan and the United States will not
be affected by this unfortunate affair, have frankly stated as
above their sincere attitude which I beg Your Excellency to make
known to your Government. I avail myself, etc., signed Koki Hirota."

2. Yoshizawa then read to me portions of the official Japanese naval
report on the disaster the purport of which is that the disaster was
not caused by deliberate intention to bomb American vessels but was
due to the inability of the aviators to distinguish the nationality of the
vessels bombed. I informed Yoshizawa that his explanation does not
cover the fact that, notwithstanding information in Japanese hands
that foreign vessels were in the neighborhood of Nanking, bombard-
ing and shelling operations by both naval and military forces were

carried out without any precautions taken against attack upon foreign vessels. I also pointed out that the bombing and shelling was carried out in the face of repeated assurances that measures had been taken to safeguard against attacks upon American nationals and property.

3. I also stated to Yoshizawa that I had just received instructions to present to the Minister for Foreign Affairs a note from the American Government. I added that, although I appreciated the action of the Japanese Government in delivering to me its note, I would proceed with the instructions which had been given to me.

4. I am still waiting for an appointment to call on Hirota which I asked for at 4 o'clock.

GREW.

Questions for Discussion:

1. What does this document reveal about Japanese foreign policy in the 1930s?

2. What evidence is there that the attack on the USS *Panay* and the three Standard Oil tankers was something other than a mistake?

3. What excuses do the Japanese offer for the sinking of the American shipping on the Yangtze River?

U.S. Department of State, Publication 1983, *Peace and War: United States Foreign Policy, 1931–1941* (Washington, D.C.: Government Printing Office, 1943), 394–97.

Franklin D. Roosevelt, "Rattlesnakes of the Atlantic" (1941)

The SS *Robin Moor* had the dubious distinction on May 21, 1941, of being the first American merchant ship sunk by a German submarine in World War II. The United States and Germany were still at peace, but the commander of the German submarine U-69 claimed the clearly marked American vessel was carrying war materiel to the British (with whom Germany was at war) and so sank the freighter with a combination of torpedoes and shellfire after ordering its crew and passengers to abandon ship.

As 1941 progressed, relations between the United States and Hitler's Germany steadily worsened. The United States clearly favored Britain in its war against Germany, and German hostility grew as larger amounts of American supplies and weapons found their way to Britain. Waldo H. Heinrichs, in his book *Threshold of War,*[1] convincingly argues that President

---

1   Waldo H. Heinrichs, *Threshold of War: Franklin D. Roosevelt and American Entry into World War II* (New York: Oxford University Press, 1988).

Roosevelt slowly but steadily prepared the nation for war, despite the public's inclination to stay out of what it saw as a European war. Roosevelt's efforts may have been most apparent on the waters of the North Atlantic, where the U.S. Navy and Coast Guard fought what amounted to an undeclared war against German submarines.

In this radio speech, one of Roosevelt's famous "fireside chats," the president explains to the American public the attack on the American destroyer *Greer*, and enumerates other Nazi attacks on American shipping. It was another step closer to war for the United States and Germany.

My fellow Americans:

The Navy Department of the United States has reported to me that on the morning of September fourth the United States destroyer *Greer*, proceeding in full daylight towards Iceland, had reached a point southeast of Greenland. She was carrying American mail to Iceland. She was flying the American flag. Her identity as an American ship was unmistakable.

She was then and there attacked by a submarine. Germany admits that it was a German submarine. The submarine deliberately fired a torpedo at the *Greer*, followed later by another torpedo attack. In spite of what Hitler's propaganda bureau has invented, and in spite of what any American obstructionist organization may prefer to believe, I tell you the blunt fact that the German submarine fired first upon this American destroyer without warning, and with deliberate design to sink her.

Our destroyer, at the time, was in waters which the Government of the United States had declared to be waters of self-defense—surrounding outposts of American protection in the Atlantic.

In the North of the Atlantic, outposts have been established by us in Iceland, in Greenland, in Labrador and in Newfoundland. Through these waters there pass many ships of many flags. They bear food and other supplies to civilians; and they bear material of war, for which the people of the United States are spending billions of dollars, and which, by Congressional action, they have declared to be essential for the defense of our own land.

The United States destroyer, when attacked, was proceeding on a legitimate mission.

If the destroyer was visible to the submarine when the torpedo was fired, then the attack was a deliberate attempt by the Nazis to sink a clearly identified American warship. On the other hand, if the submarine was beneath the surface of the sea and, with the aid of its listening devices, fired in the direction of the sound of the American destroyer without even taking the trouble to learn its identity—as the official German communiqué would indicate—then the attack was even more outrageous. For it indicates a policy of indiscriminate violence against any vessel sailing the seas—belligerent or non-belligerent.

This was piracy—piracy legally and morally. It was not the first nor the last act of piracy which the Nazi Government has committed against the American flag in this war. For attack has followed attack.

A few months ago an American flag merchant ship, the *Robin Moor*, was sunk by a Nazi submarine in the middle of the South Atlantic, under circumstances violating long-established international law and violating every principle of humanity. The passengers and the crew were forced into open boats hundreds of miles from land, in direct violation of international agreements signed by nearly all nations including the Government of Germany. No apology, no allegation of mistake, no offer of reparations has come from the Nazi Government.

In July, 1941, nearly two months ago, an American battleship in North American waters was followed by a submarine which for a long time sought to maneuver itself into a position of attack upon the battleship. The periscope of the submarine was clearly seen. No British or American submarines were within hundreds of miles of this spot at the time, so the nationality of the submarine is clear.

Five days ago a United States Navy ship on patrol picked up three survivors of an American-owned ship operating under the flag of our sister Republic of Panama—the S.S. *Sessa*. On August seventeenth, she had been first torpedoed without warning, and then shelled, near Greenland, while carrying civilian supplies to Iceland. It is feared that the other members of her crew have been drowned. In view of the established presence of German submarines in this vicinity, there can be no reasonable doubt as to the identity of the flag of the attacker.

Five days ago, another United States merchant ship, the *Steel Seafarer*, was sunk by a German aircraft in the Red Sea two hundred and twenty miles south of Suez. She was bound for an Egyptian port.

So four of the vessels sunk or attacked flew the American flag and were clearly identifiable. Two of these ships were warships of the American Navy. In the fifth case, the vessel sunk clearly carried the flag of our sister Republic of Panama.

In the face of all this, we Americans are keeping our feet on the ground. Our type of democratic civilization has outgrown the thought of feeling compelled to fight some other nation by reason of any single piratical attack on one of our ships. We are not becoming hysterical or losing our sense of proportion. Therefore, what I am thinking and saying tonight does not relate to any isolated episode.

Instead, we Americans are taking a long-range point of view in regard to certain fundamentals—a point of view in regard to a series of events on land and on sea which must be considered as a whole—as a part of a world pattern.

It would be unworthy of a great nation to exaggerate an isolated incident, or to become inflamed by some one act of violence. But it would be inexcusable folly to minimize such incidents in the face of evidence which makes it clear that the incident is not isolated, but is part of a general plan.

The important truth is that these acts of international lawlessness are a manifestation of a design—a design that has been made clear to the American people for a long time. It is the Nazi design to abolish the freedom of the seas, and to acquire absolute control and domination of these seas for themselves.

For with control of the seas in their own hands, the way can obviously become clear for their next step—domination of the United States—domination of the Western Hemisphere by force of arms. Under Nazi control of the seas, no merchant ship of the United States or of any other American Republic would be free to carry on any peaceful commerce, except by the condescending grace of this foreign and tyrannical power. The Atlantic Ocean which has been, and which should always be, a free and friendly highway for us would then become a deadly menace to the commerce of the United States, to the coasts of the United States, and even to the inland cities of the United States.

The Hitler Government, in defiance of the laws of the sea, in defiance of the recognized rights of all other nations, has presumed to declare, on paper, that great areas of the seas—even including a vast expanse lying in the Western Hemisphere—are to be closed, and that no ships may enter them for any purpose, except at peril of being sunk. Actually they are sinking ships at will and without warning in widely separated areas both within and far outside of these far-flung pretended zones.

This Nazi attempt to seize control of the oceans is but a counter-part of the Nazi plots now being carried on throughout the Western Hemisphere—all designed toward the same end. For Hitler's advance guards—not only his avowed agents but also his dupes among us—have sought to make ready for him footholds, (and) bridgeheads in the New World, to be used as soon as he has gained control of the oceans.

His intrigues, his plots, his machinations, his sabotage in this New World are all known to the Government of the United States. Conspiracy has followed conspiracy. For example, last year a plot to seize the Government of Uruguay was smashed by the prompt action of that country, which was supported in full by her American neighbors. A like plot was then hatching in Argentina, and that government has carefully and wisely blocked it at every point. More recently, an endeavor was made to subvert the government of Bolivia. And within the past few weeks the discovery was made of secret air-landing fields in Colombia, within easy range of the Panama Canal. I could multiply instance upon instance.

To be ultimately successful in world mastery, Hitler knows that he must get control of the seas. He must first destroy the bridge of ships which we are building across the Atlantic and over which we shall continue to roll the implements of war to help destroy him, to destroy all his works in the end. He must wipe out our patrol on sea and in the air if he is to do it. He must silence the British Navy.

I think it must be explained over and over again to people who like to think of the United States Navy as an invincible protection, that this can be true only if the British Navy survives. And that, my friends, is simple arithmetic.

For if the world outside of the Americas falls under Axis domination, the shipbuilding facilities which the Axis powers would then possess in all of Europe, in the British Isles and in the Far East would be much greater than all the shipbuilding facilities and potentialities of all of the Americas—not only greater, but two or three times greater, enough to win. Even if the United States threw all its resources into such a situation, seeking to double and even redouble the size of our Navy, the Axis powers, in control of the rest of the world, would have the manpower and the physical resources to outbuild us several times over.

It is time for all Americans, Americans of all the Americas to stop being deluded by the romantic notion that the Americas can go on living happily and peacefully in a Nazi-dominated world.

Generation after generation, America has battled for the general policy of the freedom of the seas. And that policy is a very simple one, but a basic, a fundamental one. It means that no nation has the right to make the broad oceans of the world at great distances from the actual theatre of land war, unsafe for the commerce of others.

That has been our policy, proved time and time again, in all of our history. Our policy has applied from the earliest days of the Republic—and still applies—not merely to the Atlantic but to the Pacific and to all other oceans as well.

Unrestricted submarine warfare in 1941 constitutes defiance—an act of aggression—against that historic American policy.

It is now clear that Hitler has begun his campaign to control the seas by ruthless force and by wiping out every vestige of international law, and every vestige of humanity.

His intention has been made clear. The American people can have no further illusions about it.

No tender whisperings of appeasers that Hitler is not interested in the Western Hemisphere, no soporific lullabies that a wide ocean protects us from him—can long have any effect on the hard-headed, far-sighted and realistic American people.

Because of these episodes, because of the movements and operations of German warships, and because of the clear, repeated proof that the present government of Germany has no respect for treaties or for international law, that it has no decent attitude toward neutral nations or human life—we Americans are now face to face not with abstract theories but with cruel, relentless facts.

This attack on the *Greer* was no localized military operation in the North Atlantic. This was no mere episode in a struggle between two nations. This was one determined step towards creating a permanent world system based on force, on terror and on murder.

And I am sure that even now the Nazis are waiting, waiting to see whether the United States will by silence give them the green light to go ahead on this path of destruction.

The Nazi danger to our Western world has long ceased to be a mere possibility. The danger is here now—not only from a military enemy but from an enemy of all law, all liberty, all morality, all religion.

There has now come a time when you and I must see the cold inexorable necessity of saying to these inhuman, unrestrained seekers of world conquest and permanent world domination by the sword: "You seek to throw our children and our children's children into your form of terrorism and slavery. You have now attacked our own safety. You shall go no further."

Normal practices of diplomacy—note writing—are of no possible use in dealing with international outlaws who sink our ships and kill our citizens.

One peaceful nation after another has met disaster because each refused to look the Nazi danger squarely in the eye until it had actually had them by the throat. The United States will not make that fatal mistake.

No act of violence, no act of intimidation will keep us from maintaining intact two bulwarks of American defense: First, our line of supply of material to the enemies of Hitler; and second, the freedom of our shipping on the high seas.

No matter what it takes, no matter what it costs, we will keep open the line of legitimate commerce in these defensive waters of ours.

We have sought no shooting war with Hitler. We do not seek it now. But neither do we want peace so much, that we are willing to pay for it by permitting him to attack our naval and merchant ships while they are on legitimate business.

I assume that the German leaders are not deeply concerned, tonight or any other time, by what we Americans or the American Government say or publish about them. We cannot bring about the downfall of Nazi-ism by the use of long-range invective.

But when you see a rattlesnake poised to strike, you do not wait until he has struck before you crush him.

These Nazi submarines and raiders are the rattlesnakes of the Atlantic. They are a menace to the free pathways of the high seas. They are a challenge to our own sovereignty. They hammer at our most precious rights when they attack ships of the American flag—symbols of our independence, our freedom, our very life.

It is clear to all Americans that the time has come when the Americas themselves must now be defended. A continuation of attacks in our own waters or in waters that could be used for further and greater attacks on us, will inevitably weaken our American ability to repel Hitlerism.

Do not let us be hair-splitters. Let us not ask ourselves whether the Americas should begin to defend themselves after the (fifth) first attack, or the (tenth) fifth attack, or the tenth attack, or the twentieth attack.

The time for active defense is now.

Do not let us split hairs. Let us not say: "We will only defend ourselves if the torpedo succeeds in getting home, or if the crew and the passengers are drowned."

This is the time for prevention of attack.

If submarines or raiders attack in distant waters, they can attack equally well within sight of our own shores. Their very presence in any waters which America deems vital to its defense constitutes an attack.

In the waters which we deem necessary for our defense, American naval vessels and American planes will no longer wait until Axis submarines lurking under the water, or Axis raiders on the surface of the sea, strike their deadly blow—first.

Upon our naval and air patrol—now operating in large number over a vast expanse of the Atlantic Ocean—falls the duty of maintaining the American policy of freedom of the seas—now. That means, very simply, (and) very clearly, that our patrolling vessels and planes will protect all merchant ships—not only American ships but ships of any flag—engaged in commerce in our defensive waters. They will protect them from submarines; they will protect them from surface raiders.

This situation is not new. The second President of the United States, John Adams, ordered the United States Navy to clean out European privateers and European ships of war which were infesting the Caribbean and South American waters, destroying American commerce.

The third President of the United States, Thomas Jefferson, ordered the United States Navy to end the attacks being made upon American and other ships by the corsairs of the nations of North Africa.

My obligation as President is historic; it is clear. Yes, it is inescapable.

It is no act of war on our part when we decide to protect the seas that are vital to American defense. The aggression is not ours. Ours is solely defense.

But let this warning be clear. From now on, if German or Italian vessels of war enter the waters, the protection of which is necessary for American defense, they do so at their own peril.

The orders which I have given as Commander-in-Chief (to) of the United States Army and Navy are to carry out that policy—at once.

The sole responsibility rests upon Germany. There will be no shooting unless Germany continues to seek it.

That is my obvious duty in this crisis. That is the clear right of this sovereign nation. This is the only step possible, if we would keep tight the wall of defense which we are pledged to maintain around this Western Hemisphere.

I have no illusions about the gravity of this step. I have not taken it hurriedly or lightly. It is the result of months and months of constant thought and anxiety and prayer. In the protection of your nation and mine it cannot be avoided.

The American people have faced other grave crises in their history—with American courage, with American resolution. They will do no less today.

They know the actualities of the attacks upon us. They know the necessities of a bold defense against these attacks. They know that the times call for clear heads and fearless hearts.

And with that inner strength that comes to a free people conscious of their duty, conscious of the righteousness of what they do, they will—with Divine help and guidance—stand their ground against this latest assault upon their democracy, their sovereignty, and their freedom.

Questions for Discussion:

1. What does this document reveal about American attitudes toward war with Germany?

2. What does Roosevelt accuse Hitler of attempting to do to the world's oceans?

3. Although the United States did not declare war, what does Roosevelt authorize the U.S. Navy to do?

Franklin D. Roosevelt, Fireside Chat 18 (September 11, 1941), in U.S. Department of State, Publication 1983, *Peace and War: United States Foreign Policy, 1931–1941* (Washington, D.C.: Government Printing Office, 1943), 673–76.

Gerald P. Nye, "Arming Merchant Ships" (1941)

Even in the late autumn of 1941, many Americans remained isolationists who wanted nothing to do with the war in Europe. One of the most outspoken was Senator Gerald P. Nye (1892–1971), a Republican from North Dakota and leading figure in the "America First Committee," a prominent antiwar organization headed by famed aviator Charles Lindbergh. He gave this speech on October 29, 1941, as a direct reply to Roosevelt's request to arm American merchant ships. While today it is difficult to understand these *non-interventionists*, as Professor Justus D. Doenecke calls them in *Storm on the Horizon*,[1] they represented a fairly broad cross section of Americans, from all parts of the country and all political persuasions.

Nye insists that arming American merchant ships will only antagonize Nazi Germany and that the best course for the nation is to remain truly neutral and stay out of the war altogether by enforcing the Neutrality Acts, which he had been a prime mover in passing. A few short weeks later, after the Japanese bombing of Pearl Harbor, Nye voted along with his fellow senators to unanimously declare war on both Germany and Japan.

The resolution provides for the arming of American merchant ships, and removes any and all restrictions upon the movement of American ships. A surer way to get into war is not known than that of going out and looking and asking for war. That way invites incidents— not lone incidents, but incidents by wholesale. . . .

We are now told that the proposal pending here, constituting what amounts to a repeal of the large part of what remains of our neutrality laws, is in no sense a declaration of war; that it is not necessarily taking a chance on leading to a declaration of war. . . .

I suppose, strictly speaking, one must agree that this is not a declaration of war; that it need not necessarily be followed by a declaration of war. But, Mr. President, no one will deny that if we arm our merchantmen and open up the sea lanes the world over to them, encourage them to navigate in war zones, even urge them to go into the ports of belligerent nations, certain it is that we shall be extending an invitation to trouble that is very, very sure of being accepted; and we shall have instance upon instance, we shall have chance upon chance to have our hates and our fears played upon as these ships, doing what they will then do and what they are now under the law forbidden to do, invite trouble for America. . . .

The pending legislation, Mr. President, asking for a setting aside of

---

1 Justus D. Doenecke, *Storm on the Horizon: The Challenge to American Intervention, 1939–1941* (Lanham, Md.: Rowman & Littlefield Publishers, 2000).

more of our law of neutrality, is nothing more than one step to get rid of every bit of fortification America afforded herself against involvement in another foreign war. . . .

Mr. President, the proposed legislation leaves nothing to the imagination. In this instance, listening to experience and profiting from history, if we should adopt the policy laid down in the joint resolution, it would mean war for the United States. It would not be a step short of war. . . .

Up until now it has been possible for those who want our intervention in Europe's war to argue, with some plausibility and with tremendous sentimental and emotional appeal, that all we have been doing in the conduct of our foreign policy these last two years could truly be summed up in that stockworn phrase "steps short of war," or "steps to keep us out of war."

The nasty looking claws of war, with all of war's meanings, were overlooked as the ears were charmed with the gentle purrs that repealing the arms embargo and adopting a lend-lease program of aid to Britain and her allies were by no means acts of war, but really designed to preserve America's neutrality while at the same time helping a gallant people.

The idea had charm. It had sufficient charm to make it possible for many who are definitely against actual involvement in war to believe that we could really go for a stroll with the leper of war and come back without having caught leprosy. . . .

Well, the gloves are off now. The claws are out. The point and purpose of it all is clear to anyone who can read or think. The mouse, the American people, has been played with long enough. Now is the time to gobble it.

What we are faced with today is no pretty tale of how just a little help from us in the way of a few over-age destroyers and perhaps a cannon or two will settle Mr. Hitler's hash for him and permit Britain to spread the four freedoms to dong dang and the whirling dervishes, under our benign direction.

The pending question is this and bluntly this and no less than this: Shall America, deliberately and consciously, go all the way into a shooting war, perhaps upon two oceans, or shall it not.

That question has no trimmings and no qualifying phrases to go along with it. It is a question of war or no war, war with its inevitable

A.E.F.[1] and its inevitable slaughter, or no war with an America pursuing the independent destiny which it can so readily achieve, beholden to no one, afraid of nothing. . . .

It has been well established in our experience in the last war, and reestablished on this very floor from the records only this week, that an armed merchantman is less safe than an ill-armed one. Its armament is wholly inadequate to protect it from the attacks which it invites; it has not a chance. It is not of record that an armed merchant ship ever sank a submarine, but it is of record that an armed merchant ship, headed for a belligerent port, carrying goods for a country at war, is a natural target for that submarine. . . .

Certainly if we get actively into the war—as the present program would lead us into it—it is going to be our war all the way, and no longer a proposition of holding Stalin's coat and handing up the sponge and water bucket to England. It is going to be our war to a point where every American voice will demand we keep our weapons at home and our dollars at home for American purposes instead of sending them into somebody else's war. . . .

Under the Neutrality Act, how many American lives have been lost on American merchant ships? None.

There is no proof that the Neutrality Act has been a failure. Indeed, there is evidence to the contrary.

To arm merchant ships invites attack.

To arm merchant ships strips them of whatever possible immunity they might enjoy as unarmed craft.

To arm merchant ships in no way strengthens them and is a deliberate jeopardizing of American lives.

Such jeopardizing of American lives with its inevitable loss of American life is the final key to war.

It cannot be forgotten that such men as will handle the guns aboard such merchant ships would be gun crews from the United States Navy, and the Navy is under orders to shoot on sight.

This is war. Whether honestly desired here, it is what I oppose. Let the proponents of shooting on sight and of arming ships to do it be

---

1   A.E.F.: American Expeditionary Force, the name of the units sent to fight in France in the First World War.

honest with us and tell us that is what they want. If it is not what they want, at least it is what is guaranteed by this program.

Questions for Discussion:

1. What does this document reveal about American attitudes toward going to war in 1941?

2. What arguments does Nye present against arming American merchant ships?

3. What arguments does Nye put forward for enforcing the Neutrality Act?

———————

U.S. Congress, *Congressional Record*, 77th Cong., 1st sess. (Washington, D.C.: Government Printing Office, 1941), 8306–14.

TWO-OCEAN WAR

The Japanese attack on Pearl Harbor on December 7, 1941, propelled the nation into a war for which it was almost completely unprepared. The initial months of the war were not encouraging. The Navy's morale plummeted after its crushing experience at Pearl Harbor and defeat after defeat at the hands of the Japanese in the Pacific. The news was no better in the Atlantic, where German U-boats sank merchant shipping almost at will, sometimes within sight of American shores. Gradually, with more and better equipment, ships, and training the American naval forces and merchant marine responded to the German and Japanese threats and, in conjunction with its allies, slowly established control over the world's oceans.

In the Atlantic Theater, the war at sea was almost entirely an effort to eradicate the German submarine threat so that American supplies could get through to British and Soviet allies. The U.S. Navy, assisted by the Canadian and British navies, had to defend convoys of merchant ships as they crossed the ocean carrying troops and supplies. Gradually the Allies developed better antisubmarine capabilities, a hard-earned advantage based on experience, training, technology, and intelligence. Furthermore, American shipyards turned out an incredible number of merchant ships—more than 2700 of the mass-produced Liberty ship design, as well as hundreds of the more advanced Victory ships and T-2 tankers. The Allies thus gained the upper hand in suppressing the submarine threat and achieved the massive logistic effort necessary to launch an invasion of Western Europe to liberate it from Nazi occupation.

If the Battle of the Atlantic revolved around convoys of merchant ships, then it can be said that the Pacific war revolved around aircraft carriers. With the destruction or incapacitation of much of America's battleship fleet at Pearl Harbor, aircraft carriers assumed the leading role. The crucial turning point of the Pacific War was the battle of Midway (June 4–7, 1942), in which two U.S. aircraft carriers sank four Japanese carriers, with the loss of one American carrier. Midway ended the American defensive phase of the war; after June, 1942, the United States remained on the offensive and began its counterattack against the Japanese Empire in August with an amphibious landing on Guadalcanal. However, the Japanese Navy continued to exist as a serious threat until late 1944. Late in the war American naval casualties mounted to alarming numbers as Japan resorted to desperate, but effective, kamikaze attacks: Japanese pilots flew their aircraft into American ships in a suicidal effort to repel the American Navy. Aircraft carriers were the favored target of the kamikaze attack.

The American war effort succeeded not only because of success in battle, but also because of the country's astounding industrial capability. But there was a critical labor shortage, so shipyards and other industries hired tens of thousands of women to fill jobs usually performed by men. Exemplified by a new cultural icon, Rosie the Riveter, these women performed crucial wartime work.

Phil Richards and John J. Branigan, "Prepare Yourself" (1942)

Merchant mariners faced incredible dangers during the Second World War. As recounted in Jim Longhi's memoir, *Woody, Cisco & Me*,[1] cargo ships were in danger of being torpedoed as soon as they left New York Harbor. Indeed, Longhi and his friend and shipmate Woody Guthrie (1912–1967) had more than one ship sink beneath them.

The United States lost hundreds of merchant ships during the Second World War, most of them in the Atlantic. Ship losses could be replaced by the massive American shipbuilding program, but it proved harder to replace experienced merchant mariners, all of whom were volunteers. The government established training centers around the country to provide new recruits, but early in the war the merchant marine suffered appalling casualties, not only because of enemy action, but because inexperienced or untrained crews did not know how to respond when torpedoed. The following

---

1   Jim Longhi, *Woody, Cisco & Me: Seamen Three in the Merchant Marine* (Urbana: University of Illinois Press, 1997).

item, excerpted from the well-titled book *How to Abandon Ship*, was one effort to capitalize on the experiences of those who had been torpedoed to benefit others. It is a remarkably blunt and practical approach to helping merchant mariners survive enemy attack.

The *Harry F. Sinclair, Jr.* was still afloat and burning a week after she had been torpedoed. Her fo'c'sle was free from flame. Yet men were burned to death because they jumped overboard, and they jumped overboard because they were not prepared.

William Caves, the bosun, safe in a water-borne lifeboat, saw an A.B.,[1] who had leaped over the side, struggling in a sea of flaming gasoline. It was impossible to reach the man. Caves saw his shipmate suck fire into his lungs. The A.B. was still fighting while he was being cremated. Then his head nodded briefly as though he were dozing, and Caves watched the charred body float deeper into the flames.

A needless death. The A.B. died because he had no faith in his own seamanship. He did not know the simplest fundamentals of buoyancy. He did not know the treachery of a cork jacket, which is scarcely more of a safety device than a strait jacket.

ADEQUATE DRILLS.—Do not cheat yourself of life the way this tragic seaman did. Prepare yourself, which cannot be done simply by engaging in peacetime boat drills. You are not a lifeboatman unless you have had experience in lowering away. Swinging out is not sufficient. As a boat drill, the mere operation of swinging out has left men inadequately trained, resulting in the loss of many lives during emergencies.

The *Comal Rico* crewmen were prepared. They held a boat drill every other day. When the ship was torpedoed, all survived except two who were killed by a direct hit.

Do not ship out unless you have taken part in a complete abandon-ship drill. Insist on this drill. Joe Melendez from the torpedoed *Saber* reported: "In the nineteen days since we left New York there had been no lifeboat drills." Do not let this situation occur aboard your ship. Complete drills can take place in harbors and when coastwise ships lay up at night and even at sea.

Frank W. Ferguson reported: "I was on the torpedoed *E. M. Clark* as A.B. There were 26 men in my lifeboat and of this number only

---

1   A.B: Able-Bodied Seaman

three were completely familiar with handling a boat. Because of this fact we had a tough time getting clear of the ship."

More drills, more survivors.

LIFE SUIT.—Provide yourself with a life suit. It will protect you against wind, rain, spray, and cold. You can sleep and work in a life suit. In the water it will enable you to get out of the danger area more quickly. It is fire-resisting for at least three minutes. Unless the suit is torn, it will prevent blood from a body wound getting into the water and attracting sharks. The dark color itself will lessen the danger of a shark attack. If the wearer is also clothed in heavy woolen underwear and takes care to keep his circulation active, a life suit will cut down the danger of frostbite and all but eliminate the possibility of death from exposure.

When the *Independence Hall* foundered off Sable Island, the vessel split in two, and a heavy sea prevented the launching of lifeboats. Ten men were lost. Reported Vincent A. Slivjak: "If these men had life suits, their lives would have been saved."

Captain Erling Vorberg, master of the torpedoed Norwegian motor tanker *Barfonn*, reported: "The boatswain, wearing the life suit, was washed into the sea by the first explosion. Due to the weight of the boots, he was kept floating in a standing position by the kapok[1] jacket, even though he was unconscious."

Of the other crewmen who jumped overboard wearing life suits, Vorberg reported: "They were floating around in the water like rubber balls and could easily swim and advance with a rather good speed. When they were picked up in the lifeboats, they were all dry and warm."

In the same convoy, all the men aboard the *Ila* were lost. They did not have life suits. Only two men were saved from the 30 aboard the Greek ship *Evros*. They did not have life suits.

R. G. Wallace, a watertender[2] from the torpedoed *Collamer*, reported: "One man was standing on the poop deck when the well deck was already under water. If this man had a life suit, he would be living today.

"A man was adrift on an old crate, and as close as we could maneuver the boat was ten feet. We asked him to jump, but he was afraid to

---

1 Kapok: a plant fiber used in lifejackets to provide flotation.

2 Watertender: member of the engineering department who tended to the ship's boilers.

do it, and after we drifted away, we heard his cries for a while, but then they were silenced."

INSPECTION.—Inspect the equipment and provisions yourself. Do not take anything for granted. Three days at sea an A.B. aboard the *Jupiter* discovered that the water tanks in four liferafts were dry.

John Larson, A.B. from the torpedoed *Allan Jackson*, reported: "The turnbuckles were frozen and it took anywheres between five and ten minutes to release the gripes."

Julius L. Schwartz from the torpedoed tanker *China Arrow* reported: "Two of the lifeboats had no rudder. The #3 lifeboat was without water."

Do not forget to inspect the screws which hold the mast step in place. In old boats these are sure to be badly rusted. The *Prusa*'s #1 boat nearly capsized when the step pulled loose at night while the boat was under full sail.

One of the breakers in the *Prusa*'s #1 lifeboat contained a top layer of fresh biscuits, but the balance of the contents was old and moldy.

FIRST-AID.—Ashore, you should take a course in first-aid; at sea you should practice what you have learned. You should provide yourself with a first-aid manual.

CLOTHING.—Whether you are bound for the Tropics or the Arctic regions, supply yourself with heavy woolen underwear.

CORK PRESERVERS.—Do not trust your life to a cork preserver. Men have drowned in them. This type of preserver rides high on the wearer's back, and sometimes it actually forces the head under water. Men who have jumped overboard wearing cork preservers have had ribs, arms, and shoulders broken. The front of the preserver strikes the chin, knocking the wearer unconscious.

Albert Pfisterer, a wiper from the torpedoed *Gulf America*, reported: "We saw bodies in the water, face downwards and feet up. This was the fault of the life preservers. The men could have been saved if it were not for the life preservers crawling up."

The bosun of the *Casper*, which sank in the Baltic Sea years ago, advised that a piece of nine thread be used to lash the cork preserver around the body to keep it snug and low.

SHIP'S MEETINGS.—John J. Smith, veteran pumpman[1] from the

---

1 Pumpman: a type of seaman found on tanker vessels tasked with taking on and discharging liquid cargo.

torpedoed Pure Oil tanker *E. W. Hutton*, strongly advocates ship's meetings. Though Smith's ship was torpedoed twice, and men were killed by direct hits, there was an absence of panic among the crew. The discussions aboard the *E. W. Hutton* had much to do in aiding the men, when the emergency came, to keep their heads.

The meetings included the entire crew, divided into two off-watch groups. Besides these meetings, a committee composed of one representative from each department conferred with Captain Carl Flaathan on safety measures.

It was agreed that if no officer were present to take command, the first capable man to reach his lifeboat station, regardless of his rating, was to act as the leader until relieved by a licensed officer. It was also understood that once launched, the lifeboat was to remain nearby until it was certain all survivors had been picked up from the rafts and the water.

The discussions should take place under pleasant circumstances. If dwelling on the subject of abandoning ship causes the men to grow fidgety, discontinue the discussions for a day or two.

TEXTBOOK.—It is suggested that you use this manual, which has been written out of the sweat and blood of actual experience, as the textbook for your meetings. For instance, read Chapter 3 on *Buoyancy*, and then ask the captain or chief engineer to explain the buoyancy conditions of your own vessel. After this discussion it is likely that you will be able, in an emergency, to put down any impulse to jump into a flaming oil slick or icy water or a shark-infested sea.

DEMONSTRATION.—Thirty-one survivors escaped in a 28-foot lifeboat from the torpedoed *City of New York*. Because of the boat's crowded condition, John Adams, the carpenter, could not get to the mast, and those around it were unable to rig the sail. One adequately trained lifeboatman among 31 persons! The sail had to be passed back to Adams for him to bend on. Then Adams had to shout instructions on how to step the mast.

It is vitally important that the crew—particularly the new seamen, the Black Gang,[1] and those in the steward's department—learn by practice and demonstration the seamanship required in handling a lifeboat. The proper distribution of weight in the lifeboat should be demonstrated, to emphasize the importance of maintaining a low cen-

---

1   Black Gang: those mariners who worked in the engine room.

ter of gravity. Everyone not trained in navigation should read Chapter 9 on *Navigating,* and practice shaping courses on a Pilot Chart before the need to do so arises.

ORDINARIES.[1]—It has been the experience of veteran seamen at ship's meetings that the youngsters are inclined to grin. Consequently the old-timers are equally inclined to drop the discussions. Yet a foolish grin does not make a person's life any less precious.

Actually these ship's boys are grinning to cover their embarrassment, to hide their sense of inadequacy. Perhaps some of them are even incapable of comprehending danger before it reaches them. Whatever the reason, the real seamen are not to allow an irresponsible attitude to affect their zeal in passing on the benefits of their experience.

MORALE.—B. A. Baker, the *Prusa's* third mate, advises: "The most important thing for any lifeboatman to do, is to school his own mind. Make up your mind not to get excited and stick to it. Don't say you won't be afraid, for you will. When the torpedo explodes you will get a sinking sensation in the pit of your stomach, and your knees may become a bit weak. The best cure for this is action."

SLACKNESS.—When you review the statistics regarding marine disasters, it is difficult to understand how there ever could be any slackness in lifeboat drills. Yet many a seaman can tell of attending hundreds of drills without once having a chance to lower away and handle a waterborne boat.

Arthur LaBarge, an oiler aboard the *Oneida,* reported on a North Atlantic trip in March: "No lifeboat drills during the entire voyage, going or coming."

Questions for Discussion:

1. According to the authors, what are the greatest dangers facing merchant seamen?

2. What does this excerpt reveal about the merchant mariners who served in World War II?

3. How could merchant mariners prepare themselves for being torpedoed?

Phil Richards and John J. Branigan, *How to Abandon Ship* (New York: Cornell Maritime Press, 1942), 9–17.

---

1 Ordinaries: Ordinary Seamen, inexperienced entry-level seamen who worked in the deck department.

Joseph Matte III, "Action at ICOMP" (1942)

Coast Guard Ensign Joseph Matte III wrote this journal during his time on the Coast Guard cutter *Ingham* from early 1942 through April, 1943, operating out of Iceland to escort Allied merchant vessels in the North Atlantic at ICOMP—Iceland Ocean Meeting Point. It was grueling duty: tedious, stormy, dangerous, isolated, and with few opportunities for shore leave. Happily, the *Ingham* was a Secretary-class cutter (sometimes called 327s, for their length), which were known for their ability to endure heavy seas; even so, Matte makes frequent comments about the rough weather he experienced. Matte broke with regulations that strictly forbade keeping journals to prevent such information falling into the hands of the enemy.

The *Ingham* remained on active duty until 1988; it is now part of the Patriots Point Naval and Maritime Museum near Charleston, South Carolina. For a complete history of the Coast Guard in the Battle of the Atlantic, especially the Secretary-class cutters, see Michael Walling's *Bloodstained Sea.*[1]

> Thursday, 27 August—At Torpedo Junction.[2] (0400) Relieve the watch. Still dark, with dense fog; visibility about 500 yards. Zigzagging on starboard flank of *Pan York* at a distance of 3500 to 5000 yards, keeping contact by radar. *Bibb*[3] similarly on port flank. (0417) Radar operator reports first one, then many "targets" in the vicinity of *Bibb*. (We have been awaiting meeting with the westbound convoy, running on opposite course to hers). We close in on *Pan York* to avoid losing her, almost running her down in doing so. Then we reduce speed and run alongside. After swinging about-face to the course of the main convoy, we ask *Bibb* for information on its location. *Bibb* reports that she narrowly averted head-on collision with another escort ship (*Bibb*'s radar must have been out). By the time we have the *Pan York* and the *Bibb* squared away, the convoy is out of radar range, so we increase speed in pursuit of it. (0730) The fog is lifting; the *Bibb* finally emerges, about where she should be. (0800) The convoy has just been relocated by radar and can be just made out through the lifting fog.

---

1 Michael Walling. *Bloodstained Sea: The U.S. Coast Guard in the Battle of the Atlantic, 1941–1944* (Camden, Maine: International Marine/McGraw-Hill, 2004).

2 Torpedo Junction: any area with heavy U-boat activity, in this case a part of the North Atlantic south of Iceland.

3 *Bibb*: U.S. Coast Guard cutter *Bibb*, a sister-ship of the *Ingham*.

And so another convoy has come to "Icomp," met the transatlantic convoy, and gone on its way. This feat of effecting a juncture between two convoys in the middle of the ocean, with only rather meager and not-too-accurate information to go by, is one of the most amazing features of the convoy system, as wonderful as it is commonplace.

(1100) Having delivered our charge, we leave the transatlantic convoy and head westward with the *Bibb* in search of an eastbound convoy, from which we will take a group of ships to Iceland.

Friday, 28 August—According to radio press, the U.S. destroyer *Ingraham* was sunk in a collision in a fog. I wonder if it happened between 0400 and 0500 GCT yesterday morning. I also wonder if the U.S. destroyer *Ingram* was in a fog yesterday morning.

Saturday, 29 August—(0745) Rain and fog. Visibility ½ to 1 mile. We have just picked up radar interference ahead, indication of an approaching convoy. (0815) An escort vessel is sighted. (0830) *Ingham* and *Bibb* join the escort group under Commander Task Unit 24.1.12, bound to the eastward with 54 ships in convoy. We take station on starboard half of van, zigzagging at 14½ knots. Convoy speed 7.5 knots. (Last winter *Ingham* was in Task Unit 24.1.1).

Sunday, 30 August—Our QC underwater sound machine[1] has been out of order all day, robbing us of at least 80% of our effectiveness as an anti-submarine unit. This single device, which enables us to locate and track submerged targets, is by far our most potent anti-submarine device, for without it, it is almost entirely a matter of blind luck to "get" a submarine with depth charges. A corollary is that the six enlisted men who operate this machine are probably the most important men on the ship.

The QC machine was fixed this evening.

Monday, 31 August—The week started off with a bang, for two ships in our convoy were torpedoed this morning about 0815. Several of our lookouts sighted a torpedo track between *Ingham* and another escort just before the explosions. Within 15 or 20 minutes both ships had gone to the bottom. Within an hour and a half the survivors had been rescued and we were on our way. The sub (or subs) was not sighted.

Wednesday, 2 September—Monday and yesterday were the kind

---

1 QC underwater sound machine: a sonar device located in a dome on the ship's bottom. It could detect submarines in passive mode by listening for propeller noises, or in active mode by sending out a distinctive pinging sound.

of days that keep us from going batty from monotony. Monday afternoon we sighted a mine and sank it with about 2,100 rounds of .30 caliber rifle and machine gun fire. It looked like an old British mine and probably was unrelated to the attack in the morning.

About 0100 Tuesday a corvette in the rear of the convoy sighted a sub and attempted to ram it, then depth charged it. This was listed as a probable kill. On the theory that other subs might be around, all the other escorts and some of the merchantmen opened up with star shell fire. This was a fantastic, dream-like scene, with star shell bursts now in one sector, then in another, some of the shells whining by the ship, apparently close by. After some time at General Quarters, we secured and resumed our station.

During the day on Tuesday we received air coverage by patrol bombers from Iceland. These planes reported submarines on the surface at various times through the day; as many as four having been reported at times. The destroyers spent most of the day chasing these contact reports.

Just after breakfast yesterday we went to General Quarters twice as contact was reported astern. In the course of our prowls at this time we went down the center of the convoy on our way astern. It was interesting to see the strange deck loads of ambulances, jeeps, trucks, landing barges, etc., and the gun crews on every ship waving to us as we passed.

At 2000 yesterday the Iceland group of 11 ships broke away and headed north. The escort group consists of *Ingham*, *Bibb*, and the old U.S. destroyer *Schenk*, which joined us yesterday. Last night was uneventful. This morning we dropped one 600 lb. depth charge on a sound contact. The captain conned the ship for the first time, during this run, and did a poor job of it, for whatever the target was, it was inside our turning circle when the charge was dropped. We had air coverage since dawn this morning, which no doubt accounts for the quiet time we have had lately.

Thursday, 3 September—Quiet day today. Dropped one depth charge in a school of fish this afternoon. Rain all day. Sighted land about 1700; visibility about four miles.

Dropped our convoy off Reykjavik about 2030 and proceeded to Hvalfjordur (a fjord near Reykjavik which is protected by anti-submarine nets) where we moored to the tanker *Sapelo* at 2230.

Friday, 4 September—RED LETTER DAY!!—I finally got mail from home! Letters from Dad, Marie, John Cameron, and Russ Serenberg, (dated July 26 to August 8.). Magazines—*Yachting, Mid-West Yachting News, Naval Institute Proceedings. New York Yacht Club, Rules & Regulations for the Construction of Racing Yachts.*

Monday, 7 September—Received a big batch of mail this morning, (July 12 to 29); lots of magazines, clippings, letters, and the planimeter[1] I ordered from Boston.

Went to the (anti-submarine) "attack teacher" this morning, aboard the HMS *Blenheim.*

Wednesday, 9 September—Took a boat under oars (for the first time) this morning, assisting in mooring the ship to a buoy. Until then *Ingham* has been laying alongside the U.S. supply ship *Melville.*

Received mail from June 3 to July 9, tonight.

Monday, 14 September—Commander George E. McCabe came aboard tonight to relieve Cdr. Greenspun. Also Lieut. J. Van Heuveln reported aboard for engineering duty. They flew from Presque Isle, Maine by Ferry Command plane, via Newfoundland and Greenland; total travel time, 6 days.

Wednesday, 16 September—Commander McCabe and the Captain held a joint inspection of the ship today, preparatory to a change of command.

Thursday, 17 September—Unmoored this forenoon and proceeded to Reykjavik, where we fueled. Came to anchor about 6 PM, after fueling.

Friday, 18 September—Went through all emergency drills today; (another part of the change of command routine).

Saturday, 19 September—Commander McCabe relieved Commander Greenspun in the morning. In the afternoon, I went sailing in one of the ship's lifeboats. A fairly nice day.

Sunday, 20 September—Commander Greenspun left for Argentia, Newfoundland.

Monday, 21 September—(1530) Got underway out of the harbor of Reykjavik in a gale, in company of *Bibb*, to escort ten merchantmen to Torpedo Junction.

Friday, 25 September—Log of a sea-sick sailor: Ate a hearty supper Monday night, but after writing my log after coming off watch at 8 PM, I offered my supper up to the storm. Up again at 4 AM Tuesday

---

1 Planimeter: an instrument designed to measure the area of a two-dimensional shape.

for the Morning watch, but slept all day without eating. Tried some supper Tuesday night, but couldn't keep it. Turned in again after the 4–8 A.M watch. Felt better Wednesday morning and held on to my breakfast.

The gale slowly backed around from SE to NW and steadied there. About 1900 Thursday (yesterday) we met the westbound transatlantic convoy and delivered our ships intact, except for one which put back into Iceland. Then last night we started off to the westward to try to find survivors of three ships torpedoed out of an eastbound convoy. This convoy was being escorted by the *Campbell* and *Spencer* (sister ships to the *Ingham*) and Canadian corvettes. The storm broke up the convoy, and then the subs went to work.

Shortly after 4 AM this morning, we (and the *Bibb*) increased to full speed, between 18½ and 19 knots. The wind had abated and shifted to southwest, smoothing out the sea. However, the wind increased shortly and a new sea has been building up all day, so that by now (3 PM) the ship is again pitching and quivering furiously. The motion in my room, the last one aft, is so violent that writing is difficult and it is even hard to keep my eyes on the penpoint.

During the second dog watch[1] we decreased speed to 13 knots due to fog setting in. This effectively kills any chance of finding anything before daylight. Ship is now comfortable for the first time since leaving Reykjavik.

I beat the Doc 2 games out of 3 in dominoes this evening!

Saturday, 26 September—About noon today 3 boats were sighted and their occupants picked up by the *Bibb*. They were 51 people of the *Penn Mar.* At 3 PM a life raft was sighted with 8 men aboard. Lieut. Masters took our No. 1 boat (under oars) to the raft and took off the men. The boat falls were led aft "married," with about a hundred men tailed off along the falls. On its return, when the boat had hooked on to the falls, the order was shouted and instantly the men ran the boat out of the waves and up two-blocked in about 2 seconds! The survivors were from the *Tennessee*; they had been clinging to their little raft since Tuesday night.

Sunday, 27 September—(0400–0800) Still proceeding east watching for survivors. Westerly wind building up a sizeable sea astern. About 0530, picked up two radar targets astern which closed from

---

1 Second dog watch: from 6 p.m. to 8 p.m.

two miles to one mile, possibly subs trailing us. Manned the after 3" guns and searched astern with star shells and 18" searchlight but saw nothing. Then we manned Gun No. 3 (forward) and countermarched at 18 knots. However we took so much solid water as to make any action or gun fire impossible, so we again turned eastward and reduced speed to 13 knots, as before. Daylight came not long after, relieving the tension.

In the afternoon we turned westward to meet an eastbound convoy. The wind had increased steadily to about Force 8 or 9, and the sea was running high, occasional combers topping 35 feet. Speed was reduced successively to 11, 10, and 8 knots, and even so we were making heavy weather of it and taking considerable solid water on deck. The old destroyer *Leary* joined us today and was plugging along with us, taking a considerable beating, reporting boats smashed etc., and a plate on the starboard bow below the waterline cracked. On the *Ingham* the principal casualty was the No. 4 boat (port side), the weather bow of which was smashed by a sea, at the same time smashing the bottom by driving part of its cradle through the bottom.

Monday, 28 September—After plugging along all day with the *Bibb* and *Leary* through high seas and fog, we found our convoy, just reforming after yesterday's storm. About 4 o'clock a few of the ships were sighted through the fog; shortly after we were assigned a station about 5 miles out, which was kept by radar, of course.

By evening it quieted down so that I wrote a couple of letters, the first time this trip I could sit on my chair without hanging on.

Wednesday, 30 September—Still zigzagging along this morning in uninterrupted fog. Have had practically no visual contact with our convoy. About 0800, the Iceland group of seven ships, including a transport, broke off from the main body, and we set our course (028 deg.) for Reykjavik.

The wind picked up again from the west building up a high and uncomfortable sea. The weather this trip has been totally miserable.

Friday, 2 October—Sighted Rekjanes light in the 4–8 watch this morning. Made our landfall off Skagi Point about 0700 and proceeded into the inner harbor of Reykjavik, where we went to General Quarters for an air raid alarm just after docking. *Bibb* tied up alongside, and "our" survivors and hers were landed into Army ambulances. They were all carried off in stretchers for some unknown reason, though all of them were locomoting about ship alright before we tied up! In the afternoon we proceeded into Hvalfjordur, where we fueled from the British tanker *Empire Garden*.

Questions for Discussion:
1. What does this document reveal about the Battle of the Atlantic?
2. What sort of problems seem to concern Matte the most?
3. What concerns should historians have in working with a journal such as Matte's?

Joseph Matte III, "Journal of Joseph Matte, III, onboard the USS *Ingham*, CG, while on convoy duty in the North Atlantic from 16 February 1942 to 19 April 1943." U.S. Coast Guard Historian's Office, http://www.uscg.mil/history/Matte%20on%20Ingham.html, accessed January 1, 2007.

George Gay, "Torpedo Squadron Eight" (1942)

With the advent of aircraft carriers, World War II witnessed battles in which naval vessels never saw the enemy ships they were fighting. The Battle of Midway was one such battle largely fought by carrier-launched aircraft. But early in the war, American pilots proved inexperienced and their aircraft proved inadequate. For example, Japanese fighters completely destroyed the aircraft of Torpedo Squadron Eight (VT-8) as it approached to attack the Japanese fleet, and only one man, Ensign George Gay, USNR, (1917–1994) survived, and even his aircraft was shot down. Floating in the ocean, he witnessed later successful attacks on the Japanese aircraft carriers, and was rescued a day after the battle. He was subsequently awarded the Navy Cross and the Presidential Unit Citation for his actions. This piece is an adaptation of an interview conducted by the Navy later in the war after Gay's promotion to lieutenant. Gay later wrote a book about his wartime experiences, appropriately entitled *Sole Survivor*.

I didn't get much sleep the night of June the 3rd, the stories of the battle were coming in, midnight torpedo attack by the PBYs[1] and all kinds of things, and we were a little bit nervous, kind of, like before a football game. We knew that the Japs were trying to come in and take something away from us and we also knew that we were at a disadvantage because we had old aircraft and could not climb the altitude with the dive-bombers or fighters and we expected to be on our own. We

---

1 PBY: a twin-engine patrol bomber seaplane, sometimes known as a *Catalina*.

didn't expect to run into the trouble that we found of course, but we knew that if we had any trouble we'd probably have to fight our way out of it ourselves.

Before we left the ship, Lt. Comdr. Waldron[1] told us that he thought the Japanese Task Forces would swing together when they found out that our Navy was there and that they would either make a retirement in just far enough so that they could again retrieve their planes that went in on the attack and he did not think that they'd go on into the Island of Midway as most of the Squadron commanders, and air group commanders, figured and he told us when he left not to worry about our navigation but to follow him as he knew where he was going. And it turned out just exactly that way. He went just as straight to the Jap Fleet as if he'd had a string tied to them and we thought that morning, at least I did when I first saw the Japanese carriers, one of them that was afire and another ship that had a fire aboard and I thought that there was a battle in progress and we were late.

I was a little bit impatient that we didn't get right on in there then and when it finally turned out that we got close enough in that we could make a contact report and describe what we could see the Zeros[2] jumped on us and it was too late. . . . It's been a very general opinion that the anti-aircraft fire shot our boys down and that's not true. I don't think that any of our planes were damaged, even touched by anti-aircraft fire, the fighters, the Zeros, shot down everyone of them, and by the time we got in to where the anti-aircraft fire began to get hot, the fighters all left us and I was the only one close enough to get any real hot anti-aircraft fire, and I don't think it even touched me and I went right through it, right over the ship.

I think we made a couple of grave mistakes. In the first place, if we'd only had one fighter with us I think our troubles would have been very much less. We picked up on the way in a cruiser plane, a Japanese scout from one of their cruisers, and it fell in behind us and tracked us and I know gave away our position and course, and speed. We changed after he left but then I know that they knew we were coming. If we'd had one fighter to go back and knock that guy down, catch him before he could have gotten that report off, I believe the Japs might have been fooled some, quite sometime longer on the fact

---

1   Lt. Comdr. Waldron: Lieutenant Commander John C. Waldron (1900–1942), the commander of VT-8, who died at the battle of Midway.
2   Zero: Japanese carrier-based fighter planes.

that our fleet was there. I think that might have been one of their first contacts warning them that we had a fleet in the vicinity and that got us into trouble, I'm sure.

Also, we went in to a scouting line out there when we were still trying to find them and didn't and the skipper put us in a long scouting line which I thought was a mistake at the time. I didn't ever question Comdr. Waldron, of course, he had his reason for it and I know that he expected to find them but he wanted to be sure that we did and that is the reason that we were well trained, and when he gave the join-up signal we joined up immediately. I was only afraid that in the scouting line in those old planes we would be caught by Zeros spread out and it would be much worse. As it turned out, it didn't make a whole lot of difference anyway, but we joined up quickly and we got organized to make our attack, the Zeros got after us.

I remember the first one that came down got one of the airplanes that was over to the left. Comdr. Waldron on his air phone asked Dobbs and came out over the air if that was a Zero or if it was one of our planes and I didn't know whether Dobbs answered him or not, but I came out on the air and told him that it was a TBD[1]. . . .

Personally, I was just lucky. I've never understood why I was the only one that came back, but it turned out that way, and I want to be sure that the men that didn't come back get the credit for the work that they did. They followed Comdr. Waldron without batting an eye and I don't feel like a lot of people have felt that we made mistakes and that Comdr. Waldron got us into trouble. I don't feel that way at all. I know that if I had it all to do over again, even knowing that the odds were going to be like they were, knowing him like I did know him, I'd follow him again through exactly the same thing because I trusted him very well. We did things that he wanted us to do not because he was our boss, but because we felt that if we did the things he wanted us to do then it was the right thing to do.

The Zeros that day just caught us off balance. We were at a disadvantage all the way around.

Interviewer: Do you think that the attack would have been any more

---

1 TBD: an American airplane, the Douglas TBD-1 "Devastator" Torpedo Plane. The Naval Historical Center states that by the time of the battle of Midway they were "Old and slow, with a weak defensive armament and without self-sealing fuel tanks, the TBD had proven horribly vulnerable to enemy fighters."

successful if the planes had been more or less spread out. Wasn't Torpedo 8 rather close together as they went into the attack?

Lt. Gay: Well, that might be true had it been that we were being shot down by anti-aircraft fire, but being jumped, as we were, by a squadron of Zeros, our beliefs were, and I think they were very well founded, that our only protection would be to stick together and let each plane's gun try and help the other plane.

In other words, in a TBD, with as few guns as they've got, the idea was to let, to stay together as a formation and fight them off as a pack rather than to try and spread out. We could have spread out all right, but they could have spread out too, and it would have been just that much worse on us.

I never have understood why it's been the general opinion in designing torpedo planes that it is not an offensive weapon. They don't seem to feel like they ought to put guns in it, and I disagree with that very thoroughly, and I can give my reasons for that.

When the Zeros attacked us that day, I was able, with my one fixed gun, to hit one; I know because I saw the tracers going into him. Of course, it couldn't hurt him with one .30 caliber [machine gun].... That day, I got a chance to shoot at other airplanes that just got in my way. It wouldn't have been that I would go out of my way to try and act as a fighter plane, it was just that the targets were there and they will be there every time a torpedo plane makes an attack, those targets will get in his way and he ought to have something to shoot at them with.

I had to fly right over destroyers that were shooting at me. If I had machine guns forward and plenty of them, I'd have been able to give them a little trouble. Then as I got in close enough to drop my torpedo, I could see everything on the port side shooting at me. If I had had some machine guns to shoot back at them, I might not have been able to silence those guns, but I could have made the gunners a little nervous. As it was, they were just sitting there shooting at me and I wasn't shooting back at them. Then after I pulled up over the ship and did a flipper turn, I dove down right at the fantail of this big carrier where they were rearming and regassing the planes. Gas hoses were scattered all over the place out there, and I know they were full of gasoline. If I'd had forward guns, I could have set that ship afire right there myself.

I had no guns to shoot with except that one little pea shooter, the .30 caliber putt-putt and by the time I got there it jammed, it either jammed or was shot up. Then after I went out, I flew over another destroyer and every time there was a target and every time I had no guns to work on it. They seem to feel that they don't put the guns in the torpedo planes because we'll go off and fool around and get ourselves in trouble. I don't think they'll have that trouble with the pilots because I do think that they should have fire power forward and also aft to take care of themselves so that when the targets get in the way you can at least have the self satisfaction, if nothing else, of shooting at them. I really strongly recommend them forward. I find a lot of people who disagree with that, but that's my personal opinion on it. . . .

Interviewer: What happened to your torpedo when you launched it?

Lt. Gay: Well, I was very lucky. Of course, I said it was the first one I'd ever carried and naturally the first one I've ever dropped. . . . Well, when I got in close enough to think about dropping a torpedo, I saw that she was in this hard turn and I pulled out to the right and swung back and gave her a lead and it was a perfect set up. I couldn't have missed it if I'd wanted to . . . by the time the torpedo got to her she was broadside and when I shot at her she was coming to me and turning hard, so I just veered off to the left a bit and, I was to her port by this time see, and she was in the turn to starboard and I laid off left and she just turned right around into it. It was easy.

Interviewer: Right after that, as I understand it, you flew directly over the ship and circled about and finally was downed by a Zero. Do you want to go on from there please?

Lt. Gay: Well, yes, I dropped the torpedo and was fortunate enough to get away from the anti-aircraft fire although everything was shooting at me. I flew right down the gun barrel on one of these big pom poms up forward. I think it must have been about 20 mm [anti-aircraft guns] stuff. I looked in the sights and tried to get a shot at that fellow but my gun was jammed by then and I figured the only way that I could evade all that anti-aircraft fire was not to throw my belly up in a turn away from the ship, but was just to go right straight to her and offer as small a target as I could. So I flew right down the gun barrels, pulled up on the port side, did a flipper turn right by the island, I could see the little Jap captain up there jumping up and down raising hell, and I thought about wishing that I had a .45[1] so that I could take a pot shot at him. I couldn't hit him, but, if nothing else, thrown the gun at him, just something, but I then dropped right back down on the deck and flew aft looking at these airplanes.

By the way, I had a thought right in a split second there to crash into those planes. That I don't feel is any suicidal instinct at all. I know that if I had been shot up to the extent where I felt that I'd only go over those planes and fall in the ocean on the other side, feeling that I was pretty near gone, just a matter of seconds, that I would have crashed right into those planes, because I could have started a beautiful fire and I figured that's the way the Japs do it when they crash into a ship. It's when a fellow is just gone and knows it, it is just crash into the ship or crash into the sea, and you have enough control to do a little bit more damage, why you crash into the ship.

I dropped down after going over these ships, I didn't feel very badly, I had a left leg that was burned and a left arm that was gone, the plane was still flying and I felt pretty good and I didn't see any sense in crashing into those planes. I thought maybe I'd get a chance to go back and hit them again someday and as long as there's life there's hope, so I pulled up and went over them, dropped back down next to the water, just after I passed over the fantail and then I heard the torpedo go off. Just a little bit after that the anti-aircraft fire hadn't picked up anymore, but the Zeros jumped on me and I was trying to get out of the fleet. Before I got away from them though, the five Zeros dived right down on me in a line and about the second or third one shot my rudder control and ailerons out and I pancaked into the ocean. The hood slammed shut, I couldn't keep the right wing up. It had hit the water first and snapped the plane in, and bent it all up and broke it up and the hood slammed shut and it was in the sprained fuselage. I couldn't hardly get it open. That's when I got scared. I was afraid I was going to drown in the plane.

I got out of there and thought about my rear gunner, made a dive to try and pick him up, but I couldn't get to him. The first thing I saw after I came to the surface was the other of those two large carriers headed right straight for me and she was landing planes. . . . They went right by me about 500 yards to the west of me and the cruiser that

---

1   .45: the U.S. Navy's standard sidearm, the semi-automatic US Pistol, caliber .45, M-1911A1.

was with her was only a thousand yards, screen and I presume, went by about 500 yards to the east of me headed north and they circled back.

After the [U.S. Navy] dive bombers came in and beat those carriers up and got them burning good and they lost control of them and they stopped pretty close to me, there was another [Japanese] cruiser that patrolled up and down on the north and south line that came by me first to the east, I guess about two miles away, and turned to me, and I thought they saw me and were coming over, but instead of that she just ran a 180 degree reversal and went back to the south. The next time she came up, she went by me much closer, but still to the east, went up and made her turn, and in her turn she got to the west of me and came back down by me on the other side. And then the third time that she came up, she came almost to me and made her 180 degree turn and went back, and on her way back that time, a patrol plane came by over to the west and she circled around the [Japanese aircraft carrier] *Kaga* to get on the other side and help throw up a screen against the patrol planes. They were trying to knock her down and she didn't come back anymore.

Then during the afternoon, there was a [Japanese] destroyer came pretty close to running me down. It came closer to me than any other ship. If there had been anybody aboard that I knew I could have recognized them as they went by. Of course, I was hiding under this cushion and instead of having my head above and out of the water, I presented the side of this little black cushion to him and hoped that they'd figure out that I was a piece of the wreckage. Pretty fair estimate about that time anyway, so I managed to not be picked up by them somehow.

My main troubles in the water, outside of my leg burning very badly in the salt water, I didn't know exactly what was the matter with it until after I got into the hospital the next day. My hand was bleeding and I thought about sharks and then I remembered the concussions of the bombs and things and I knew that the sharks didn't like those things and I figured that they would be run off and I think that this is the case, but I swallowed an awful lot of salt water, I lost an awful lot of weight and my main difficulty was keeping my eyes open. The salt water finally got in my eyes to such an extent that I could only with very great difficulty open my eyes and I would open them and scan the horizon 360 degrees and then shut them again and leave them that way unless I heard something or unless I figured it was maybe a ship might have gotten close since I looked the last time and I'd force them open and look again. I got better on that score, much better after I got out of the water and was able to kind of clean my eyes out and get the salt water out of them.

Interviewer: How about those heavy explosions you heard at night, didn't you experience some heavy explosions?

Lt. Gay: Well, not too many at night. The carriers during the day resembled a very large oil field fire, if you've ever seen one. The fire coming out of the forward and aft end of the ship looked like a blow torch, just roaring white flame and the oil burning, the crude oil, boil up, I don't know how high and just billowing big red flames belch out of this black smoke. The dive bombers told me they saw this smoke at 18,000 feet that day and really did make a nice fire and they'd burn for awhile and blow up for awhile and I was sitting in the water hollering "Hooray, Hooray."

I was in a funny position to be cheering for the thing, but I was really tickled to see the dive bombers really pasting them even though they were in pretty bad shape. But during the afternoon after they pretty well burned themselves up, the larger one close to me there, the [Japanese aircraft carrier] *Akagi*, sank just after dark, the [Japanese] cruisers raked her with fire finished her off, and the other two, the [Japanese aircraft carriers] *Kaga* and the *Soryu*, burned all night, but they didn't necessarily explode. As a matter of fact, the Japs were there trying to put the fires out. I could seem them playing around, searchlights, picking up people and trying, I think they were trying to salvage these two ships; but the explosions that I heard the next morning turned out to be our submarines putting torpedoes into these things and they finished them off. That was early the next morning just as dawn was cracking.

Interviewer: Another question. Going back to your rescue at Midway, how did you identify yourself to your rescuing planes?

Lt. Gay: Well, I was sitting up in the middle of this battle area and there was all kinds of things around, oil slick and barrels and lumber and the Japanese life rafts were black. I was in a big four-man yellow rubber life raft and I am sure he knew, as soon as he saw that yellow boat, that I was an American. Of course, I waved to him and had my regular Navy T-shirt, took my khaki shirt off and just figured if he saw that Navy T-shirt, me in that yellow boat, that he'd know it was one of his buddies.

Questions for Discussion:

1. What does this account reveal about the experiences of American naval aviators fighting in the Pacific Theatre?

2. Assess the reliability of Ensign Gay's recounting of his experiences: what are its strengths and weaknesses?

3. What enabled Ensign Gay to survive the Battle of Midway?

"Ensign George Gay, USNR, interview," box 11, World War II Interviews, Operational Archives Branch, Naval Historical Center.

Office of War Information, "Rosie the Riveter" (1943)

During both world wars women stepped forward to work in shipyards, releasing young men to join the armed services or other vital war-related work. In the First World War, a few women worked as welders, but in the Second World War many thousands of women worked in shipyards on the nation's coasts and the Great Lakes. The generic name for these women in

"Welder-trainee Josie Lucille Owens plies her trade on the ship, 1941–1945." With nearly one thousand African American women employed as burners, welders, scalers, and in other capacities at the Kaiser Shipyards in Richmond, California, women war workers played an important part in the construction of the Liberty Ship SS *George Washington Carver*, launched on May 7th, 1943. Photo by E. F. Joseph, courtesy of the Library of Congress #LC-USW3-028671-C.

"Welders Alivia Scott, Hattie Carpenter, and Flossie Burtos await an opportunity to weld their first piece of steel on the ship SS *George Washington Carver*," ca. 1943. Photo by Arthur S. Siegel, courtesy of the Library of Congress # LC-USW3-028676-C.

"Women shipfitters worked on board the USS *Nereus*, and are shown as they neared completion of the floor in a part of the engine room. Left to right are Shipfitters Betty Pierce, Lola Thomas, Margaret Houston, Thelma Mort and Katie Stanfill. U.S. Navy Yard, Mare Island, CA.," ca. 1943. Photo by the Department of the Navy, courtesy of the National Archives, ARC #296892.

"First women to attain rate of Electric Welder, 3rd class, were Alyce R. Sawyers (on the left) and Josephine L. Hollingworth, in 1942. U.S. Navy Yard, Mare Island., CA.," ca. 1942. Photo by the Department of the Navy, courtesy of the National Archives, ARC #296887.

the Second World War was *Rosie the Riveter*, however, most photos emphasize the role women played as welders, rather than riveters, and the term *Wendy the Welder* was also used; at some shipyards, up to half the women employed were welders. One of the photos included here shows a female worker with a welding mask labeled *Rosie*, even though her name was Josie and she was a welder, not a riveter.

About half of all female workers were married, and many had children. Faced with a labor shortage and absenteeism by women struggling to hold down a job and take care of their children, shipyard operator Henry J. Kaiser established housing, daycare, schools, and the nation's first HMO to care for workers and their families. The demand for labor at Kaiser's West Coast shipyards resulted in enormous population growth: the shipbuilding community of Richmond, California, more than quadrupled in size during the war. But as detailed in Amy Kesselman's *Fleeting Opportunities*,[1] after

---

1 Amy Kellerman, *Fleeting Opportunities: Women Shipyard Workers in Portland and Vancouver During World War II and Reconversion* (Albany: State University of New York Press, 1990).

the war women quickly found themselves displaced from heavy industry as male-dominated labor unions excluded them from shop floors across the nation.

Questions for Discussion:
1. What do these photos tell us about the ethnicity or race of women who worked in American shipyards?
2. What do these images tell us abut the work women performed in ship-yards during World War I and II versus that performed by men?
3. What clues do these images give about the conditions and attitudes ex-perienced by women on the Home Front in World War II?

National Archives and Records Administration, RG 208: Records of the Office of War Information, 1926–1951 and RG 181: Records of Naval Districts and Shore Establishments, 1784–1981.

3

COLD WAR AND BEYOND

The end of the Second World War saw the United States Navy the undisputed master of the world's oceans and the American merchant marine the largest and most modern in the world. But there were some dramatic changes in the postwar world that threatened the Navy and American shipping.

The Cold War created challenges for the Navy and the merchant marine. The advent of the atomic bomb caused some in the defense establishment to question the need for a navy. The Navy escaped elimination and found new roles for itself, both in conventional areas and as part of the nation's nuclear deterrence program. The merchant marine, although always recognized as a vital strategic asset, did not fare as well. Government policy, changing markets, and labor issues dogged the American-flagged merchant fleet, which is now only a shadow of its former self.

While American shipping declined, the American public rediscovered the sea. The sea was a playground for wealthy Americans who traveled across the Atlantic on ocean liners and also for an increasing number of people who took inexpensive pleasure cruises in the Caribbean. In the 1960s American leaders, scientists, and the public also rediscovered the sea as an important resource to be utilized carefully. Part of this recognition came about because valuable fish stocks were harvested to near-extinction, and marine disasters such as the *Exxon Valdez* grounding brought home to many Americans the need to protect coastal zones from environmental disaster.

Into the twenty-first century, the United States continues to wrestle with what its relationship should be with the world's seas, the Great Lakes, and western rivers. The American-flagged merchant marine has virtually ceased to exist, commercial fishing has diminished, invasive species have altered the marine environment, and pollution remains an issue. The U.S. Navy remains the most powerful in the world, but has struggled to remain abreast of societal changes and faces a new enemy in the War on Terror.

POSTWAR MERCHANT MARINE

At the end of World War II the U.S. merchant marine comprised some 60 percent of the world's merchant tonnage, most of it built between 1942 and 1945. Things looked rosy for both shipowners and maritime labor. But things went sour fairly rapidly as Congress, in the Merchant Ship Sales Act of 1946, essentially gave away large numbers of war-built merchant ships to friendly foreign nations in an effort to bolster their economies against the threat of communist insurrection. This was compounded by the Marshall Plan of 1947, which permitted cargoes sent to Europe to be shipped in for-eign-flagged vessels. This decline has been effectively captured by René De La Pedraja. In his book, *The Rise and Decline of U.S. Merchant Shipping in the Twentieth Century*,[1] he places much of the blame of this decline on the inability of shipping companies to organize, coordinate, and make short-term sacrifices for long-term gains.

Merchant mariners also suffered after the war. The federal government denied merchant mariners the generous veteran's benefits granted to re-turning GIs, leaving many embittered. Furthermore, as the Cold War pro-gressed, the government embarked on a program to weed out merchant seamen with communist sympathies. The U.S. Coast Guard stripped many merchant mariners of the seaman's documents that permitted them to work on U.S.-flagged vessels, and the FBI continued to monitor labor unions for communist infiltrators.

The Korean War ameliorated these circumstances as the military real-ized its need for the merchant marine to deliver troops and supplies. Steam-ship companies and labor unions rallied to the war on communism, not only for military sealift, but for humanitarian missions such as the evacu-ation of refugees. Congress rewarded the effectiveness and loyalty of the merchant fleet by passing the 1954 Cargo Preference Act, which guaranteed that at least 50 percent of government-generated cargoes would be shipped in U.S.-flagged vessels.

The early postwar era was a golden age for labor unions: by 1955 an estimated 17.5 million Americans belonged to labor unions. Maritime la-bor unions won improved working conditions and higher wages than ever. The unions were led by tough men who had risen during the equally tough 1930s. Joe Curran continued to dominate the National Maritime Union (NMU), Harry Bridges led the International Longshore and Warehouse

---

1   René De La Pedraja, *The Rise and Decline of U.S. Merchant Shipping in the Twentieth Century* (New York: Twayne Publishers, 1992).

Union (ILWU), and Paul Hall assumed leadership of the Seamen's International Union (SIU). Each man wielded enormous power, not only in the union halls, but politically as well. Shipowners increasingly came to appreciate that these labor leaders were not to be trifled with and sometimes found themselves allied with the unions in lobbying Congress to support the diminishing merchant fleet.

The merchant marine was also active in the Vietnam War, providing supplies to American forces through a new container facility at Cam Ranh Bay, often facing enemy attack in so doing. The last incident of the war involved the capture of the American containership *Mayaguez* in 1975.

Frazer A. Bailey, "The Marshall Plan and the Merchant Marine" (1948)

Frazer A. Bailey (1888–1960) is representative of the conservative steamship owners of the mid-twentieth century. Publicly supportive of private enterprise, deeply suspicious of labor unions, they nonetheless sought out every possible scrap of government aid they could. Bailey himself had been involved in shipping from age twelve, starting at the Newport News Shipbuilding Company and working his way up to president of the Matson Steamship Company, which dominated shipping between Hawaii and the mainland U.S. and still exists today.

In this address, Bailey, as president of the National Federation of American Shipping, Inc., a major lobbying group for the shipping industry, addressed the Advertising Club of Washington, D.C., on February 3, 1948, concerning the impact of the Truman administration's Marshall Plan, officially known as the *European Recovery Program* (ERP). The Marshall Plan, named after U.S. Secretary of State George Marshall, was a massive American effort to rebuild the war-torn European economy so that governments friendly to the United States could successfully resist communist takeover. The Marshall Plan is generally considered to have been not only a generous act by the American people, but crucial in rebuilding the economies of western Europe and one of the first steps toward European unification. Bailey was clearly anticommunist, but in his speech he expresses concerns for the impact of the Marshall Plan on American shipping.

I shall speak to you briefly upon the ocean shipping features of the Marshall Plan.

First, I would like to say clearly, and with considerable emphasis, that American shipping favors the Marshall Plan. There is every reason why it should.

We favor a sound and comprehensive plan which will enable these nations to recover their economic footing, without, however, doing substantial damage to any particular American industry, or to our American economy as a whole. We believe this should be the generous act of the whole American people.

Even though it involves some sacrifices on the part of American industry and labor, as it inevitably must, we believe these unfortunate European nations should be assisted to a position approaching their prewar condition, and from there they should go forward to any stability and prosperity which their own energies and ingeniousness can provide.

We are not in favor of wrecking any part of our own economy in the process, and we do not wish to change places with them.

Since before the Civil War, (for approximately a century) we have not occupied a position upon the seas commensurate with our position as a leader among nations. If history shows anything whatever, it clearly demonstrates that nations which allow their merchant fleets to decline and disintegrate are soon relegated to a lesser position in world affairs. The outstanding examples are Spain, Portugal and the Netherlands.

During the present times when America is endeavoring to assist in a program of world peace and stability through the United Nations we can ill afford to do anything which will weaken our influence.

To our thinking it is idle to talk of restoring our merchant fleet to some formula of prewar relativity. Just before World War II we were carrying less than 30 percent of our own commerce. We have no ambition to dominate world shipping, but we feel it is not over-ambitious to aspire to transport in our own ships approximately one-half of our imports and exports. We are not speaking now of world trade we are speaking; of American commerce. Now that we have the fleet, even though somewhat unbalanced by types, we should begin to make progress in that direction.

Since its earliest days, the great leaders of our country have recognized the need of a strong merchant marine to carry on the nation's commerce, and for national defense. To list these statesmen and military leaders would be to catalog history's foremost figures from Washington and Jefferson through two Roosevelts and down to Eisenhower and Nimitz.

Recently one of our naval heroes said that in time of war we never have had sufficient merchant ships. In two World Wars we have spent 17 billion dollars in the necessarily desperate and extravagant building of merchant fleets to defend not only our own country, but civilization itself. Certainly two such lessons should suffice.

What then are the shipping proposals contained in the latest European Recovery Program? It is proposed to transfer to the sixteen Marshall-Plan nations, by sale or charter, 500 additional U.S. war-built vessels.

It is well to understand just what is involved in a proposal of that magnitude. Five hundred war-built vessels of the size and type suggested represent 5 million deadweight tons of shipping, an amount equal to one-half of our merchant marine before the war and approximately one-half of our present privately-owned shipping fleet. It represents 25 percent of our reserve fleet, which the Keller Committee estimates will equal 2,000 ships when our chartered ships are returned. As far as we know, no competent authority has determined whether a reserve fleet of this size is deficient, is proper, or is surplus of our defense requirements. Please bear in mind that at the end of the last World War the Maritime Commission had under its control about 4,500 large merchant ships.

The merchant fleets of the participating nations, now in operation and under construction, already exceed the capacity of their prewar fleets by 1.5 million tons, and their projected fleets in 1951 will exceed prewar capacities by more than 7 million tons according to their own figures. In 1951 the 16 Marshall-Plan nations will possess 7 percent more of the aggregate world active merchant fleet than they possessed in 1938.

To the average citizen the shipping proposals contained in the European Recovery Program would seem to indicate a shortage of ships to transport relief cargoes. However, such is not the case. There are ample ships now in operation to transport all of the relief cargoes which the European Relief Program proposals say are now moving in maximum volume. This is borne out by the fact that during the last few months almost two ships per day have been returned to the Maritime Commission by charterers, from the fleet of U.S. vessels which are primarily carrying bulk dry cargoes to Europe. This fleet of chartered vessels reached a maximum figure of 1,405 ships in July 1947 and had been reduced to 1,128 on January 1 of this year.

All that is contemplated in the ERP proposals is the transfer of these same ships from U.S.-flag, U.S. manning, and U.S. management, to foreign-flag, foreign manning, and foreign management, together with loss of employment to some twenty to twenty-five thousand American seamen in favor of an equal number of European seamen and a corresponding drain upon their manpower resources.

It would, of course, be wasteful both in time and money to withdraw 500 additional ships from the present reserve fleet and have them placed in operation by these participating nations only to force, as they inevitably would, 500 other American ships out of business and into lay-up status.

The question of transferring one-fourth of our reserve fleet under this program appears to raise serious questions of national defense. It would result in placing 25 percent of our reserve fleet under the control of European nations, some with governments not too stable, some who are, through economic necessity, bartering ships to nations behind the iron curtain for coal, timber, corn and other necessities from eastern Europe. There is nothing in the international situation today to justify such a hazardous gamble.

We are aware that the program suggests what is termed "chartering," as to 300 ships and that under it there would normally be the expectation that these vessels will be returned. We find no one in the shipping industry who believes this would eventuate. We cannot escape the memory of what has happened to 95 ships delivered to Russia under lend-lease when she was our ally, and we would have great concern, not only about the return to the United States of the vessels transferred under charter, but also the possible use of these ships, or other ships for which they may substitute, in the hands of an unfriendly nation.

Economy in dollar credits is predominantly, if not the sole, reason suggested in the ERP proposals for turning over these ships to foreign control. There have been loose statements made that a saving of some 300 million dollars would result from the sale of the ships proposed, and that the program would be further reduced by many millions if additional vessels were chartered as therein suggested.

We have made a very careful estimate of these costs based upon the individual factors of which they will be composed, and we find the total saving to be less than 200 million dollars. It is our feeling that so modest a saving in a program of these proportions, equaling as it does slightly more than 1 percent of the aggregate amount, falls far short of justifying the damaging results which are certain to follow in both the fields of American shipping and of national defense.

The only possible saving is in the lower operating cost of the foreign ship due to the employment of cheap foreign crews, food and repairs, and in the use of foreign currency. We hear of no suggestion to similarly economize in other phases of the Marshall Plan through the use of cheap foreign labor. There is to be no effort to reduce the cost of wheat, coal, or other commodities, or of their transportation to seaboard by such means. We are strongly opposed to the application of this principle, but if it must be availed of, it should have universal application.

Fortunately, the President appointed a Committee of 19 distinguished citizens under the Chairmanship of the Secretary of Commerce to advise him, and I shall quote the language:

"to advise . . . on the limits within which the U.S. might safely and wisely plan to extend economic assistance to foreign countries and on the relation which should exist between such assistance and our domestic economy."

Let me read you two short quotations from the report:

"The U.S. needs an active merchant marine for national defense and we must not create conditions in which that merchant marine cannot survive."

and again:

"The limited financial savings are not sufficient to justify the drain on U.S. resources for national defense which such transfers would involve."

Unfortunately this report appears to have been ignored by the authors of the European Recovery Program in preparing their suggestions to the Congress. We, however, have great faith that it will *not be ignored*, nor will the American shipping industry nor the American economy be ignored by Congress in its final decisions.

The greatest deterrent to war is strength and preparedness. From hiding places throughout Germany secret documents have been assembled at Nuremberg in connection with the trials of Nazi criminals. Throughout these documents it was shown with compelling clarity that unpreparedness of the western democracies persuaded Hitler to attack in 1939. On April 4, 1941, (Document 1881PS) Hitler solemnly assured Matsuoko that his (Hitler's) program against merchant tonnage transportation was such he could guarantee the utter impossibility of a single American landing in Europe.

Donation of a part of our reserve fleet is a step in the direction of weakness and unpreparedness.

Questions for Discussion:
1. What arguments does Bailey make about American shipping and the European Recovery Plan?
2. What concerns does Bailey have about handing over American merchant ships to other nations?
3. What connections does Bailey make between the merchant marine and American strategic needs?

Frazer A. Bailey, "The Marshall Plan and the Merchant Marine" before the Advertising Club of Washington, Hotel Statler, Washington, D. C., February 3, 1948. Typed manuscript, Schuyler Otis Bland Library, USMMA, Kings Point, NY.

J. Robert Lunney, "Korean Refugees" (1950)

The Korean War came as an unsuspected and unwelcome surprise to the United States. Starting with a sudden attack on June 25, 1950, North Korean forces quickly overran almost the entire Korean peninsula, only to be thrown back by General Douglas MacArthur's amphibious landing at Inchon on September 15. United Nations forces had advanced almost to the Chinese border when the Chinese People's Volunteer Army attacked, sending the American, South Korean, and allied troops on a long retreat southward.

Many of these U.N. forces evacuated through the port of Hungnam, along with tens of thousands of North Korean refugees fleeing Communist persecution. At Hungnam the U.S. Navy and merchant marine evacuated them all while concentrated naval gunfire and aerial support kept back the Communist forces. The United Nations forces loaded some 105,000 soldiers, 98,000 civilians, 17,500 vehicles, and 350,000 tons of supplies onto ships in Hungnam harbor in an astonishingly effective example of the utility of sea power. J. Robert Lunney (1927–), a twenty-three-year-old merchant mariner on board the freighter S.S. *Meredith Victory* witnessed the evacuation firsthand. The *Meredith Victory*, one of the last ships to leave Hungnam, rescued fourteen thousand refugees, earning it the distinction *Gallant Ship* from Congress, the only vessel deemed such in the Korean War. The next day the last Marines left and Communist forces claimed Hungnam. The full story of this remarkable event is recounted in Bill Gilbert's *Ship of Miracles*.[1]

Dear Folks:

Before we completed discharging all of our cargo we were sent to Hungnam from Pusan[2] on the 19th. We arrived at Hungnam the next day and anchored. From our anchorage we could see all of the planes and naval attacks on the shortening perimeter. The first rocket ships in the area sailed right past us to get into position for a rocket attack. At night all you could hear were the five- and eight-inch guns plus the rockets being fired into the Chinese lines. During the heaviest part of the firing, I got out of the rack[3] and made for my door and only realized what happened when the cold air hit me and I woke up. Luckily, all the firing was from our guns, and there was no harbor attack by the Reds while we were there. We went into the docks Friday nite the 22nd; the harbor was then packed with approximately fifty ships (both merchant and naval). We had already taken on provisions to feed a thousand troops for two days. The original plan was to fill our lower holds with cargo, then take about a thousand troops on top of the cargo. Upon arriving at the pier, where we tied up with another ship, we got the word that we were to load North Korean refugees: 10,401, and this did not count babies on their mothers' and fathers' backs which seemed to be between three and four thousand more, making a final total of refugees about 14,000. They were instructed to bring food and water (whatever the poor people could scrape together is beyond me, for the whole dock area was completely leveled). In the meantime, an intense naval and air barrage was going on. The perimeter was two miles in depth now. So we were within two miles of the front lines. Naval shells kept flying over our heads and bursting in the near distance, and one could see the planes on their diving runs spurting rockets and machine gun fire. The military constructed a wooden ladder and causeway over the other ship right to us, and the people piled on by the thousands.

It was now dusk and you could see the lineup of people as far as

---

1 Bill Gilbert, *Ship of Miracles: 14,000 Lives and One Miraculous Voyage* (Chicago: Triumph Books, 2000).
2 Pusan: a port in southernmost South Korea.
3 Rack: bunk.

you could look. Old people, maimed, on crutches, kids still nursing at their mother's breast, old men with children strapped to their backs; eighteen came aboard in litters, expectant mothers, carrying crying children.

It was truly a pitiful sight. . . . In the sick bay one mother had already given birth. . . . The people were all fed in Pusan by the military who came aboard about eighteen strong, including some South Korean MPs.[1] One poor fellow cut his foot badly and had to be put ashore in Pusan, and as we sailed he was still crying to have his wife put ashore with him.

I just wonder how many homes this mass evacuation has broken up. They just all had to be evacuated or be killed by the Reds for cooperating with the Americans. There were 30,000 in all, and it took three Victory ships to load them. We originally got orders to take them to Pusan but received diversion orders while under way for Koje-Do (an island just to the S.W. of Pusan), but as luck would have it, the message never came thru, so into Pusan Christmas Eve with the poor lot. We stayed there overnight as I mentioned before (where we removed the sick and fed everyone). Luckily we had good weather the twenty-four hour journey down from Hungnam and exposure for the people on deck was not too bad. On the way north I saw an LST[2] loaded with people sailing south and they were all huddled together on deck, protecting themselves against the wintry blasts and I felt sorry for them. But now I realize that the people on deck are the lucky ones, for the people are packed together so tightly in the lower holds that they cannot move, much less get fresh air. They are packed just like sardines. No toilet facilities and no water or food, much less an occasional change of air thru the ventilators rigged for cargo—but never a human cargo. The decks are just littered with filth and human feces. The whole ship just stinks to high heaven and you cannot turn without meeting the odor. Just imagine a city of 15,000 people jammed together on this ship without facilities to handle them and the dirt and disease that will ensue.

We are now anchored off Kyosai To[3] and awaiting LSTs to come

---

1   MPs: Military Police.
2   LSTs: Landing Ship Tank, a kind of transport vessel designed to load or unload vehicles directly onto a beach.
3   Kyosai To: Koje-Do, an island off Pusan, Korea.

alongside to remove them. . . . They have been aboard now seventy-two hours and even if they start discharging immediately it will take twenty-four hours to get them all off.

Never have I felt the want to be home as I have this Christmas. With all this death and destruction looking you in the face everywhere, you turn with a feeling of utter helplessness; one just feels that he has had enough of war. I just imagined and read of the heartrending sights of modern war, but this exposure has given me my fill. I have gone out on deck and walked around, looking at the people, all huddled together, trying to keep warm, mothers with babies clutched tightly and fathers trying to keep their sons warm under their own coats, and one cannot help but swell up emotionally and cry. I have given all my chocolate out and the ship has given them water as best they can, while the crew gives out as much food as is permissible, but as is true in all these cases, 14,000 people cannot all be fed and watered. . . .

As it was, we got out of Hungnam in the nick of time with the people because it was all evacuated within twenty-four hours after we left, and at least we have saved them from the hands of the Communists. You can imagine what it must be to live under Communist rule, if all these people who have lived under it for five years are willing to endure this to get away from them.

Our Christmas dinner was fine, and I know that Mother prepared a good one for all of you back home, and don't think I wouldn't have liked to have been there. This reminds me of a sentence I read in the Steward's cookbook which the boys will appreciate—"'when do we eat?' Thru out the years this loud and lusty call of the 'inner man' has been a challenge and an inspiration to good cooks everywhere" . . . Mother, please take note.

Pusan, Korea
December 28, 1950:

Did not have a chance to send my last letter till now, so this postscript. Anchored off Pusan the 26th, after discharging refugees into two LSTs, within six hours (much faster than we had all expected) off an island where I think all 91,000 evacuated from Hungnam were dumped. We came into the pier at Pusan this morning and are trying to clean up the vessel. I don't think we will be too successful, for what we really need is a fumigation. They are busily engaged in discharging the rest of our cargo (jet fuel) now and will be finished within the next two days.

The latest is that we go to Sasebo, Japan, from here. For what, I don't know. It is only about ten hours from Pusan, so it may be for another war cargo for Korea.

About now all the fellows are wanting to go home and I don't blame them. . . . But hopes for going home or staying do no good with the Military running things. Ship's agents just came abd. with 600 bucks for advance to the crew, so must sign off and have them mail this for me (and besides, I have to get to work, doling out the dough).

Love to all,
Bob.

Questions for Discussion:

1. How did Lunney and his crewmates regard the Korean refugees crowded onto the *Meredith Victory*?
2. What options did the North Korean refugees have at Hungnam?
3. What strengths or weaknesses does this document have in understanding the merchant marine's role in the Korean War?

Used with permission of J. Robert Lunney.

Paul Hall, "Big Labor Comes to the Fourth Coast" (1959)

Paul Hall (1915–1980), the cigar-smoking, tough-talking leader of the Seafarers International Union (SIU), made it the nation's largest and most powerful seafaring union, outstripping Joe Curran's National Maritime Union (NMU). Hall encouraged labor and management to work together because he recognized that strikes hurt both sides and made the American merchant marine less competitive, hurting everyone in the business.

Hall, born to poverty in rural Alabama, had little education and shipped out mostly as a wiper in the black gang.[1] In the 1940s his skills as a union organizer brought him forward in the SIU leadership, and he soon developed a reputation for his ability to get concessions from shipowners at the bargaining table. He also understood that unions had to become involved in politics in order to succeed. The SIU training facility at Piney Point, Maryland, is named the *Paul Hall Center for Maritime Training and Education* in his honor.

In this speech to the largely conservative Propeller Club in 1959, Hall

---

1   Black gang: crew members who shoveled coal to fuel the ship, exceptionally hot and brutal labor.

berates management for its poor leadership and encourages shipowners to work with the SIU and other large labor unions on the Lakes rather than oppose them.

Our industry, on the Atlantic and Gulf, is looking up. Labor is now more consolidated. It is more in a mood to cooperate. It is desirous to have cooperation with you. If we can have that reciprocated, we can then go a long way.

On the Great Lakes you have a different problem, an entirely different problem. The Great Lakes operator, for many years, has been very successful in resisting legitimate Union organization. He has built around himself, in many instances, a hodge-podge of little company unions and so-called independent unions, anything to keep a so-called outside Union out. Very clever. But it hit them in the pocketbook. Look at the Lake wage scale. Who have you really beat? What have you really beat? You haven't beaten anybody but yourself. When you figure it out, you're paying the same dollar across the board. Look at your wage scale; look at the cost of your shipping operation. You have built the foundation of your Labor relations on quicksand. That is what you have done.

I don't know how many of these little fink unions are up here. I know for a fact that most, if not all, of them have been created by the various segments of this management. I am no expert on the Great Lakes and I don't claim to be. But I know the waterfront a little bit and I know seamen a little bit and I know when something is being manipulated. It is quite evident that that is what has happened here.

Now, for many years, the offshore industry, as far as Labor was concerned, regarded the Great Lakes as an entity unto itself, it was in the hinterlands, too far away and they were different and everything else. This was brought about partly because of the fact that the operators, certain kinds of operators, not everybody, preached this to the people that worked for them. This type of Lakes operator said, "Don't you do this and don't you do that. If you go Union these salt water sailors will take your jobs, they will bring in undesirables to take your jobs. Hate them, oh, we gotta hate them and beat them." That was the kind of stuff that went on and for all these years because of this and because of its effect on the Great Lakes' sailor's feelings, he didn't want to talk about these things. Many of them resisted legitimate unions. Well, this is the blind reasoning of the ostrich with his head in the sand.

When the Seaway[1] opened, as I heard some previous speaker say, it was a new thing. Whether anyone likes it or not, the offshore sailor has to come into the Great Lakes. We are here. And we are not here to leave. We are here to stay.

In our own organization we are responsible . . . we are a responsible Union. There are those among you with whom we have done business over the years. Our word is our bond. We supply competent and qualified people. If there's any way for us to help you make a better management operation, we do it. We would like to see our SIU Great Lakes District Union do the same thing. We are not here to take anybody's job on those ships. We are not here to push management around. We are not here to hurt management in one manner or even blast them. We are here to help them because we are not kidding ourselves after all the years it took to stabilize things in the deep-sea field; after all the years it has taken to create an attitude of responsibility toward the people with whom we work, management. We are not going to leave our flanks open up here, coming in, if for nothing else, to protect the deepwater ship, to protect their operation, to protect their contracts, to protect the relationship between ourselves and the operators who bring those ships up here.

I could not help but observe the foundations that you have so very cleverly built on quicksand. I will tell you something, you have fooled yourselves very badly because now the Unions, the National Maritime Union and the Seafarers International Union, the International Longshoremen's Association, and every one of the labor groups that speak for this industry, all of the trade unions, are going to come up here in strength. We are the first of many to come. We will not be driven from this field because the creature of some operator beats us in an election. We knew before we went into it we were going to take some bad beatings. We have taken bad beatings in our day. We have been lucky, literally, to get off of the field alive. As one of the operators with whom we deal on the Great Lakes asked me, "Paul, you fellows are going to organize or try to organize on the Lakes?" I said, "Yes." Well, as well as I can recall, he said to me, "What do you think will happen?" I said, "Well, I think it will happen something like this:"—if you gentlemen

---

1 Seaway: the St. Lawrence Seaway opened in 1959. It connected the Great Lakes to the Atlantic Ocean via the St. Lawrence River, for the first time allowing oceangoing ships to traverse the Great Lakes.

pardon my language—"to start with, for the first thirty-nine rounds we will get knocked on our behinds so many times that we are going to have calluses as thick as the palms of our hands and the blood will be running down around the cuts over our eyes. But, about the fortieth round, we are going to start getting the know-how. We are going to start understanding what the rules of the game are. And from that fortieth round, on, somebody better watch out; somebody had better be careful. We want to be cooperative and we are cooperative, but as far as assassins are concerned, we don't like."

We are not going to be defeated or driven from these Lakes by those tactics. We are going to go into every company with an "independent" company union every opportunity we have. We are going to ask that this Landrum-Griffin bill,[1] which was meant to kill decent unions, be invoked against those company unions. We are going to ask the law to look at those kind of unions. That is what we want. We want to know who wrote their handbills, who wrote their constitutions and who put the money into them. When the legislators of this country devised the Landrum-Griffin bill it was to hurt the legitimate labor unions. But the legitimate labor movement in this maritime industry is capable of handling itself.

If you walk into our union headquarters, you will see an accounting department there that is not second even to that of a good top corporation. If you walk into the National Maritime Union, you will see the same thing. The union that I'm talking about, the company union, can't take scrutiny, gentlemen, because when these legislators were making laws against bona fide unions, some of them forgot that some of the Management people owned unions. Standard Oil forgot it.

One of the unions in Standard Oil just affiliated with our international and is now demanding a full Federal investigation of the creation of a new company union. All we want is reasonable treatment. Those of you who imagine that because a seafarer's union is composed of sailors that those sailors cannot have available the same technical knowledge and the same techniques and the same practical knowledge you have, are kidding yourselves. We are going to have our day in court on it, and when we do, they are going to regret it because these little company unions that have been so cleverly devised to defeat le-

---

1   Landrum-Griffin bill: a bill that restricted union efforts to organize workers and to engage in political fund-raising.

gitimate unions are going to hang around some necks like an albatross and they are going to get mighty heavy.

This does not go, by any means, for the legitimate operator, and there are a great number of them. Take it from one who has campaigned in every labor war on the waterfront for a long time; every experience I have ever had on the waterfronts makes me see and understand very clearly, whether you, as management on the Great Lakes can see it or not, that even though the company union pattern has been successful there is a new day in labor-management relations coming here on these Lakes.

You have been successful in trying to divide some of our unions, the longshore groups. From one end of the Lakes to the other, I don't know how many bargaining patterns you have got. The quality of the performance of the work varies just as much as it differs in the wage scale zone. You don't want this.

I'm not a management man. I don't really think I could ever be one. Not only for philosophical reasons, but for the lack of education. But there is one thing that I do know: If I were a management man on these Lakes today, I would take a good look at this labor picture. I would ask myself, "Where are we going?" You are now bringing in here the philosophies and the psychological attitudes of the deepwater sailor who will never be your man. He is bound to be in and out of here and his influence will be felt.

The conditions of the offshore ports are going to be your conditions; the problems of the offshore ports are going to be your problems.

I have heard it said up here in discussion that this is a Fourth Coast.[1] That's right. And with that Fourth Coast will come to you, as business people, all of the opportunities that come from the opening of the new area of business; but with that opportunity to improve or help yourself, don't forget that it also brings on the other side of that coin, the problems of the Fourth Coast. The labor problem is just one. Panlibhonco[2] is another. I don't know how many grain shipments that you have lost to those runaway flag ships. I dare say it is more than

---

1   Fourth Coast: with the completion of the St. Lawrence Seaway in 1959, some called the Great Lakes the *Fourth Coast*, after the Atlantic, Pacific, and Gulf coasts.

2   Panlibhonco: ships registered under the flags of Panama, Liberia, Honduras, or Costa Rica, so-called flag of convenience nations whose low taxes and lack of regulation make them more profitable than U.S.-flagged ships.

two or three. Here we have a common enemy. That is why you should take a second look at the Great Lakes, at this labor relations picture.

Now, some of you might say, "Who is that big fat bum sitting up there and talking like that to us?"

Well, listen, I never had a good meal in my life until I came into this industry. I never did. The only job I ever had—I haven't always been a union official—since I was grown was a job in the maritime industry. I think I have an obligation to this industry. If I were associated with or working for you, I would have an obligation to the thing that has made it possible for me to live better and to eat better, be able to educate my children. This is the point from which I speak to you, not as a big, arrogant labor skate, but as a guy that has a feeling for this industry. I tell you you can make this Great Lakes a good industry and a healthy addition to the total industry if you but examine yourself. Examine yourself on these matters. Examine yourself on the Panlibhonco issue, the fink unions.[1] Try to work together on the problems of a common nature.

I'm not going to give you that old saw that you either live together or hang separately, it's too obvious; you should know that. You have basic problems that present a tough combination. Labor is one; the foreign carriers of grain is another; and there's going to be a longshore[2] problem and I could go on and on down the line. You have got to get together. Don't make the ghastly mistake that the ship owners on the Atlantic and Gulf coasts made. Don't make the ghastly mistake that the West Coast ship owner made, which was a classic example of what you seem to be doing here. The West Coast owner was also a clever fellow. He used Lundeberg[3] against Bridges,[4] and Bridges against Malone,[5] and Malone against the other union heads involved. Yes, the West Coast owner was a very smart guy. He put one against the other and, in the process, today it takes almost twenty per cent more to run a West Coast ship than it does an East or Gulf Coast ship.

---

1 Fink unions: company-run labor unions.
2 Longshore: Hall is hinting at a future problem with dockworker's unions.
3 Lundeberg: Harry Lundeberg, Hall's predecessor as head of the SIU.
4 Bridges: Harry Bridges, long-time leader of the left-leaning International Longshore and Warehouse Union (ILWU).
5 Malone: Vincent J. Malone, leader of the Marine Firemen, Oilers, Watertenders, and Wipers' Union (MFOWW).

He was clever, real clever. He could not have done more damage to himself if he had been his own worst enemy.

That is what happened with the West Coast industry. Don't you be the West Coast industry. Don't try to play tic-tac-toe in the labor field, gentlemen, because it will cost you and it will cost this industry.

There are a lot of things that I would like to say because my vocation is my avocation; my job is my hobby. Some people like to go to a play or a movie; I like to go to any kind of a meeting where there is a bunch of guys from the industry where I live. I like to talk to them.

Questions for Discussion:
1. What does this document reveal about relations between management and maritime labor unions?
2. What changes were underway in Great Lakes shipping in 1959?
3. According to Hall, what benefits are there for shipowning companies to cooperate with big labor unions like the SIU?

Paul Hall, "Labor Management Co-operation," in Propeller Club of the United States, *American Merchant Marine Conference Proceedings* 25 (1959): 43–50.

Jesse Calhoon, "Foreign Flag Rustbuckets" (1977)

In December, 1976, four separate Liberian-flagged oil tankers sank in or near U.S. waters, sparking an outcry from a number of groups. One of these tankers exploded in Los Angeles harbor, one grounded in the Delaware River, one spilled 5,000 gallons of oil into the Thames River in Connecticut, and most famously of all, the *Argo Merchant* grounded off Nantucket and broke apart, spilling 7.3 million gallons of oil into the Atlantic. Further groundings and accidents in January, 1977, provoked further outrage.

Labor unions were among the most vocal critics of how the major oil companies transported their cargoes. Labor leaders such as Jesse Calhoon of the Marine Engineers' Beneficial Association (MEBA), a longtime critic of unregulated foreign-flagged ships and of the oil industry in general, pressed Congress for new and stricter regulations, such as those requiring oil bound for American markets to be carried in U.S.-flagged vessels with American crews and the use of double-hulled tankers. Calhoon was particularly incensed by the use of Liberian "flags of convenience." Liberia, a small nation in Africa, generated revenue for itself by registering vessels under its flag. Shipping companies and operators flocked to the Liberian flag because it offered considerable cost savings to them due to lax or almost nonexistent safety regulations and very light taxation.

Mr. Chairman, I am here on behalf of the members of the Marine Engineers' Beneficial Association, a union which represents engineers aboard U.S.-flag vessels. Because of the importance of oil to the economy and well-being of this country, our union believes that the recent foreign flag tankers casualties have an importance which goes far beyond the millions of gallons of petroleum products carried aboard those ships.

If we fail to take immediate action which results in reducing the danger to our ports and coastal regions posed by unsafe foreign ships, we will endanger the ability of the United States to establish a viable national energy program based on energy independence and the maximum use of domestic energy materials. Already, voices are being raised in opposition to increased reliance on tankers to transport oil from the North Slope of Alaska to the lower forty-eight States and from new areas of offshore production to coastal refining regions.

These voices come from people who are understandably concerned when they view eight tanker casualties within just one month. What they must understand—and what the American people must come to realize—is that tanker transportation of oil can be environmentally sound. We have proved this with U.S.-flag tankers. Their record of oil spills in 1973 was 1 gallon spilled for every 100,000 gallons transported. Since that year, new environmental regulations have resulted in a reduction of oil spills from U.S.-flag ships.

Mr. Chairman, for the sake of our national energy policy and the safety and environmental protection of our coastal areas and ports, we must act unilaterally and in concert with other nations to enforce strict safety standards for any and all foreign flag vessels which enter U.S. territorial waters.

It may seem to be a coincidence that eight tankers flying foreign flags have been involved in major casualties during one month. Mr. Chairman, let me assure you. These casualties are no coincidence. They are the direct and almost inevitable result of the use of flags of convenience by major U.S. oil companies and others. They are the direct and almost inevitable result of the failure of the U.S. Coast Guard to exercise its authority and responsibility to assure that any vessel coming into a U.S. port—no matter what flag it flies—be in good condition and equipped with adequate and operational navigation equipment. They are the direct and almost inevitable result of the influence which multinational U.S. oil companies have over the policies of the federal government. And they are the direct and almost inevitable result of the increasing reliance which this country has placed on imported oil and our failure to require that a reasonable portion of that oil be carried in U.S.-flag ships.

This country is in the grips of an energy crisis. Most of the public lost sight of that fact when the long lines at gasoline stations disappeared. But the shortage of available energy supplies is even more acute today than it was during the Arab oil embargo three years ago. Domestically, we are producing less and consuming more oil than we were then. As a result, we must import more and more oil from foreign countries.

Today, more than half of all oil consumed in the United States comes from foreign sources, and more than 40 percent of our crude imports come from the very countries which cut off our oil supply three years ago. The only way this imported oil can reach the United States from the Middle East and Africa is by tanker. And the largest fleet of tankers in the world flies the Liberian flag—1,014 ships accounting for 89½ million deadweight tons.

This committee knows all-too-well how this tiny country of Liberia, with no natural harbors of its own, acquired such a massive fleet of ships. The first ingredient of the Liberian recipe for instant maritime supremacy is composed of U.S. tax laws which permit American shipping companies to hide their foreign-flag shipping profits from being taxed. Add to this the fact that Liberian law does not require the recording of ownership of corporate holdings and Liberia's tax and mortgage laws are also quite favorable to foreign shipping companies, and mix with the generous desire of the major U.S. oil companies and others to avoid U.S. requirements for safety, environmental protection, and crew qualifications and it is easy to see why the Liberian tanker fleet has doubled in the past ten years.

There have been statements by the Coast Guard and the Department of Transportation to the effect that the worldwide Liberian fleet is at least as safe as any other fleet of vessels. In these and other actions, officials of the present have proved themselves to be effective spokesmen for foreign flag shipping interests. The facts, Mr. Chairman, reveal a different conclusion.

Most U.S. ports can only handle smaller vessels. The largest tanker which can call directly on an East or Gulf Coast port, for example, is a 70,000 [ton] ship. It is a fact that very few ships of this small size are being built anywhere in the world except the United States. As a result, most of the foreign flag tankers calling at U.S. ports were built during the 1950s. Only these smaller ships are capable of making it into our ports. And it was these smaller ships which were involved in the eight casualties during the past month. Mr. Chairman, many of these ships were rustbuckets which should not be allowed in or near U.S. waters.

A brief examination of the Liberian-flag vessels of 70,000 deadweight tons or less which are operated by some of the major U.S. oil companies reveals the advanced age of these Liberian vessels which are capable of calling directly on Gulf and East Coast ports.

Gulf Oil Corporation has fourteen Liberian-registered ships with an average age of seventeen years. SoCal has nineteen of these ships and Phillips has another four, with an average age of seventeen years. Getty has eight Liberian-registered ships with an average age of eighteen years. Of course, there are also older vessels flying the U.S. flag, but they must meet standards and requirements which foreign vessels can avoid.

Mr. Chairman, this committee took testimony nearly a year ago which cited the failure of the Coast Guard to adopt and enforce adequate tanker safety measures to protect the environment. As long as four years ago, this committee initiated legislation, eventually signed into law, which gave the Coast Guard authority to adopt navigation and safety regulations which would apply to any vessel in U.S. waters. If the Coast Guard, and the Department of Transportation of which it is part, had implemented the authority which Congress delegated in 1972, it is very possible that these recent casualties would not have occurred.

One of the reasons for the failure of these agencies to act is a direct result of what president-elect Carter[1] has called the *revolving door*

---

1   Carter: James "Jimmy" Carter (1924–) officially took office as president of the United States on January 20, 1977.

policy which permits industry officials to assume government positions having a direct effect on the industry from which they came; and government officials going to the industry which they formerly regulated. It is a clear fact of American government that the U.S. oil industry has an excessive degree of influence in the executive branch. Ending the revolving door policy can go a long way toward reducing that influence.

In testimony before this committee yesterday, Secretary Coleman[1] cited a long string of international treaties and conventions as both strengthening tanker safety and limiting U.S. ability to act unilaterally to enforce tanker safety. We believe that the United States must enter into international agreements governing maritime transportation. But we also recognize the clear limits of multilateral approach.

The Inter-Governmental Maritime Consultative Organization[2] was created in 1948. IMCO has had many accomplishments, but it takes years to agree on policies and even more years before those policies become adopted in practice. For example, Secretary Coleman referred to IMCO's adoption of procedures designed to give attention to the problem of substandard ships. The procedures and guidelines to which he referred are not likely to be put into practice until 1985. If we wait until then, the United States will be at the mercy of foreign flag rustbuckets for another eight years.

After citing a host of international agreements which permitted the Coast Guard to intervene in the *Argo Merchant* casualty, Secretary Coleman concluded by saying that, inasmuch as the incident occurred in international waters and involved a ship of Liberian registry, the investigation must be conducted by the Government of Liberia and not by the United States.

Mr. Coleman, the Coast Guard intervened in the *Argo Merchant* grounding because that ship and its cargo posed a direct threat to U.S. territory. We see no reason for our government to refrain from undertaking an investigation of its own to determine the cause of that grounding.

---

1   Coleman: William T. Coleman Jr., (1920–), an African American attorney who served as secretary of transportation under President Gerald Ford.

2   Inter-Governmental Maritime Consultative Organization: a group that the United Nations charged with overseeing maritime commerce, now known as the International Maritime Organization (IMO).

We must not shrink from unilateral action in maritime affairs. Ships carry more than $80 billion of cargo to and from the United States each year. We would not shrink from stopping the entry of unwanted insects, diseases and crops into our country. The same logic must be applied to prevent substandard ships from entering our waters.

It is time that we adopted standards which required adequate safety and navigational equipment on vessels of all sizes and of all flags making use of U.S. waters.

It is time that we upgraded our construction requirements for tankers to require double bottoms just as we do for dry cargo ships. The danger of a gas explosion can be eliminated by requiring the installation of an inert gas system.

It is time that Congress mandated that the National Transportation Safety Board conduct independent investigations of maritime accidents occurring in U.S. waters, whether or not they involve U.S. flag ships.

It is time that we took the Bureau of Marine Inspection out of the Coast Guard and placed it under the Maritime Administration, which has overall responsibility for merchant marine affairs. In addition to being a sound reorganization proposal, this recommendation would make it possible for the inspection of merchant vessels to be done by those with merchant marine experience—a situation which has not existed under the Coast Guard despite a statutory requirement that at least half of the inspectors come from the merchant marine.

And it is time that we adopted cargo preference requirements for imported oil. Among the many reasons to support this proposal is the fact that we will always have a greater degree of control over ships which fly our own flag. That control includes construction, operation, equipment and crew requirements and standards which will provide the American people with far more assurance and protection than will ever be possible under any international agreement affecting foreign flag ships.

Finally, Mr. Chairman, we believe that the oil spill liability law should be changed to provide that the character[1] of any oil tanker be jointly liable together with the owner of that vessel for any damages resulting from an oil spill involving the chartered ship. Far more than any international agreements, this one measure will assure that the oil

---

1   Character: the company that charters an oil tanker.

companies which charter these vessels exercise due care in inspecting the tankers which carry their oil.

Mr. Chairman, the world's oil supply is limited. But it is also clear that the United States will be depending on oil for many more years, and tankers will play a major role in transporting that oil. We urge this committee to consider the measures which we have recommended so that we can continue to have access to the oil we need in a manner which gives adequate protection to the environment and the people of the United States.

Questions for Discussion:
1. What does this document reveal about transporting oil circa 1976?
2. Whom does Calhoon blame for the oil tanker problems?
3. What is Calhoon's unstated agenda in criticizing foreign-flagged oil tankers?

Statement of Jesse M. Calhoon, President, National Marine Engineers' Beneficial Association, January 12, 1977, to the Senate Committee on Commerce, *Recent Tanker Accidents* (Washington, D.C.: Government Printing Office, 1977), 161–63.

THE NAVY'S COLD WAR

After the Second World War, the U.S. Navy possessed virtual hegemony over the world's oceans. But there were numerous challenges, too, not the least of which was that the advent of nuclear weapons meant any confrontation with the Soviets could result in a nuclear war. Furthermore, the Navy had a powerful domestic opponent in the U.S. Air Force, which saw naval forces not only as obsolete, but as an impediment to developing expensive new weapons like the long-range B-36 bomber that was designed to carry thermonuclear weapons deep into enemy territory. Thus at the moment of the Navy's apotheosis to dominant world naval power, it faced the question from Congress, why does this country need the Navy?

The reaction of some top naval officers to such criticism is known as the *revolt of the admirals*, which is also the title of Jeffrey G. Barlow's analysis of postwar naval policy.[1] One of the key players in this so-called revolt was Rear Admiral Daniel V. Gallery (1901–1977), a highly decorated veteran of

---

1   Jeffrey G. Barlow, *Revolt of the Admirals: The Fight for Naval Aviation, 1945–1950* (Washington, D.C.: Naval Historical Center, 1994).

World War II and a major player in postwar squabbling between the Navy and Air Force over the funding of so-called supercarriers versus the B-36 bomber. In a series of articles for the *Saturday Evening Post* in 1949, Gallery argued that the next "war will be won by whichever side is able to deliver the Atom Bomb to the enemy, and at the same time protect its own territory against similar delivery" and that carrier-based aircraft were the ideal weapons platform to do so.

As it turned out, the Navy, with its large fleet of nuclear submarines and forward-deployed aircraft carriers, was often at the forefront of Cold War operations. Since the early days of the Cold War, when the Truman administration sent the USS *Franklin D. Roosevelt* to Greece in 1946 to symbolize support for anticommunist forces, the aircraft carrier had acted as a powerful reminder of American military might. Carrier-based aircraft played important roles in both the Korean and Vietnam conflicts and in virtually every other crisis up to the present.

Furthermore, because the Soviet Union embarked on an aggressive naval program of building up a formidable surface and submarine fleet, there were numerous confrontations between American naval forces and the Soviets. Sometimes these were direct confrontations, as during the Cuban Missile Crisis in 1962, and sometimes by Soviet proxy, as when North Vietnamese torpedo boats attacked an American destroyer in 1962, thereby initiating direct American involvement in Vietnam. The Navy's Cold War intensified in the 1980s when the Reagan administration responded to Soviet naval expansion with an attempt to create a six hundred–ship navy.

John F. Kennedy, "Cuba Quarantined" (1962)

The Cuban Missile Crisis was the moment when the Cold War came closest to escalating into a nuclear war that could have destroyed all life on the planet. The main issue was the Soviet deployment of nuclear missiles in Cuba. On October 16, 1962, U.S. reconnaissance revealed Soviet nuclear missile installations on the island. The Kennedy administration reacted strongly to the presence of Soviet nuclear missiles so close to the American mainland. In a dramatic television appearance, President John F. Kennedy announced that the U.S. Navy had imposed a "quarantine on all offensive equipment" coming to Cuba, carefully avoiding the word *blockade*, the use of which could have been interpreted as an act of war.

The following is an excerpt from a meeting of the executive committee of the National Security Council, 10:00 a.m.–11:15 a.m., October 24, 1962. The secretary of defense reported the plans for naval interception, noting the presence of a submarine near the Soviet ships considered most likely to be carrying nuclear missiles for delivery to Cuba. President Kennedy and his advisers discussed the Soviet submarine problem and the Navy's procedures for signaling the submarines with practice depth charges. It was understood that if a Soviet submarine interfered with the quarantine, the U.S. Navy might have to sink it, possibly starting World War III or a nuclear holocaust.

In the middle of the meeting there were reports that certain Soviet ships had stopped or turned back, and Kennedy directed that there be no interception of any target for at least another hour while clarifying information was sought. By 3:25 p.m., six of the "most interesting" Soviet merchant ships had turned around. Four days later, on October 28, 1962, Soviet premier Nikita Khrushchev announced that the installations would be dismantled. Nuclear war had narrowly been averted.

McNamara:[1] The second point, Mr. President, is the present position of the Soviet vessels, and our plans for intercepting them. There are two vessels that I'll be discussing. One is the *Gagarin*, and the other is the *Kimovsk*, of which these are pictures.

Both of these will be approaching the barrier, by which I mean, they are about 500 miles from Cuba at approximately noon today, roughly the present time, eastern daylight time. I say they will be approaching it—they will be approaching it if our dead reckoning is correct. . . .

The *Gagarin* appears to be about 30 to 50 miles behind the *Kimovsk*. . . .

The *Gagarin* declared technical material at Conakry. This is a typical declaration of an offensive weapons–carrying ship from the Soviet Union. We have checked back the records, and this appears to be a typical way by which they propose to deceive. Both of these ships, therefore, are good targets for our first intercept. Admiral Anderson's plan is to try to intercept one or both of them today.

There is a submarine very close, we believe, to each of them. Between. One submarine relatively close to both of them. The submarine will be at the barrier tonight, late today. It's traveling 8 knots an hour, and therefore it should be 20 to 30 miles from these ships at the time of intercept

And hence it's a very dangerous situation. The Navy recognizes

---

1   McNamara: Robert S. McNamara, secretary of defense between 1961 and 1968.

this, is fully prepared to meet it. Undoubtedly we'll declare radio silence. And therefore neither we nor the Soviets will know where our Navy ships are for much of today.

And that, I think, summarizes our plan.

President Kennedy: Which one are they going to try to get? Both of them?

McNamara: They are concentrating on the *Kimovsk*, but we'll try to get both. The *Kimovsk* has the 7-foot hatches and is the most likely target.

President Kennedy: If the . . . one of our ships. . . . what kind of ship is going to try to intercept? A destroyer?

McNamara: Last night, at about midnight, the plan was to try to intercept the *Kimovsk* with a destroyer. Previously it had been thought it would be wise to use a cruiser. But, because of the Soviet submarine, at the time of intercept, it's believed that it would be less dangerous to our forces to use a destroyer. The *Essex*,[1] with antisubmarine equipped helicopters, will be in the vicinity, and those helicopters will attempt to divert the submarine from the intercept point.

McCone:[2] Mr. President, I have a note just handed to me. . . . It says that we've just received information through ONI[3] that all six Soviet ships currently identified in Cuban waters—and I don't know what that means—have either stopped, or reversed course.

Rusk:[4] What do you mean, Cuban waters?

McCone: Dean, I don't know at the moment.

McNamara : Most of these ships are outbound from Cuba to the Soviet Union. There are several, and I presume that that's what that refers to. There are only—

President Kennedy: [interrupting] Why don't we find out whether they're talking about the ships leaving Cuba or the ones coming in?

McCone: I'll find out what this guy [unclear. He leaves the room.]

Rusk: [drily] Makes some difference. [A few people laugh.]

Bundy:[5] It sure does.

---

1   *Essex*: the aircraft carrier USS *Essex*, lead ship of Task Force 136, which was tasked with enforcing the "quarantine" of Cuba.

2   McCone: John A. McCone, director of the Central Intelligence Agency, or CIA, from 1961 to 1965.

3   ONI: the Office of Naval Intelligence.

4   Rusk: Dean Rusk, secretary of state from 1961 to 1969.

5   Bundy: McGeorge Bundy, special assistant to the president for national security affairs from 1961 to 1966.

McNamara: There were a number of ships so close to the harbors in Cuba this morning that we anticipate their entering the harbors at the present time, inbound from the Soviet Union. There were a number of ships outbound also relatively close to the harbors.

Gilpatric:[1] There is one other ship, a tanker, which is now passing through one of the straits, one of the channels through the islands, a tanker. . . .

President Kennedy: If this submarine should sink our destroyer, then what is our proposed reply?

Taylor:[2] Well, our destroyer, first, will be moving around all the time and the submarine is going to be covered by our antisubmarine warfare patrols. Now we have a signaling arrangement with that submarine to surface, which has been communicated I am told by . . . to—

Alexis Johnson:[3] I sent it last night, yes.

Unidentified: But is that . . . ?

Taylor: Could you describe this, I just—

Alexis Johnson: I sent the identification procedures for a submarine. I sent a message to Moscow last night saying that, in accordance with the President's proclamation, the Secretary of Defense has issued the following procedures for identification of submarines, and asked the embassy to communicate this to the Soviet government, and said this is also being communicated to other governments, this would be a general regulation. Whether they . . . I have not got acknowledgment of receipt of that.

As far as our proclamation is concerned, it was delivered to the Soviet foreign office last night and very promptly returned.

Rusk: I presume they took a look at it.

Alexis Johnson: It was also delivered to the embassy here last night. We have not yet received it back. But these identification procedures should be in their hands.

They are standard. . . . I understand they are an addition to standard international practice accepted by the Soviets?

McNamara: No. This is a new procedure I asked them to set up yesterday, Alex.

---

1   Gilpatric: Roswell L. Gilpatric, deputy secretary of defense from 1961 to 1964.
2   Taylor: General Maxwell D. Taylor, U.S. Army, president's military representative until October 1962, then chairman of the Joint Chiefs of Staff.
3   Alexis Johnson: Ural Alexis Johnson, deputy undersecretary of state for political affairs from 1961 to 1964.

Alexis Johnson: It is a new procedure.

McNamara: Here is the exact situation. We have depth charges that have such a small charge that they can be dropped and they can actually hit the submarine without damaging the submarine.

Taylor: They're practice depth charges.

McNamara: Practice depth charges. We propose to use those as warning depth charges. The message that Alex is talking about states that, when our forces come upon an unidentified submarine we will ask it to come to the surface for inspection by transmitting the following signals, using a depth charge of this type and also using certain sonar signals which they may not be able to accept and interpret. Therefore, it is the depth charge that is the warning notice and the instruction to surface.

Taylor: I believe it's the second step, Mr. Secretary, as Anderson[1] described it.

McNamara: Yes.

Taylor: First the signals and then after—

McNamara: Right. The sonar signal very probably will not accomplish its purpose.

Alexis Johnson: The time element being what it has been, I am not sure that we could assume . . .

McNamara: I think it's almost certain they didn't. [Unclear] didn't see ours, but you and I were working on it at 1:30 [unclear]. I'm sure that it got to the Soviet Union back to the submarine. Now—

Alexis Johnson: That's what I mean. Yes.

McNamara: I neglected to mention one thing about the submarine, however.

[Nineteen seconds excised as classified information]

President Kennedy: Kenny?

Kenneth O'Donnell:[2] What if he doesn't surface, then it gets hot?

President Kennedy: If he doesn't surface or if he takes some action—takes some action to assist the merchant ship, are we just going to attack him anyway? At what point are we going to attack him?

I think we ought to wait on that today. We don't want to have the first thing we attack as a Soviet submarine. I'd much rather have a merchant ship.

---

1   Anderson: Admiral George Whelan Anderson, Jr., Chief of Naval Operations (CNO) from 1961 to 1963.

2   Kenneth O'Donnell: Kenneth Phillip O'Donnell, Kennedy's special assistant.

Taylor: Well, we won't get to that unless the submarine is really in a position to attack our ship in the course of an intercept. This is not pursuing [unclear] on the high seas.

McNamara: I think it would be extremely dangerous, Mr. President, to try to defer attack on this submarine in the situation we're in. We could easily lose an American ship by that means. The range of our sonar in relation to the range of his torpedo, and the inaccuracy, as you well know, of antisubmarine warfare is such that I don't have any—

President Kennedy: [Unclear] imagine it would.

McNamara: —great confidence that we can push him away from our ships and make the intercept securely. Particularly, I don't have confidence we could do that if we restrict the commander on the site in any way. I've looked into this in great detail last night because of your interest in the question.

Rusk: Can you interpose the Soviet merchant vessel between the submarine and yourself? Or does he have torpedoes that can go around and come in from the other side?

Taylor: He can maneuver any way he wants to.

Rusk: I know. But I mean, suppose that you have air observation, you keep the Soviet ship—

Unidentified: Right underneath.

Unidentified: I don't think—

McNamara: What the plan is, Dean, is to send antisubmarine helicopters out to harass the submarine. And they have weapons and devices that can damage the submarine. And the plan, therefore, is to put pressure on the submarine, move it out of the area by that pressure, by the pressure of potential destruction, and then make the intercept. But this is only a plan and there are many, many uncertainties.

Rusk: Yeah.

President Kennedy: OK, Let's proceed.

Questions for Discussion:
1. What does this document reveal about the likelihood of nuclear attack during the Cold War?
2. What signs of confusion are there among President Kennedy's advisors?
3. What are the strengths and weaknesses of a transcription like this for historians studying the Cuban Missile Crisis?

Based on *The Presidential Recordings: John F. Kennedy, The Great Crises*, ed. Philip Zelikow and Ernest R. May (New York: W. W. Norton, 2001) 3: 190–94.

Lyndon B. Johnson, "Tonkin Gulf Speech" (1964)

In early August of 1964, the destroyer USS *Maddox* came under attack on an intelligence mission in the Gulf of Tonkin off the coast of North Vietnam. Three Soviet-built North Vietnamese torpedo boats attacked the *Maddox*, which returned fire. The next night, the *Maddox*, now joined by the USS *Turner Joy*, reported another attack by Communist gunboats.

In response to these attacks on the American destroyers, President Johnson ordered retaliatory air strikes from American aircraft carriers on North Vietnam that destroyed an oil storage facility at Vinh and damaged or sank about thirty vessels. In the following pieces, President Johnson reports to Congress on his actions. Congress replied with the "Tonkin Gulf Resolution," which empowered the president to employ military force in Southeast Asia. The Vietnam War had started in earnest for the United States.

Postwar analysis has since revealed that North Vietnamese naval forces did not attack *Maddox* and *Turner Joy* on the second night. A full account and the context of the Tonkin Gulf incident can be found in Edwin E. Moise's *Tonkin Gulf and the Escalation of the Vietnam War*.[1] Notably, while Moise concluded there was no second attack, he finds that there was no attempt to deceive—that the report of an attack was a mistake unconnected with any political efforts to force an escalation of the conflict in Southeast Asia.

To the Congress of the United States:

Last night I announced to the American people that the North Vietnamese regime had conducted further deliberate attacks against U.S. naval vessels operating in international waters, and therefore directed air action against gunboats and supporting facilities used in these hostile operations. This air action has now been carried out with substantial damage to the boats and facilities. Two U.S. aircraft were lost in the action.

After consultation with the leaders of both parties in the Congress, I further announced a decision to ask the Congress for a resolution expressing the unity and determination of the United States in supporting freedom and in protecting peace in southeast Asia.

These latest actions of the North Vietnamese regime have given a new and grave turn to the already serious situation in southeast Asia. Our commitments in that area are well known to the Congress. They were first made in 1954 by President Eisenhower. They were further defined in the Southeast Asia Collective Defense Treaty approved by the Senate in February 1955.

This treaty with its accompanying protocol obligates the United States and other members to act in accordance with their constitutional processes to meet Communist aggression against any of the parties or protocol states.

Our policy in southeast Asia has been consistent and unchanged since 1954. I summarized it on June 2 in four simple propositions:

1. America keeps her word. Here as elsewhere, we must and shall honor our commitments.

2. The issue is the future of southeast Asia as a whole. A threat to any nation in that region is a threat to all, and a threat to us.

3. Our purpose is peace. We have no military, political, or territorial ambitions in the area.

4. This is not just a jungle war, but a struggle for freedom on every front of human activity. Our military and economic assistance to South Vietnam and Laos in particular has the purpose of helping these countries to repel aggression and strengthen their independence.

The threat to the three nations of southeast Asia has long been clear. The North Vietnamese regime has constantly sought to take over South Vietnam and Laos. This Communist regime has violated the Geneva accords for Vietnam. It has systematically conducted a campaign of subversion, which includes the direction, training, and supply of personnel and arms for the conduct of guerrilla warfare in South Vietnamese territory. In Laos, the North Vietnamese regime has maintained military forces, used Laotian territory for infiltration into South Vietnam, and most recently carried out combat operations—all in direct violation of the Geneva agreements of 1962.

In recent months, the actions of the North Vietnamese regime have become steadily more threatening. In May, following new acts of Communist aggression in Laos, the United States undertook reconnaissance flights over Laotian territory, at the request of the Government of Laos. These flights had the essential mission of determining the situation in territory where Communist forces were preventing inspection by the International Control Commission. When the Communists attacked these aircraft, I responded by furnishing escort fighters with instructions to fire when fired upon. Thus, these latest North Vietnamese attacks on our naval vessels are not the first direct attack on armed forces of the United States.

As President of the United States I have concluded that I should now ask the Congress on its part, to join in affirming the national determination that all such attacks will be met, and that the United States will continue in its basic policy of assisting the free nations of the area to defend their freedom.

As I have repeatedly made clear, the United States intends no rashness, and seeks no wider war. We must make it clear to all that the United States is united in its determination to bring about the end of Communist subversion and aggression in the area. We seek the full and effective restoration of the international agreements signed in Geneva in 1954, with respect to South Vietnam, and again in Geneva in 1962, with respect to Laos.

I recommend a resolution expressing the support of the Congress for all necessary action to protect our Armed Forces and to assist nations covered by the SEATO Treaty.[1] At the same time, I assure the Congress that we shall continue readily to explore any avenues of political solution that will effectively guarantee the removal of Communist subversion and the preservation of the independence of the nations of the area.

The resolution could well be based upon similar resolutions enacted by the Congress in the past—to meet the threat to Formosa in 1955, to meet the threat to the Middle East in 1957, and to meet the threat in Cuba in 1962. It could state in the simplest terms the resolve and support of the Congress for action to deal appropriately with attacks against our Armed Forces and to defend freedom and preserve peace in southeast Asia in accordance with the obligations of the United States under the Southeast Asia Treaty. I urge the Congress to enact such a resolution promptly and thus to give convincing evidence to the aggressive Communist nations, and to

---

1   SEATO: South East Asia Treaty Organization, an alliance of several Asian nations and the United States created to oppose further Communist gains in Southeast Asia.

the world as a whole, that our policy in southeast Asia will be carried forward—and that the peace and security of the area will be preserved.

The events of this week would in any event have made the passage of a congressional resolution essential. But there is an additional reason for doing so at a time when we are entering on three months of political campaigning. Hostile nations must understand that in such a period the United States will continue to protect its national interests, and that in these matters there is no division among us.

Questions for Discussion:

1. What does this document reveal about American strategic concerns in the Cold War?

2. What does this document reveal about the utility of the U.S. Navy in the Cold War?

3. How did naval events get the United States involved in a land war in Asia?

United States Department of State, *Department of State Bulletin* 51, no. 1313 (August 24, 1964): 268.

Ronald Reagan, "600-Ship Fleet" (1982)

Ronald Reagan (1911–2004) was a popular but controversial American president known for his persuasive speaking style. Reagan connected comfortably with ordinary Americans with his straightforward patriotic speeches that placed the United States in a titanic struggle with the evil Soviet Union and advocated a massive rebuilding of the American military. Creating a six hundred–ship navy was a key component of rearming the country, and central to that program was recommissioning several World War II battleships. Reagan made the following remarks during the recommissioning ceremony for the USS *New Jersey* in Long Beach, California, on December 28th, 1982. The *New Jersey*, now refitted with modern weapons systems (including thirty-two Tomahawk missiles), served in U.S. operations during the Lebanese Civil War in 1983 and 1984. With the fall of the Soviet Union in the 1990s, the *New Jersey* was once again decommissioned. It is now a floating museum in Camden, New Jersey.

Surrounded by all this Navy blue and gold, I've had the strange feeling that I'm back on the set filming "Hellcats of the Navy."[1] [Laughter] That was a picture that was based on a great, victorious operation of the Navy in World War II in the Sea of Japan called "Operation Hellcat." I remember at the time I was in love with my leading lady. She is Nancy, my wife, and I'm still in love with her, but I have to confess that today I find myself developing a great respect for the leading lady in these ceremonies. She's gray, she's had her face lifted, but she's still in the prime of life, a gallant lady: the *New Jersey*.

I'm honored to be here for the recommissioning of this mighty force for peace and freedom. Putting this great ship back to work protecting our country represents a major step toward fulfilling our pledge to rebuild America's military capabilities. It marks the resurgence of our nation's strength. It's a strength we can afford. We cannot afford to lose it.

Since the founding of our Armed Forces during the Revolutionary War, our country has always done without large standing armies and navies. Our great success story—unique in history—has been based on peaceful achievements in every sphere of human experience. In our two centuries of continuous democracy, we've been the envy of the world in technology, commerce, agriculture, and economic potential.

Our status as a free society and world power is not based on brute strength. When we've taken up arms, it has been for the defense of freedom for ourselves and for other peaceful nations who needed our help. But now, faced with the development of weapons with immense destructive power, we've no choice but to maintain ready defense forces that are second to none. Yes, the cost is high, but the price of neglect would be infinitely higher.

Another great power in the world sees its military forces in a different light. The Soviet Union has achieved sheer power status only by—or I should say superpower status only by virtue of its military might. It has done so by sacrificing and ignoring achievement in virtually any and every other field.

In contrast, America's strength is the bedrock of the Free World's security, for the freedom we guard is not just our own. But over the

---

1 "Hellcats of the Navy": Reagan starred with his wife Nancy in this 1957 film about a submarine in World War II.

past years we began to drift dangerously away from what was so clearly our responsibility. From 1970 to 1979, our defense spending, in constant dollars, decreased by 22 percent. The Navy, so vital to protecting our interests in faraway troublespots, shrank—as you've been told by the Secretary—from more than a thousand ships to 453.

Potential adversaries saw this unilateral disarmament, which was matched in all the other services, as a sign of weakness and a lack of will necessary to protect our way of life. While we talked of detente, the lessening of tensions in the world, the Soviet Union embarked on a massive program of militarization. Since around 1965, they have increased their military spending, nearly doubling it over the past 15 years.

In a free society such as ours, where differing viewpoints are permitted, there will be people who oppose defense spending of any kind at any level. There are others who believe in defense, but who mistakenly feel that the Department of Defense is inherently wasteful and unconcerned about cost cutting. Well, they're dead wrong.

Waste in government spending of any kind is an ever-present threat. But I can assure our fellow citizens there is no room for waste in our national defense. A dollar wasted is a dollar lost in the crucial effort to build a safer future for our people. Secretary Weinberger[1] and the members of this administration are committed to spending what is necessary for defense to secure the peace and not a penny more. As the recommissioning of this ship demonstrates, we are rearming with prudence, using existing assets to the fullest.

To those who've been led to believe that we've gone overboard on national security needs and are spending a disproportionate share on the military, let me state: This is not true.

In spite of all the sound and fury that we hear and read, defense spending as a percentage of gross national product is well below what it was in the Eisenhower and Kennedy years. The simple fact is that, by reforming defense procurement, by stressing efficiencies and economies in weapons system production, we have been able to structure and fund a defense program our nation can afford. It meets the threat, and it provides wages and benefits that are more akin to what our men and women in uniform deserve.

---

1   Weinberger: Caspar "Cap" Weinberger (1917–2006) was secretary of defense from 1981 to 1987.

Already, we're realizing tremendous dividends from our defense program. The readiness of our forces is proved. The readiness of our forces is dramatically improved. As you've just been told, we're more than meeting our recruitment goals. And we've had congressional support for such key initiatives as the purchase of two aircraft carriers, the B-1 bomber, and the C-5 transport plane.

As a nation, we're committed to take every step to substantially reduce the possibility of nuclear war, while providing an unshakable deterrent to such a war for ourselves and our allies. To this end, we're closing the window of vulnerability by instituting a comprehensive strategic force modernization program.

But while we do this, we're advancing vigorous arms control proposals aimed at deep and verifiable reductions in strategic nuclear missiles. We have proposed that intermediate-range nuclear missiles in Europe be reduced to zero on both sides at the same time we cut conventional forces in Europe to balanced levels. And I may say, the news is encouraging. The Soviet Union has met us halfway on the zero option. They've agreed to zero on our part. [Laughter]

We can't shut our eyes to the fact that, as the Soviet military power increased, so did their willingness to embark on military adventures. The scars are plainly evident in a number of Third World countries. We're also aware that, though the Soviet Union is historically a land power—virtually self-sufficient in mineral and energy resources and land-linked to Europe and the vast stretches of Asia—it has created a powerful, blue-ocean navy that cannot be justified by any legitimate defense need. It is a navy built for offensive action, to cut the Free World's supply lines and render impossible the support, by sea, of Free World allies.

By contrast, the United States is a naval power by necessity, critically dependent on the transoceanic import of vital strategic materials. Over 90 percent of our commerce between the continents moves in ships. Freedom to use the seas is our nation's lifeblood. For that reason, our Navy is designed to keep the sealanes open worldwide, a far greater task than closing those sealanes at strategic choke-points.

Maritime superiority for us is a necessity. We must be able in time of emergency to venture in harm's way, controlling air, surface, and subsurface areas to assure access to all the oceans of the world. Failure to do so will leave the credibility of our conventional defense forces in doubt.

We are, as I said, building a 600-ship fleet, including 15 carrier battle groups. But numbers are not the final test. Those ships must be highly capable.

The *New Jersey* and her sister ships can outgun and outclass any rival platform. This 58,000-ton ship, whose armor alone weighs more than our largest cruiser, is being recommissioned at no more than the cost of a new 4,000-ton frigate. The "Big J" is being reactivated with the latest in missile electronic warfare and communications technology. She's more than the best means of quickly adding real firepower to our Navy; she's a shining example of how this administration will rebuild America's Armed Forces on budget and on schedule and with the maximum cost-effective application of high technology to existing assets.

The *New Jersey's* mission is to conduct prompt and sustained operations worldwide, in support of our national interests. In some cases, deployment of the *New Jersey* will free up our overstressed aircraft carriers for other uses. While the aircraft carrier remains the foundation of American naval power, the battleship will today be the sovereign of the seas. In support of amphibious operations, the *New Jersey's* 16-inch guns can deliver shells as heavy as an automobile with pinpoint accuracy. And with a speed of 35 knots, the *New Jersey* will be among the fastest ships afloat.

History tells us that a delegate to the Continental Congress called the creation of our Navy "the maddest idea in the world." Well, we've been questioned for bringing back this battleship. Yet, I would challenge anyone who's been aboard or even seen the *New Jersey* to argue its value. It seems odd and a little ironic to me that some of the same critics who accuse us of chasing technology and gold-plating our weapons systems have led the charge against the superbly cost-effective and maintainable *New Jersey*. I doubt if there's a better example of the cost-consciousness of this administration than the magnificent ship that we're recommissioning today.

However, even with maximum efficiency and an eye toward making every dollar count, we must not fool ourselves. Providing an adequate defense is not cheap. The price of peace is always high, but considering the alternative, it's worth it.

Teddy Roosevelt said it well. "We Americans have many grave problems to solve, many threatening evils to fight, and many deeds to do if, as we hope and believe, we have the wisdom, the strength, the courage and the virtue to do them. But we must face facts as they are. Our nation is that one among all nations of the Earth which holds in its hands the fate of the coming years."

Today, I'd like to take this opportunity to thank all of those who worked on the *New Jersey*. You're a great team, and you did an outstanding job in putting her back into fighting trim. You represent a new spirit, a new sense of responsibility that we must have in all our shipyards and defense-related industries if public support for our vital task is to be maintained.

This ship, as the Secretary told us, was brought in on time and on budget. And from all reports, the craftsmanship and professionalism of those involved in the project were superior, and I'm pleased to have the opportunity to extend the thanks of a grateful nation.

The *New Jersey*, like any ship in our fleet, will depend on the ability, dedication, and, yes, patriotism of you here who are her crew. You're the elite. Six thousand applied for 1,500 crew spaces on the *New Jersey*. I have no doubt, too, that from among your ranks will come the Spruances and the Halseys and the Thompsons of tomorrow.

A few moments ago I quoted Teddy Roosevelt. Most people remember him as a man of strength and vitality, and, yes, some have an image of a warlike man always spoiling for a fight. Well, let us remember, he won the Nobel Peace Prize, an honor bestowed upon him for his courageous and energetic efforts to end the Russo-Japanese war. He knew the relationship between peace and strength. And he knew the importance of a strong navy.

"The Navy of the United States," he said, "is the right arm of the United States and is emphatically the peacemaker. Woe to our country if we permit that right arm to become palsied or even to become flabby and inefficient."

Well, the *New Jersey* today becomes our 514th ship and represents our determination to rebuild the strength of America's right arm so that we can preserve the peace.

After valiant service in Vietnam and after saving the lives of countless marines, the *New Jersey* was decommissioned in 1969. During that solemn ceremony, her last commanding officer, Captain Robert Penniston, spoke prophetically when he suggested that this mighty ship "Rest well, yet sleep lightly, and hear the call, if again sounded, to provide firepower for freedom."

Well, the call has been sounded. America needs the battleship once again to provide firepower for the defense of freedom and, above all, to maintain the peace. She will truly fulfill her mission if her firepower never has to be used.

Captain Fogarty, I hereby place the United States Ship *New Jersey* in commission.

God bless, and Godspeed.

Questions for Discussion:

1. According to President Reagan what benefits does recommissioning the USS *New Jersey* bring to American defense abilities?

2. How does Reagan deal with the critics of his rearmament program?

3. According to Reagan, what is the relationship between a strong navy and American ideals?

Ronald Reagan, *Public Papers of the Presidents of the United States: Ronald Reagan, 1982* (Washington, D.C.: Government Printing Office, 1983), book 2 (July 3 to December 31, 1982): 1647–50.

SEA CHANGE IN SOCIETY

Postwar American society was largely conservative, and change proved incremental rather revolutionary. For example, the military officially desegregated in 1948 when President Harry S Truman (1884–1972) signed Executive Order 9981. But Secretary of Defense Robert S. McNamara had to issue a directive in 1963 banning all racial discrimination on and off U.S. military bases, indicating that problems still existed.

Civilian changes were no faster. Like many Americans, African Americans were eager to go to the beach, but in many states laws either banned them from beaches or relegated them to segregated "blacks only" beaches. The issue was a serious one; Chicago experienced a major race riot in 1919 that left 38 people dead and 537 injured when blacks attempted to use a "white" beach. After the Second World War, the civil rights movement began in earnest with the Supreme Court's *Brown v. Board of Education of Topeka* decision that overturned the principle of "separate but equal" facilities for blacks and whites. Soon African American leaders like Dr. Gilbert Mason of Biloxi, Mississippi, began demanding the desegregation of beaches in a series of "wade-ins" that sometimes resulted in mob violence.

The American public had also proven unwilling to challenge the status quo when it came to military spending and nuclear armaments in the 1950s. But slowly the American public awakened to the idea that the Cold War's nuclear arms race might result in a nuclear war that could incinerate the planet. Novels like Neville Chute's chilling apocalyptic novel *On the Beach* and its subsequent 1959 movie version starring Gregory Peck proved both popular and alarming. Pacifist groups, inspired by the nonviolent civil disobedience of Indian leader Mohandas Gandhi, donned their swimsuits to interfere with the launching of nuclear submarines, enduring chilly waters to bring attention to their cause and presaging the widespread pacifism of the later 1960s.

Bob Thomas, "Biloxi Beach Wade-In" (1960)

Beaches were the scenes of considerable tension and violence during the desegregation struggles of the 1960s. In Mississippi, some of the earliest and bloodiest riots occurred as the result of one black physician's efforts to integrate Biloxi's "whites only" beaches. Dr. Gilbert Mason (1928–2006) began protesting the segregation of the region's beaches in 1959. Subsequent wade-ins ignited some of the bloodiest white rioting in Mississippi history, complete with burning crosses, crowd violence, and random shootings. Opposing Dr. Mason was the white establishment, including the Mississippi State Sovereignty Commission, a state agency dedicated to defending racial segregation. Historian J. Michael Butler has recently exposed the chillingly detailed reports of the Sovereignty Commission and compared their tactics to those of the Gestapo or KGB.[1]

The following piece is an excerpt from a report by a Mississippi State Sovereignty Commission agent. The report is rambling and poorly organized but reflects the chaos Dr. Mason's wade-ins brought to Biloxi. If anything, it underreports the scale of the violence: whites attacked some 125 black men, women, and children with clubs, chains, and brass knuckles as Biloxi's police looked on, doing nothing to protect the protestors. The value of this document is that Thompson had access to all the elected officials of Biloxi, giving invaluable insights into their reactions to the violence on the beach.

---

1   J. Michael Butler, "The Mississippi State Sovereignty Commission and Beach Integration, 1959–1963: A Cotton-Patch Gestapo?" *Journal of Southern History* 68, no. 1 (February, 2002): 107–48.

Mason's efforts toward beach integration were slow to bear fruit. Wade-ins in 1959, 1960, and again in 1963 did not bring immediate results, and the response of Biloxi's black community was complex; not all African Americans agreed with his tactics. Thus Biloxi's beach only became offi-cially integrated in 1972 after a long national campaign and legal battle.

On Sunday Morning at 9:00, I met inspector Jacobs at Highway Patrol Headquarters, along with about twelve other Patrolmen, and we started checking on the beach. The Patrolmen had instructions to patrol the highways and not interfere with anything not on the main highways. At 2:00 p.m., we got a call that the Negroes had hit the beach at the White House in Biloxi. When we got there, we saw a group of Negroes, among whom was Dr. Mason, who seemed to have a pretty rough cut above his left eye which was bloody. He had put some other Negroes in his car, a 1959 Buick, license #322-193. Infor-mation is that the Negroes Dr. Mason put in the car were pretty well roughed up, too, and I understand he was taking them to the hospital. Also, a car, a 1959 Oldsmobile, license #324-195 belonging to a Negro, Herbert Caliste of 310 Washington Street, Biloxi, was there in this group. There was a Negro Airman[1] on the front lawn of a house close to the beach that was out cold and they were trying to get an ambu-lance, but up until I left some twenty minutes later, they had not been able to get one. I did not see the actual fighting, but I did notice that the Biloxi Police was scarce. Sheriff Dedeaux[2] and his deputies were at the scene, and some of the Highway Patrolmen heard him tell his deputies that he did not want any arrests on the beach.

Earlier in the morning, Highway Patrol Car 80 stopped three mo-torcycles loaded with Negroes and took them to Harrison County jail and while they were booking these Negroes, Movie Star John Carroll[3] walked up and put his arm around one of the Negroes and asked him if he wanted him to bail him out. The Negro said that he didn't know him, and Carroll gave him his name and address, and told him he was

---

1   Airman: member of the U.S. Air Force, from nearby Keesler Air Force Base.
2   Sheriff Dedeaux: Harrison County Sheriff Curtis Dedeaux, who attempted to control the beach disturbances by manipulating Dr. Felix Dunn, the head of the local chapter of the NAACP who often favored accommodating white interests versus open con-frontation.
3   John Carroll: (1906–1979) a white movie star who reached his peak in the 1940s; he was born in nearby New Orleans.

going to pay him out and he would go and raise some more money to get his buddies out, and all he asked was that he send the money back to him. Charges against these two Negroes were expired drivers license and obstructing traffic. Patrol officers Vernon and Fairley made the arrest. The Negro bailed out was named W. L. Richardson, 616 Fourth Street, New Orleans, La. Sheriff Dedeaux was showing Carroll around the jail. It was noticed that Carroll kept his arm around the Negro or on his shoulder all the time he was talking to him. A friend who was with Carroll said that he did this for public relations all the time. Patrolman Archie Fairley said he was standing with Curtis Dedeaux last summer during the election when Dedeaux promised a lot of help to the Negroes if he were elected. Enclosed with this report will be found a copy of a statement that came out in a Negro newspaper that was attributed to Sheriff Dedeaux during this campaign last year. One of the Negroes involved in this incident got out of the car with Patrolman Jack Anderson, and on the main street in Biloxi, I stopped and talked with this Negro whose name is David Hamilton, age 16, address is #2 Bunyan Courts, he goes to M. F. Nichols High. This Negro boy works part time for the Past Time Café in Biloxi. He stated that morning, Dr. Mason asked different ones to go on the beach and twelve cars of Negroes went to the beach and got there at 2:00 p.m. They were asked by Dr. Mason to leave all their knives, clubs, etc., at McDaniel's Funeral Home in Biloxi. They were to meet back at McDaniel's Funeral Home at approximately 3:30 or 4:00, where they would disburse.

Two Negroes by the name of Galloway and Dickey went with these boys to carry them. Galloway is a disabled veteran in Biloxi, and Dickey is an embalmer at Brown Funeral Home. Dr. Mason told them to go on out into the water and if the police came, to go further out until they called and told them to get out that they were under arrest. This boy stated that his mother had told him not to go down on the beach and that he had not paid any attention to her, but after what happened, that he would definitely listen to her from then on that he was not going back down there any more or any where else that Dr. Mason said. This boy stated that Dr. Mason had had several meetings in his home that he had heard of, but he knew of no particular ones that were present at these meetings and that Dr. Mason was stirring up all this trouble as he was the only one that was really interested in carrying this further. I asked the boy if he did not have a swimming pool of his own or if one was not available there in Biloxi for the Negroes. He stated that there was one at the high school and that he would be perfectly satisfied to use that one and no other from now on.

The following Negroes were hurt: (on beach) Kenneth Thames, age 17; Marzie Thomas, age 21; Lucell Bullock, 38; and W. B. McDaniel, age 35. McDaniel is the operator of the funeral home where the Negroes gathered to begin with. They were all taken to the new Biloxi Hospital.

While at the scene, I observed that the Actor John Carroll, who paid the Negro on the motorcycle out of jail, was with Sheriff Dedeaux all the time as an observer.

After this, a crowd of Negroes gathered on the beach. It was estimated that from four to five hundred Negroes assembled in front of Dr. Mason's home, but they gradually broke up. This Negro, W. P. McDaniel, age 35, from the Undertaking Parlor where the group first started from, had quite a bit to say. He said that the move by the white groups were well planned and he recognized the first person that struck him, and he said that he intended to file a complaint with the police. He said that his group went swimming in front of the hospital because they thought that there would be fewer people there than any other place. He, also, stated that people had been talking about the NAACP[1] and that now, they would see something of it.

Later, Dr. Mason, also, stated that the officers refused to do anything and said he heard one say that the Negroes were getting what they deserved.

During the night, taxi-cabs and automobiles in the Negro section of the town were bombarded with rocks and bottles and bricks. A seventeen-year-old white youth, Andrew Parker, was wounded in the back from ambush by a shotgun blast while riding his bicycle. He was not seriously injured.

I understand from a reliable source that this boy had just been released from Columbia and he was in the Negro section, in a place where he was not suppose to be. Six white and Negro Airmen were beaten up during a fight on a downtown street. A Negro bar was shot up by a unknown gunman shortly after Midnight, however, no one

---

1   NAACP: National Association for the Advancement of Colored People, one of the oldest and best organized groups that led the struggle for equal rights for African Americans.

was injured because the bar had closed earlier. Police, also, stated that a shotgun blast was fired into a service station earlier today, but no one was injured. A white man said he was attacked by five Negroes, but he managed to escape without serious injury. Quite a few Negroes remained on the job during the night because they were afraid to walk on the city streets. The Police Station was swamped with phone calls from Negro citizens asking for protection for their homes. Also, working Negroes were asking for escorts to protect them to their homes.

On Monday morning, Inspector A. D. Morgan and myself talked to Sheriff Dedeaux in his office and he said that the Friday preceding, he had had a conversation or meeting with Dr. Dunn and Wilson Evans, who is head of the I.L.A., labor organization here, and a Reverend McIlhanny. They stated that they were going on the beach at about three different spots on that Sunday, but that they were not going to have any violence of any kind. Sheriff Dedeaux stated that he had made arrangements for them to come back the first of the week and get with him and he would try to work out something plausible between them and the Board of Supervisors. The Sheriff, also, stated that he blamed Clayton Rand[1] for being the Daddy of the whole situation since Rand had raised so much fuss with the Negroes out in front of his home there on the beach that the people had to do something. Sheriff, also, stated that Roy Wilkins came to Mt. Bethel Baptist Church sometime last year and brought two Negro lawyers with him to discuss the sand beach proposition. They, also, got with and discussed this situation with white Attorney, Knox Walker.

While I was in the Sheriff's office, a man came in from Sears Roebuck and reported that Negroes in droves were inquiring about buying firearms. Dedeaux stated that he would like for this man to, before he sold firearms of any kind, make the people come over and get permission from him and register this stuff before they bought it. The man said that he would. Dedeaux, also, said that he believed that charges at Biloxi should be dropped and will be all over with; that Mason would mouth-off quite a bit after that, but after he got knocked in the head Sunday, he wouldn't attempt to go back on the beach any more. Also, while A. D. Morgan and myself were in Sheriff Dedeaux's office, Dr. Dunn called. From the conversation, I gathered that Dunn

---

1   Clayton Rand: a local journalist and owner of a beach house who opposed integration.

was complaining about the two Constables in Gulfport closing up a lot of Negro joints. The Sheriff told Dunn that he blamed him for this trouble, that he had promised to keep things quiet until the group met back with him the first part of the week to try to work things out and that he did not keep his word, and that he could not and would not try to interfere with the Constables and what they were doing. The conversation, also, seemed to center around a request from the Negroes to get with a Mrs. Brown, who runs the Broadwater Beach Hotel to build a colored motel and swimming area in the vicinity of the Broadwater Beach, at a cost of a quarter million dollars. The Sheriff had arranged a meeting with Mrs. Brown, but he told Dunn that after the disturbance, he doubted whether or not she would be interested at all in this plan. The Negroes seem to be of the opinion that they would be satisfied if this could be worked out providing the county had nothing to do with it.

Questions for Discussion:
1. What does this document reveal about racial tensions in 1960?
2. How does Bob Thomas's position as an officer of the Mississippi State Sovereignty Commission impact his view of events?
3. What can be surmised from this document about the effort to desegregate Biloxi's beaches?

Bob Thomas, "Beach Disturbances, Biloxi, Harrison County, Mississippi," May 2, 1960, Mississippi State Sovereignty Commission 5–4–0–50, Mississippi Department of History and Archives, Jackson, Mississippi.

Polaris Action, "All Aboard *Ethan Allen*" (1960)

To many Americans, the Navy's nuclear submarines were a technological triumph. These nuclear-powered submarines could remain submerged for months at a time. According to Admiral Burke, chief of naval operations, these submarines, which were armed with intermediate range Polaris ballistic missiles that could be launched while the submarine remained submerged, were "purely a weapon for massive retaliation" against any Soviet nuclear first strike.

But to a determined minority, nuclear submarines—and more especially the nuclear missiles they carried—were a threat to world peace and security. The most outspoken and active of the antinuclear submarine groups was Polaris Action, established by the pacifist group Committee for Nonviolent Action (CNVA) in 1960 to protest the launching of the new *Ethan Allen* class of nuclear submarines, the first to be designed specifically to launch nuclear missiles against targets in the Soviet Union. The following firsthand account, written by Polaris Action activist Bill Henry, recounts his experience in civil disobedience. Other groups, notably the environmental group Greenpeace, have adopted similar tactics to bring attention to various issues, and protests against nuclear submarines became common again in the 1980s.

From the New London City Dock we could see the first two of our boats—a canoe and a dory—towed away by the Coast Guard. They had set out to obstruct the launching of the *Ethan Allen*. About 11:35 AM, a third boat named *Leo Tolstoy*[1] and manned by Vic Richman and Larry Orenstein, left City Dock and headed for the launching ways of EB.[2]

Don Martin and I had planned to begin swimming toward the sub from the Groton shore when the third boat restricted the area surrounding the launching site. Our timing was poor. The boat left too soon and arrived at our jumping off place rather late. Only two minutes remained before the *Ethan Allen* was to be launched. We quickly stripped down to bathing trunks. Then we walked absurdly through the sunny, cool November air onto the shore which was grouped with people gathered for the launching. Into the calm, dark, icy water we strode. The cold pierced us and we gasped for air. The numbness which began to pierce us was forgotten as whistles blew and the *Ethan Allen* slid smoothly and cautiously down the ways into the silent waters with the occupants on her deck presenting themselves in beautiful symmetry.

"We're too late," I thought, but Don and I agreed to survey the situation from a piling near the ways before making our next move. As we swam, shipyard workers waved warnings to halt. Others shouted to us to stay out. A C.G.[3] boat pulled up to us and just as we reached the pilings a Guardsman yelled at us to come aboard. "Are we under ar-

---

1 Leo Tolstoy: (1828–1910), the famous Russian author of *Anna Karenina* and other influential works was an advocate of pacifism.
2 EB: the Electric Boat Corporation, of Groton, Connecticut, built many of the Navy's nuclear submarines.
3 C.G.: Coast Guard.

rest?" I asked. "Yes," he replied, but unconvincingly. He said the same when asked again.

I swam over, grabbed on to the boat and pulled myself up. Suddenly the Guardsman stopped me and ordered, "Hold it." A voice over the ship's radio instructed, "Let them swim." The Guardsman I understood to say, "Navy says let them swim so you have to go back." I soon rejoined Don in the water. He had decided not to go aboard in the first place. We pushed off in the direction of the sub, situated in the center of the river with its colorfully draped bow[1] pointing toward us about 250 yards away.

A number of C.G. launches were in the area. Don and I talked and decided that we could both swim way across the estuary to the other side if it were necessary. With this confidence in mind we struck out toward the sub. Almost immediately a C.G. launch moved into our path. But our swimming battle of three pacifists against four boats at Newport News served us well.[2] A word between us and we split up. I headed around the rear of the launch while Don headed around the bow. One boat cannot stop two swimmers. The launch retreated. The launch regrouped with another launch, bow to bow. This time we didn't even slow down. We swam for the point where the two bows nearly touched and because neither launch could move ahead without ramming the other, we were able to swim between the bows.

Another boat blocked us. Don headed for the bow and I went around it. I headed for the stern but the launch backed up. I headed for the bow but the launch went forward. I was blocked. I swam in close to the launch in order to try and pull myself around the bow by holding on to projections from the hull and pulling myself forward even while the launch moved. I held to a water escape valve temporarily and then made a lunge and several quick strokes to pull myself in front of the boat before it would move ahead. I got around it as it moved ahead and then I pushed off from its hull. It moved in position ahead of me again. Don had disappeared.

The considerate young skipper of the launch asked me to come aboard. I told him that I felt obligated to keep trying until I was exhausted. Someone said "you'll never make it." Just then, another

---

1   Colorfully draped bow: on launching, the submarine's bow was covered in red, white, and blue bunting.

2   Newport News: Newport News in Virginia was also the site of Polaris Action protests.

Guardsman said, "Look, his buddy is there already." I reached up and grabbed the horizontal edge of the deck and by swinging hand over hand I was able to move around the bow to open water. I could see Don clinging to the drapery halfway up the sub's bow 150 feet away.

The launch blocked me again. I was wearying and numb as two launches created waves which wearied me further. The considerate young skipper threw me a buoyant ring but I avoided it. He told me very nicely that he felt responsible for my life and I told him that I would be careful but that I felt I had a duty just as he had a duty. After several minutes I was able to swim around the stern. Maybe I was permitted to do so.

As I moved closer to the sub a huge section of launching cradle[1] bobbed to the surface. A man amidships yelled, "You'll be killed if you stay there." I moved toward the bow and the ship seemed to start moving ahead. I grabbed the red, white and blue streamers and pulled myself up. The slope of the hull was about 45°. I climbed to the same point Don had. An official on deck kindly warned me of the weakness of a thick string I was depending on. I grasped a different hold and pulled my stiff body up to the rope guardrails around the deck.

The coldness had penetrated so far and so long that the outside of me was stiff like the exoskeleton of a bug. I shivered violently and the numbness seemed to move deeper and deeper. I had to concentrate to walk straight. My body weaved and my consciousness was barely with me. I took a life jacket in a vain effort to retain body heat. I arose when directed. A rope was tied around my waist and I voluntarily proceeded down a steel ladder to a waiting Navy boat. There Don was being held. He was in no sense waiting.

We were taken to the Coast Guard Station where we joined the seven other disobedients. They greeted us with shouts of "How close did you get?" Dick Zink offered his warm coat. Military personnel volunteered in a very considerate manner a hot radiator, a warm blanket and a hot cup of coffee.

Questions for Discussion:
1. What does this document reveal about American attitudes toward nuclear arms in 1960?

---

1   Launching cradle: when a vessel is launched it rests on a cradle of large timbers that also slide into the water.

2. What can be inferred about the values and methods of Polaris Action from this account?

3. How does this account blur the line between journalism and activism, and is this a useful approach?

Bill Henry, "All Aboard *Ethan Allen*," *Polaris Action Bulletin* #16, December 3, 1960.

Elmo Zumwalt Jr., "Z-Gram #66: Equal Opportunity" (1970)

The U.S. Navy officially became racially integrated after President Harry S Truman issued Executive Order 9981 in 1948, which established a policy of equal treatment in all the armed services. In practice, racism and other forms of discrimination continued. Lingering racism, low morale at the end of the Vietnam War, and young African Americans radicalized by various black power movements created increasingly tense interracial relations in the Navy.

Admiral Elmo Russell Zumwalt Jr. (1920–2000), the unorthodox chief of naval operations (CNO) from 1970–1974, moved to alleviate these racial tensions. A highly decorated war veteran, Zumwalt disseminated his ideas in Navy-wide communications known as *Z-grams*, an unusual move that bypassed the chain of command and directly communicated the CNO's ideas to the entire Navy. Zumwalt recorded his contentious career in his autobiography entitled *On Watch*.[1]

In this Z-gram, Zumwalt attempts to create a more welcoming environment for all minorities in the Navy. However, racial tensions remained; in 1972 there was a race-based "riot" on board the aircraft carrier USS *Kitty Hawk*, and Congress mounted a major investigation of racial problems in the Navy. Ultimately the Navy began a recruiting drive aimed specifically at African Americans, featuring slogans such as "Your Son can be Black, and Navy, too."

EQUAL OPPORTUNITY IN THE NAVY

1. THE PURPOSE OF THIS NAVOP IS TO EXPRESS MY WHOLE-HEARTED SUPPORT OF THE POLICIES ON EQUAL OPPORTUNITY STRONGLY REAFFIRMED BY THE SECRETARY OF THE NAVY IN ALNAV 51, TO EXPRESS MY GENERAL GUIDANCE FOR IMPLEMENTATION OF THESE POLICIES, AND TO DIRECT

---

1 Elmo R. Zumwalt Jr., *On Watch: A Memoir* (New York: Quadrangle/New York Times Book Co., 1976).

IMPLEMENTATION OF A FEW OF THE ACTIONS WE CAN TAKE IMMEDIATELY.

2. LAST MONTH, SECRETARY CHAFEE[1] AND I, ALONG WITH OTHER SENIOR OFFICIALS OF THE NAVY DEPARTMENT, MET ON ONE OCCASION WITH REPRESENTATIVE BLACK NAVY OFFICERS AND THEIR WIVES AND LATER WITH A REPRESENTATIVE GROUP OF BLACK ENLISTED MEN AND THEIR WIVES. PRIOR TO THESE MEETINGS, I WAS CONVINCED THAT, COMPARED WITH THE CIVILIAN COMMUNITY, WE HAD RELATIVELY FEW RACIAL PROBLEMS IN THE NAVY. HOWEVER, AFTER EXPLORING THE MATTER IN SOME DEPTH WITH THESE TWO GROUPS, I HAVE DISCOVERED THAT I WAS WRONG—WE DO HAVE PROBLEMS, AND IT IS MY INTENTION AND THAT OF SECRETARY CHAFEE TO TAKE PROMPT STEPS TOWARD THEIR SOLUTION.

3. WHAT STRUCK ME MORE THAN ANYTHING ELSE WAS THE DEPTH OF FEELING OF OUR BLACK PERSONNEL THAT THERE IS SIGNIFICANT DISCRIMINATION IN THE NAVY. PRIOR TO THESE MEETINGS, I SINCERELY BELIEVED THAT I WAS PHILOSOPHICALLY PREPARED TO UNDERSTAND THE PROBLEMS OF OUR BLACK NAVYMEN AND THEIR FAMILIES, AND UNTIL WE DISCUSSED THEM AT LENGTH, I DID NOT REALIZE THE EXTENT AND DEEP SIGNIFICANCE OF MANY OF THESE MATTERS.

4. THERE ARE TWO KEYS TO THE PROBLEM. FIRST, WE MUST OPEN UP NEW AVENUES OF COMMUNICATION WITH NOT ONLY OUR BLACK PERSONNEL, BUT ALSO WITH ALL MINORITY GROUPS IN THE NAVY SO THAT WE MAY LEARN WHAT AND WHERE THE AREAS OF FRICTION ARE. SECOND, ALL OF US IN THE NAVY MUST DEVELOP A FAR GREATER SENSITIVITY TO THE PROBLEMS OF ALL OUR MINORITY GROUPS SO THAT WE MAY MORE EFFECTIVELY GO ABOUT SOLVING THEM. OUR MEETINGS HERE IN WASHINGTON WERE A BEGINNING, BUT NO MORE THAN THAT. MUCH REMAINS TO BE DONE.

5. FOR EXAMPLE, I AM PARTICULARLY DISTRESSED BY THE

---

1   CHAFEE: John Chafee, Rhode Island politician and secretary of the Navy from 1969 to 1972.

NUMEROUS EXAMPLES OF DISCRIMINATION BLACK NAVY FAMILIES STILL EXPERIENCE IN ATTEMPTING TO LOCATE HOUSING FOR THEIR FAMILIES. THIS SITUATION AND OTHERS LIKE IT ARE INDICATIVE IN SOME CASES OF LESS THAN FULL TEAMWORK BEING BROUGHT TO BEAR BY THE WHOLE NAVY TEAM ON BEHALF OF SOME OF OUR MEMBERS AND FAILURE TO USE EXISTING AUTHORITY AND DIRECTIVES TO ENFORCE THEIR RIGHTS (SECNAV INST 5350.12). IN SOME PLACES HOUSING PERSONNEL ARE TACITLY CONTRIBUTING TO DISCRIMINATION IN HOUSING.

6. SECRETARY CHAFEE AND I HAVE ASKED OUR STAFFS TO BEGIN WORK WITH OTHER MEMBERS OF THE NAVY DEPARTMENT TO MAKE AN IN-DEPTH INVESTIGATION OF THIS PROBLEM AND PRESENT TO US WITHIN 60 DAYS PROPOSALS WHICH WILL HELP ALLEVIATE THE MOST ACUTE HOUSING PROBLEMS. MEANWHILE, THERE ARE MANY THINGS THAT CAN BE ACTED UPON IMMEDIATELY. THEREFORE, BY 15 JANUARY 1971 I EXPECT ACTION TO BE TAKEN AS FOLLOWS:

A. EVERY BASE, STATION AND AIRCRAFT SQUADRON COMMANDER AND SHIP COMMANDING OFFICER SHALL APPOINT AN AWARE MINORITY GROUP OFFICER OR SENIOR PETTY OFFICER AS HIS SPECIAL ASSISTANT FOR MINORITY AFFAIRS. THIS OFFICER OR PETTY OFFICER SHOULD HAVE DIRECT ACCESS TO THE COMMANDER/COMMANDING OFFICER AND WILL BE CONSULTED ON ALL MATTERS INVOLVING MINORITY PERSONNEL. EXCEPTING THOSE COMMANDS ALREADY HAVING MINORITY-AFFAIRS OFFICER BILLETS, THE INITIAL ASSIGNMENT WILL BE ON A CONCURRENT DUTY BASIS. (I CAREFULLY WEIGHED THIS ITEM WITH MY DESIRE, AS EXPRESSED IN REF A, TO REDUCE COLLATERAL DUTY ASSIGNMENTS. HOWEVER, AFTER DISCUSSING THIS WITH SEVERAL BLACK OFFICERS I BECAME CONVINCED THAT THEY WOULD IN FACT, CHERISH THIS AS A COLLATERAL DUTY.)

B. ALL SHORE BASED COMMANDERS SHALL ENSURE THAT A MINORITY GROUP WIFE IS INCLUDED IN THE NAVY WIVES OMBUDSMAN CONCEPT SET FORTH IN REF B.

C. THE PROGRAMS ALREADY BEGUN BY COMNAVSUPSYSCOM TO ENSURE THAT THE SPECIAL NEEDS OF MINORITY

GROUPS ARE RECOGNIZED AND PROVIDED FOR SHALL BE EXPEDITED, NAMELY:

(1) SUITABLE COSMETICS AND OTHER PRODUCTS FOR BLACK PERSONNEL AND THEIR DEPENDENTS WILL BE STOCKED IN NAVY EXCHANGES.

(2) SHIP'S STORES WILL STOCK BLACK GROOMING AIDS.

(3) EVERY BASE AND STATION, WILL EMPLOY, AS SOON AS POSSIBLE, AT LEAST ONE QUALIFIED BLACK BARBER/BEAUTICIAN IN MAJOR BARBER AND BEAUTY SHOPS, AND WILL WORK TOWARD THE GOAL OF HAVING SUFFICIENT BARBERS/BEAUTICIANS QUALIFIED IN HAIR CARE FOR BLACK PERSONNEL TO PROVIDE SERVICE FOR ALL BLACK PATRONS.

(4) ALL MAJOR COMMISSARIES SHALL STOCK FOODS AND PRODUCE FREQUENTLY REQUESTED BY MINORITY GROUPS. AS A MINIMUM, SPECIFIC RECOMMENDATIONS SHOULD BE SOLICITED FROM MINORITY PERSONNEL AND THEIR FAMILIES AND ACTED UPON BY LOCAL COMMISSARY MANAGERS.

A. SPECIAL SERVICES OFFICERS WHICH DEAL IN DISCOUNT TICKETS FOR VARIOUS ENTERTAINMENT PROGRAMS WILL ALSO OBTAIN DISCOUNT TICKETS TO EVENTS OF SPECIAL INTEREST TO MINORITY GROUPS WHENEVER SUCH TICKETS ARE AVAILABLE.

B. A REPRESENTATIVE SELECTION OF BOOKS, MAGAZINES AND RECORDS BY AND ABOUT BLACK AMERICANS WILL BE MADE AVAILABLE IN NAVY LIBRARIES, WARDROOMS, CLUBS AND OTHER READING AREAS.

ANY OF THE ABOVE WHICH CAN'T BE ACCOMPLISHED WITHIN THE TIME SPECIFIED ABOVE WILL BE REPORTED VIA CHAIN OF COMMAND TOGETHER WITH A SUMMARY OF CIRCUMSTANCES PREVENTING TIMELY IMPLEMENTATION.

1. IN ORDER THAT I MAY REACH A MORE COMPLETE UNDERSTANDING OF THE PROBLEMS EXPERIENCED BY OUR MINORITY PERSONNEL, IN ADDITION TO SECNAV/OPNAV/BUPERS TEAM VISITS I AM DIRECTING MY SPECIAL ASSISTANT FOR MINORITY AFFAIRS, LCDR NORMAN, TO VISIT

MAJOR NAVAL ACTIVITIES WITHIN CONUS[1] TO MEET WITH
INDIVIDUAL COMMANDING OFFICERS AND WITH MINOR-
ITY MILITARY PERSONNEL AND THEIR DEPENDENTS. BY
LEARNING IN DEPTH WHAT OUR PROBLEMS ARE, I BELIEVE
WE WILL BE IN A BETTER POSITION TO WORK TOWARD
GUARANTEEING EQUAL OPPORTUNITY AND TREATMENT
FOR ALL OF OUR NAVY PEOPLE.
2. THIS IS THE FIRST OF MY REPORTS TO YOU ON MINOR-
ITY AFFAIRS. SECRETARY CHAFEE AND I WILL BE LOOKING
INTO ALL AREAS OF MINORITY AFFAIRS AND WILL BE ISSU-
ING FURTHER REPORTS AS OUR PROBLEMS BECOME MORE
CLEAR AND THEIR SOLUTIONS BECOME MORE APPARENT.
IT IS EVIDENT THAT WE NEED TO MAXIMIZE OUR EFFORTS
TO IMPROVE THE LOT OF OUR MINORITY NAVYMEN. I AM
CONVINCED THAT THERE IS NO PLACE IN OUR NAVY FOR
INSENSITIVITY. WE ARE DETERMINED THAT WE SHALL DO
BETTER. MEANWHILE, WE ARE COUNTING ON YOUR SUP-
PORT TO HELP SEEK OUT AND ELIMINATE THOSE DEMEAN-
ING AREAS OF DISCRIMINATION THAT PLAGUE OUR MI-
NORITY SHIPMATES. OURS MUST BE A NAVY FAMILY THAT
RECOGNIZES NO ARTIFICIAL BARRIERS OF RACE, COLOR OR
RELIGION. THERE IS NO BLACK NAVY, NO WHITE NAVY—
JUST ONE NAVY—THE UNITED STATES NAVY.
E. R. ZUMWALT, JR., ADMIRAL, U. S. NAVY,
CHIEF OF NAVAL OPERATIONS.

Questions for Discussion:
1. What does this document reveal about the sort of problems minority
personnel were experiencing in the U.S. Navy?
2. What underlying beliefs compelled Zumwalt to act on discrimination in
the Navy?
3. What concrete changes does Zumwalt propose to improve minority living conditions for Navy personnel and their families?

Elmo R. Zumwalt Jr., "Z-gram # 66: (Equal Opportunity); 17 December 1970,"
Navy Historical Center, http://www.history.navy.mil/faqs/faq93–66.htm (last
accessed February 18, 2007).

---

1   CONUS: Continental United States.

TAILHOOK AND BEYOND

Like the rest of American society since 1945, the Navy has struggled with change. Ideals of equal opportunity in society as a whole meant that the armed services had to deal with messy issues such as racial and ethnic integration, the role of women, and permitting gays and lesbians to serve in the military. While some issues were handled smoothly, the Navy has always been the most tradition-minded of the services, and some changes did not come easily. True equality for African Americans proved elusive until the 1970s, women faced limited careers and sometimes sexual predation, and the issue of gays and lesbians remains unresolved in the "don't ask, don't tell" policy abhorred by liberals and conservatives alike. That is not to say that the Navy has not changed thanks to active reformers, but outsiders often find it hard to understand the emphasis on tradition and reluctance of some to change the Navy's culture and attitudes toward minorities and women.

The single most prominent event for the Navy in the 1990s was the so-called Tailhook scandal. The 1991 Tailhook convention was the worst sex scandal in the military's history, one that damaged the morale and prestige of the Navy. Tailhook, a private organization of past and present naval aviators and their supporters, held its annual convention in 1991 at the Las Vegas Hilton. During the convention, a number of sexual assaults occurred on both civilian and military women. The Navy and Congress launched a major investigation into Tailhook '91; ultimately the scandal ended or damaged the career of a secretary of the Navy, fourteen admirals, and hundreds of other officers. Nor did the scandal go away. The PBS investigative reporting show *Frontline* episode "Navy Blues: The Clash of Values and Politics in the Post-Tailhook Navy" released in 1996 further fanned the controversy.

Inspector General's Office, "Victim 50" (1993)

Lieutenant Paula Coughlin suffered a sexual assault while passing through a gauntlet of men lining the hallway of the convention hotel. Coughlin complained officially to her superiors of her fellow officers' behavior, but the complaints were initially ignored. After she went public with her story, other attendees and female naval officers came forward. Coughlin's own career suffered, and she resigned from the Navy in February 1995. While many credit Coughlin with changing the Navy's culture, others have criticized her for playing "sexual politics." A full analysis of the sometimes troubled history of women in the Navy since 1945 can be found in Jean Ebbert and Marie-Beth Hall's book, *Crossed Currents.*[1]

Status/Service/Rank: Lieutenant (0–3) United States Navy/Female
Date/Time of Incident: Saturday, September 7, 1991 11:30 p.m.
Place of Incident: Hallway, Third Floor, Las Vegas Hilton

Victim 50 is LT. Paula Coughlin. At the time of Tailhook '91, she was aide to Rear Admiral John W. Snyder, United States Navy, Commander, Naval Air Test Center. According to LT. Coughlin, she arrived at the third floor hallway of the Hilton Hotel alone at approximately 11:30 p.m. Saturday evening. She entered the hotel from the pool patio through the doors at the main passenger elevators, turned right and proceeded up the hallway.

As she approached the hallway, she found it to be loud and rowdy. Both sides of the hallway were lined with men leaning on the walls. As she began to walk up the hallway, there were approximately six to eight of the young men on each side of the hallway and two in the center of the hallway. Each had their backs to her at the head of the group. As she attempted to pass the man on the right side the man intentionally bumped into her with his right hip. LT. Coughlin excused herself, and one of the men lining the hallway yelled loudly, "Admiral's Aide!"

LT. Coughlin turned to look at the man who yelled. She described the man who had first bumped into her as having dark skin with short dark hair, perhaps Hispanic or a light skinned black. She was grabbed by the buttocks with such force that it lifted her off the ground and ahead a step.

LT. Coughlin turned around and yelled at the man, "What the f—— do you think you are doing?" As she said that, she was grabbed on the buttocks by someone from behind. She turned and asked that individual the same question. The men in the group began grabbing her breasts as well as her buttocks. LT. Coughlin described the assault as follows:

"The man with the dark complexion moved in immediately behind me with his body pressed against mine. He was bumping me, pushing me forward down the passageway where the group on either side

---

1   Jean Ebbert and Marie-Beth Hall, *Crossed Currents: Navy Women From WWI to Tailhook* (New York: Brassey's, 1993).

was pinching and then pulling at my clothing. The man then put both his hands down the front of my tank top and inside my bra where he grabbed my breasts. I dropped to a forward crouch position and placed my hands on the wrists of my attacker in an attempt to remove his hands . . . I sank my teeth into the fleshy part of the man's left forearm, biting hard. I thought I drew blood . . . I then turned and bit the man on the right hand at the area between the base of the thumb and base of the index finger." The man removed his hands, and another individual "reached up under my skirt and grabbed the crotch of my panties. I kicked one of my attackers . . . I felt as though the group was trying to rape me. I was terrified and had no idea what was going to happen next."

LT. Coughlin attempted to escape into one of the administrative suites, but her route was blocked by men who stood in the doorway and would not allow her through. The men in the crowd continued to grab at her buttocks and breasts, and she noticed that one of the men in the crowd turned and began to walk away. "I reached out and tapped him on the right hip, pleading with the man to just let me get in front of him. The man stopped, turned . . . and pivoted to a position directly in front of me. With this action, the man raised both his hands and put one on each of my breasts."

LT. Coughlin broke free and ran past him into an open door that led to one of the administrative suites. She sat in the room in the dark, "attempting to understand what had happened to me . . . I was appalled not only by the brutality of the incident, but the fact that the group did that to me knowing I was both a fellow officer and an admiral's aide."

According to one witness, a male Federal Government civilian employee, "I remember Coughlin enter the hallway. Coughlin stood in the hallway for a couple of minutes and then proceeded down the hall. As she advanced through the area, the gauntlet collapsed around her blocking her from my view. I recall Coughlin wrenching around as she disappeared from sight. I never saw her exit the gauntlet." There were approximately 100 men in the hallway at the time, none of whom the witness recognized.

A male Navy lieutenant stated that he saw a woman walk into the crowded hallway. He saw her get pinched on the buttocks by an unknown male. As the woman turned to confront the man, another male from the other side of the hallway pinched her on the buttocks. During the confrontation, he heard someone yell "Admiral's Aide!" Later, when the witness saw LT. Coughlin on television, he realized that she was probably the woman he witnessed being assaulted in the hallway.

Another male Federal Government employee witnessed part of the assault on LT. Coughlin. The witness saw a man standing in the hallway whom he described as the "master of ceremonies." The man appeared to be moving about in an animated fashion, trying to get women to walk through the gauntlet where the men in the hallway would then surround them. If a woman did not want to walk down the hallway, the man would physically pick them up and carry them down the hallway. The witness saw LT. Coughlin conversing with the "master of ceremonies," and it appeared that she was telling him she was a lieutenant and an admiral's aide. The witness saw a man come up behind LT. Coughlin and grab her from behind, wrapping his arms all the way around her. LT. Coughlin started to struggle, bending over forward. At the same time LT. Coughlin was being assaulted, another woman standing behind the witness was being grabbed by men in the hallway. The witness left the area before LT. Coughlin emerged from the hallway.

During the course of our investigation, we received several allegations indicating that LT. Coughlin engaged in improper activity while at Tailhook '91. We investigated all such allegations but found that the allegations were based on hearsay testimony or were otherwise without merit. None of the people who told us about the alleged incidents or improper conduct involving LT. Coughlin actually witnessed the incidents themselves nor could they provide the identity of any eyewitnesses.

When interviewed, LT. Coughlin denied all allegations of impropriety. No credible information was found to support the allegations of misconduct on the part of LT. Coughlin. As noted by one male officer, it appeared the allegations were fabricated to discredit LT. Coughlin for her public disclosure of facts concerning assaults at Tailhook '91.

Questions for Discussion:
1. How did Tailhook '91 reveal larger issues both within American society and the Navy?
2. What does this scandal reveal about the Navy's attitudes toward women in the early 1990s?

3. What strengths or weaknesses does this document have in revealing sexual harassment and discrimination in the Navy?

Department of Defense, Inspector General's Office, *Tailhook 91: Review of the Navy Investigations* part 2, appendix F: "Individual victim/assault summaries" (Washington, D.C.: Government Printing Office, 1993), F26–F28.

James Webb, "Defending the Navy's Culture" (1996)

This speech, delivered by James "Jim" Webb (1946–) on April 25, 1996, at the Naval Institute's 122nd Annual Meeting and Sixth Annapolis Seminar, received a standing ovation. It is a powerful but controversial statement about the Navy as a distinct culture. Webb, a former secretary of the Navy in the Reagan Administration, was a 1968 graduate of the Naval Academy who served with distinction as a marine in Vietnam and was already notorious for his 1979 article entitled "Women Can't Fight."

In this speech, Webb blamed the Navy's leadership for "failing to defend the Navy's culture and of abandoning the very ideals of their profession to save or advance their careers," a thinly veiled attack on Admiral Jeremy "Mike" Boorda (1939–1996), himself a controversial figure who had risen from the enlisted ranks to become chief of naval operations (CNO). Webb and other tradition-minded Navy and Marines veterans criticized Boorda for his "politically correct" stands against all forms of sexual harassment, his support for opening virtually all Navy jobs to women, his handling of the Tailhook '91 scandal, and Boorda's wearing of devices on his service ribbons to which some thought he was not entitled.

> Like so many graduates of this institution, I am flooded with memories each time I drive through the Naval Academy gates and see the monuments and the buildings that have by now become a constant in my life. The memories remain incredibly vivid, filled with an emotion that has never passed, making it hard to believe sometimes that it has now been a full generation since those first days after I raised my hand and took the oath to defend my country, and at the same moment forever abandoned what remained of my youth.
>
> Some of them are happy, some are not. Some are personal, some are not. But all of them are tied in some way to service, and more specifically to the greatness of America's Navy and Marine Corps. And when I think of where the country and the Navy and indeed I myself have journeyed, in my memory I always return to the evening lecture

series in the musty, hallowed darkness of Mahan Hall. An integral part of our plebe[1] summer training, the lectures were our first formal introduction to the leaders and the history of our new and special calling.

Packed into the dankness of Mahan Hall with our new classmates sitting all around us, sweating and hacking and sneezing, exhausted from the day's activities that had begun well before dawn, reeking of mildew from the whiteworks uniforms[2] that never seemed to get entirely dry, dozing now and then from the constant, unrelenting pressure of our new calling, the pressure that challenged us to be men at eighteen, to assume responsibility and accept the consequences of our acts, the pressure that it seemed would never in the rest of our young lives abate, never let up perhaps even until we were finally old men nodding and hacking on different benches, bent and exhausted from our journey, the journey that would take us off to sea or under it or above it or into the jungles that bordered it, the journey that would find us, as that magnificent song we all learned to sing so aptly puts it, by the service called away, scattered far and wide.

They were giants, the men featured in those lectures, and we felt their presence as we sat in the seats where some of them once sat and learned of the battles they had fought and of the courage they had shown. Their words and, most importantly, their example sank into me so deeply that for as long as I shall live, I know they will never cease to bring shivers of pride and awe to me when I remember them, those bold mirrors of an increasingly distant past.

The young lieutenant on Guadalcanal who asked his loved ones always to pray, not that he came back, but that he would have the courage to do his duty. The chaplain on a sinking ship who gave his life preserver to a young sailor, telling him, take it, lad, you need it more than I do. The admirals of the greatest sea battles in history who faced enormous decisions that had to be made on gossamers of information, with thousands of lives and indeed a nation in the balance. And above all, the inarguable first commandment of naval leadership, shown time and again by leaders young and old when their defining moment came: where principle is involved, be deaf to expediency.

---

1   Plebe: a first-year student at the Naval Academy.
2   Whiteworks uniforms: the uniform worn by the most junior midshipmen at the Naval Academy during their first, plebe year.

I resolved to prepare myself so that when my time came, I could honor this heritage, show that I had the same physical and moral courage, the identical dedication to my country and to the people whose lives were being entrusted to me. I wanted more than anything to have the courage to do my duty, to take care of my people, to speak the truth no matter how it hurt, no matter what the consequences. And I was not alone. In the mess hall, on the parade field, walking to class, I could look around me and see thousands who felt the way I did.

Some might say we were naive, that we aspired to some unreachable, romantic standard that human nature in its tilt toward accommodation cannot consistently maintain. My own journey tells me otherwise, that we were right, that for the long-term good there is no substitute for an insistence on ethics, loyalty, accountability, and moral courage. And yet today I must say I am sadly astounded to see our Navy struggling for its soul, too often unanchored from these simple yet demanding notions, many of whose leaders have advanced themselves through a blatant repudiation of these very ideals. There are still exceptional leaders in our Navy, some of whom are my classmates, others whom I can see in this audience today. But too often the best leaders are not being heard. Something almost unexplainable happened in the decades since we sat in those seats in Mahan Hall. Some of it happened to the country as a whole, but some of it did not. A great deal of it happened to the Navy as an institution. It happened gradually, issue by issue, argument by argument, compromise by compromise.

Over time, getting worse as the years went by, an increasing percentage of the naval leaders who were promoted into the highest sanctums of government somehow lost their way, until finally, in recent years, many whose very duty it was to defend the hallowed traditions and the unique culture of their profession declined to do so when their voices were most urgently needed. Some are guilty of the ultimate disloyalty: to save or advance their careers, they abandoned the very ideals of their profession in order to curry favor with politicians.

I frequently find myself wondering how this possibly could have happened. To be fair, these have been uniquely difficult times for military leaders. Our generation's complex and volatile political debates resulted in unprecedented intrusions into command relationships because of new concepts of limited warfare, increased judicial oversight, and a variety of programs mandated under the rubric of equal opportunity. The all-volunteer system, with its emphasis on targeted bonuses and specialty pay, fostered greater rewards for individual skills than for group values. But the other services faced these same issues with far less chaos. The inescapable difference has been the approach of the Navy's top leadership, particularly during this decade.

And so I go back to those dank, sweltering teenage evenings in Mahan Hall, and I ask myself, what would Nimitz[1] have said and done in these situations? Or King?[2] Or Admiral McCain?[3] Or, dare I be presumptuous, Tom Moorer,[4] one of the great living admirals of our time? Indeed, what should any true leader who believes in the system that advanced him and in the people who serve that system feel compelled to do? And why has it not been done?

Perhaps over time moral courage became less important as a promotional criterion than political correctness, so that many of the most capable simply did not get promoted in the first place, couldn't make the cut in an environment where politicians more and more frequently played favorites.

Perhaps some kept their courage but became confused regarding their jurisdiction in this ever-widening gray area where military and political control overlap. Perhaps, some chose to hide behind the notion of civilian control as a way to duck the hardest issues facing them, issues they feared might be dangerous to their personal advancement, issues that might even affect their ability to get a good corporate job when they retired. Perhaps for some, loyalty became personal rather than institutional, directed at saving the boss rather than the service itself, and along the way getting one's self a fine fitness report. Or, just maybe, all of the above, in varying amounts, depending on the individual and the crisis of the moment.

Allow me a reflection. I resigned as Secretary of the Navy after repeated arguments over force structure reductions that I believed were strategically unwise. I had presented the new Secretary of Defense

---

1   Nimitz: Fleet Admiral Chester William Nimitz (1885–1996), commander in chief of Pacific forces during the Second World War.

2   King: Fleet Admiral Ernest Joseph King (1878–1956), commander in chief, United States fleet, during the Second World War.

3   McCain: Admiral John Sidney McCain Jr. (1911–1981), commander-in-chief of the U.S. Pacific command from 1968 to 1972, and father of Senator John S. McCain III.

4   Moorer: Admiral Thomas Hinman Moorer (1912–2004), chairman of the Joint Chiefs of Staff from 1970 to 1974.

three alternative ways of meeting an eleven billion dollar budget reduction without taking apart the Navy's shipbuilding program. I made a series of presentations and speeches, including one at the National Press Club, where I indicated that it was time for the United States to return to its traditional strategic role as a maritime power by reducing its overly large Army and Air Force commitment to NATO.

At that time, we were fielding 60,000 more Army soldiers alone in Germany than Britain had in its entire army worldwide, and almost as many Air Force personnel in Germany and the U.K. as Britain had in its entire Air Force. Repeatedly I made the point that the static defensive bases overseas were an historical anomaly that were due to be reduced, but it was vital for our country to maintain a vigorous and sizeable fleet in order to meet continuing geopolitical demands around the world, particularly in Asia, the Indian Ocean, and the Persian Gulf.

Instead of offering or responding to a strategic vision, the new Secretary of Defense ordered each department to offer up force structure reductions in approximately equal shares, largely to avoid political fights inside the JCS[1] and the Congress. I could not agree with this. The stakes for the Navy were similar to those in 1949 when Louis Johnson, within weeks after becoming Secretary of Defense, abruptly canceled the Navy's aircraft carrier program, prompting the immediate resignation of Navy Secretary John Sullivan and his undersecretary, and after that the famous "Revolt of the Admirals." The revolt cost Admiral Denfield his position as CNO,[2] but in the process it saved carrier-based naval aviation, to the benefit of the Navy and certainly of the country.

I lost my debate, and I regrettably resigned from the best job in the world. There was no second revolt of the admirals, nor did I expect one, but the lack of vigorous argument on behalf of their Navy, frankly, amazed me. And where are we now? The troop levels in Europe were going to be reduced in time, anyway. Failing to advance a vigorous strategic vision simply allowed the Navy to shrink as well. And today in the Congress, the think tanks, and the professional journals, the media, so-called military experts argue almost without rebuttal that navies exist simply to fight other navies, as if the geographical

---

1   JCS: Joint Chiefs of Staff.
2   CNO: chief of naval operations, the highest-ranked officer in the Navy.

makeup, national security needs, and lanes of commerce of all nations are the same.

The bases in Subic[1] are gone, with no visible movement to replace them elsewhere. The bases in Japan and Okinawa are in jeopardy. The Korean peninsula is a tinderbox, on the verge of war. China is mocking American power as it builds its economy with the help of American business at the same time developing a strategic axis with the Muslim world, intimidating its neighbors, proliferating nuclear weapons, and aggressively growing its own fleet. Libya is building a massive poison gas facility. Pakistan and Iran are increasing their military and even nuclear aspirations, bidding to become major powers.

These events are occurring against a backdrop where the fleet is moving toward three hundred ships, a third the size of the Navy when I was commissioned and half of the nearly six hundred we were able to rebuild it to during the Reagan era. Not surprisingly, over the past seven years our national presence in Pacific Asia has become ever more tenuous. Our allies are wondering whether and for how long we will be dependable. Our competitors and potential enemies have begun to discount us, both politically and militarily. Few in Asia missed the significance of China's recent warning that American naval vessels not sail through the international waters of the Taiwan Strait, and the Clinton administration's compliance with that warning.

These issues play along the most vital sea lanes of our country and its key allies. Who is willing to bet his reputation and his career on the need to preserve Navy force structure?

Or consider another example, less personal, more specific.

Whenever a crisis erupts that threatens our country's security interests, most of us know the first question usually asked by the President's national security advisers: where are the carriers? And the answer is always the same. They are either on station or proceeding with all due speed into harm's way. I was in Asia during the tensions that flared just before the Taiwanese elections. Whether the Administration used them properly or not, the carriers were there, ready to strike, just as they have been in or near every other hot spot in the last fifty years.

To be more specific, the officers and sailors were there, showing once again why the carrier battle group is the most potent and for-

---

1   Subic: Subic Bay in the Philippines was an American naval base until 1992.

midable tactical assemblage in history. As always, the finest combat pilots in the world were in their ready rooms or on the catapults, prepared to do whatever it took to defend the national security interests of the United States. They have never failed our nation, not once. They are smart. They are tough, they are dedicated, they are loyal, they are truly the best we have.

So when the Tailhook investigation began, and certain political elements used the incident to bring discredit on naval aviation as a whole, and then on the Navy writ large, one is entitled to ask, on behalf of these magnificent performers who have never failed their leaders, where were their leaders?

When the acting Secretary of the Navy, who had never spent a day in uniform, called a press conference and announced that the antics of one group of aviators at Tailhook was an indication that the Navy as a whole had cultural problems—cultural, as in ethos, as in the overall body of traits that constitutes an institution's history and traditions— how could the CNO stand next to him and fail to defend the way of life he had spent a career helping to shape?

When Paula Coughlin's commanding officer, who had previously received dual honors as the Navy's outstanding fighter pilot and as commander of its outstanding fighter squadron, was relieved of his command based on a letter she wrote, without being given so much as five minutes to explain his own actions in her case to the admiral who summarily dismissed him, who risked his career by taking Jack Snyder's[1] side?

When one of the finest candidates for Commander in Chief of the Pacific in recent times, a man who flew more than five hundred combat missions in Vietnam and then in the Gulf War commanded the largest naval armada since World War II, is ordered into early retirement by the Chief of Naval Operations because one Senator asked on behalf of a constituent why Stan Arthur as Vice Chief of Naval Operations had simply approved a report upholding a decision to wash out a female officer from flight school, who expressed their outrage? Who fought this? Who condemned it?

When a whole generation of officers is asked to accept the flawed wisdom of a permanent stigma and the destruction of the careers of some of the finest aviators in the Navy based on hearsay, unsubstanti-

---

1   Jack Snyder: Rear Admiral John Snyder, Coughlin's commanding officer.

ated allegations, in some cases after a full repudiation of anonymous charges that resemble the worst elements of McCarthyism, in effect, turning over the time-honored, even sacred, promotional process which lies at the very core of military leadership to a group of Senate staffers, what admiral has had the courage to risk his own career by putting his stars on the table and defending the integrity of the process and of his people?

When the captain of a ship that experienced a significant pregnancy rate while deployed overseas stands in front of the entire world and announces that none of these incidents happened at sea, is there a sailor in the Navy who honestly believes him? Indeed, what would have happened to the captain's career had he said otherwise? How does that reality affect loyalties and even one's own belief in a code of ethics? It should surprise no one that this type of conduct has the result of killing morale down the chain of command and building up resentment, not only against the leadership but also against politically protected sub-groups. Top leaders who seek to minimize or reverse problems in this way simply cause them to become more severe, even among those who otherwise might support the policies.

One wonders whether these admirals really believe that political staffers in the Senate possess more wisdom and judgment than their own officers on matters relating to discipline and qualifications for promotion. If they do, they should resign immediately. If they don't, then they should fight back, not with a memo here and there but by being willing to bet their careers on the soundness of the institution that gave them a career in the first place. Or is there an insinuation here, that their own careers are more important than the dozens that are being ruined, and the thousands that are either deciding to become civilians or are waiting in the balance to see whether leadership can survive in the U.S. Navy?

I was recently shown a very disturbing statistic. Last year, 53% of the post-command commanders in naval aviation left the Navy rather than continue their careers. In no other year, in peace and war, has that number reached even 25%. These were the cream, the very future of the Navy, officers who had performed for two decades in a manner that marked them as potential admirals. They took their commands, they saw how the Navy's being led, and they walked. And who is willing to accept responsibility? The aftermath of Tailhook was never about inappropriate conduct so much as it was about the lack of wisdom among the Navy's top leadership. Tailhook should have been a three- or maybe a five-day story.

Those who were to blame for outrageous conduct should have been disciplined, and those who were not to blame should have been vigorously defended, along with the culture and the mores of the naval service. Instead, we are now at four years and counting, and its casualty list reads like a "Who's Who" of naval aviation.

These kinds of problems are fixable. It's not difficult to identify them, which is one reason morale has sunk in the fleet. What is difficult is finding people who will insist that they be fixed.

Our system still produces such leaders. In 1987 my predecessor as Secretary of the Navy tried to order Admiral Bruce DeMars to change the results of a promotion board on which he had sat as president. In the weeks just before my confirmation hearing, I watched Admiral DeMars put his career at great risk by refusing to do so, on the grounds that civilian control ended with the precepts given to the board. I not only supported that position, I admired it.

On a more recent note, Admiral Chuck Larson has been faced with a panorama of difficult decisions right here at the Naval Academy, having inherited the results of years of politically oriented leadership that threatened the very fabric of this institution. National media attention has been intense. He and the senior officers he put into place here including one of my classmates, Captain Randy Bogle, a man that I have known as a midshipman on the Brigade Honor Committee together and have admired for years have truly begun to bring the Academy back to its rightful place as the heart of naval leadership, the cradle of its values.

I'd like to say just one quick thing about the recent events that have attracted so much media attention. I have never been shy about offering criticism of Academy policy when warranted. But we are not seeing a cheating scandal. We are not seeing a drug scandal. We are not seeing the failure of discipline. We are seeing leadership at work, taking the grist that society offered it, openly dealing with a variety of offenses by people who—if you add them up—make up less than 1% of the Brigade.

As one example, when three midshipmen were arrested for sale and distribution of LSD, Admiral Larson immediately ordered the entire Brigade of Midshipmen to take a urinalysis. All at once. The media was flabbergasted, but never more so than when no drug users turned up. None. Admiral Larson had no way of knowing that in advance, but he believed in his people, and they did not let him down.

It's fair to say that with this decision Admiral Larson bet the Brigade—and bet on the Brigade—and won. At Tailhook, a long succession of high-rankers bet against the traditions and the respect of the naval service—and everyone has lost.

If the Navy is to regain its soul and its respect, the answer lies not in some additional program but in the right kind of leaders, at every level of command. Leaders who understand that the seemingly arcane concepts of tradition, loyalty, discipline, and moral courage have carried the Navy through cyclical turbulence in peace and war. Leaders who are imbued with a solemn duty to preserve sacrosanct ideals and pass them on to succeeding generations, leaders who know that this obligation transcends their own importance and must outlast their individual careers. Leaders with the courage to articulate the inviolability of these ideals to the political process. Leaders who will never allow a weakening of these ideals in exchange for self-preservation.

It's time to give the Navy back to such leaders. There can be no more important task over the next few years. Without officers who will defend the Navy's culture and take decisive action when it is needed, there will be nothing but continuing chaos. With them, as they have shown throughout the Navy's history, no challenge is too great; anything is possible.

Questions for Discussion:
1. What does this document reveal about the Navy as a culture distinct from the rest of American society?
2. What criticism did Webb have of the Navy's top leadership?
3. According to Webb, what role does the Naval Academy at Annapolis play in fostering ideals of naval leadership?

James Webb, "Defending the Navy's Culture," *U.S. Naval Institute Proceedings*, July 1996, 91–93; reprinted with permission; © 1996 U.S. Naval Institute/www. usni.org.

Patricia Schroeder, "Too Many Captains" (1996)

The suicide of Chief of Naval Operations Admiral Jeremy Boorda on May 16, 1996, was the final tragic act of the Tailhook scandal. Boorda was the only CNO ever to rise from the enlisted ranks, and many high-ranking naval officers, especially tradition-minded graduates of the Naval Academy, considered him an outsider. Boorda's demands that the Navy reform itself in the aftermath of the Tailhook scandal further alienated him. Hounded by critics, Boorda became despondent and shot himself in the chest. This speech by Democratic Congresswoman Patricia Schroeder (1940–) on May 30, 1996, in the House of Representatives reflects the anger many felt about Boorda's death and the tactics of his opponents. The first woman to be elected to Congress from Colorado, she specialized in military matters, was the first woman to sit on the House Armed Services Committee, and ran for president of the United States in 1988. Schroeder was a powerful advocate for women in the military, having once declared that the chairman of the Armed Services Committee was a sexist who "doesn't believe that anyone with a uterus can make a decision on military affairs."

Mr. Speaker, Adm. Jeremy Boorda's suicide was a tragedy for his family and the Navy. But that hasn't stopped the vultures from circling. They were out in force before he died, and they're still hovering.

First, former Navy Secretary John Lehman,[1] who was fired by the Reagan administration, has been making the rounds—the *Wall Street Journal* and the Sunday morning television talk shows—with the spin of spins: He blames Boorda's suicide on the Navy's enemies. Guess who the Navy's enemies are? Anyone, myself included, who tried to clean up the Tailhook scandal.

With friends like Mr. Lehman, the Navy needs no enemies. Left out of his disingenuous assertion is the fact the he participated in and condoned the Tailhook debaucheries. Gregory Vistica relates in his recent book, *Fall From Glory, The Men Who Sank the U.S. Navy,*[2] that then-Secretary Lehman gyrated with a naked stripper in a room full of Naval officers at the 1986 Tailhook convention. That is the tawdry standard Mr. Lehman set for the Navy on his watch. Is it any wonder the orgies continued until they involved assaults on female Naval officers? Is it any wonder that by the time Tailhook hit the fan in 1991 it splattered Navy leaders at the highest echelons?

---

1   John Lehman: John Lehman Jr., (1942–), secretary of the Navy under President Ronald Reagan.
2   Gregory L. Vistica, *Fall from Glory: The Men Who Sank the U.S. Navy* (New York: Simon & Schuster, 1995).

Worse, once Tailhook became public, senior Naval officers who had known of and ignored the Tailhook excesses tried to contain the scandal and shift blame down ranks. The admirals were first into the lifeboats, leaving junior officers to go down with the ship. It is any wonder that Tailhook generated a storm of bitterness that continues to this day?

On ABC's "This Week with David Brinkley" last Sunday, Mr. Lehman responded to questions about his behavior by accusing reporters of "gutter journalism." He was half right. He was in the gutter, not the reporters.

Mr. Lehman went on to add to the Navy's list of enemies the White House—I don't know if he meant the Reagan White House, which forced his resignation, the Bush White House, or the Clinton White House. Probably all three—and the Senate Armed Services Committee, headed up by Strom Thurmond (R-SC) and Sam Nunn (D-GA). He implied that the committee did my bidding. Don't I wish.

In the final analysis, Mr. Lehman, whose motto as Secretary was loyalty is agreeing with me, can't tolerate anyone who disagrees with him.

Then we have former Secretary of the Navy James Webb, who replaced Mr. Lehman in 1987, but abruptly quit his post 2 years later when things didn't go his way. He wanted a larger Navy and a smaller Army and Air Force—no surprise there. And a bigger Navy with no women. In a recent speech—April 25—at the Naval Academy, Mr. Webb erupted with a volcanic attack on today's Navy, Mr. Lehman, and Admiral Boorda. The audience cheered. Go figure.

Finally, we have the disgraceful case of Comdr. John E. Carey. After being relieved of his command for improper conduct, Commander Carey wrote an anonymous letter that the *Navy Times* unfortunately published. Did Commander Carey take issue with the action of his superiors? Did he argue the merits of his dismissal? No, he didn't mention that he had been sacked. Instead he launched a personal attack, a tabloid mugging, on Admiral Boorda, ridiculing his short stature—referring to him as little Mickey Boorda. Acting as if he represented the entire Navy, rather than one disgruntled, bitter individual, he made the lunatic claim that not a single officer in the Navy respected the admiral.

So there you have it, a debaucher, a malcontent, and a calumniator. One was fired by President Reagan, one quit in a huff, and the other was relieved of his command. Yet they all claim to represent the Navy. They can't all be right.

The Navy suffers from a command fixation. Everyone thinks they are captain of the ship. The ship is the Navy. It goes where the captain commands it. We've got a rabble of captains, some like Lehman and Webb outside the service and others inside, all jockeying to speak for the Navy, but all denouncing it and each other because the Navy's not sailing where they want it to go.

Compare the antics of this trio with the thoughts expressed Tuesday by Bettie Moran Boorda, the admiral's widow. Her statement apparently sprang directly from Admiral Boorda's final message to the Navy he loved. "Take care of each other. Be honorable. Do what is right."

Questions for Discussion:
1. What does this document reveal about the impact of the Tailhook scandal on the Navy?
2. What is the basis of Schroeder's anger in this speech?
3. What does this document reveal about the relationship between the Navy and the rest of American society?

___

Patricia Schroeder, "Too Many Captains," Library of Congress, "Thomas" http://thomas.loc.gov/cgi-bin/query/D?r104:10:./temp/~r1044a1bsZ (last accessed November 22, 2007).

THE SEA AROUND US

The 1960s were a crucial decade in the growing awareness of the importance of the world's oceans. The Cold War was at its height, and American and Soviet submarines patrolled areas of the ocean that were previously inaccessible, such as below the arctic ice cap. So too, the writings of marine biologist Rachel Carson (1907–1964), such as her 1951 best seller *The Sea Around Us*,[1] profoundly impacted how the American public regarded the ocean. American television picked up on this new interest in the sea with shows like *Sea Hunt*, which ran from 1958 to 1961 and featured a plea to protect the ocean environment at the end of each episode. The National Geographic Society's television specials featuring the activities of Jacques-

___

1   Rachel Carson, *The Sea Around Us* (New York: Oxford University Press, 1951).

Yves Cousteau (1910–1997) further excited Americans about ocean science and environmentalism.

The federal government also took a keen interest in the oceans. Some of that interest was strategic, attempting to understand the world's oceans as a battlefield in the Cold War. But so, too, there were economic concerns, and a scientific idealism that the world's oceans were the last frontier on earth. Blessed with ample federal funds, interest and research in ocean science took off in the 1960s, dramatically changing how human societies understood and interacted with the marine environment.

Despite growing awareness of the fragility of marine ecosystems, abuses continued. Pollution slowed as activists and legislators moved to curb pollution of the nation's lakes, rivers, and harbors, but certainly did not stop. Overfishing continued to plague the country's waters, and the centuries-old cod fishery off New England all but ceased to exist. Even shipwrecks, considered by many to be submerged cultural resources, were plundered by treasure hunters who recklessly pursued the gold and silver to be found on a handful of such wrecks.

John F. Kennedy, "National Effort in Oceanography" (1961)

President John F. Kennedy (1917–1963), a lifelong yachtsman and former naval officer, was a powerful advocate for researching and protecting the world's oceans. Whether it was building a fleet of oceanographic vessels or supporting the creation of National Seashores. In a speech in Newport, Rhode Island, in September, 1962, President Kennedy briefly reflected on the pull of the ocean, commenting

> I really don't know why it is that all of us are so committed to the sea, except I think it is because in addition to the fact that the sea changes and the light changes, and ships change, it is because we all came from the sea. And it is an interesting biological fact that all of us have, in our veins the exact same percentage of salt in our blood that exists in the ocean, and, therefore, we have salt in our blood, in our sweat, in our tears. We are tied to the ocean. And when we go back to the sea, whether it is to sail or to watch it we are going back from whence we came.

In this letter to the president of the U.S. Senate, Kennedy clearly lays out his vision on the importance of the ocean to the nation.

March 29th, 1961

My dear Mr. President:

The seas around us, as I pointed out in my message to the Congress on February 23, represent one of our most important resources. If vigorously developed, this resource can be a source of great benefit to the Nation and to all mankind.

But it will require concerted action, purposefully directed, with vision and ingenuity. It will require the combined efforts of our scientists and institutions, both public and private, and the coordinated efforts of many Federal agencies. It will involve substantial investments in the early years for the construction and operation of ship and shore facilities for research and surveys, the development of new instruments for charting the seas and gathering data, and the training of new scientific manpower.

We are just at the threshold of our knowledge of the oceans. Already their military importance, their potential use for weather predictions, for food and for minerals are evident. Further research will undoubtedly disclose additional uses.

Knowledge of the oceans is more than a matter of curiosity. Our very survival may hinge upon it. Although understanding of our marine environment and maps of the ocean floor would afford to our military forces a demonstrable advantage, we have thus far neglected oceanography. We do not have adequate charts of more than one or two percent of the oceans.

The seas also offer a wealth of nutritional resources. They already are a principal source of protein. They can provide many times the current food supply if we but learn how to garner and husband this self-renewing larder. To meet the vast needs of an expanding population, the bounty of the sea must be made more available. Within two decades, our own nation will require over a million more tons of seafood than we now harvest.

Mineral resources on land will ultimately reach their limits. But the oceans hold untapped sources of such basic minerals as salt, potassium and magnesium in virtually limitless quantities. We will be able to extract additional elements from sea water, such as manganese, nickel, cobalt and other elements known to abound on the ocean floor, as soon as the processes are developed to make it economically feasible.

To predict, and perhaps some day to control, changes in weather and climate is of the utmost importance to man everywhere. These changes are controlled to a large and yet unknown extent by what happens in the ocean. Ocean and atmosphere work together in a still mysterious way to determine our climate. Additional research is necessary to identify the factors in this interplay.

These are some of the reasons which compel us to embark upon a national effort in oceanography. I am therefore requesting funds for 1962 which will nearly double our government's investment over 1961, and which will provide $23 million more for oceanography than what was recommended in the 1962 budget submitted earlier. A summary and comparison of the 1960, 1961 and 1962 budgets is contained in two tables[1] which are enclosed with this letter.

1. Ship Construction.

The proposed program for 1962 includes $37 million for ship construction, an increase of $23 million over 1961. This will provide for 10 oceanographic vessels. Only two will replace existing ships. The others will be used to meet needs that have long existed in Federal agencies and other oceanographic institutions conducting research for the Government.

The present United States oceanographic fleet is composed of 27 research ships and 17 survey vessels. All but two were constructed prior to the end of World War II; many are over thirty years old. Only two of the ships were designed specifically for research purposes; the remainder has been converted from a variety of ships designed for other uses. Thus the success of the national oceanographic program will depend heavily on the construction of the new specially designed vessels proposed for 1962.

2. Shore Facilities and Data Center.

Shore facilities are urgently required to provide laboratory space for analysis and interpretation of data and to train new oceanographers. In oceanographic research about five scientists and technicians are required ashore for each scientist aboard ship.

For 1962, $10 million is being requested for laboratories and wharf-side facilities. This represents a five-fold increase over 1961. It in-

---

1   Tables: not shown here.

cludes, for example, funds for a new Bureau of Commercial Fisheries laboratory to replace a forty-year-old structure and additional laboratory space at universities and other oceanographic institutions.

An essential part of the shore establishment is the new National Oceanographic Data Center which will begin its first full year of operation in 1962. This Center will make available to the scientific community oceanographic data collected throughout the world.

3. Basic and Applied Research.

The conduct of research is the central purpose of our whole national effort in oceanography. New ships and shore facilities are essential tools of scientific research, but it is the research itself that will yield new knowledge of the earth's "inner space," and new uses of the sea. The proposed program includes $41 million for basic and applied research in oceanography. This is an increase of $9 million over the 1961 level.

Basic research is the cornerstone on which the successful use of the seas must rest. Progress here is largely dependent on the work of scientists at many universities and laboratories throughout the United States and on ships at sea. Their investigations cover all aspects of the marine environment, the motion and composition of ocean waters, the evolution and distribution of marine plants and animals, the shape and composition of the ocean bottom, and many other geophysical and biological problems. Of timely significance is the attempt to penetrate to the earth's mantle to better our understanding of the origin and history of our planet. This undertaking, known as Project Mohole, involves the development of new drilling methods that can be used in the deep seas. This project has recently resulted in a spectacular achievement. Samples from nearly a thousand feet beneath the sea floor were obtained by drilling in three thousand feet of water.

Considerable attention will also be given to applied problems in the marine sciences. Oceanographers will be studying such problems as sound propagation in water, the effects of changes in ocean conditions on the movement of ships, weather forecasting, and fisheries management. Methods of predicting changes in ocean conditions also are being developed. Eventually they may lead to maps of "weather within the sea" much like the atmospheric weather maps of today.

Many advances are being made in methods of exploring the seas.

Oceanographers are now able to descend to the great depths in bathy-scaphes.[1] New electronic equipment will allow them to probe the ocean and to "see" with sound pulses what before has been opaque. Using these new techniques, our scientists already have discovered vast currents below the ocean surface a thousand times larger than the flow of the Mississippi.

4. Training of Oceanographers.

The most important part of our long-range program in oceanogra-phy is the training of young scientists. Scientific manpower of every sort will be needed—technicians, college graduates, and post-graduate researchers—and they must be trained in many scientific disciplines. This training should go hand in hand with the conduct of research at universities and other oceanographic institutions. By their support of these institutions, the programs of the National Science Founda-tion, the Office of Naval Research, and the Department of Health, Education and Welfare will be of major importance to an expanding program in oceanography; for they can result in the education of new young scientists as well as in the production of new knowledge. In the coming year, these agencies are undertaking to increase the number of fellowship awards and graduate student research contracts, and they also will encourage the development of new university programs in oceanography.

5. Ocean Surveys.

World-wide surveys of the oceans—their properties, their contents and boundaries—are needed to make charts and maps for use of sci-entists in their research programs and for a variety of commercial and defense applications. The United States' ocean survey program for FY[2] 1962 is being increased within the limits of ships available for this purpose. I am requesting additional funds to allow the Coast and Geodetic Survey to extend the operating season of its existing ships, thus making the maximum use of limited ship resources. As already mentioned, funds are included for a new survey ship which will in-crease our deep-sea survey capability.

6. International Cooperation.

Oceanography is a natural area of opportunity for extensive inter-national cooperation. Indeed, systematic surveys and research in all

---

1   Bathyscaphe: a submersible vessel especially designed for exploring ocean depths.
2   FY: fiscal year.

the oceans of the world represent tasks of such formidable magnitude that international sharing of the work is a necessity.

Our present maps of the oceans are comparable in accuracy and detail to maps of the land areas of the earth in the early part of the 18th century. Precise methods of measuring ocean depths have become available during the last ten years, and these, when combined with new developments in navigation, should make possible for the first time modern maps of the topography of the entire sea floor. An accurate mapping of the oceans will require international cooperation in ship operations and in establishing a world-wide system of navigation. In these endeavors the United States can play a leading part.

This year an Intergovernmental Oceanographic Commission is being established under UNESCO[1] to provide a means whereby interested countries can cooperate in research and in making surveys and maps of the deep sea floor, the ocean waters, and their contained organisms. Membership on the Commission is open to all countries of the UN family that desire to cooperate in oceanography. The United States intends to participate fully in the activities of the Commission.

The United States also will participate in the International Indian Ocean Expedition. Many nations, including the Soviet Union, are cooperating in this expedition under the non-governmental sponsorship of the International Council of Scientific Unions. Over a quarter of the world's people live in the countries surrounding the Indian Ocean. If more can be learned of the Indian Ocean's extensive food resources, these nations can be helped to develop and expand their fishing industries as part of their general economic development.

7. The Coast Guard.

At present, the Coast Guard–enabling legislation limits the extent to which the Coast Guard can engage in scientific research. Only the International Ice Patrol is authorized to make such studies. I recommend that the statutory limitations restricting the participation by the Coast Guard in oceanographic research be removed. With ocean weather stations, deep sea thermometers, and other data collection devices, our Coast Guard can make a valuable contribution to the oceanographic program.

---

1   UNESCO: United Nations Educational, Scientific, and Cultural Organization.

CONCLUSION

Knowledge and understanding of the oceans promise to assume greater and greater importance in the future. This is not a one-year program—or even a ten-year program. It is the first step in a continuing effort to acquire and apply the information about a part of our world that will ultimately determine conditions of life in the rest of the world. The opportunities are there. A vigorous program will capture those opportunities.

Sincerely,

JOHN F. KENNEDY

Questions for Discussion:

1. How does Kennedy underscore the importance of the world's oceans to the nation's future?

2. What does Kennedy have to say about the importance of oceanography in this document?

3. What does this letter reveal about changing attitudes toward the ocean environment circa 1961?

"Letter to the President of the Senate on Increasing the National Effort in Oceanography," in *Public Papers of the Presidents of the United States: John F. Kennedy; Containing the Public Messages, Speeches, and Statements of the President, 1961–1963* (Washington, D.C.: Government Printing Office, 1962), 240–44.

Stratton Commission, "Our Stake in the Uses of the Sea" (1969)

For much of our history, Americans have viewed the ocean as a limitless resource. We now know that ocean life is finite, but it has taken decades of work to educate the public about our impact on the marine environment. This change in attitudes goes back at least as far as 1961, when, in a message to Congress, President John F. Kennedy boldly stated, "Knowledge of the oceans is more than a matter of curiosity. Our very survival may hinge upon it."

Taking up this challenge was Julius A. "Jay" Stratton (1901–1994), a former president of the Massachusetts Institute of Technology and the presidentially appointed head of the Commission on Marine Science, Engineering, and Resources. Under his leadership, the commission investigated a broad array of marine problems then made recommendations in the form of the 1969 report, *Our Nation and the Sea: A Plan for National Action*, often known as the *Stratton Report*. Driven by the need to ensure the "full and wise use of the marine environment," Stratton focused on oceans as a frontier with vast resources, and his commission made over one hundred recommendations that paved the way for the creation of the National Oceanic and Atmospheric Administration (NOAA) in 1970 and the Coastal Zone Management Program in 1972. It remains as close to a comprehensive ocean policy as has yet existed in this country. What follows is an excerpt from the introduction to the report.

How fully and wisely the United States uses the sea in the decades ahead will affect profoundly its security, its economy, its ability to meet increasing demands for food and raw materials, its position and influence in the world community, and the quality of the environment in which its people live.

The need to develop an adequate national ocean program arises from a combination of rapidly converging and interacting forces.

The world population is expected to approximately double by the year 2000, but even a lesser rate of growth would intensify the already serious food supply problem. The need for supplemental animal protein sources is critical and is growing daily. The sea is not the only source of additional protein but it is an extremely important one.

The United States itself faces no serious protein shortage, and its rate of population growth shows a promising decline. Nevertheless, it is expected that by the end of the century the population of our country will reach 300 to 350 million people and that the Nation will rely increasingly on food from the sea.

As the population grows, new means must be developed to expand the economy, to generate new jobs and products, and to pay the costs of publicly rendered services. Although land-based activities will continue to dominate the economy for many years to come, new and expanded ocean industries offer some of the Nation's most inviting opportunities for economic growth.

The recent achievements of technology in the sea have focused national attention on ocean resources to a greater extent than ever before. The sea's potential as a source of food, drugs, and minerals has been much publicized, and the oceans have been depicted as a "last frontier" to be conquered by man. The Commission's appraisal is more modest than many of these glowing assessments, but even hard estimates show great possibilities for the future.

The potential for expanded economic activities is evident in today's marine industrial operations. Offshore petroleum, gas, and sulfur re-covery attests that the wealth in the land under the sea is available to man; the mining of tin, diamonds, sand, gravel, and shell from the seabed shows the possibilities of recovering other important miner-als. Deep submersibles and undersea habitats demonstrate the ability of man to live and work under the sea. Yet technological development for economically important work in the sea remains largely in the fu-ture.

Vital though marine economic development is, it must be tempered by other considerations. There is increasing concern over the need to understand our physical environment, of which the oceans are but one part. This concern is based on growing appreciation that the en-vironment is being affected by man himself, in many cases adversely. It is critical to protect man from the vicissitudes of the environment and the environment, in turn, from the works of man.

Today, man's damage to the environment too often is ignored be-cause of immediate economic advantage. To maximize the present economy at the expense of the future is to perpetuate the pattern of previous generations, whose sins against the planet we have inher-ited.

If adequately protected, the sea and shoreline can provide unique and valuable opportunities for recreation. The growth of the country's population, most pronounced in urban areas along the shoreline, and the increased wealth and leisure of many of our people, are creating inexorable pressures for access to the sea. Contamination or destruc-tion of beach, marsh, waterway, and shoreline aggravates these pres-sures by denying use of the sea and shore to a growing population.

The pollution problem pervades all aspects of our expanding tech-nological society. Even with stronger abatement programs, it appears likely that pollution will increase alarmingly in the years ahead. Much of our unwanted waste will find its way into our lakes and estuaries and ultimately into the sea. Intensified use of the marine environ-ment is also generating its own polluting effects, which must be kept in check in order to preserve the sea for a diversity of human uses. Because the rate of marine-related activity is increasing very rapidly, delay may mean excessive, irreversible damage to some parts of the marine environment, particularly in the coastal zones near the great centers of population and in the estuaries of major rivers.

The oceans and marine-related activities must be viewed in the context of the total land-air-sea environment. In many ways, the oceans are the dominant factor in this total environment. However, intervention by man in any one element produces effects on the others, frequently through processes we do not yet understand. Mankind is fast approaching a stage when the total planetary environment can be influenced, modified, and perhaps controlled by human activities. The Nation's stake in the oceans is therefore an important part of its stake in the very future of man's world.

The oceans impartially wash the shores of most of the world's nations, whose interests in the uses of the sea mirror ours. Means for reaching reasonable accommodation of competing national interests must be found to achieve efficient and harmonious development of the sea's resources. The atmosphere, which is so influenced by the oceans, knows no national boundaries; the nations of the world share a common interest in its monitoring and prediction and in its modification.

The Marine Resources and Engineering Development Act of 1966 recognized that the national interest in marine programs is intertwined with the interests of the peoples of the whole world. The United States has sought to carry out the policy stated in the Act by advancing a proposal to the nations of the world for an International Decade of Ocean Exploration. Through the President and the Congress, the United States also has given its support to the World Weather Program in which all nations of the world are seeking to explore and monitor global atmospheric processes.

The Commission shares the conviction that marine scientific inquiry and resource development, as well as meteorological prediction, offer many real opportunities to emphasize the common interests of all nations and to benefit mankind. The gap between the living standards of the rich and poor nations is ever widening. The world cannot be stable if a handful of nations enjoy most of the planet's riches while the majority exists at or below subsistence levels, and many of the efforts to aid the less fortunate nations will involve uses of the sea.

Because instabilities in the world situation cannot be remedied quickly, military power will continue to be a central factor in world affairs. As naval technology increases, the depth and variety of undersea operations require detection systems of ever increasing power and complexity. Today's advances in military undersea technology forecast an increasingly important role for U.S. defense and deterrence capabilities in the global sea. As the uses of the sea multiply, the Navy's defense mission will be complicated by the presence of structures, vehicles, and men. The resulting problems can be resolved only by the closest cooperation between civil and military users of the sea. Furthermore, military and civil science and technology for undersea operations can and should be mutually supporting, emphasizing the need for cooperative action.

The Commission believes strongly that the Nation's stake in the uses of the sea requires a U.S. Navy capable of carrying out its national defense missions anywhere in the oceans, at any desired depth, at any time.

However, the oceans must not provide a new dimension for the nuclear arms race. The official position of the United States declares that the seabed and deep ocean floor should be used exclusively for peaceful purposes, with the understanding that the test of whether an activity is "peaceful" is whether it is consistent with the United Nations Charter and other obligations of international law. Further, the United States has requested the U.N. Disarmament Committee to take up the question of arms limitation on the seabed and ocean floor with a view to defining those factors vital to a workable, verifiable, and effective international agreement which would prevent the use of this new environment for the emplacement of weapons of mass destruction. The Commission supports this position, as well as the U.S. proposal that any agreement prohibiting the deployment of nuclear and other weapons of mass destruction designed for use on the bed of the seas should be negotiated in a broader arms control context and not in relation to devising international arrangements for the exploration and exploitation of marine resources.

Questions for Discussion:

1. What does the document reveal about changing attitudes toward the ocean?

2. What are the Stratton Commission's primary concerns about the world's oceans?

3. What role does the Stratton Commission foresee for scientists in shaping government ocean policy?

_____

Commission on Marine Science, Engineering and Resources, *Our Nation and the Sea. A Plan for National Action* (Washington, D.C.: Government Printing Office, 1969), 1–4.

Daniel L. Muir, "Defending American Fisheries" (1977)

Fish, especially the North Atlantic codfish, are a highly valued resource that nations have even fought wars over. Mark Kurlansky brings this topic to public attention in his important and enjoyable work, *Cod*.[1]

But most Americans do not appreciate the importance of the nation's fisheries, even though the United States has the world's fourth largest coastline, the third largest continental shelf, and some of the best fishing grounds in the world. The commercial fishing industry failed to grow much between 1945 and 1970, while foreign fleets increased their catches off the U.S. coast threefold during that period. Many of these foreign fishing fleets belonged to communist Soviet-bloc nations, a fairly alarming idea during the Cold War made more alarming by the efficiency with which these large modern vessels reduced fish stocks.

To counteract the depletion of fishing stocks, the 1976 Magnuson Fishery Conservation and Management Act (FCMA) allowed the U.S. government, on March 1, 1977, to declare an Exclusive Economic Zone (EEZ) of two hundred nautical miles that allowed it to take a more aggressive role in protecting fisheries. The Magnuson Act thus put 10 to 20 percent of the world's fish resources under sole American jurisdiction. United States Coast Guard cutters and aircraft patrolled the nation's fishing grounds, boarding fishing vessels to ensure compliance with American regulations. Between March 1 and December 1, 1977, the Coast Guard issued 353 citations as follows: Bulgaria, 2; Italy, 11; Spain, 90; USSR, 106; USA, 106; Japan, 28; East Germany, 3; West Germany, 2; Poland, 4; France, 1. At least for a little while, American fishermen could rejoice that the government protected "their" fish, especially in New England, where fish landings doubled and new fishing boat construction boomed.

Captain Daniel L. Muir, USCG, provided the following information to a Senate committee investigating small business conditions in the fishing industry. The investigating senators seem especially displeased that the State Department intervened in a number of cases to avoid diplomatic incidents with Soviet-bloc nations.

---

1   Mark Kurlansky, *Cod: A Biography of the Fish That Changed the World* (New York: Walker and Co., 1997)

I. SEIZURES FOR VIOLATION OF THE FCMA.

Date	Vessel Name (Nationality)	Summary
9 APR	TARAS SHEVCHENKO (UR[a])	CGG[b] DECISIVE boarded the Soviet stern trawler at 1222 on 9 APR in a position 124 miles SE of Nantucket, MA. The vessel had previously been boarded on 4 MAR and cited for using improper log codes and given a copy of U.S. codes. Boarding officers from the DECISIVE discovered that log codes were not used until 12 MAR and that it had caught and processed approximately 50 metric tons of river herring since 4 MAR. It should not have retained more than seven and one half tons of herring. At 2220, the DECISIVE and COMLANTAREA (Commander, Atlantic Area) both recommended seizure. COMDT (Commandant) forwarded recommendation for seizure to SECSTATE (Secretary, Department of State) at 0125 on 10 APR and SECSTATE concurred with seizure of the subject at 0349. Due to this vessel's gross violation of river herring by-catch quota, catching and retention of a large amount of squid since 1 APRIL and disregard for proper log keeping procedures from 4–12 MARCH, the F/V[c] TARAS SHEVCHENKO was officially seized on 10 APR at 0010R.
28 JUL	ADRIANA (MX[d])	CG utility boat 41390 boarded the Mexican fishing vessel approximately 20 miles offshore and 2 miles north of the U.S./Mexican border at 2115 on 27 JUL. The subject vessel was found to have its fishing gear in the water and not in possession of a permit to fish within U.S. Fishery Conservation Zone. At 0727 on 28 JUL, COMDT recommended seizure. At 0758, SECSTATE concurred with the proposed action. The F/V ADRIANA was seized for fishing illegally in U. S. waters.
1 SEP	HIGHLY NO. 301 (TW[e])	CGG CONFIDENCE boarded the Taiwanese side trawler on 1 SEP and found a large amount of prohibited species including 5.9 metric tons of arrow-tooth flounder, 5 halibut, 30 kg of squid and one salmon. At 1110, on 2 SEP, COMDT recommended seizure to SECSTATE. At 1517, SECSTATE and the White House reported they concurred with the seizure. Consequently, at 1744, the CONFIDENCE seized the F/V HIGHLY NO. 301 for gross violations of the FCMA.

Notes: a. the USSR, or Union of Soviet Socialist Republics.

b. Coast Guard cutter.

c. fishing vessel.

d. Mexico.

e. Taiwan.

II. *NON-SEIZURES (Commandant, U.S. Coast Guard Disapproved)*

Date	Vessel Name (Nationality)	Summary
15 MAR	PESCAPUERTA TERCERO (SPa)	CGC ALERT boarded the Spanish stern trawler at 0820 and discovered the last haulback had been at 1900 the previous day. The net was on deck with 100 kg mackerel and a few invertebrates still in it. The ALERT and COMLANTAREA recommended seizure at 0111 on 16 MAR. COMDT did not concur with the seizure and ordered appropriate reports of violation/citations be issued. ACTIVE issued reports of violations for failure to sort catch and possession of prohibited species as well as citations for failure to minimize incidental catch and failure to return prohibited species to the sea with a minimum of injury.
8 APR	FOTON (UR)	CGC RELIANCE on a routine boarding of the Soviet stern trawler discovered that it had retained and frozen 160 kg flounder and 36 kg squid (both prohibited species). At 0555 on 9 APR, COMLANTAREA requested COMDT to concur with seizure of the subject. 0759 COMDT objected to the seizure and ordered the F/V FOTON be issued a report of violation for retention of prohibited species.
10 APR	ANTANES SNECHKUS (UR)	CGC RELIANCE boarded the Soviet freezer transport at 0840 on 10 APR. Boarding officers found 17 tons of cod, 93 tons of redfish and 16 tons of river herring, all of which are in violation of the retention of prohibited species section of the FCMA. At 0535 on 11 APR, COMDT requested SECSTATE's concurrence in the seizure of prohibited catch only and directed the vessel into port to unload. 0634 SECSTATE concurred with proposed action. The R/T ANTANES SNECHKUS was escorted to port where the 16 tons of herring were confiscated and a report of violation was issued for retention of other prohibited species.
14 APR	VASILY YAKOVENKO (UR)	CGC TAMAROA conducted a routine boarding of the Soviet stem trawler and discovered that its log indicated 13.8 percent of its processed fish had been river herring, a prohibited specie. At 1720 on 16 APR, after all catch had been searched, TAMAROA recommended seizure for retaining 20 tons of river herring (7 percent more than allowed). At 2333 COMLANTAREA requested COMDT to concur with the proposed action. At 0220 on 17 APR COMDT objected to seizure and ordered TAMAROA to issue report of violations for retention of prohibited species and improper reporting procedures.

continued

Table II—*Continued*

| 18 APR | EIKYU MARU NO. 2 (JAb) | CGC JARVIS boarded the Japanese side trawler at 1552 on 18 APR and discovered from its log that it had on two occasions fished illegally within the 12 mile limit off our coast. Penetrations of 0.5 and 2.5 nm inside the limit were evidenced from the subject's logs. At 0607 on 19 APR, CCGDSEVENTEEN (Commander, Seventeenth Coast Guard District) requested no objection to seize the subject vessel. At 0935, COMDT objected to the seizure of F/V EIKYU MARU NO. 2 and ordered two reports of violations be issued for fishing illegally within the 12 mile limit. |

Notes: a. Spain.
b. Japan.

III. *NON-SEIZURE (Forwarded to Department of State)*

Date	Vessel Name (Nationality)	Summary
28 MAR	GEROY ELTIGENA (UR)	CGC BIBB obtained radar contact of a vessel outside the eastern boundary of fishing window, Hake window "B."a Contact was plotted to be 8.3 nm outside authorized fishing area. BIBB intercepted contact and it was found to be F/V GEROY ELTIGENA. At 1425 on 28 MAR, a boarding party was put on the subject vessel and discovered that she was in fact fishing outside authorized area. The BIBB and COMLANTAREA recommended seizure of the vessel. At 2014, COMDT requested SECSTATE's concurrence to seizure. SECSTATE objected to seizure, consequently COMDT directed BIBB to issue appropriate reports of violations/citation. Reports of violations for retention of prohibited species and fishing outside of authorized area were issued.
2 APR	YUHAN SUTISTE (UR)	CGC ACTIVE conducted a routine boarding of the Soviet stern trawler to check for compliance of the FCMA. Boarding party found 25 lbs of prohibited species (redfish) in fishmeal grinder, 75 lbs. of pickled redfish in a locked compartment, and its fishing logs in a state of "complete disaster." At 1425 on 2 APR, the ACTIVE and COMLANTAREA recommended seizure of subject vessel. At 0025 on 3 APR COMDT requested concurrence in seizure from SECSTATE. 0322-SECSTATE did not concur in seizure and recommended report of violation/citation be issued. 0423 ACTIVE issued reports of violations for retaining prohibited species, failure to record discards by species, failure to record proper catch composition, and failure to record catch disposition.

continued

Table III—*Continued*

4 APR	SOVREMENNY (UR)	On 10 MAR COMLANTAREA received a message from this enforcement vessel stating it was entering FCZ.[b] On 15 MAR COMLANTAREA received a second message from the subject stating it was departing Loading Zone No. 1 (an authorized fishery support activity area). Consultations concerning the subject determined she was a UR fisheries enforcement vessel and not subject to FCMA as long as she did not operate in any action defined as "fishing." CGC DECISIVE was ordered to observe operations of the subject and report results. On 0500, 4 APR the subject vessel was observed alongside another UR fishing vessel and transferring personnel and hoses rigged between the vessel. 1155 boarding party aboard subject reported that logs indicated it had delivered personnel, fruit/vegetables and took on water from several vessels. Based on evidence of conducting support activities without a permit area commander recommended seizure. 1311 COMDT requested concurrence with seizure from SECSTATE. 1732 SECSTATE objected to seizure and consequently COMDT ordered DECISIVE to issue the F/V SOVREMENNY for conducting fishery support activity in the FCZ without a permit (violations to 8 counts).
30 MAY	IVAN SHISKIN (UR)	On 29 MAY COMLANTAREA informed CGC BIBB that the Soviet fishing vessel was one of the UR vessels that had its permit cancelled and that they should board her at the first opportunity. With the aid of another CG cutter it was learned that the subject ceased support activities 7 hours and 20 minutes after announcing intentions to do so and 11 hours after receiving messages instructing her to cease immediately. 0200, 31 MAY COMDT requested SECSTATE for concurrence in seizure. 0317 SECSTATE transmitted nonconcurrence and COMDT ordered reports of violation/citation to be issued. CGC BIBB issued report of violation to the IVAN SHISKIN for conducting fishery support activity in the FCZ without a valid permit (3 counts).
10 SEP	LASKARA (PL)[c]	CGC ACTIVE boarded the Polish Stern Trawler at 0815, 10 SEP and discovered it had recently completed a trawl. Investigation revealed that no attempt was made to sort prohibited species and return them to the sea. Estimated total catch was 17 tons squid and 3 tons other prohibited species. At 1620 ACTIVE recommended seizure of subject vessel for gross violations of FCMA. At 2200 COMDT requested SECSTATE for concurrence of seizure. On 11 SEP at 0057 SECSTATE informed COMDT that they and White House did not concur and recommended report of violation/ citation be issued. COMDT ordered at 0223 on scene commander to issue appropriate reports of violations. At 0345 the CGC ACTIVE issued to the F/V LASKARA reports of violations for failure to return prohibited species to the sea with a minimum of injury and conducting a bottom trawl in a prohibited area.

Notes: a. certain species could only be fished in certain zones, which appeared as "windows" on nautical charts.
b. Fisheries Conservation Zone.
c. Poland.

Questions for Discussion:

1. Based on the above evidence, what is the United States' primary interest in creating and enforcing the FCMA?

2. What evidence is there that foreign fishermen attempted to conceal illegal fishing activity?

3. What difficulties does the U.S. Coast Guard have in enforcing and prosecuting violators of the FCMA?

U.S. Senate Select Committee on Small Business, *Economic and Small Business Conditions in the Fishing Industry.* 95th Cong., 1st sess., (Washington, D.C.: Government Printing Office, 1977), 56–60.

Melvin A. Fisher, "Wreck of the *Atocha*" (1988)

The phrase *greed is good* was coined in the 1980s. This was also a decade during which many shipwrecks came to light, including the wrecks of treasure ships loaded with gold. Under ancient marine salvage laws, whoever found the wreck was entitled to keep what they found. Improved diving technology and the growth of scuba diving meant that previously untouchable shipwrecks were now vulnerable to plunder. For a time, it was thought that treasure hunters and underwater archaeologists could work together, but as detailed in Stephen Kiesling's *Walking the Plank*,[1] that effort proved a complete failure. Archaeologists and others increasingly called for the protection of what they saw as invaluable cultural resources, and the treasure salvors had to defend their practices.

Foremost among the treasure salvors was Mel Fisher (1922–1998), a colorful treasure hunter best known for finding the wreck of the Spanish treasure galleon *Nuestra Señora de Atocha* in 1985 about thirty-five miles west of Key West, Florida. After the discovery, the federal government claimed title to the wreck, and the State of Florida seized many of the items Fisher had retrieved from his earliest salvage expeditions. After eight years of litigation, the U.S. Supreme Court ruled in favor of Fisher. Now a variety of state and local laws offer more protection to shipwrecks as cultural resources.

In the following transcript of his testimony before Congress, Fisher vigorously defends what he sees as his right to salvage treasure.

---

1   Stephen Kiesling, *Walking the Plank: A True Adventure Among Pirates* (Ashland, Ore.: Nordic Knight Press, 1994).

Mr. FISHER. Thank you, Mr. Chairman and distinguished members of the committee.

My name is Mel Fisher. I come before you today from Key West, FL.

Back in the early 1800s, the island city of Key West was known as the rescue and salvage or wrecking capital of the world. Its wealthiest citizens were salvors of many ships that ran aground upon the dangerous reefs of the Florida Keys. The island of Key West was first charted by that famous explorer, Ponce de Leon.

It is right and fitting I should be from Key West and testifying before this committee today about shipwrecks. The occurrences of the last two years, in particular, have revived for the world the tradition of the searchers and salvages of the 1800s. During the past ten to fifteen years, millions of Americans and millions more people around the world have experienced with us, through the media and knowing us, the thrill of searching for and finding one Spanish galleon and part of her sister ship off the Florida Keys. Final discovery of the main ballast pile of the *Nuestra Señora de Atocha* was widely reported and publicized in July of 1985.

This was after 17 years of searching hundreds of thousands of miles and investing millions of dollars and much more.

The publicity and information produced to the general public both here in the United States and around the world as the result of our efforts on the *Nuestra Señora de Atocha* and her sister galleon, *Santa Margarita*, have put more archaeology and more history before more people than any governmental progress that ever has been or ever could be envisioned by the individual States or the Federal Government.

In fact, more than one half of the total salvage from the *Atocha* is ending up in public ownership because of donations by the many investors who, with their private risk capital, have made my dream and the dreams of so many who have worked with me become possible.

If you have any doubt about whether the American people are in favor of keeping the incentive and the dreams that I stand for a reality of our great nation, then I suggest asking your constituents when you go back home. Or, if you want to know how to spend more Federal and State tax dollars on bureaucratic treasure hunts, then you could ask the few public employees who are the real motivators behind this bill called H.R. 74, and they certainly will let you know how. They need Government grants, big ones.

In contrast, because it seems to preserve such things as the constitutional intent of our Nation's founding forefathers in establishing Federal district court jurisdiction over admiralty and maritime matters, I would like to suggest the acceptability of H.R. 2071. That bill is sponsored by Mr. Shumway,[1] [and] reflects some real study of the lessons of the past that we look toward preserving our heritage for the future generations while preserving as well the greatest incentive of all, the American dream of free enterprise.

These are some of the things I strongly urge should be part of responsible legislation regarding shipwrecks:

Responsible archaeological salvage of ancient or historic abandoned shipwrecks should be encouraged by promoting, through private investment and public participation, cooperative recovery efforts between government and private enterprise with guaranteed public access to unsalvaged wrecks by responsible sport divers, shipwreck salvors, and professional and amateur archaeologists who are willing to ensure the maintenance of archaeological integrity.

Federal district courts, sitting in admiralty and applying the laws of salvage, are best suited by constitutional designation and resulting heritage of judicial decisions to remain the forum for the resolution of disputes among competing salvors and between States and private entities, including large and small salvage companies, for fair and equitable enforcement of legal requirements designed to ensure preservation of the archaeological integrity of historic shipwrecks.

Individual States should continue to have the right to intervene in a Federal admiralty action to assert a claim to archaeological data and historically important artifacts for public display, but the private person or enterprise, whether a salvage company or association of sport divers, must also continue to have the right to appeal unfair tactics by a State or other governmental body to some higher and wholly unbiased body such as the Federal court system.

There should be—and my team of many years which includes archaeologists and divers has helped formulate some with me—a set of responsible guidelines which can be embodied in Federal legislation with continued enforcement by Federal admiralty courts and judges.

---

1 Shumway: Congressman Norman D. Shumway (1934–).

If you don't put in guidelines ahead of time, the ones that the States invent will be just horrible.

Today, you have two distinctly different pieces of proposed legislation before you. One, H.R. 74, also known as the Bennett bill, would totally gut the constitutional mandate for the Federal district courts to have exclusive jurisdiction of admiralty and maritime affairs. I beg you before you consider anything, this matter should be taken before the Judiciary Committee, because this affects the Constitution.

The other bill, H.R. 2071, known as the Shumway bill, would preserve the constitutional jurisdiction of the Federal district courts over admiralty and maritime matters and seems to fairly balance the need for incentive with the need for enforcement.

It was mentioned a while ago that the admiralty court does not allow for archaeology, and that is not true. In the case of *Cobb v. the State of Florida*, admiralty law does describe archaeological balance and protection.

The late Judge William Marvin who was the Provisional Governor of Florida and the U.S. district court judge sitting in admiralty in Key West way back in the 1840s summed it up as well as anyone could. Judge Marvin asked as part of one of his opinions which ultimately went to the Supreme Court of the United States, "What court other than a court of admiralty would have jurisdiction over salvage?"

Judge Marvin was right in the 1840s, and he is right now. H.R. 2071 goes into preserving the archaeological and historical integrity of an ancient wreck by putting out a lot of requirements for salvors. It has been my experience that any salvor worth their salt realizes that good archaeology and good history are required in order to maximize the profit and other benefits of the recoveries from an ancient vessel.

The best example of this that I can give to you is the fact that you can buy a silver coin from some unknown, unidentified galleon in the Bahamas for $150 while a very similar silver coin from the *Atocha* sold for more than $1,000. The only difference between these two coins is that good archaeology and good history have added to the value of the salvaged items.

The increase in value is not only ascertainable in the private market, but also in the public collections that, to the greatest extent, are nothing more than donations by private salvors and private investors.

The admiralty courts have always been in the position of determining the proper way to salvage a vessel and, historically, whether all efforts went first to the saving of lives. In the case of an ancient historic vessel, the courts have determined that the proper way to salvage is to require that the salvor adhere to certain standards for the protection of the archaeological and historical data revealed during the recovery of items from the shipwrecks.

I know and you know that archaeology is a very important part of history. I believe all of us realize that the reason history is so important to our society is that we can learn from the past. Hopefully, the mistakes of the past can be carefully analyzed, documented, compiled, and studied so that, with the knowledge gained, the mistakes of the past can be avoided in the future.

Studying about my past struggles to fulfill my dream at the greatest of costs will lead to the point where we now stand—looking back at the past so that we can navigate the future course of archaeological recovery from shipwrecks.

Over two hundred years ago, our forefathers put in the U.S. Constitution that admiralty and maritime claims were exclusively under the jurisdiction of the U.S. district courts. Now, I beg you, do not try to change the Constitution by passing H.R. 74. What you would do is turn all admiralty and maritime claims over salvage of all shipwrecks of a certain age to the individual States and their courts which, because of the Constitution provision, would not have jurisdiction over salvage which is a uniquely maritime claim.

What you would end up doing is to put all private salvors and private risk capital at the hands and under the time consuming jurisdictions of the administrative laws and administrative bureaucracies of the various coastal States with no recourse except the State's own courts.

Federal admiralty law as it now exists encourages the salvaging of derelict, wrecked, and abandoned vessels, and the Federal courts are ready, willing, and able to protect the individual rights of the finder and salvor.

The Federal district courts also protect the interests of the public in the archaeological and historical data retrieved from shipwrecks. With their own great heritage rooted in the Constitution, [the] U.S. district court system and its jurists are very well aware of the public responsibility that is the cloth of their robes. The process is relatively simple and straightforward.

My presence before you here today shows that it does work, even when the State and Federal Governments at the time tried their best and their dirtiest tricks, to take it away from the people who have spent so much time and so much money and lives to make the dreams come true. The system we have works well enough so that in my case, at least, the good guys won.

If you have any questions that today's testimony does not fully answer, I invite all of you to come to Key West and get a first-hand look at this dream come true.

What has made this country great is that I can pursue as an adult the dreams I first had in grade school and high school. I was just honored down in Palm Beach County last week at a science museum where a lot of talented young people were explaining about their own dreams. One young lady explained about how she plans to find *Atlantis*. I would sure like to get her on my payroll.

Incentive, and the freedom to pursue it, are part of what this country is still about. Let's keep the incentive and the freedom intact to explore the oceans and rivers and lakes of our great Nation and not have to be only a bureaucrat or a lettered scientist or academic before we can touch the face of history.

We have many archaeologists working for us under contract and on our payroll. We have many preservationists working for us full-time. We have the most advanced computerized archaeology in the world today, state of the art. We scan religious objects. They go into the computer. All the data as to weight, date, everything else is entered in. It can be faxed off to the Vatican museum in a matter of twelve seconds. They can compare it with their religious items and let us know what we have found.

Motivation is the main thing. I am motivating millions of kids and millions of adults as well to be able to pick out their goals in life and follow their dreams, persevere, and accomplish what they want to do. If the State owns shipwrecks, it will put everything back twenty-five years. We will have to start back in the beginning. . . .

Title is the main thing. Mr. Bennett was right, we should tighten up his bill. We should eliminate title to the government from his bill. You see, if they get title to shipwrecks, then next year they will have title to all of our homes that are more than fifty years old, all of our antique airplanes, automobiles, and trains. Shipwrecks are no different. They do not belong to the Federal Government. . . .

I don't think there is any treasure hunter or salvor who is in this business for private gain only. Several of them mentioned that. Most of them are much more interested in the history and the archaeology.

. . .

The States, if they own title, harass you tremendously. I know. I have been there. I have been in the business twenty-six years. The first five years was beautiful because they had no State law. Once I found gold, they made a State law saying they owned all the shipwrecks and the treasure. From then on, the stuff hit the fan.

They arrested my men, put us in jail, put me in jail, they stopped us from working. Then, once they let us go back to work again, they would only let us work eight hours a day and five days a week, and we had to go by thousands of rules and regulations that they invented which did put us out of business, so we had to go outside the country and outside the State.

Questions for Discussion:
1. What does this testimony reveal about the importance of submerged cultural resources such as shipwrecks?
2. What does Fisher's testimony reveal about how some Americans felt about property and government regulation of shipwrecks?
3. How does Fisher support the idea that his approach to shipwreck salvage promotes public interest in history?

U.S. Congress, House Committee on Merchant Marine and Fisheries, Subcommittee on Oceanography, *Historic Shipwrecks*, 100th Cong., 1st sess., April 21, 1987, H.R. 74 and 2071, 44–49.

OCEAN LINERS TO CRUISE SHIPS

The manner in which most Americans went to sea changed dramatically in the postwar decades. Immediately after the war, Americans crossed the ocean in fast oceangoing vessels called *ocean liners*, primarily as a form of transportation and often on American-flagged and -crewed vessels. Jet aircraft overtook ships as a form of travel in the early 1960s, and by 1970 ocean liner service was a thing of the past.

But a handful of clever businessmen bought the obsolete liners and converted them into cruise ships, a fascinating story detailed in Kristoffer

Garin's *Devils on the Deep Blue Sea*.[1] While ocean liners were primarily a means of transportation, cruise ships were more akin to floating resorts. There was little need for speed, and the vessels themselves generally operated in sheltered waters rather than the North Atlantic. They were a tremendous hit with middle-class Americans, who flocked in ever-increasing numbers to cruise ships for their vacations.

While the heart of the ocean liner business had been Manhattan, the primary American cruise ship port became tropical Miami, Florida. While many ocean liners had flown the American flag, the cost-conscious cruise industry operated mostly foreign-flagged vessels, thereby avoiding expensive American regulations and labor costs. Like in other industries, consolidation has been the rule: one Miami family, the Arisons, founded Carnival Cruise Lines (now known as CCL) and has gradually taken over Holland America Line, Princess Cruises, and even the famous Cunard Line. But the rapid expansion of cruising has not been without its costs, especially environmental, and safety concerns have also plagued the industry, which explains at least to some extent the revival of American-flagged cruise ships in the first years of the twenty-first century.

American Export Lines, "Brings American Living Standards to Sea" (1950)

The Second World War brought a new prosperity to the United States. American business and industry, bolstered by technological advancements and the absence of major foreign competition, created more and better jobs. The new, large middle class had a taste for European travel and more vacation time than ever before. Before the advent of jet airlines, the best way to get to Europe was by ocean liner. Travel on the newest and best ocean liners meant bragging rights (an important aspect of the new consumer culture) in the country's affluent suburbs.

This piece, released by American Export Line's publicity department, typifies the expectations that the affluent society had for its leisure time. With a strong faith in American technological know-how, the public demanded amenities such as air-conditioned staterooms and swimming pools.

---

1   Kristoffer Garin, *Devils on the Deep Blue Sea: The Dreams, Schemes and Showdowns that Built America's Cruise-Ship Empires* (New York: Viking, 2005).

NATION'S FASTEST PASSENGER LINER TO BE LAUNCHED
JUNE 3

S.S. *Independence* of American Export Lines is to be First Transatlantic Luxury Liner to be Fully Air-Conditioned

The 1000-passenger, 25-knot S.S. *Independence*, fastest vessel in the American Merchant Marine, will be launched June 3 at the Quincy, Mass., shipyard of Bethlehem Steel Company, John E. Slater, president, American Export Lines has announced.

Largest passenger vessel to be constructed in this country in more than a decade, the *Independence* is also the first transatlantic luxury liner to be completely air-conditioned. Incorporating advanced ideas in interior design as well as in engineering detail, the *Independence* has been acclaimed by government and industry leaders for meeting and exceeding the world's highest safety standards. Cost of the *Independence* and her sister ship, the *Constitution*, to be launched in September, is about $50,000,000.

Upon completion in January 1951, the *Independence* will enter American Export Lines' New York–Mediterranean express service and make the 4000-mile crossing to Genoa in less than eight days. The speedy vessel, with 22,000-mile cruising radius will be capable in time of emergency of transporting 5,000 troops and their equipment on a continuous voyage to any port in the world.

Rated at about 26,000 gross tons by transatlantic passenger standards, the *Independence* is 683 ft. in length, 89 ft. molded breadth, and will draw 30 ft. when loaded. When launched the vessel will be about 60 percent completed with more than 14,000 tons of steel erected, according to D. D. Strohmeier, vice president of Bethlehem Steel Company. The streamlined twin funnels and mainmast will be stepped following launching, since they are too tall to clear the lofty structure of the giant shipway.

—SHIP WILL HAVE 25 KNOTS SPEED—

Scheduled for a trial run off the New England coast in mid-December, the *Independence* is guaranteed by her builders to deliver 25-knots top speed, thus making her the fastest vessel in the American merchant marine. Bethlehem steam turbines developing 55,000 horsepower will drive twin 27-ton propellers, most powerful to be installed in an American passenger vessel. There are two engine rooms separated by water-tight bulkheads and capable of being operated independently.

The hull is divided into 14 water-tight safety zones. A double bottom extends full length from the sharp, rakish bow to the stern. Automatic, mechanical and visual fire-detecting, fire alarm and fire-fighting systems cover the entire ship. Fireproof and fire resistant materials have been used throughout, including all partitions, draperies and floor coverings. Safety measures meet or exceed all regulations of the U.S. Coast Guard and other government agencies.

Hull and mechanical designs were developed by Bethlehem Steel Company shipbuilding technicians in association with L. S. Andrews, vice president, American Export Lines and his operating staff. Interiors were developed by Henry Dreyfuss,[1] prominent American designer, following his extensive research into contemporary American living habits.

—BRINGS AMERICAN LIVING STANDARD TO SEA—

The designer, charged to provide utmost comfort for every passenger in each of the three classes of the *Independence*, as well as American living standards for the 575 officers and crew, has produced innumerable refinements that set new standards for living at sea. Spaciousness, bright color combinations, exclusive fabric designs and weaves for drapery and upholstery, private baths, ample dresser, wardrobe and baggage storage space and air-conditioning are stateroom features. Over-sized folding wall and sofa berths permit instant conversion of bedrooms into spacious living rooms.

The atmosphere of a fine American home is evidenced further in the magnificent series of public rooms that occupy the entire Promenade Deck. Forward is a circular observation lounge 65 ft. in diameter with broad windows looking out to sea for two-thirds of its circumference. Aft is the library with a special niche to enshrine a copy of the "Declaration of Independence," and with an interesting furniture arrangement to provide conversational privacy for many small groups. Still farther aft are cocktail lounges for first and cabin class passengers. Surrounding the sweep of rooms is a broad promenade deck. There are eight large suites, two of which have private enclosed verandahs.

A large theatre, sunken-floor dining room, gymnasium, electric

---

1   Henry Dreyfuss: Henry Dreyfuss (1904–1972) was a famed American industrial designer known for his streamlined ergonomic designs of many household items.

baths, gay shops, elevators, intra-ship and ship-to-shore telephones are among the additional attractions.

—TWO SWIMMING POOLS PROVIDED—

There are large swimming pools for first and cabin class passengers and a saltwater cascade for tourists. The first class pool of Hollywood design, tapered, with rounded corners and under-water illumination for nighttime use, is the center of interest of the two-level Sun Club sports area that covers over 9000 sq. ft. The deck above the vast pool area extends aft in two broad wings to multiply the lounging area for spectators who wish to view the swimming. Forward of the pool is the Sun Club café which includes an American soda bar. Large sections of the glass after wall and roof of this room can be rolled back to convert it into an open-air terrace.

"The *Independence* and her sister ship, S.S. *Constitution* which soon will follow, represent our all-out bid to win and hold transatlantic travelers by providing American flag ships tailored to the American standard of living," Mr. Slater said. "The names *Independence* and *Constitution*, rich in our tradition, were chosen to inspire respect for the American way of life, afloat as well as ashore."

Questions for Discussion:

1. How does this piece reflect American social ideals as they existed in 1950?

2. How does this piece reflect the postwar American consumer culture?

3. How does this piece reflect the American obsession with technological advancement?

Typed manuscript, vertical files, Schuyler Otis Bland Library, U.S. Merchant Marine Academy, Kings Point, NY.

United States Lines, "The End of an Era" (1969)

The introduction of transatlantic commercial jet passenger service in the late 1950s signaled the end of American-flagged ocean liners. Ocean liners—ships that specialized in crossing the ocean as fast as possible as a form of transportation—died within a decade. Many tried to make the transition to cruise ships, which were a form of leisure rather than transportation, but it proved difficult for American-flagged vessels to compete with the lower labor costs of foreign-flagged ships. The glamorous age of movie stars and millionaires crossing the North Atlantic by steamship ended.

That fact became abundantly clear at the end of 1969 when United States

Lines announced it was laying up the S.S. *United States*, a ship often referred to as the "flagship of the United States merchant marine." Launched in 1952, the *United States* was both the largest passenger ship ever built in the United States and the fastest, with a top speed of almost forty knots. The *United States* has passed through several hands since lay-up, but has never operated since 1969. The present owner is NCL (formerly Norwegian Cruise Lines), which has announced plans to return the ship to service sometime in the future.

The United States Lines announced today that four scheduled voyages of the S.S. *United States*—one in December and two in January, also one in March have been cancelled.

The Company said that the cancellation could mean the end of operations for the "greatest and fastest ship ever to have flown the American flag."

Cancelled were the Christmas cruise and the Grand Pacific cruise, scheduled to depart from New York on December 19th and January 21st, respectively, and the ship's one January and one March transAtlantic crossings.

As a result, the vessel, which is presently undergoing its annual overhaul, will remain in a lay-up status indefinitely.

The Company said that the decision to cancel the voyages was made with great regret. However, the Company has made the announcement well in advance of the original sailing dates in order to give passengers time to make other arrangements.

It had been the original intent to carry out an extensive overhaul and refurbishing of the ship during the present shipyard overhaul period. However, two factors led to the decision to cancel the cruises and the transatlantic crossings.

One was the fact that President Nixon's newly announced Maritime Program has the objective or reducing operation subsidies, and this compounds the economic problem for passenger ships because they obviously require higher subsidies. The second is the expiration, on December 31st, of the Company's Operating-Differential Subsidy[1] Agreement with the Federal Government.

---

1 Operating-Differential Subsidy: government funds (subsidies) given to shipping companies to offset the additional costs associated with flagging with the U.S. This helped employ American mariners and encouraged shipowners to register their ships under the American flag. In return, the government could use those vessels in times of trouble or need. The SS *United States* was designed to carry American troops in time of war.

The Company explained that for the last year, it had sought to develop various plans together with the Maritime Administration and Union representatives for the continued operation of the S.S. *United States* on an economically feasible basis.

At the present time, the Company has an application pending in Washington for a new subsidy contract since the present one expires at the end of this year. The purpose of the subsidy under this application is to offset the difference between foreign and American operating costs.

In addition, another application has been pending in Washington for many months for a countervailing subsidy under the provisions for Section 604 of the Merchant Marine Act.[1] The subsidy being sought under this application is intended to offset subsidies paid by foreign governments to vessels competing with the S.S. *United States*.

The Company called attention to the fact that United States Lines has continued to operate the vessel and has lived up to its contractual commitment to the Government despite mounting losses for a number of years. These losses reached a peak of $4.8 million in 1968 and will be over $4 million in 1969.

The announcement also expressed the view that competition for North Atlantic passengers will increase, now that the airlines are offering round-trip fares at less than half of what passengers must pay on ocean-going vessels.

Unless the Government is prepared to assist the ocean operators to offset losses, the future of American-flag passenger vessels is bleak.

The Operating-Differential Subsidy Agreement of United States Lines, which was signed 20 years ago, is the first of the subsidy contracts to come up for renewal.

There has been a reasonable question as to the wisdom of operating this passenger ship for the last few years but, because of the obligation which United States Lines has under the Operating-Differential Subsidy Agreement with the Federal Maritime Administration, it continued operating the ship until the termination of the Agreement. In view of the fact that the next scheduled sailing of the ship would

---

1   Merchant Marine Act: the Merchant Marine Act of 1936 provided various subsidies for American ship construction and operation. Section 604 permitted additional subsidy funds at the discretion of the federal government.

be the Christmas cruise, and since increased subsidy for the passenger ship has not been renewed, there would no longer be subsidy on the ship after December 1st, making it economically impossible for United States Lines to operate the ship after that date. The economic situation is worsened as a result of the fact that starting January 1, 1970, United States Lines will not receive operating subsidy on the North Atlantic containerships.

The marketing program of United States Lines for this vessel has been quite successful during 1969 (resulting in more million-dollar voyages than in any other previous season on the North Atlantic during the summer months). However, the losses of United States Lines for 1969 after a Federal subsidy of approximately $12 million will be between $4 and $5 million.

Over the years, while total revenues have increased only slightly, the crew wages have increased about 2½ times, while the subsidy rate as determined by the Maritime Administration has decreased. The losses on passenger-ship operations have been a direct burden on the container and break-bulk cargo ships, the profits from which had to first offset passenger-ship losses.

Although United States Lines has been willing to operate the ship, it does not feel it must accept a continued operating at a loss, especially after the termination of the present Operating-Differential Subsidy Agreement.

A recent calculation by United States Lines indicated that it would require a crew reduction of at least 30% and a significant increase in the Operating-Differential Subsidy on wages from the present 62% to at least 92% in order to break even. Since neither condition was possible to achieve, the conclusion to cancel the two cruises is an economic reality.

Early this year, United States Lines attempted to join together with a number of other steamship companies in order to form a consolidated passenger-ship operation. However, for various reasons the plan was not accepted by the authorities involved.

Subsequent to this decision, a number of companies laid up their passenger ships immediately but United States Lines felt it had an obligation under its Operating-Differential Subsidy Agreement with the Government and continued to operate the ship.

The S.S. *United States* entered service in July, 1952, and established every conceivable type of record in the North Atlantic. The ship was the recipient and is still holder of the North Atlantic Blue Ribbon, represented by the Hales Trophy for the highest speed, and technologically, it is still the world's fastest and safest passenger ship.

The ship has, since her maiden voyage, been the symbol of first-class service and cruises. If the cancellation of these cruises leads to her permanent retirement from transatlantic service, it represents the end of an era.

The objective of the new maritime policy, which will be the subject of legislation during the present session of Congress, is to maximize the results of not only the construction-differential subsidies but also the operating-differential subsidies. Since the amount of the present annual operating subsidy of the S.S. *United States* would permit the Federal Maritime Administration to subsidize approximately fifteen large, high-speed cargo ships, each of these would have a far greater possibility of improving the balance of payments situation and increasing the influence of American-flag participation in world commerce. Therefore, there can be no question that the decision of the new Maritime Program to concentrate on cargo is understandable, although it is emotionally and philosophically disappointing.

The first passenger ships operated by United States Lines in 1921 were the *George Washington, America, Susquehanna, Hudson, Princess Matoika*, and the *Potomac*, which were mainly German ships taken over at the end of World War I.

The list of famous passenger ships operated since that time by United States Lines includes, *President Pierce, President Taft, President Roosevelt, President Harding, President Adams, President Monroe, President Van Buren, President Fillmore, President Polk, President Garfield, President Arthur, Leviathan, Republic, President Grant, Manhattan, Washington*, and the *America*, launched in August, 1939.

Each of these great passenger-ship names can evoke memories, not only on the part of the many passengers who sailed them over the past forty-eight years but also among the many American servicemen who reached the shores of Europe during World War II aboard three of these ships, known during that period as the *West Point, Wakefield*, and *Mount Vernon*, and who returned home on them at the termination of hostilities in 1945.

Fortunately, United States Lines recognized that the era of trans-

Atlantic passenger transportation on American-flag ships was being threatened by the introduction of the jet airplane and focused its attention away from passenger operations and onto commercial carriers with the development of large, high-speed containerships. Their advanced equipment and systems permit the expansion of American commercial influence into the hinterlands of practically all of the countries of the world.

Actually, it was just such American innovativeness and the influence of such sea power which led to the formation of the Merchant Marine in the first place. In the last few weeks, the Company withdrew its applications for the renewal of a subsidy contract for its North Atlantic containerships which will commence operating without any government subsidy in January, 1970. While there are many who see de-activation of that great passenger ship, the S.S. *United States*, as the termination of an era, there are just as many who recognize the introduction of United States Lines' large Lancer-class containerships[1] on the North Atlantic as the rebirth of perhaps a much more important era of American sea power. In addition to the six large containerships already in service, the Company is building two additional Lancers and converting eight large Mariner vessels to containerships.

Dr. John J. McMullen, President of United States Lines, however, characterized himself as an eternal optimist, and expressed hope that somehow a solution will be found so that the S.S. *United States* will soon return to an operating status.

Questions for Discussion:
1. What does this document reveal about economic changes in the 1960s?
2. How were shipping subsidies both a blessing and a curse to companies like United States Lines?
3. What changes did United States Lines make to keep itself economically viable?

United States Lines press release, November, 1969, vertical files, Schuyler Otis Bland Library, U.S. Merchant Marine Academy, Kings Point, NY.

---

1   Lancer-class containerships: United States Lines built the first container ships built specifically as such from the keel up, with a service speed of twenty-two knots and capable of carrying twelve hundred containers, making them the largest and fastest containerships in the late 1960s.

Al Levett, "Cruise Ship Garbage" (1991)

The international cruise ship industry grew from carrying 500,000 passengers in 1970 to carrying 9,500,000 passengers in 1998, with half of all ships traveling to the Caribbean. But the sleek white hulls of the cruise ships belied the ugly cost-cutting practices that made them so affordable yet profitable at the same time. In particular, cruise ships, like many other commercial vessels, dumped garbage, especially plastic, into the ocean illegally, in direct contravention of an international agreement known as MARPOL 1978. But regulating the cruise ships proved difficult. Foreign-flagged and largely staffed by workers from developing countries, the cruise ships largely fell outside of federal regulation. But environmentally conscious Americans were shocked and angered when they saw trash dumped at sea.

In this piece, an ordinary American recounts to Congress how he videotaped the crew of a cruise ship dumping bags of trash at sea in 1991. While it took the U.S. Coast Guard many months to act on this matter, it was one of several incidents that revealed the extent to which cruise ships polluted the world's oceans. Between 1993 and 2003 the cruise ship industry paid nearly $50 million in environmental fines. The International Council of Cruise Lines (ICCL) has since moved strongly to meet federal and international environmental standards.

> Mr. Levett.   Good morning. I am pleased to be invited here today to speak to you on this important subject. We hope that our experience and the videotape that we took may serve to shine the light on the illegal practice of marine pollution and ultimately contribute to positive changes in the way that business is conducted at sea.
>
> I will briefly outline the major events of the case and the actions that we took over the past eighteen months which ultimately led to criminal charges against Princess Cruise Lines. As you will see, the videotape, while a critical element in this case, taken by itself might not have resulted in the case being successfully resolved. It took an active role and determination on our part as well as encouragement from the Center for Marine Conservation[1] and the efforts of the FBI and Justice Departments to make the system work.
>
> On October 25, 1991, my wife and I witnessed and videotaped the disposal at sea of trash in plastic garbage bags. The incident took place

---

1   Center for Marine Conservation: a Washington, D.C., organization committed to protecting ocean environments.

off the *Regal Princess*, approximately six miles south of the Florida Keys. Once on shore, we reported the incident and submitted a copy of our videotape to the Coast Guard Marine Safety Office in Miami for review.

We followed the progress of our complaint through regular and periodic calls to the Marine Safety Office. I must tell you that the slow responsiveness and lack of progress that the Coast Guard made in investigating this well-documented incident was irritating. Equally troubling was the incomplete or lack of knowledge that Coast Guard officials displayed about the MARPOL agreement. I spoke to several officers in the Miami office and found that they did not appear to understand where Coast Guard jurisdiction began.

In January of 1992, in an effort to exert some pressure on the Coast Guard to move the case along, we granted an interview to the *St. Louis Post Dispatch*. In April, with little progress reported, we again went public granting an interview to *Condé Nast* Magazine. The story appeared in the June 1992 issue.

Our continued calls to the Marine Safety Office and the published articles appeared to do little to accelerate this investigation. With a great amount of reluctance, my wife and I agreed to provide NBC news with the videotape scenes from our cruise and grant them an on-screen interview. It was our feeling that the threat of public pressure and [the] embarrassment of having to explain the eight-month delay in the processing of our complaint through the national media would pressure the Coast Guard to action, and, in fact, it did.

In July of 1992, within a few weeks of when the Coast Guard learned of NBC's interest in the story, the case was processed through the Coast Guard's legal office to the U.S. Attorney's Office for prosecution. On April 15, 1993, the U.S. Attorney for the Southern District of Florida filed a criminal charge against Princess Cruises for discharging plastic bags filled with garbage into the sea. On April 26, Princess, as part of a plea agreement, pled guilty to the crime and was fined $500,000, [the] maximum under the law.

Although we are pleased that our videotape played a major role in the successful outcome of this case, it is distressing to us to recall the significant additional effort that went into moving this case along. If the Coast Guard would not take action on a well-documented and videotaped incident, how will they respond to a less well-documented case?

Perhaps the lack of responsiveness on the part of the Coast Guard was due to the fact that this was the first well-documented case of this nature presented to them. The thought of a few bags of garbage thrown overboard may have taken low priority given their wide range of responsibilities. Now that the first case has been successfully concluded and the Coast Guard's role clarified, we would hope that procedures have been established and formalized so that citizen complaints are handled more aggressively in the future.

The Center for Marine Conservation and the U.S. Attorney's Office are to be commended for their professional, intelligent, and diligent efforts that went into the successful outcome of this case, in our opinion.

We do have two thoughts that we would like to share with the committee. First, it seems to us that the financial penalty is an insignificant deterrent to a large carrier. Over the course of a year, the maximum penalty of $500,000, if spread over the number of passengers sailing Princess ships out of U.S. ports, might average only a dollar or two per passenger. This is not a severe financial penalty to a company the size of Princess. Perhaps the law should be broadened to include the loss of port privileges to repeat offenders. This would represent an economic threat great enough to truly discourage the prohibited practices.

Secondly, we believe that a citizen ombudsman[1] needs to be established. Passengers must have a direct channel to report incidents of this nature. Someone to cut through the bureaucracy, follow the progress of investigations, and report to Congress and the responsible Federal agencies on a regular basis.

I would like to thank the committee for this opportunity to share our experiences.

Mr. Tauzin. Thank you, Al. We are going to interrupt the panel and allow questions at this time in order to facilitate air travel that Al must meet. Al, in your testimony, you indicate that the film was taken on October 25, 1991. Charges were not filed 'til April of '93. That is eighteen months. That is enough time to have two children, not twins. That is an awful long time. Do you think it should ever

---

1   Ombudsman: an agency or person that investigates and resolves complaints.

take that long again to bring a case to prosecution when there is a film of the violation available to the authorities?

Mr. Levett. I certainly believe that a reasonable amount of time is necessary to thoroughly investigate the matter and do the research, the Coast Guard should not be jumping to conclusions. We feel that the initial investigation that took some eight months or more to get to the Justice Department was excessive.—Once the facts were in hand, from our perspective, it could have been immediately turned over to the Justice Department for criminal investigation, and that is what we didn't understand.

Simply—I would make phone calls every three weeks or each month to follow the progress of the case. I was given a variety of stories why the case had not been moved along yet. In one instance the computer system was unable to accommodate the necessary information. We were told that the Coast Guard expected to walk the case file across to their legal division within a few days. In fact, a month later it still hadn't been walked across. There were simply no explanations provided.

Mr. Tauzin. Did anyone in this case ever say whether this was just a single incident or this was common practice? Was there any discussion of that in the plea bargaining that occurred?

Mr. Levett. I was not involved with the plea bargaining.

Mr. Tauzin. Well, not involved. You were simply involved in bringing the case and pushing the authorities along?

Mr. Levett. Yes, sir.

Mr. Tauzin. And in terms of your involvement, do you think that the case would have been prosecuted if you hadn't stayed on it?

Mr. Levett. The indication the Marine Safety Office gave us initially was that they felt that this was probably a civil fine, if that, and that was their preliminary sense of it. I encouraged them to consider a criminal investigation on the matter because I felt that the—I believe it was a $25,000 civil fine they told me. I just felt that was insignificant given the nature of the incident.

Mr. Tauzin. Now, we have been asked this question so maybe you can answer it—is there a financial reward for the citizen service you performed in this case?

Mr. Levett. The U.S. Attorney has informed us that under the law we are entitled to a portion of the reward at the discretion of the Court.

Mr. Tauzin. So that the Court can or cannot? It is entirely up to the Court to decide whether to reward you and your wife for the video you took and the efforts you took to ensure prosecution this case?

Mr. Levett. That is correct, sir.

Mr. Tauzin. Do you know what the limits of that Court discretion are? How far can they go?

Mr. Levett. They can go up to half of the fine, which is $250,000.

Mr. Tauzin. Mr. Coble for questions.

Mr. Coble. Thank you, Mr. Chairman. Al, let me be sure I have this right in my mind. On 25 October 1991, once you and your wife came ashore, you immediately reported it to the Coast Guard?

Mr. Levett. That is correct. On the 26th, I believe, when we were ashore. We were in Ft. Lauderdale overnighting with our in-laws, and I made several phone calls. One of those was to the Marine Safety Office in Miami.

Mr. Coble. And you may not know the answer to this next question. Reading from your statement, then it is, you say, in July of 1992—that would be seven or eight months later—within a few weeks after the Coast Guard learned of NBC's interest, then the case was processed through the Coast Guard's legal office. So far as you know, Al, was that the Coast Guard's first involvement from October of '91 when you and your wife had discussed with them?

Mr. Levett. No. I believe I had been making periodic calls, and if I am to believe what they told me, that they were in the process of reviewing them during that period.

Mr. Coble. I was going to say, Admiral, I would be very disappointed if that were the case. I would think the Coast Guard would have been on top of it, but I am inclined to agree with Al about this, Admiral. We will talk to you later. I am very high on the Coast Guard, Al, as is the Chairman, but this appears to be an undue delay. Maybe there is a good reason for it. There may have been other matters that caused the delay, but this concerns me as it concerns you.

As an aside, Al, the Chairman asked you did you know about the provision whereby witnesses could be benefited by receiving a portion of a judgment or a penalty?

Mr. Levett. No, sir, we did not.

Mr. Coble. There would have been nothing wrong if you had known it, but it is known now, and I suspect "sailors beware" may be the signal that emanates from this hearing room, Mr. Chairman.

Mr. Tauzin. If the gentleman would yield, that is the reason I asked the question.

Mr. Coble. Yes. Just one minute, Al. I think I have one more question, but I am not sure. I think the Chairman probably touched on that. Yes. OK. We will pursue this—the delay of the Coast Guard that bothers you, Al, and it bothers me. As I say, the Admiral may have a good defense for that. Thank you, Al, for what you and your wife did. Thank you for being here today.

Questions for Discussion:

1. What does this document reveal about the cruise ship industry in the 1990s?

2. What does this document reveal about American attitudes toward dumping garbage at sea?

3. What compelled Levett and his wife to be so persistent in pursuing the garbage dumping issue?

U.S. Congress, House Committee on Merchant Marine and Fisheries, *Pollution from Cruise Ships and Coast Guard Prevention*, 103rd Cong., 1st sess., May 11, 1993, (Washington, D.C.: Government Printing Office, 1993), 6–15.

MARITIME ENVIRONMENTALISM IN THE 1990S

By the 1990s coastal counties were home to more than half of the U.S. population, putting increased strain on wetlands, mangrove forests, estuaries, coral reefs, and other coastal habitats. The American relationship to the sea was changing, a natural extension of the growing ecological awareness in society. Scientists, fishermen, and coastal residents realized that the ocean's bounty was not limitless, and that a careful conservation of ocean resources was required. Man-made disasters like the 1989 *Exxon Valdez* oil spill, the ongoing movement to save the whales, and the nuisance posed by invasive species such as zebra mussels made Americans more aware than ever that our waterways and coastal waters needed protection.

Yet these issues were complicated. The *Exxon Valdez* spill proved more difficult to recover from than anticipated, Native Americans insisted on harvesting whales, and zebra mussels seemingly took over the Great Lakes. The marine environment was changing, and while humanity was at fault, it could not seem to do anything to repair what it had damaged. Furthermore, the consequence of this environmental disaster extended far beyond the oil industry or Alaskan wildlife; it wrought considerable damage to the fragile human communities that bordered the region.

Elenore McMullen, "Subsistence Living After the *Exxon Valdez*" (1993)

The March 24, 1989, *Exxon Valdez* oil spill was one of the most devastating man-made environmental disasters ever to occur. Some eleven million gallons of oil spilled, affecting 1,900 km of Alaskan coastline and killing countless wildlife and fish. While the majority of the spill area now appears to have recovered, some environmental effects are still felt today. In addition, the continuing impact of the oil spill caused cultural changes in the communities in nearby waters, especially those reliant on commercial fishing or those who continued to live off the land, such as Native American communities. Stephen Haycox, in his controversial interpretation of the relationship of Alaskans to big oil companies, *Frigid Embrace*,[1] explores some of the tensions between Native and non-Native people on environmental protection issues.

In the following piece, taken from congressional testimony on the continued impact of the spill in 1993, a Native Alaskan leader recounts her community's struggles to cope with the disaster. For a people engaged in living off the land by hunting and gathering, the destruction of the environment was devastating, creating the possibility of cultural self-doubt that could further erode traditional values and customs integral to their identity.

My name is Elenore McMullen and I am Chief of the Village of Port Graham. I would like to thank the Committee for inviting me to testify on behalf of myself, the Native Villagers of Port Graham, and the Alaska Natives who live in Prince William Sound and other areas in south-central Alaska impacted by the *Exxon Valdez* oil spill. For seven thousand years the Alaska Natives of Prince William Sound, known as Alutiiq people, have survived by relying upon the resources of the Sound. I would like to tell the Committee what the Alutiiq people believe is the condition of Prince William Sound four years after the

---

1   Stephen W. Haycox, *Frigid Embrace: Politics, Economics, and Environment in Alaska* (Corvallis: Oregon State University Press, 2002).

Exxon Valdez oil spill and how that condition has altered and jeopardized our life.

The Native Villagers of Port Graham, as well as the Natives residing throughout Prince William Sound, are dependent upon uncontaminated, renewable natural resources for their survival. For centuries, we have lived in isolated communities surviving off the land—a manner of living non-Natives refer to as "the subsistence way of life." Until the *Exxon Valdez* oil spill, subsistence had been the cultural mainstay of my people.

The *Exxon Valdez* oil spill had far-reaching effects on the Natives of south-central Alaska and Prince William Sound. Oil hit beaches over five hundred miles from the Valdez Narrows, where the *Exxon Valdez* ran aground. In Prince William Sound, nearly 170 miles of shoreline was oiled. Oil was documented in Cook Inlet, on the Kodiak Island group and along the Alaska Peninsula. Cleanup activities were maintained as far west as Perryville and oil may have landed even farther west. . . .

According to the experts, the spill impacted the ecology of hundreds of miles of shoreline. Even though oil accumulations were cleaned from most beaches by the summer of 1992, oil residues remain beneath the surface of these beaches. According to the experts, oil residue may persist longer than twelve years in some areas. Intertidal biological impacts will likely persist more than eight years in heavily oiled sites. Recent studies show that isolated patches of highly contaminated sediment continue to bleed, producing more contamination. The potential for long-term impact on biota and retarded biological recovery is great.

The experts have determined that the *Exxon Valdez* oil spill impacted a large number of natural resources used for subsistence. The species included salmon, rockfish, dolly varden, char, herring, mussels, morays, clams, sea otters, harbor seals, killer whales, murres, black oyster catchers, murrellets, and harlequin duck. It has been estimated that over a half-million birds and over four thousand sea otters died immediately following the spill. For many species, population recovery has been slowed by continued exposure to oil that persists in inter-tidal and subtidal areas. Continuing reproductive and other injuries to harlequin ducks, sea otters, pink salmon, dolly varden and other consumers of inter-tidal invertebrates was probably caused by the ingestion of contaminated mussels. Oil in heavily contaminated mussel beds appears relatively unchanged since 1989 and will continue to harm the environment for an additional three or more years. Experts say that the rate of biologic recovery will be retarded until the oil disappears or becomes inert. Estimates of the time frame for population recovery to pre-spill levels range from a few years to many decades. Some species, such as harlequin duck, may never recover. Local extinction is very possible.

The experts' evaluation only confirms what has long been observed by my people. Since the spill, there is simply less life in Prince William Sound. Ducks are rarely seen. Seals are difficult, if not impossible, to find. Sea otters are scarce. Even the pink salmon run has gotten smaller. It now requires greater effort to harvest amounts comparable to that taken before the spill, if it can be done at all. We must now search greater lengths of shoreline to harvest chitons or find places to harvest uncontaminated clams and mussels. The large-scale kill of species by the oil forces us to harvest smaller, less mature, fish and game. Harvesting of smaller or undersized subsistence resources is wasteful and requires more effort to achieve the same subsistence harvest levels. Simply put, less edible meat will be obtained per pound of fish harvested when the fish are smaller.

Subsistence is the basis of the Alutiiq culture. When the *Exxon Valdez* oil spill destroyed wildlife and blackened beaches, this man-made disaster also damaged the culture of the people who have relied on those subsistence resources for thousands of years. There were both real and perceived changes in the quality and quantity of those resources. We became uncertain as to the safety of the resources and our ability to harvest them. For the first time ever, we questioned our knowledge of the environment. Not only did subsistence production decline, but above all, *culturally* significant components of subsistence declined, such as subsistence participation, cooperative hunting, fishing, and gathering, processing and preparing of subsistence foods, sharing, transfer of knowledge, satisfaction derived from eating subsistence foods, and our feeling of the integrity of place and autonomy. . . .

The oil spill ripped the fabric of Alutiiq community by damaging its core elements: first the natural resources and with it, the subsistence harvest. This upheaval damaged the individual people by taking away the means by which they derive order and meaning from their lives and introduced uncertainty and confusion.

The impact of the oil spill on the subsistence way of life is not yet over for my people. We have no idea how long the impact will continue to be felt. The first year of the oil spill, the Alutiiq people suffered a major loss, not only in tangible subsistence products, but also in the loss of what subsistence means. The catastrophic oil spill shocked my people and severely disrupted our way of life. In 1991, 1992, and indefinitely into the future we remain deeply concerned about the long-term impacts on subsistence species. Those who feel they can resume eating local resources have done so cautiously and worry about the risks to their health. They say they will never look at the resources with the same happiness and confidence as before the spill. Now they will always wonder if it is safe to eat their native foods. Those who feel they cannot resume eating local foods will continue indefinitely to experience a serious disruption to their subsistence life.

The governments formed an Oil Spill Health Task Force as part of an emergency response to provide the best information available regarding the safety of subsistence resources. Although the Task Force did a credible job with the information and resources available, it was unable to alleviate concern among residents of the impacted areas. Native persons were excluded from the study while Exxon was closely involved. Inconsistencies caused poor public acceptance of the Task Force recommendations and a loss of the Task Force's credibility. For example, commercial fishing guidelines indicated that fish were unacceptable if oil was found on fish or equipment, yet Natives were advised that fish were edible if their smell, taste, and appearance was satisfactory. Moreover, the Task Force's newsletters raised questions that were never answered which further contributed to uncertainty. To date, no definitive scientifically recognized health risk assessment has ever been completed for native subsistence foods.

Because we are so uncertain about the safety of the resources, we are uncertain about the ability of the Alutiiq culture and people to rebound from this event. As one Native has said, "If the water is dead, maybe we are dead. Our heritage, our tradition, our ways of life and living in relation to nature and to each other." The world has recognized that there has been an environmental disaster caused by the spill. What is overlooked, however, is the human disruption. Until the natural resources have fully recovered, the Alutiiq people who depend upon the resource will not recover.

The problems my people face have not at all been addressed by the Trustees who are administering the money received by the governments' settlement with Exxon. Approximately a billion dollars is being spent on natural resource recovery throughout the Prince William Sound area. The Alutiiq people, however, occupy and utilize just a small percentage of the Sound. Unfortunately, in the physical and financial vastness of the recovery program, the needs and desires of the Native people are being ignored.

At the time of the settlement, the Native people used the courts to make known their objection that they were not full participants in the settlement process. Our fears have now become realities as we have seen that the villages have not been involved in the restoration process. I understand that one subsistence study has been conducted by the Trustees thus far; to my knowledge, no Natives were consulted or involved in its design. The bulk of the settlement money appears to be headed towards commercial fishing interests and the restoration of recreation services. Little or no attention is being paid to the impact on the subsistence way of life. The Native community, except for the two seats in the Public Advisory Group, has been essentially disenfranchised.

On behalf of the Native people, I implore this Committee to help us help ourselves. We need money to be set aside so that the Villages can undertake their own programs and conduct their own restoration of their local subsistence areas. We need money specifically ear-marked to protect, preserve and enhance our subsistence resources.

Of all the persons affected by the spill, the Alutiiq people of Prince William Sound most heavily and directly rely upon the resources of the Sound. Yet we have been given almost no opportunity to participate in its restoration and have received no assistance from anyone interested in helping to restore and preserve our way of life.

I am glad that the Committee has taken the time to listen to the pleas of the Alutiiq people and pray you will assist us in our efforts in the wake of the *Exxon Valdez* oil spill to save the Sound and save ourselves.

Questions for Discussion:
1. What long-term impact did the *Exxon Valdez* oil spill have on the ecology of Prince William Sound?
2. How did the *Exxon Valdez* oil spill impact the distinctive culture of the Alutiiq villagers?

3. What evidence is there that the Alutiiq villagers suffered discrimination in the aftermath of the *Exxon Valdez* oil spill?

U.S. Congress, *Prince William Sound: Hearing Before the Committee on the Merchant Marine and Fisheries*, 103rd Cong., 1st sess., (Washington, D.C.: Government Printing Office, 1993), 146–54.

Keith Johnson, "Makah Whaling" (1998)

The Makah are the only Native Americans in the continental United States with a treaty-protected right to whale. The 1855 Treaty of Neah Bay guaranteed the Makah fishing, whaling, and sealing rights, but the last documented Makah whale hunt occurred in 1926. In 1996, with the recovery of local whale stocks, the Makah sought permission from the International Whaling Commission to take up to five gray whales annually, a move supported by the U.S. government. Their return to whaling has been resisted by whaling opponents, and the Makah have accused environmentalist groups of racism. On May 17, 1999, the Makah had their first successful whale hunt since 1926, using largely traditional methods.

Forced to defend their cultural traditions in the court of public opinion, Keith Johnson, president of the Makah Whaling Commission, sets forth the Makah view on whaling. Johnson has consistently connected the whale hunt to the identity of his people, stating "No one can say we don't have the right to whale, or that we are not a whaling people . . . It's who we are."

My name is Keith Johnson. I am a Makah Indian and President of the Makah Whaling Commission, made up of representatives from twenty-three traditional whaling families of our Tribe. For the past three years we have been reading the attacks made on us by animal rights organizations, aimed at stopping our whale hunt. These attacks contain distortions, exaggerations and outright falsehoods. Reading these things has sickened and angered me and I feel I must speak out.

What We Plan to Do

We plan to conduct a whale hunt this year, sometime in October or November. While we are legally authorized to take up to five whales per year, our management plan limits the number of landed whales over a five year period to twenty, or an average of four per year. But I want to point out that our Whaling Commission will issue a permit only if there is an unmet need in the community, so it is possible that as little as one whale per year will be taken if that will suffice to meet our needs.

Why Does the Tribe Want to Do This?

Whaling has been part of our tradition for over two thousand years. Although we had to stop in the 1920s because of the scarcity of gray whales, their abundance now makes it possible to resume our ancient practice of whale hunting. Many of our Tribal members feel that our health problems result from the loss of our traditional seafood and sea mammal diet. We would like to restore the meat of the whale to that diet. We also believe that the problems which are troubling our young people stem from lack of discipline and pride and we hope that the restoration of whaling will help to restore that discipline and pride. But we also want to fulfill the legacy of our forefathers and restore a part of our culture which was taken from us.

How Did the Makahs Get a Legal Right to Hunt Whales?

Before entering into negotiations with the Makah for cessions of our extensive lands on the Olympic Peninsula in 1855, the United States government was fully aware that our people lived primarily on whale, seal and fish. They knew that we hunted several species of whales and had a substantial commerce in whale oil which had brought us prosperity.

When the United States Territorial Governor, Isaac Stevens, arrived at Neah Bay in December of 1855 to enter into negotiations with our leaders, he was met with strong declarations from them that in exchange for ceding our lands to the United States they demanded guarantees of their rights on the ocean and specifically, of the right to take whale. The treaty minutes show Governor Stevens saying to the Makahs: "The Great Father knows what whalers you are—how you go far to sea to take whale."

He went on to promise U.S. assistance in promoting our whaling commerce. He then presented a Treaty containing the specific guaranty of the United States securing the right of the Makahs to continue whaling. The Treaty was accepted by us. It is the only treaty ever made by the United States that contained such a guaranty. The Treaty was ratified by the Congress in 1855 and has since been upheld by all the Courts and the Supreme Court. To us it is as powerful and meaningful a document as the U.S. Constitution is to you, because it is what our forefathers bequeathed to us. In fact, one of our whalers has said that when he is in the canoe whaling, he will be reaching back in time and holding hands with his great grandfathers, who wanted us to be able to whale.

Will the Makahs Sell Any of the Whale Meat?

Absolutely not! Yet animal rights groups like Sea Shepherd continue to insist that we secretly plan to sell whale meat to Japan. That claim has been repeated endlessly by other animal rights groups. It is utterly false.

Although our Treaty guaranteed a commercial right, we have agreed to limit ourselves to non-commercial whaling. We are bound by Federal Law and our own Tribal Law not to sell any whale meat. We have no plan to sell whale meat in the future. We also believe that Sea Shepherd is well aware of this but chooses to continue to accuse us of planning to sell whale meat in order to generate continued financial contributions.

Though it may be difficult for some people to accept, we are acting out of purely cultural motives. In fact, it is costing our Tribe an enormous amount of money to carry on the whale hunting program. It is conducted solely because that is our Treaty right and because it fulfills a deep cultural need in our members. It is, if you please, part of our religion, because for us, culture means religion.

Is There Any Conservation Issue if We Take Whales?

Absolutely not. The Eastern Pacific or California gray whale has been studied by scientists around the world and it is established that the gray whale population is currently at an all-time high of around 22,000. The population continues to increase at 2½% per year, despite an annual harvest which has gone as high as 165 by Russian aborigines, called Chukotki.

The gray whale was removed from the endangered species list in 1994 and the population is now considered to be at its maximum level. In fact some biologists have raised the question of whether the number of gray whales may be nearing the carrying capacity of their range, that is, the number that can be supported by the food resources in that range. No reputable biologist or whale scientist has suggested that our taking five whales a year will present any conservation threat whatsoever to the gray whale stock.

The fact that no one can legitimately argue that this is a conservation threat is one of the main reasons why two of America's leading conservation organizations have refused to join in the attack on our whaling: The Sierra Club and Greenpeace. There are animal rights activists within those organizations who are trying to get them to come out against our whaling, but they have steadfastly refused because they do not see this as a conservation issue, they refuse to be drawn into the animal rights issue and they will not oppose indigenous people's rights.

The Wishes of the Tribe

Our attackers continue to claim that we are disregarding the views of the majority of our members. They repeatedly publicize in the media and elsewhere the views of two women who are members of the Tribe and are outspoken opponents of whaling. While we respect the right of all of our members to hold and to express their views on any subject, I must respectfully point out that these two women do not speak for anywhere near the majority of the Tribe and there are other Elders who strongly support whaling.

In the last opinion poll we held on the issue, 85% of those voting favored whaling. There is a faction within our Tribe which is opposed to whaling, but they are a distinct minority.

I can say proudly that the Makah Tribal Council and the Makah Whaling Commission represents the strongly held views of the vast majority of our members that we should go back to whaling as our ancestors did before us and as they wished us to do when they negotiated the treaty right which we have.

We were the premier whalers on the American continent and were able to enjoy a prosperous life because of our whaling trade. Our forefathers bequeathed our right to whale to us in our Treaty and we feel that a treaty right which cannot be exercised is no right. I can tell you that our Tribe is not prepared to abandon our treaty right.

How We Plan to Conduct the Hunt

We will hunt the whale from one or two sea going canoes, each carved from a single cedar log by Indian carvers. Each canoe will be manned by a crew of eight whalers and will include a harpooner and rifleman. Both these men will be stationed in the bow. The harpooner will use a stainless steel harpoon mounted on a wooden shaft. It will be connected to the canoe by a rope with floats attached. The harpooner will throw the harpoon at the whale. Immediately afterwards, or simultaneously, the rifleman will fire a special high-powered rifle using a .50 caliber round. We are using this specially designed rifle and this ammunition on the specific recommendation of Dr. Allen Ingling, a Veterinarian. Dr. Ingling is also a specialist in arms and the humane killing of animals. This weapon has been tested by Dr. Ingling, who has worked with the National Marine Mammal Laboratory of the National Marine Fisheries Service. Dr. Ingling has instructed us on the target area to be hit so as to bring about almost instantaneous loss of consciousness and death of the whale.

The use of the special rifle has been attacked by many animal rights groups as brutal and non-traditional. I believe these attacks are dishonest. In the 19th century, we didn't use such a weapon; we used harpoons and spears. The whale often died after a prolonged and agonizing period of time from internal bleeding. That was not humane. Groups such as Sea Shepherd will not be deterred by our showing that we are using a humane method. I wonder what they would say if we could dispatch the whale by using a hypodermic needle that would bring about swift and instantaneous death? I think they would condemn that because a hypodermic needle was not a traditional weapon of the Makahs.

I don't hear any of these animal rights groups attacking us for conducting the hunt with a canoe. The lives of at least eight people will be at risk on the dangerous waters of the Pacific in October and November to hunt the whale. That is our traditional method. If we wanted to abandon all cultural tradition, we would simply use a deck mounted cannon firing a harpoon into the whale. No, our canoe has been carved by traditional carvers and will be paddled by eight whalers who have sanctified themselves by rituals that are ancient and holy to us. The hunt is being conducted in a manner which is both traditional and modern.

The Dire Prediction That Our Whale Hunt Will Threaten the Whale
Watching Industry

The Sea Shepherd organization has been making sweeping claims that if we hunt a whale, whales will begin attacking humans throughout the waters of the State of Washington and devastate the whale watching industry throughout the state. This is complete nonsense.

First of all, most of the whale watching in Washington State is focused on orcas, not gray whales, and takes place in Puget Sound and the eastern area of the Strait of Juan de Fuca. As for gray whales, whale watching on this species is primarily concentrated in Westport, far from any area where we will be hunting whales.

The idea that whales will somehow begin to act aggressively against humans in boats or change their migratory path to avoid boats is false. The whales passing through the waters of Washington State have come here after being hunted and attacked in the Bering sea by Russian indigenous people called Chukotki. The Chukotki have been hunting the gray whale for over forty years and there is no evidence that gray whales have attacked other boats after having been struck by Chukotki whalers. Nor is there any evidence that whales communicate with each other and spread the message that humans are the enemy, to be attacked or avoided. This is a fantasy promoted by animal rights activists to advance their argument that our activities will harm the whale watching business. The charge that our whaling somehow presents a threat to marine activities on the waters of the State of Washington is a gigantic fiction dreamed up by imaginative animal rights activists who will go to any lengths to stop our whaling.

What Is Our Cultural Need for Whaling?

It is hard for us to explain to outsiders our "cultural" attitudes about whaling. Some of us find it repugnant to even have to explain this to anyone else. But let me tell you about my own case.

I have a Bachelor's Degree in Education from Central Washington University. I was the first Makah teacher in the Neah Bay School System from 1972 through 1976. I received my principal's credentials from Western Washington University in 1975 and served as Vice Principal of the Neah Bay Schools in 1976 and between 1990 and 1997.

Have I lost my culture? No. I come from a whaling family. My great grandfather, Andrew Johnson, was a whaler. He landed his last whale in 1907. My grandfather, Sam Johnson, was present when the whale was landed and told me he played on the whale's tail. I lived with my grandfather for sixteen years and heard his stories about our whaling tradition and the stories of family whaling told by my father Percy and my uncle Clifford. When I was a teenager I was initiated into Makah whaling rituals by my uncle Clifford. While I cannot divulge the details of these rituals, which are sacred, they involve isolation, bathing in icy waters and other forms of ritual cleansing. These rituals are still practiced today and I have been undergoing rituals to prepare me for the whaling which is to come this year. Other families are using their own rituals.

When the idea of resuming whaling first spread through our village, I was intensely excited, and so was my whole family. In fact, I can say I was ecstatic about the idea of resuming the hunt; something my grandfather was never able to do. I am proud to carry on my family legacy and my father is overjoyed because he is going to see this in his lifetime.

I can tell you that all of the Makah whalers are deeply stirred by the prospect of whaling. We are undergoing a process of mental and physical toughening now. I feel the cultural connection to whaling in my blood. I feel it is honoring my blood to go whaling. We are committed to this because it is our connection to our Tribal culture and because it is a treaty right—not because we see the prospect of money. We are willing to risk our lives for no money at all. The only reward we will receive will be the spiritual satisfaction of hunting and dispatching the whale and bringing it back to our people to be distributed as food and exercising our treaty right.

Recently the Progressive Animal Welfare Society (PAWS) distributed a brochure in which they implied we have lost our cultural need for whaling because we have adapted to modern life. They cite our "lighted tennis courts . . . Federal Express . . . and other amenities." Well, excuse me! I want to tell PAWS that the two tennis courts on our high school grounds have no lights. How about the fact that Federal Express makes deliveries to our reservation? Does that mean that we have lost our culture?

These attacks on our culture and our status are foolish. No one can seriously question who we are; we are a small Native American Tribe who were the whalers of the American continent. We retain our whaling traditions today. It resonates through all of our people from the youngest to the oldest, and we don't take kindly to other people trying to tell us what our culture is or should be.

The Domino Effect

Animal rights groups have been scaring each other and pumping up the claim that if we whale, it will mean the collapse of all restrictions against commercial whaling and whaling will be resumed everywhere. This is nonsense. If there are other indigenous peoples who have a legitimate whaling culture and whaling tradition, then they should be allowed to whale just as we do. The rest is all hype promoted by anti-whaling organizations to try to stop us from killing a single whale.

Sea Shepherd

The leader of the pack attacking us is The Sea Shepherd Conservation Society. They have been responsible for a steady stream of propaganda aimed at inflaming the public against us, some of which has been repeated by other anti-whaling groups, who have assumed it was factual.

Who is Sea Shepherd? They are a California-based organization which has for years operated on the fringe of mainstream conservation groups. They have built a flourishing organization supported by contributions from around the world. They portray themselves as the swashbucklers of the ocean because they have sunk whaling ships. This action has earned them the label of a terrorist organization and they have been barred from attending the deliberations of the International Whaling Commission even as observers since 1987. They applied for readmission in 1995 and the IWC again denied them admission. They threatened to sink our boats if we whaled without IWC sanction, smug in the assumption (wrong as turned out) that we would never get approval from the IWC. They have since churned out reams of material attacking us.

We can't hope to keep up with this barrage by Sea Shepherd and others. These groups are well financed. Sea Shepherd, for example, is sufficiently well financed to operate two ocean going vessels, a submarine, an airplane, a helicopter and other water borne craft. It seems to me that Sea Shepherd is actually in the commercial whaling business themselves and we're their best ticket now.

The Ethical Issue

The arguments and claims put out by Sea Shepherd and the other anti-whaling groups are designed to inflame the public against us and to attack the honesty of our motives. They mask the real aim of these groups: to prevent the killing of a single whale.

Some people honestly believe that it is wrong to kill one of these animals. Maybe their minds are made up, but I want to say to them that we Makahs know the whales, probably better than most people. We are out on the waters of the ocean constantly and we have lived with and among whales for over two thousand years. We are not a cruel people. Some of us have even gone into the water to free whales who became entangled in nets—a dangerous undertaking. But we have an understanding of the relationship between people and the mammals of the sea and land. We are a part of each of each other's life. We are all part of the natural world and predation is also part of life on this planet. So orca whales attack and eat whales and whale calves as well as seals and fish. Those who regard the orcas simply as cute may prefer to ignore this side of their nature. But there is a reason they are called "killer whales." In fact, they were originally called "whale killers."

I want to deal with the claims of those who would romanticize the whale and ascribe almost human characteristics to it. To attribute to gray whales near human intelligence is romantic nonsense—as any professional whale biologist can tell you. The photographs of gray whales surfacing to be petted by people are all taken in the calving lagoons of Baja, California and Mexico. This behavior is not exhibited by gray whales anywhere else, particularly by migrating whales passing through our waters. The whales we will hunt are migrating whales and we will not hunt any mother whale with a calf.

Whales have captured the public's fascination. Whales are definitely "in." Does that mean that Indians are "out"? The world has had a similar fascination with us and our cultures, but whenever we had something you wanted or did something you didn't like, you tried to impose your values on us. The Federal government even tried to stamp out our potlatch tradition because they thought it was backward and impoverishing. Too often white society has demonstrated this kind of cultural arrogance. We don't take well to Sea Shepherd or PAWS telling us we should rise to a "higher" level of culture by not whaling. To us the implication that our culture is inferior if we believe in whaling is demeaning and racist.

We feel that the whaling issue has been exploited by extremists who have taken liberties with the facts in order to advance their agenda. We understand that there are many people who legitimately believe that it is wrong to kill a whale. But we feel that the zealousness and self-righteousness which emanates from the animal rights community has led to dishonesty and extremism. To them I would say that we may have deeper feelings for the whale than you or your forebears. We ask that you show some respect for Indian culture and that you stop the lies and distortions. The Makah people have been hurt by these attacks, but nevertheless we are committed to continuing in what we feel is the right path.

We Makahs hope that the general public will try to understand and respect our culture and ignore the attacks of extremists.

Questions for Discussion:

1. What does this document reveal about the maritime culture of the Makah?

2. How does protecting a natural resource sometimes become a racial issue?

3. What does this document reveal about the American public's attitudes toward conservation?

Keith Johnson, "An Open Letter To The Public From The President of the Makah Whaling Commission," August 6th, 1998. By permission of the author.

Bruce Babbitt, "Counterattack Against the Pathogens of Global Commerce" (1999)

One of the unintended consequences of modern maritime commerce is the spread of species from one region of the world to another. For example, when the St. Lawrence Seaway opened in 1959, no one dreamed that ships from Europe would inadvertently carry invasive species such as the zebra mussel into the Great Lakes. By the 1990s, it became clear that invasive species were killing or crowding out native species of fish and changing the environment. The consequences have been hard to predict and even harder to prevent.

The following is a speech made by Bruce Babbitt (1938–), secretary of the interior during the Clinton administration and an ardent conservationist, at the First National Conference on Marine Bioinvasions at the Massachusetts Institute of Technology on January 26, 1999.

At the outset, let me congratulate the conference sponsors. You are taking the initiative in a much neglected field. Marine bioinvasions have large consequences for our food supply, our economy, our fishing industry, and human health. These invasions also threaten to degrade and homogenize coastal waters in every corner of the seven seas.

Ten years ago, just after midnight on March 24, the *Exxon Valdez* crashed into a reef in Prince William Sound. Eleven million gallons of crude oil poured into the pristine waters, casting a shroud over hundreds of miles of shoreline. Television crews on the scene broadcast images of seabirds, otters, and sea lions, slicked black with oil. Those images fixated the world on the dangers of oil spills and led to many new laws and regulations designed to prevent another such tragedy.

Yet the biological spills taking place in Prince William Sound from oil tankers go virtually unnoticed. Just over a year ago the U.S. Fish and Wildlife Service discovered four new species of zooplankton spreading through the sound, released from ballast water brought by tankers from East Asia via San Francisco Bay. In the long run, these zooplankton, feeding on phytoplankton utilized by the Dungeness crab, may change the sound more extensively and permanently that any oil spill. And no one has a clue—or a dime—to contribute toward a massive "clean up." Were that even possible.

With just four, small bioinvasive species, Prince William Sound is relatively lucky. So far. But look farther south, where a prolific and hungry European stowaway has disembarked. The green crab has begun to infest Pacific coastal waters, devouring anything, from commercially valuable oysters and clams to barnacles, algae, and snails. And it's not alone. In the northwest nearly forty percent of all aquatic species are exotic, including the spartina that has choked Willapa Bay and decimated the shellfish industry. This particular invader came from our own Atlantic coastal estuaries.

It gets worse inside the Golden Gate. There, as Interior Secretary, I have worked with environmentalists, irrigation farmers and cities to get more freshwater down California's main rivers into the Delta and San Francisco Bay. Our goal is to help restore endangered native fish like chinook salmon and Delta smelt. Only now I know that it is not enough to ensure healthy flows downstream; our real threats may be coming *upstream*.

Specifically, some thirty species of exotic fish—Asian goby, Atlantic shad, Mississippi catfish, carp, bass, perch, sunfish . . . *gold*fish—are swarming the bay, a veritable marine zoo. An additional two hundred bioinvasive species suffocate native fisheries and helped drive the thicktail chub to extinction. Those are only the *documented* cases, with new arrivals every ten weeks.

Moving eastward, the Gulf of Mexico is being mugged by the brown mussel, which displaces native mollusks, threatens mangroves, and fouls water intake systems. In the Chesapeake, a hotspot for over 150 documented bioinvasive species, oyster beds now succumb not only to polluted runoff, or overharvest, but to the new arrival of a predatory whelk. I'll let the courageous researchers detail what's happening less than a mile away from here, in North America's oldest coastal port and fishery. It's too depressing for me.

It might be easier if we could simply blame the rest of the world for our troubles. But the truth is ballast water sloshes both ways. In the early 1980s, a small, luminescent blob called Leidy's comb jelly was pumped aboard ships along our coast, then discharged weeks later into the Black Sea. With no predators, it mushroomed into one of the most intense marine invasions ever recorded, nearly wiping out anchovies and other fisheries. Zebra mussels exchanged for jellyfish: the maritime law of reciprocity at its darkest.

No place on earth is immune from the twin threats of extinction and alien invaders. In the mid-nineteenth century, when wooden whaling ships criss-crossed the seas in bloody pursuit, Herman Melville pondered: "whether Leviathan can long endure so wide a chase and so remorseless a havoc; whether he must not at last be exterminated from the waters." He took note of how we were pushing the buffalo to extinction on the prairies, but dismissed it as impossible on the high seas, rationalizing that, surely, whales could escape to polar regions and thus become "immortal in his species."

Mankind never used to navigate such frozen regions, even though the fouled wooden hulls like Ahab's surely carried a few unwelcome guests. To be sure, bioinvasion from ships is as ancient as the Vikings and the Phoenicians. Even when ballast consisted of stones, dirt and iron, some exotic bioinvasive species hitchhiked along.

What has changed in the past half century is the rate of spread, leading to faster, wider, more complex dispersal. We reach remote ports on a weekly, daily, hourly basis. From more diverse trade routes. Loaded with much larger volumes of ballast. Discharge of that ballast is nothing more than "point source pollution" and must be treated as such.

Global aquaculture—shrimp farms, public fish hatcheries, commercial oyster beds—also bears responsibility for the spread of epibionts, parasites, predators, and pathogens. So does the aquarium industry. The outbreak of giant African snails in Florida or the *Caulerpa taxifolia* clone, an alga taking over the Mediterranean, originated not in ballast, but from aquarium tanks.

All these sources must be included in our response, policy, and research. But at a more immediate level, we must grasp the root of the problem. That root lies not in isolated incidents, but in scope: the dramatic rate of spread, the increasing vectors of pathogens that carried cholera to Alabama and seem to multiply toxic "red tides" around the world.

As a very crude rule of thumb, ten percent of invasive species will establish breeding populations; ten percent of those will launch a major invasion. At first, that "one percent" factor seems negligible. Then consider how San Francisco Bay is approaching three hundred exotics.

Consider also that ships this century have grown from 3,000 tons to 300,000 tons, and the volume of ballast water slurry—pumped and sucked at 20,000 cubic meters an hour—has kept apace. Faster crossings let more species survive, reproduce, make connections, and take baggage. The fall of trade walls brings global exposure to once quiet seaside ports, and vice-versa. In the ballast water of timber cargo ships traveling between Coos Bay, Oregon, and Japan, researchers found 367 species of living animals and plants.

That's a single route. Consider how larger ports, say Norfolk and Baltimore, receive more than 12 million metric tons of foreign ballast water per year, originating in 48 different foreign ports, and 90 percent of them carried live organisms, including barnacles, clams, mussels, copepods, diatoms, and juvenile fish. Worldwide, it is estimated that tens of thousands of ships carry several thousand species daily. Let me put this another way: In the time it takes me to deliver this speech, two million gallons of foreign plankton will have been discharged somewhere in American waters. We'd better get busy. And fast.

How? What is our response? So far it has been pitiful. Frankly, in light of the economic and ecological devastation, we have been too timid. We restrain ourselves with voluntary guidelines, a scattered approach, and limited, unenforced codes. No longer.

In 1997, President Clinton, responding to concerns of scientists like yourselves, asked the Departments of Interior and Agriculture to draft an executive order for his consideration. That order, which is now before the President, will contain two broad initiatives. First, it will require federal agencies to review their existing authorities and activities to reduce the risk of bioinvaders. Second, it will create an interagency working group to draft a plan—possibly including regulatory and legislative change—necessary for a coordinated response to bioinvaders.

What will this look like in practice? I'll sketch the rough outlines in pencil. For there are existing models, and while there is still much to learn, we do know this: the first and best line of defense against bio-invaders is to keep them out in the first place. Period. Not one marine bioinvasive species, after it has taken hold, has ever been eliminated or effectively contained. There is simply no silver bullet. This is a so-bering fact. It means our efforts must be focused primarily on prevention. And that, in turn, means effective regulation and enforcement.

In 1990, in response to the damage caused by the zebra mussel in the Great Lakes, the Congress enacted [the] Nonindigenous Aquatic Nuisance Prevention and Control Act. Among other provisions, the Act now requires ballast water exchange at sea rather than in the Great Lakes system. We should now move toward mandatory ballast exchange for not just the Great Lakes, but for all shipping in all American ports. In California water districts whose systems are threatened by invaders working their way upstream out of San Francisco Bay have begun to call for ballast water regulation by federal and state agencies.

We need to mount a coordinated research program to better understand the threats posed by alien invaders including fish, crustaceans, mollusks, and pathogens and to guide programs of prevention and control. Perhaps we can find economical and safe means to decontaminate ballast water and sediments in situ. The Agricultural Research Service and APHIS[1] in the Department of Agriculture, the Coast Guard, the National Oceanic and Atmospheric Administration, and the Biological Research Division of the United States Geological Service should mount a coordinated effort to understand agricultural threats, threats to natural ecosystems, and new methods of prevention and control.

Does this mean our agency budgets must catch up to, and keep pace with, the ecological devastation they target? Yes. Because that devastation is economic as well. Vast as they are, the Great Lakes are easy compared to the task ahead, and offer few unqualified success stories. Yet as a case study, it makes a strong case why an aggressive, well-funded public response to bioinvasion is well worth the expense and effort.

---

1   APHIS: the federal government's Animal and Plant Health Inspection Service.

We spend several million dollars a year sterilizing, catching, poisoning, [and] putting up barriers to suppress the sea lamprey. Well, it's still there. And it may never go away. But for every dollar we invest, the Great Lakes earn $30.25 in increased fisheries revenue. Your stock portfolio should perform as well.

Global cooperation is an imperative. Our joint efforts with Canada on the Great Lakes provide an example. Two global entities—the Convention on Biological Diversity and the World Trade Organization—should play a major role in international cooperation. The Convention on Biological Diversity is the place to begin, and indeed preliminary discussions pursuant to section eight of the Biological Diversity Treaty are underway. Those discussions underline the need for Senate ratification of the Biodiversity Treaty. The World Trade Organization must also take an active role in the movement to develop and harmonize regulations in this area.

Let me conclude on a cautious note of hope. You've all heard that the flip side of crisis is opportunity? Well, the *Exxon Valdez* crash gave us such an opportunity. It led Congress to require double hulled tankers and stiffen training, navigation, and technology within the shipping industry. It prompted state, federal, and private agencies to establish habitat restoration programs and undertake comprehensive research on the North Pacific ecosystem.

We face an even greater opportunity now. The time is at hand for scientists, policy makers, and industry and the public to join together for an intensive coordinated counterattack on the threat of bioinvasions. You have initiated that process, and we in the public sector must now respond in kind. Thank you.

Questions for Discussion:
1. According to Babbitt, what are the implications of marine bioinvasions?
2. What regions of the country does Babbitt say are most endangered by marine invasive species?
3. What is the relationship of invasive marine species to commercial shipping?

Bruce Babbitt, "Launching a Counterattack Against the Pathogens of Global Commerce" http://www.doi.gov/news/archives/990126.html (last accessed January 13, 2007).

THE WAR ON TERROR

After the attack on the World Trade Center the morning of September 11, 2001, the United States found itself embroiled in a conflict that President George W. Bush labeled the *War on Terror*. This conflict immediately brought concerns about the security of American ports. Many believed terrorists could easily smuggle a weapon of mass destruction into the country onboard a ship. The result was the new, cabinet-level Department of Homeland Security, which Congress charged with securing American ports.

The United States Coast Guard became one of the most important agencies of Homeland Security. Ideally suited for coastal and port security, the Coast Guard enjoyed a surge in funding and prestige. But Coast Guardsmen also found themselves fighting terror in the Middle East, and some, such as Nathan Bruckenthal, were killed in action.

In the United States, the issue of securing American ports proved complicated. Homeland Security officials had to deal with millions of cargo containers entering through the nation's busy port facilities. As if that were not challenge enough, in 2006 the problem became politicized when an Arab company moved to buy the management contract of some of the nation's biggest cargo facilities. That deal ultimately failed in the face of popular and congressional opposition.

Nathan Bruckenthal, "Operation Iraqi Freedom" (2003)

The following is an interview of Coast Guard Petty Officer 3rd Class Nathan Bruckenthal (1970–2004) done by PAC Peter Capelotti of the U.S. Coast Guard Reserve on April 25, 2003. The interview took place in Bahrain and was part of the Coast Guard Historian's Office Iraqi Freedom Documentation Project. Capelotti interviewed Bruckenthal during his first tour of duty in Iraq. During Bruckenthal's second tour, he was killed in action at the Khawr Al Amay Oil Terminal off the coast of Iraq on April 24th, 2004, in a terrorist suicide bombing when a dhow that he and his team intercepted near the terminal exploded. The explosion overturned the boarding team's rigid hull inflatable, killing Bruckenthal and two U.S. Navy sailors and wounding another Coast Guardsman and three other Navy personnel. Bruckenthal was the first Coast Guardsmen killed in combat since the Vietnam War; he was posthumously awarded the Bronze Star, the Purple Heart, and the Global War on Terrorism Expeditionary Medal and buried with full military honors at Arlington National Cemetery. He left behind a wife pregnant with their only child, a daughter born months after Bruck-enthal's death.

DC3[1] Bruckenthal: We do a lot of . . . we have mock boardings that we do. Down in Miami they have some boats that we'd be doing, you know, some tugs down in the river that we do mock boardings on. We use paintball guns and stuff like that for simulation. You know, what we've got to do. We also have platforms on land that we work with. They'd use a lot of noise simulation and stuff like that, and it is very intense, very hardcore training for a long time, and you just get it done, and we do that. We train every day when we're in port. I mean we just train and train and train.

Q: Do you get a lot of policy to go along with your training; like why you're doing certain things?

DC3 Bruckenthal: Oh definitely. The Coast Guard policy is always in effect. We always go with Coast Guard policy.

Q: And "Use of Force" and all that?

DC3 Bruckenthal: Force Continuum, Use of Force Policy, and that's just our job and we have to live by it.

DC3 Bruckenthal: Had you been on a number of boarding missions in the Caribbean before you came here?

DC3 Bruckenthal: I did one deployment for 70 days. We had a four-ton cocaine bust down there. It was my first patrol with the TA-CLET[2] so I was pretty psyched about that. It gets you built up. You know you're like, I'm finally doing something that's, you know, going from a housing DC to doing something like that where it's like you're stopping drugs from coming into the country. It's just a great feeling and now I'm coming out here and doing this. It's like I'm on a high horse right now.

Q: When did you get here?

DC3 Bruckenthal: I got here the end of February.

Q: And can you describe sort of the run-up to that first night of the war; your experiences on different vessels, different . . . was this the first time you had to interact with people from other navies in the coalition?

DC3 Bruckenthal: For me it was. We worked with the New Zealand

---

1   DC3: Damage Controlman, Petty Officer Third Class.
2   TACLET: Tactical Law Enforcement Team

Navy. We did some boardings down here at the pier; some mock boardings with them, just running through with their boarding teams showing them what we do. We don't try to change their policy or anything.

Q: Uh hum.

DC3 Bruckenthal: We just show them what we do and see if we can help them in any way.

Q: Was there anything that they did that was that much different from what you guys are doing?

DC3 Bruckenthal: It's all basically the same. It seems like all the navies that we've worked with, everybody has the basic same rules of engagement and use of force policies and stuff. It's really cool to interact with another navy to see what they do. Also though, just to catch up on things like that. So we did that and then we went and worked with the Polish Special Forces and they're great guys. I learned a lot from them. They have the same "Use of Force" as us. They do the same job as we do.

Q: Did you do any combined boardings with them?

DC3 Bruckenthal: We did. We did some UN[1] boardings with them down in the holding area; pretty compliant boardings. Just basics; checking the holds. We did a few—I can't recall how many we did—but we did a few boardings with them. We were on there for about a week doing boardings with them.

Q: As tensions got a little bit higher and the war started to get closer, can you describe that night that the war started; where you were and what you were doing?

DC3 Bruckenthal: We were, I believe at the mouth of KAA[2] River. We were tasked to do a boarding on a tug that was allegedly broke down in the middle of the river, and we went onboard and just. . . . I stood security with the crew and we did make sure that the . . .

Q: When you say, stood security, you were actually keeping them in place?

DC3 Bruckenthal: Just keeping them in place, keeping an eye on them, and they were really compliant, pretty scared.

Q: How about you?

DC3 Bruckenthal: I get "amped up" when I'm put into something like

---

1   UN: United Nations.

2   KAA: Kwahr 'Abd Allah River.

that. It's just my nature. I mean don't get me wrong. Your nerves are always there just like you do anything. I mean if you're not scared or if you're not nervous about doing something then there's probably something wrong with you. You know you've probably been in the job too long.

Q: Or not long enough.

DC3 Bruckenthal: Or not long enough, exactly. So we just did that boarding, made sure that what they were saying that their engines were totally dissembled, and they were, and we went ahead and got off that vessel.

Q: And that was the night the war started?

DC3 Bruckenthal: That was the night, I believe, yes.

Q: Could you see it and feel it, hear it, from where you were?

DC3 Bruckenthal: Yes.

Q: Yeah. What was it like being in the middle of a naval bombardment?

DC3 Bruckenthal: It's pretty . . . for a person like me who's never really seen anything like that before, it was pretty interesting. I mean the sounds of war, and the colors of war you could say is how the . . . the color of the sky. I remember the sky was a big factor. You could see . . . it was very hazy from the smoke and very loud. Our ship; we were on the PC-10.[1] It's the *Firebolt*; a naval ship, and it would shake every once in a while from some of the sounds; some of the noises that were coming off. So we were pretty close. It was . . . it gets to you. You know you're thinking of, hey yeah, we're doing this. I agree with what we're doing and I stick by my country totally, but at the same time you've got to think of where the end of that noise is coming from. But you just do your job and you just make sure everything . . . your crew and your team is safe, and stuff like that.

Q: Did you have any sensation that these things were coming from behind you, over your heads, or . . . ?

DC3 Bruckenthal: Not really. Like I said, that night was real dark. You couldn't really see much except for the haze in the sky.

Q: Uh hum.

DC3 Bruckenthal: So you would see flashes but you really couldn't tell where they were coming from, but we knew.

---

1 PC-10: USS *Firebolt*, a Cyclone-class coastal patrol boat.

Q: Can you describe what you guys did the next day when you encountered these tugs?

DC3 Bruckenthal: Like I said, I'm just a boarding team member, so they told me to get dressed along with the other seven team members on our team. They said, get dressed. We have a boarding to do. We went ahead and saddled up. We went out, did this boarding on the tug with a barge next to it. We tied up next to the alongside tow and went onboard, mustered the crew—again I stood security back aft with the crew—and then the Australian Marines were there and we had a couple of Navy EOD[1] guys there. They went and took a look at the mines and stuff like that. I wasn't really involved with much of that because I was making sure that . . . the security; made sure nobody was, you know, the demeanor of the crew. You've got to look to see, you know, hey, are they acting funny or whatever? But you're always looking for something like that, and the crew was pretty nervous.

Q: Do you think they felt in fear of their lives?

DC3 Bruckenthal: I don't think I can say whether or not they did. The demeanor of them; they just seemed like they were pretty nervous; whether they got caught or they'd known they got caught, or whatever. They were pretty nervous sitting there. They wouldn't talk much. They wouldn't talk with each other.

Q: They didn't try to talk with you guys at all?

DC3 Bruckenthal: The only thing they'd ask us for is water and if they could use the bathroom.

Q: Uh hum.

DC3 Bruckenthal: We would take them to the bathroom if they needed to go and stuff like that.

Q: They were taken EPW?[2]

DC3 Bruckenthal: I believe so. I'm not sure.

Q: But they passed out of your control?

DC3 Bruckenthal: They passed out of our control and went onto a different ship. They took them . . . I'm not sure where they took them to or what they did with them after that.

Q: And after that what sort of things was your team doing?

DC3 Bruckenthal: We did another quick sweep of the vessel to make

---

1   EOD: Explosive Ordnance Detachment, specialists in bomb and mine disposal.
2   EPW: Enemy Prisoner(s) of War.

sure that it wasn't sinking; just to make sure it was intact. We made sure . . . we found another automatic weapon that hadn't been found before. We were down on the barge. We had all the weapons lined up on the barge and everything like that, and it was pretty scary standing on top of 60-something mines, you know, like uggghhh, let's get off this thing. (Laughter)

Q: You like to have EOD guys when . . .

DC3 Bruckenthal: Exactly. It was great having them there. You know, it's like, hey, we trust you guys.

Q: Yeah, and after that day, as the war progressed, what do you recall now as significant operational highlights of what the unit did? Did you continue your boardings off the *Firebolt*?

DC3 Bruckenthal: Continue boardings off the *Firebolt*?

Q: Did you serve on the *Firebolt* from that point to the end of hostilities?

DC3 Bruckenthal: Well until we came back into port.

Q: Okay, which is now?

DC3 Bruckenthal: Which was now, yes.

Q: Okay, so you've been on there since then.

DC3 Bruckenthal: Yes.

Q: Because the war started up until whenever you got off?

DC3 Bruckenthal: Yes.

Q: Okay, so you weren't on another vessel after that?

DC3 Bruckenthal: Not until the end when they were transferring us around.

Q: Right.

DC3 Bruckenthal: We did a lot of escort duties back and forth from Umm Qasr. We actually pulled into Umm Qasr.

Q: Did you go ashore there?

DC3 Bruckenthal: I just stepped ashore and then went back to the conn[1] just pretty cool.

Q: What was Umm Qasr like when you stepped ashore there?

DC3 Bruckenthal: It was sandy; pretty deserted; a lot of Marines; a lot of coalition forces were there but you could tell it was deserted. Pretty eerie, and that was when we escorted one of the . . . the first humanitarian ships.

Q: Do you remember what vessel that was you escorted?

---

1   Conn: the ship's bridge area.

DC3 Bruckenthal: I can't recall off the top of my head.

Q: What do you take from this that you'll take with you for the rest of your career in the Coast Guard and your civilian career?

DC3 Bruckenthal: I think, work-wise, my career-wise I take the tactics that we used; the communications with other coalition forces, how it really was. I mean there were times when there was a language barrier. I mean when we were with the Polish . . .

Q: Almost like the NYPD.[1] (Laughter)

DC3 Bruckenthal: Exactly. You know it's like you really couldn't communicate with them because they don't speak English and we don't speak Polish. So you use a lot of hand signals and a lot of stuff like that, and it seemed that it worked out perfectly.

Q: Uh hum.

DC3 Bruckenthal: I mean nothing's perfect I know, but still it seemed to be rolling. Even when we would be training with the Aussies or the New Zealand folks, I mean the accents still . . . I mean like, you know, I don't have much of an accent but we have guys on our team that have accents and they have really thick accents, so it's like you have to learn how to slow down and stuff like that.

Q: Can you tell the difference between a New Zealander and an Aussie?

DC3 Bruckenthal: Not really.

Q: Not really. (Laughter)

DC3 Bruckenthal: So I think I take that for work-wise just that things work. You know the training that we get, the training that we do is—as tedious as it sometimes is—it works. I mean there's always something there. And for my personal life; just the way it felt that first day of war, just that you're feeling that, okay, yeah, this is getting done and this is getting done for a reason.

Q: Are you glad it's over?

DC3 Bruckenthal: Well it's not over yet, but . . .

Q: Until you get home, yeah.

DC3 Bruckenthal: Well not even until I get home. I mean I still have family over here.

Q: Do you?

DC3 Bruckenthal: So I mean there are still things that just need to get

---

1 NYPD: New York Police Department.

done. So until this whole thing is over with, you know, there's still going to be that feeling; something to tell my kids.

Q: Is there anything that you'd like to add or anything we haven't covered that you wanted me to comment on or add?

DC3 Bruckenthal: Not really. I think we've pretty much covered everything.

Q: Well DC3, I really appreciate this.

DC3 Bruckenthal: Alright Chief.

Q: Thanks for hanging around and . . .

DC3 Bruckenthal: No problem.

Questions for Discussion:

1. What does this interview reveal about the maritime dimensions of the War on Terror?

2. What does this interview reveal about Americans serving overseas in Operation Iraqi Freedom?

3. What strengths or weaknesses does this sort of interview have for historians?

"Operation Iraqi Freedom and the U.S. Coast Guard," U.S. Coast Guard Historian's Office, http://www.uscg.mil/history/WEBORALHISTORY/IF_DC3_Bruckenthal.html (accessed January 1, 2007).

Tom Ridge, "Port Security" (2004)

Following the 9/11 attack, Congress created the Department of Homeland Security (DHS) in 2002 to prepare for, prevent, and respond to domestic emergencies, especially terrorism. The new department absorbed a number of older agencies, including the United States Coast Guard. From its inception, port security was of paramount concern. Many believed terrorists could send a nuclear bomb or other device in a cargo container into an American port and detonate it with dire consequences.

In this piece, a speech by the first secretary for homeland security, Tom Ridge (1945–), the necessity and complexity of port security is explained. Notably, this speech took place at Long Beach, California, the nation's most important container facility.

Thank you for that introduction; it is a pleasure to be with you— here at America's busiest seaport.

I know that you know how important the entire maritime industry is to the health of our nation's economy—contributing more than one trillion dollars to the annual GDP.[1]

And ports like this one are the gateway into the vastly interconnected global economy. Ninety-five percent of all international overseas trade moves through our Nation's ports.

Much of it—$1 billion a day of economic activity—happens right here at the Ports of Los Angeles and Long Beach.

In addition, more than eight thousand foreign flag vessels make 60,000 port calls annually in our country. And nearly 200 million passengers on cruise ships and ferries travel in and out every year.

You are helping to lead the Nation's port security effort—in part because of the healthy competition between Los Angeles and Long Beach, but also on account of your unprecedented cooperation when it comes to security.

This port has been involved with the development, implementation, and success of nearly every initiative from point of origin to destination—all the while protecting the vital commerce that passes through these docks and slips every day.

Los Angeles/Long Beach was home to one of the first Maritime Safety and Security Teams; has participated in the pilots for several security initiatives such as the Transportation Worker's Identity Card; deployed officers overseas, and hosted foreign officials as part of CSI;[2] and have set the standard for partnership with the local community, including 100 C-TPAT accounts[3] with area businesses.

You've also served as an important test bed for Operation Safe Commerce. We are looking forward to the arrival of the first containers under this program in just a few days.

The Department has been proud to partner with you on so many occasions as we layer our port security measures across the nation and around the globe. But we have been even more proud to watch as these two competing facilities partner with each other to ensure the security of this entire complex.

---

1   GDP: Gross Domestic Product, a measure of a nation's wealth.
2   CSI: Container Security Initiative.
3   C-TPAT accounts: Customs-Trade Partnership Against Terrorism, a partnership between private corporations and the federal government to increase transportation security.

It's not difficult to recognize the critical importance of our seaports not only to a thriving economy, but also to a safe and secure homeland.

Behind each ship is a long journey—and a long story—one that can rarely be understood by just observing from the dock.

For instance, shortly after I began serving as the President's Homeland Security Advisor, I boarded a ship in New Orleans Harbor. The vessel was registered in Singapore; the crew was from India; the cargo was American grain, on its way to Japan!

And that is just the beginning. Nine million containers arrive on those ships into our Nation's 361 seaports every year—more than 30 percent of them here in Los Angeles and Long Beach.

Once they reach shore, they are stacked and stored in facilities like this . . . then carried on trains and trucks across the country . . . and their contents are delivered to warehouses and waiting customers . . . all across the country.

The story doesn't end with the ships themselves. To this picture add the critical infrastructure at and around our ports, plants, refineries, warehouses, stockyards, and, of course, nearby port communities.

Shipping is a global industry; terrorism is a global problem; and our collective security requires a global solution.

In the past, efforts to secure this vast global industry—both here in America and throughout the world—were isolated, scattered, and uncoordinated.

Like other areas of critical vulnerability, we recognized this problem, coordinated with stakeholders and partners, identified best practices, and took specific actions to secure our homeland—and the global economy.

But for the first time ever, through an international effort there will be one world standard for ship and port security. This will help create a culture of security at ports around the world and mandate specific improvements.

I am pleased to announce that as of today, the United States is in full compliance with the requirements of this new standard—just in time to meet the July 1st deadline. In the past, we have been forced to rely on a patchwork of security procedures. With the implementation of these comprehensive new standards, we will now be able to rely on our international partners.

We will now be better able to harden physical infrastructure, verify the security of individual vessels before they approach a U.S. port, and better restrict access to our port areas.

We will be able to verify the security of individual vessels before they call on a U.S. port . . . before they can pose a threat. And those not in compliance may not be allowed to enter our ports.

On top of the standards of the international code, the United States has required vessels and port facilities to conduct vulnerability assessments, submit action plans, and increase security by the same July 1st deadline.

Leading this effort has been the U.S. Coast Guard. The Coast Guard has received nearly one hundred percent of the security assessments and plans required under this law. The Coast Guard has reviewed thousands of security plans from ship owners and terminal operators. Some will be obvious to the public, others will remain known only to the professionals charged with safety and security.

You might notice increased identification checks, additional screenings, more canine teams, and higher fences. Behind the scenes, facilities might install surveillance cameras, establish restricted areas, provide additional training, and increase or improve security personnel and patrols.

No plan is one size fits all. Each was designed to meet the unique security needs of a specific port.

Going forward, The U.S. Coast Guard will conduct assessments with teams of experts who simulate terrorist attacks on port facilities—to determine which vulnerabilities still exist and where. Then, they can work with individual ports on additional training and security measures to further solidify our efforts in and around America's ports.

Thanks to these new standards—and the work of so many of you here today—we now have a robust baseline of security in place for all of our nation's ports . . . and a certification program to ensure that foreign flagged vessels docking in U.S. ports have met U.S. generated security requirements.

Of course, these new security standards are just one tool in our worldwide layers of defense.

Those layers begin thousands of miles away . . . even before a container is loaded or a ship pushes off for the United States . . . and they continue until we can be sure that our ports, and the people they serve, are safe and secure.

In the time that I have been speaking, more than 100 containers will have entered this port. I'd like to take you along on the voyage of just one of these containers, and explain some of the layered defenses that have been put in place along the way.

The cargo supply chain is a complex system of movements; and security must start long before the container is loaded on to a ship for transport and must be present throughout the supply chain.

From the cutting floor in Thailand to final delivery in the "Heartland," we are ensuring that security is infused at every step of the process.

Twenty-four hours before a container is even loaded onto a cargo vessel, the Department of Homeland Security's Customs and Border protection unit receives electronic transmission of advance cargo manifests for all U.S.-bound containers.

Early reports from industry show that this 24-hour rule is aiding not just security, but productivity.

This advance information is then analyzed by our National Targeting Center, to compare against law enforcement data, the latest threat intelligence and the ships' history, in order to identify potentially high-risk cargo.

Accurate information at every stage of this process is critical to our overall security.

Next, Homeland Security officials use advanced technologies and risk analysis to begin our first layers of security far from American shores.

Under the Container Security Initiative, we have placed CBP[1] inspectors at 19 foreign seaports from Vancouver to Rotterdam to Singapore. These officers work alongside our allies to target and screen containers aboard cargo ships headed for the United States.

During a trip across the high seas, information about a container or its contents can be monitored and mapped against possible threats.

The Coast Guard uses this real time information to track high risk vessels, and when necessary, further screen or board potentially threatening ships. These intelligence based actions help prevent problems long before a ship enters our waters.

Once in transit, the next layer is the container itself. The Depart-

---

1   CPB: Customs and Border Protection.

ment is working closely with industry partners to create a more secure container.

Also, through Operation Safe Commerce, we are testing additional container technology devices and business processes that will help create a smarter, more secure container.

Once a container arrives at our shores, CBP officers thoroughly scan 100% of the high-risk containers using advanced x-ray and radiation screening equipment. Containers that need further screening are taken to a secure location.

There, the higher-risk shipments are physically inspected for terrorist weapons and contraband prior to being released from the port of entry.

Sometimes, however, regular common sense can be our greatest security tool. A great example of the effectiveness of our people and programs occurred at a port like this one last summer.

Customs and Border Patrol Agents—using the electronic information they were provided about a ship transiting from China to El Salvador—seized a cache of weapons worth more than $421,000.

The ship was traveling without a permit and the cargo was mismarked as frozen trout! Problem was that frozen trout was making the long trip across the Pacific in an un-refrigerated cargo container.

We are increasing security to ensure that our ports remain open, but we must do so while continuing to facilitate the flow of commerce.

Of course, we cannot do this alone. In addition to working with foreign governments, we must partner with business to help secure the supply chain.

We do that with our Customs-Trade Partnership Against Terrorism [to] enlist the private sector to help secure the entire supply chain. To date, more than 6,000 manufacturers, forwarders, brokers, carriers, and other key supply chain actors are participating in C-TPAT.

Programs like C-TPAT are helping our industry partners reach a higher degree of security across their entire supply chain.

Those that succeed qualify for time- and money-saving incentives such as "FAST" lane access[1] and reduced inspections. *Traffic World*

---

1   "FAST" lane access: Free and Secure Trade (FAST) lane access allowed qualified trucking companies to move more quickly through security and border checkpoints.

magazine reports that C-TPAT has "drawn some of the strongest praise business has ever heaped on a government program."

As owners and operators, the private sector can play an even larger role in the development and funding of advanced security procedures and technologies.

Securing our ports and waterways is a team effort—everyone, from local government and private citizens to the international community, plays an important role in ensuring that our waterways remain open for business.

All of these efforts—each and every layer of security—are geared toward finding that critical balance between security, freedom, and prosperity. We must find a way to keep our ports open to legitimate trade and travelers but closed to terrorists. I believe we have made significant progress toward that goal.

We've become more confident and more aware. As you know, homeland security is a national strategy, not a federal one; a world-wide effort, not just an American one. It's about the integration of a nation and a world—driven by a philosophy of shared responsibility, shared leadership, and shared accountability—in essence, a renewed commitment to the federalism upon which our nation was founded.

I'm quite grateful for the resolve and responsibility shown by all Americans—especially those of you here today who work hard to protect this country and its citizens. And I ask that we continue to work together as we have time and again to achieve our dreams and goals—and preserve America as the world's greatest home for freedom.

Questions for Discussion:
1. According to Ridge, what complications does a global economy have for port security?
2. What challenges does containerization offer to the Department of Homeland Security?
3. What kind of partnerships does Ridge claim are necessary to secure American ports from terrorist attack?

Remarks by Secretary Tom Ridge at Port of Los Angeles, June 21, 2004, http://www.dhs.gov/xnews/speeches/speech_0185.shtm, last (accessed January 14, 2007).

Scott McClellan, "Dubai Ports Press Briefing" (2006)

The Dubai Ports controversy began in February, 2006, when Dubai Ports World (often known as *DPW*, or *DP World*), a company owned by the government of Dubai in the United Arab Emirates, purchased the management contracts for U.S. port facilities in New York, New Jersey, Philadelphia, Baltimore, New Orleans, and Miami, as well as operations in sixteen other ports. The federal government, the Bush administration, and most of the maritime industry approved the move.

However, Democratic New York Senator Chuck Schumer called for a review, and Republican leaders including Speaker of the House Dennis Hastert and Senate Majority Leader Bill Frist publicly questioned the deal, too. Opposition was based on the idea that no foreign government should be permitted to own such strategic assets, and some even argued that port management should remain under American control even though a foreign (British) company already possessed the management contracts for the terminals.

In this transcript of a February 22, 2006, press conference, Scott Mc-Clellan (1968–), then White House press secretary, defends the Bush administration's position on the Dubai Ports deal. Faced with congressional opposition, Dubai Ports abandoned the deal and an American company took over management of the ports in question.

Q: Scott, you said this morning that the President wasn't made aware of the ports decision until the last several days, until after the decision had been made. Does the President wish that he'd been brought into the deliberations sooner, that he knew about it before it became a big political controversy?

Mr. McClellan: Let me mention a couple of things. First of all, there is a congressionally mandated review process that is put in place for transactions like this. It is a national security review process. It's called the Committee on Foreign Investment in the United States—the CFIUS process—that oversees such transactions. And you have some twelve departments and agencies that are involved and thoroughly reviewing such transactions and closely scrutinizing such transactions to make sure that it meets all national security concerns, to make sure that there is no national security threat.

So this was a transaction that was closely scrutinized by the experts—by the counter-terrorism experts, by the intelligence community, and those who are responsible for protecting the American people. No one in those departments objected to this transaction going forward.

Now, we have seen some concerns expressed by some members of Congress and others, and that's understandable, given that they have seen some coverage that has seemed to suggest that this company, an Arab company, would be in control of our ports. And that is a false impression. That's why it's important that we continue to talk with members and others about the facts, and that they understand the safeguards that are in place, and they understand how closely scrutinized this was. And that's what we will—that's what we will continue to do.

I mean, in hindsight, when you look at this and the coverage that it's received and the false impression that it has left with some, we probably should have briefed members of Congress about it sooner. And we are talking with members of Congress about it. There were some briefings last week; I know there are some additional briefings occurring today and there will be some additional briefings in the days going forward, so that they can have a full understanding of the facts, because when you look at the facts, we believe it should be clear to people that all the national security issues were addressed during this review process that was mandated by Congress. That is our top concern, the safety and security of the American people. And that's why it goes through a process like this.

Q: But Scott, does the President think that he should have learned about it sooner in the process?

Mr. McClellan: Well, one thing that the President did, Terry, one thing the President did—and even after all this press coverage of this transaction—was go back to every Cabinet member whose department is involved in this process and ask them, are you comfortable with this transaction going forward? And each and every one expressed that they were comfortable with this transaction going forward. We are confident in the congressional process that was put in place, because it looks at all these security issues relating to a transaction like this.

Last year—I think in any given year, there's some fifty to three hundred transactions that go through this national security review process. And this process is designed with one thing in mind: to make sure that there are no national security concerns. Last year, there were some sixty-five transactions that went through this process. This was a matter that was reported in the press going back to, I think, late Oc-tober. The financial press was covering this possible transaction. And despite the fact that it's been covered in the press and that there are some sixty-five transactions that go through this process every year, we feel like Congress probably should have been briefed on this mat-ter sooner, particularly in light of some of the false impressions that have been left in the minds of members of Congress.

Q: Scott, you talk about false impressions and that the coverage, the media coverage somehow drove that. The reality is, you had members of Congress—like Peter King of New York[1] and others—who are fa-miliar with the process, who knew about this, who didn't necessarily sound misinformed, who, nevertheless, still object to the deal. So was it a case of leaving a false impression, or the fact that you just have people who are opposed to this?

Mr. McClellan: Well, I think it could be both. But clearly there are some that have been left with a false impression, because you have some people that have gone out there and said that the Arab company would be in control of our ports and be in control of security of our ports. That's not the case. This is not about control of our ports. This not about the security of our ports. And let me be very clear: One thing we will never do is outsource to anyone the control and security of our ports, whether that's Dubai or any other entity that operates terminals at our ports.

And let's put this in a different perspective. If this transaction were blocked, this would not change port security one iota. The Coast Guard and the Customs and Border Patrol remain in charge of our security. The Coast Guard remains in charge of physical security. The Customs and Border Patrol remains in charge of cargo security. And there are a number of safeguards and security measures that we have put in place to make sure that cargo is screened before it reaches our shores.

Q: Let me just follow on this point. There's bipartisan consensus that monitoring the ports, the seaports, is very difficult, and it's a vulner-able area of our homeland security strategy. Karl Rove said, memora-bly, recently, that Democrats have a pre-9/11 view of the world; Re-publicans and this President have a post-9/11 view of the world. So a

---

1   Peter King: Republican congressman from New York who worked with Senator Chuck Schumer to oppose the Dubai Ports deal.

lot of people wonder on both sides of the aisle, how is it the President could allow a sale like this to go through with country that has clear ties to terrorism?

Mr. McClellan: The President doesn't view it as a political issue. The President views it as the right principle and the right policy. We should not be holding a country from the Middle East or a company from the Middle East to a different standard from a company from Great Britain. And the President believes very strongly that all these issues were addressed during the review process. That's why he checked with his Cabinet Secretaries—all the national security issues. We shouldn't—so it's a matter of principle. It's a principled position that the President is taking.

We also have to take into account the broader foreign policy implications something like this could have. The United Arab Emirates is a strong ally and partner in the global war on terrorism. General Pace,[1] just yesterday, talked about how the UAE is providing superb military-to-military cooperation, and how they are a very solid partner in the global war on terrorism. They provide access to their ports for our aircraft carriers, they provide access to our Air Force planes over their airspace and at their airports. The UAE is someone we have worked very closely with to crack down on terrorist financing. They work very closely with us in sharing important intelligence. And so I think you have to also look at it in that context. But the principle—

Q: But if we don't go through on this and they could retaliate, that relationship would be harmed—

Mr. McClellan: I wouldn't describe it that way. I mean, first of all, this is about a principle. And the principle is that we shouldn't be holding a Middle Eastern company to a different standard than a British company. They went through a very thorough review process before this transaction was allowed to proceed forward. And let me also mention that when it comes to Dubai Ports, there are security safeguards in the agreement that they signed with us. They committed to enforcing security standards under the Container Security Initiative, and under the Customs Trade Partnership Against Terrorism.

Now, let me mention what those are. The Container Security Initiative allows for the Customs and Border Patrol to inspect 100 percent

---

1 General Pace: General Peter Pace, USMC, chairman of the Joint Chiefs of Staff from 2005 to 2007.

of all high-risk containers at foreign ports before they are loaded onto vessels and headed into the United States. The Customs Trade Partnership Against Terrorism is a public/private partnership with some seven thousand companies that do regular business with the United States. And what they must do is increase their security to prevent terrorists from compromising their shipments. That's not only the company that's shipping this cargo, but the company that is providing the services, as well.

And I would also point out that Dubai Ports was the first Middle Eastern entity to join the Container Security Initiative. So the Customs and Border Patrol work very closely with Dubai customs to screen containers that are coming to the United States. And this is a company that operates in many countries around the world. It's a company that we are very familiar with.

[Questions about CSIUS review process]

Q: Why aren't Americans managing the ports?

Mr. McClellan: Well, let me answer your first question, and then we'll get to your next two or three questions. The President learned of this recently, he became aware of it.

Q: How recently?

Mr. McClellan: And there was no objection raised by any of the departments during the review process, or any concerns expressed about potential national security threats. And that's why it didn't rise to the presidential level.

Q: When did he find out?

Q: Scott, talk a little bit about—one of the problems here is it's a secretive process, and understanding that some things concerning national security are done in secret—

Mr. McClellan: Well, it's not just that. I mean, there's proprietary information, as well. And I think that what we're working to do is make sure that we can provide as much information as possible about this transaction. Because, as I pointed out, one thing that is key is that this company agreed to additional security measures that they would take beyond what some others do in transactions like this. And I pointed out what those are.

Q: You talked about checking cargo and that they say they'll allow cargo to be checked. There's clearly not the manpower to check cargo. About 5 percent to 7 percent coming in this country are ever checked. So what does the U.S. need for this company to do? Hiring and firing? Do they vet people? Do you know all that?

Mr. McClellan: This is the company that manages the terminals. They'll manage the terminals—

Q: So can they hire and fire?

Mr. McClellan:—the forklifts that lift the cargo off or load the cargo on to ships. And that's what their responsibility is. But that's why I pointed that there were additional security safeguards that were put in place in an agreement with Dubai Ports. And that's important to understand.

And in terms of—let me back up and make sure that people have a clear understanding of the security measures that are in place, because I think in your question you ignored some key aspects of this. First of all, we secure cargo before it gets to our shores. The Customs and Border Patrol and the Coast Guard are in charge of security for our ports, and they do a great job. And there are a number of steps and measures that we have put in place over the last few years to improve security at our ports and to strengthen security at our ports—as I pointed out, the Container Security Initiative.

Under the Container Security Initiative, the Customs and Border Patrol inspects 100 percent of all high-risk containers. And they do that at foreign ports before they're loaded on to the ship and headed to the United States. A hundred percent of all cargo is screened, using intelligence and using cutting-edge technology. Technology is very important. Technology is very important—

Q:—all of it—

Mr. McClellan: No, 100 percent of cargo is screened. There's a 24-hour rule in place. The Customs and Border Patrol is required to screen the manifest a day before cargo arrives. So what we're doing is pushing out the security before that cargo comes to our shores. And then I also mentioned the Customs Trade Partnership Against Terrorism, how that's been implemented and how we have more than seven thousand companies participating in that.

And then, finally, the technology that is used by the Customs and Border Patrol—they use large-scale x-ray and gamma ray machines and radiation detection devices to pre-screen cargo coming into this country. So there are a lot of security measures that are put in place. It is the top priority for this administration.

Q: Scott, would you just go back to the hiring? So who is running the forklifts? Do we have any control over that, or does that matter?

Mr. McClellan: Well, that's why the agreement was signed with this company. That's why I just pointed that out. Sure, it matters. And that's why it was looked at very carefully during this review process. This review process looked at all the national security issues relating to this very matter.

Q: When specifically did the President—how did he find out about this—and when specifically? Was it last week when this blew up? He read it in the paper?

Mr. McClellan: No, it was coming out last week, and he learned about it over the last several days. I couldn't pinpoint the exact time, but last several days, recently.

And—but I think it's important to keep in mind when you're reporting back to the American people what I just said. This transaction was closely scrutinized to make sure that there were no national security threats. There were no objections raised by any of the departments that are charged with being involved in this process. And that's why it didn't rise up to the presidential level. But even in spite of that, with all the attention that this transaction has received, the President felt it was very important to go back to each Cabinet Secretary who has responsibility for this process, and ask them, are you comfortable with this transaction proceeding forward. And they all said, yes. And I'm sure it's for the reasons that I spelled out to you in this very room, because of the agreements that were put in place, because of the working relationship that we have with this company, and because there were no national security threats raised. . . .

[Questions about when President Bush learned about the ports deal]

Q: Scott, it sounds like the President has lost control of the party on the Hill. It sounds like they're campaigning against George Bush.

Mr. McClellan: No, I don't think that's accurate. You're talking about this specific issue? This specific issue—let's clarify that—no, I think—the President just came back from a House Republican conference just a short time ago, and they talked about important national security priorities, and they talked about the tools we're using to protect the American people like the terrorist surveillance program. And at the end of that comment—end of those remarks, he received a standing ovation. So I think there is strong, united support for the policies that we are putting in place and that we are pursuing to make America more prosperous and to make America safer.

This President has made his number one priority winning the war on terrorism. And so let's keep in mind that the United Arab Emirates is a key partner and ally in the global war on terrorism. They work very closely with us. Partnerships are key to winning the war on terrorism. And they have followed the rules. They went through this review process, a thorough review process, that involved national security experts, that involved counter-terrorism experts. They looked at all these issues and they said they were comfortable with this transaction going forward.

And we shouldn't be creating a different standard here. But if you're going to try to block something like this, you also need to look at it in the context of those broader foreign policy concerns. It could have a real negative impact on our relations with countries like the UAE, and other allies who are following this issue very closely—allies who have helped us to save lives and prevent attacks. . . .

[Questions about briefing the administration on the CFIUS process]

Q: So is the administration concerned that the rancor on the Hill over this sends an inappropriate message overseas and that the U.S. government is divided?

Mr. McClellan: The President is concerned about the mixed message that could be sent on this matter. He said that yesterday. It sends a terrible message to our allies when you say a company from the UAE, an Arab country that has been a good ally in the war on terrorism, should be held to a different standard than a company from Great Britain, particularly when it followed all the rules, and when it went through this review process.

Questions for Discussion:

1. What does this press briefing reveal about the American economy in the early twenty-first century?

2. What does this document reveal about American security concerns in the early twenty-first century?

3. According to McClellan, why was the president confident in the abilities of DP World to run American container terminals?

White House Press Briefing, February 22, 2006, http://www.whitehouse.gov/news/releases/2006/02/20060222-5.html (last accessed January 14, 2007).

Joshua M. Smith grew up on Cape Cod and coastal Maine. He holds degrees from the University of St. Andrews, Maine Maritime Academy, East Carolina University, and the University of Maine. He is author of *Borderland Smuggling: Patriots, Loyalists, and Illicit Trade in the Northeast, 1783–1820*, which won the John Lyman Award in American Maritime History in 2007. He lives with his family in New York City and is an associate professor of humanities at the United States Merchant Marine Academy, Kings Point, New York.

New Perspectives on Maritime History and Nautical Archaeology
Edited by James C. Bradford and Gene Allen Smith

CPSIA information can be obtained
at www.ICGtesting.com
Printed in the USA
FSOW01n0428310516
20869FS

9 780813 033051